Journey of a Lifetime

Journey of a Lifetime

Friedrich Glasbrenner

ISBN: 978-0-646-99246-4

First edition, © 2019, Friedrich (Fred) Glasbrenner.

Published by F & Z Glasbrenner
603/50 Saltwater Promenade,
Point Cook, Vic. 3030.

Book design and preparation: John Litchen.
(PO Box 3503, Robina Town Centre, Qld, 4230.)

Dedication:

For Theo (Guth), Uli (Bauer) and my younger self,
we dreamed of seeing the world but had no means of doing it other
than by riding bikes...

...and for Uli, who sadly passed away in March 2018,
a lifelong friend and travelling companion whose memories of our
adventures were so much better than mine, and whose photographs
contributed so much to this book...
Part of me went to Heaven with him...

Part One
Early Journeys

*"Whatever we saw we shall never forget.
Whatever we did we should never regret."*
F Glasbrenner.

*Tante Anni, Onkel Ludwig, and Irma Illg,
my mother, as children in Kuernbach.*

Part One : Early Journeys

Chapter One

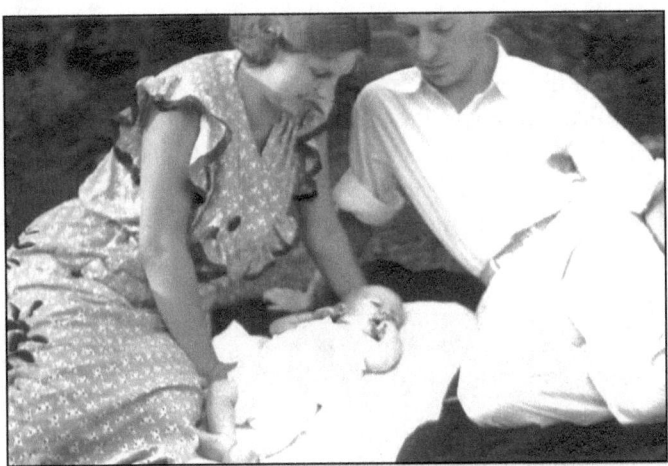

The very day I took my first breath of air was on Thursday, the 18th of June 1936, in a Hospital in Philadelphia, Pa, USA. When they put me in my mother's arms the Doctor told her, "Here Irma is your handsome Butterball."

I must have been quite something at close to 4 Kg with blue eyes (well, if one looks at me today I must certainly have been a big Baby). Apparently my Mum was assisted by a Dr Barnard who was the older brother or a close relative of Dr Christiaan Barnard who in South Africa performed the first Heart Transplant.

Dr Barnard was the House Doctor of the wealthy Zimmermann Family where my mother was employed as a 'chambermaid'.

Mum was borne in Stuttgart on the 2nd of October 1914 and grew up in a small Village called Kuernbach 70 Km north of Stuttgart, from where her ancestors came. It was famous for its good wines. During the Great Depression, my grandma lost most of her possessions, vineyards and so on. Having lost her husband in Russia during the First World War and with 9 kids to feed and clothe, she found life extremely difficult.

She decided to go to America to work and earn some extra cash for her family back home. She went there four times. On her last trip my mother accompanied her and got a job with the same Family.

The year they arrived in New York was 1928, in September just before Mum's 15th birthday. It was a whole new world for my mother, seeing all those skyscrapers and streets full of cars and people dressed totally differently to those in the small village she had left behind, where geese, ducks and chickens still roamed the streets, and cars had a 10 Km speed limit so as not to endanger kids playing on the road. Women were smoking — some even wore trousers — men wore bowler hats, and boys were selling newspapers on the streets.

It didn't take Mum very long to fit into her new way of life and when she was 16 she got her driver's license and was able to do the family's weekly shopping in one of Zimmermann's cars. I believe at that time she also started smoking, because it was the 'In Thing'. It was a totally different life compared to the one she had left behind.

Mum: ...after a few years in America.

Early Journeys

In 1932 Mum started accompanying Grandma to the German club where she was a long time member. After a while the inevitable happened; she met a young man with whom she fell in love and became engaged to.

Engaged and happy in the garden of Frederick's older sister and her husband in Philadelphia.

Finally, on the 20th of April 1935 (Adolf Hitler's birthday) she married Friedrich Glasbrenner, with Grandma's blessings of course.

Early Journeys

My Father, (Frederick John) Friedrich Gottlieb Glasbrenner was born in Murrhart on the 26th of April 1910 and did his education in Backnang near Stuttgart. After finishing high School he was lucky to get an apprenticeship at a big truck and machinery manufacturer 'Karl Kaeble' as a motor mechanic.

Unfortunately, soon after finishing his apprenticeship he was made redundant, because of the depression (15 million people were out of work in Germany). He decided to go to America to earn money so he could return and further his education at the *Machienenbauschule* in Esslingen to obtain his diploma of engineering. But like most plans, they don't often work out the way you would like.

Dad's older Sister Maria was already in America, married to Peter Biehl, a German from near Karlsruhe who happened to be a foreman at a big train factory called 'BUDD', so it was relatively easy for Dad to get a job. Besides, they were looking for experienced machine builders and Dad had the right qualifications. He was liked by everyone there, and having learned English in school he was very valuable.

It didn't take long before he spoke like a 'Yankee.' (Even when he went back to Germany he never lost his American accent). He was sent all over America for the company as a trouble-shooter and it was not long before they also made him a Foreman.

In Philadelphia he joined the German club and on a picnic he met the young and beautiful Irma Illg with whom he fell head over heels in love. They were soon married and his Brother in law Peter Biehl was his best man.

Well so much for saving money to pay for his studies for his Diploma of Engineering, but he was happy the way things had turned out.

They created a home in Newkirk Street in Philadelphia and on the 18th of June 1936, GUESS WHAT?

A not so little *Butterball* saw his first light and was happy to be able to move around, yelling his lungs out.

They named me Friedrich Ludwig Glasbrenner.

Things had changed dramatically, instead of Irma and Fritz there was now also a little 'Fritzle' who demanded all their Attention.

Dad, on the day he arrived in America.

Journey of a Lifetime

Fritzle ... very early days

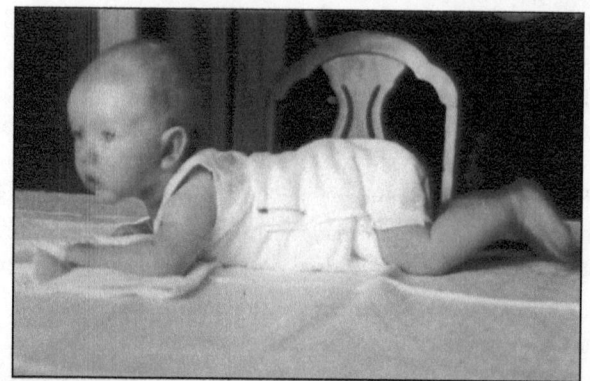

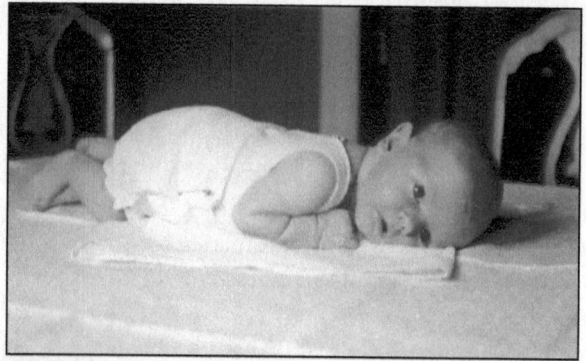

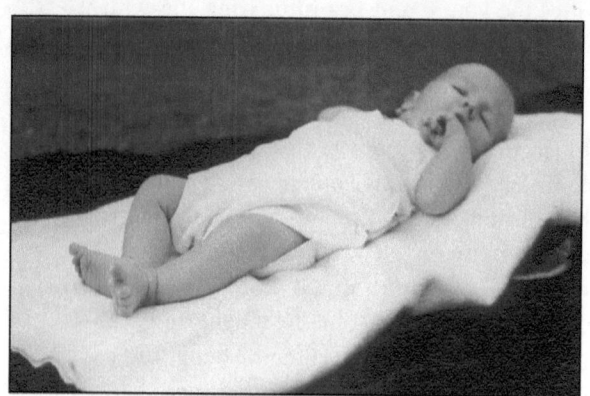

Early Journeys

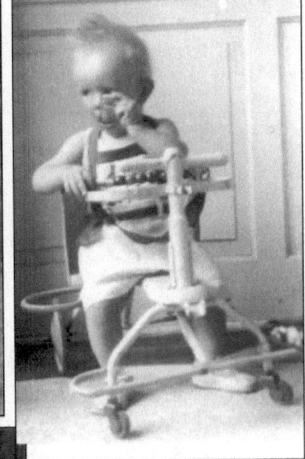

'Butterball' with Mum and Dad at home in Philadelphia.

Journey of a Lifetime

Early boating trips and camping with the family are what I hold responsible for my lifelong desire for travel and adventure.

Early Journeys

Life was always lots of fun and games with Mum and Dad on the steps in front of our house... 35 Newkirk Street Philadelphia.

By the end of 1938 my Grandma became very sick and she didn't get better. The Doctors told my parents the only way she would recuperate was to take her back home to her little village because she might also be suffering from home sickness.

Dad took some long leave from work and offered to accompany her back home to Germany, where miraculously she recovered in a relatively short time. Mum in the meantime also decided to take me to Germany, so the relatives could meet the two and half year old good looking little American blond fellow who very quickly had to learn the German language. (*Schwaebisch* – a southern German dialect.)

After some time in Stuttgart with Aunty Sophie, Grandma's sister, and her husband, the Second World War broke out and they missed the opportunity to get back to America. They had no choice but to spend the war years in Germany.

Mum's Aunt Sophia: we lived with her in Stuttgart once we arrived back in Germany.

My first outing with Mum after we ariverd in Germany in 1939.

Mum and me with newly arrived baby brother Heinz.

In the beginning of the war, life in Germany was not too bad. We lived in Stuttgart and it didn't take Dad long at all to get a good Job at Mahle, where they made pistons for war machinery. Unemployment was now virtually non-existent and there was no more Depression as before. I went to kindergarten not far from our apartment in Stoeckach Srasse 66 and Mum got a job downstairs where there was a small dairy and grocery shop.

On the radio we were told how good our soldiers were. Apparently they conquered one country after another and we were winning the war without loss of life. What a lot of Crap!

In 1942 I started School where I was a very good observant kid, but then the war started to intensify. On the 21 of October 1943 my brother Heinz was born nearby, in Bad Cannstatt so my other grandma, Dad's mother, came to look after me because Dad still had to go to work.

When the first bombs fell over Stuttgart it frightened the shit out of everybody. We thought this can't be for real, but it sure was, and it never stopped until the end of the war. We lived in a set of 6 storey apartment houses where the men dug tunnels from one house to the other in case one of them got hit.

Well, the front one got hit with the loss of 14 lives, and it would have been many more had it not been for the tunnels where the residents sheltered during air strikes. Early in September 1944, the air strikes went on for hours. It was an absolutely terrifying night; hours without electricity in the cellar with Heinz crying his heart out still having to be looked after. By the morning the bombing had stopped and I ventured out to look at the damage and could not believe what I saw. Half of the opposite side of the street was destroyed; buildings smashed and toppled over, still burning. There were human bodies half burned and still smouldering, laying in the rubble on the street amongst dead animals. The smell, the stench was shocking. I stood there trying not to vomit, not knowing what to do.

Naturally there was no more school, and being only 8 years old I was happy about that. Most of the schools were damaged or totally destroyed. At that time my parents decided to take me to my relatives in Kuernbach, a smaller country town where they believed it would be safer.

For me it was a crucial change in my life.

First I was taken to Tante Frieda and Onkel Gottlieb, Frieda being a stepdaughter to my grandma and I did not like being there. I wanted very badly to be with my family. *Only years later did Mum and Dad realise the big mistake they made in sending me to Kuernbach, but at the time they only wanted me in a safe place.* First they enrolled me in school and that's where the crap started. **The teachers were all Nazis** and very brutal. They belted shit out of us kids for no reason at all. Their excuse was to make good '***Soldiers***' out of us.

If I knew where they were buried I would still piss on their graves!

I'm the one with arms folded in the second row. School photo 1942

I did not like living at Aunty Frieda's because it was like living in the bush. At night when you wanted to go to the toilet, you had to light an oil lamp to find the way outside past the cattle barn to the so called '*toilet*' which was next to the pigs' pen, and then you just had to crap on top of the combined —*Cows' and Pigs'*— shit heap with rats running past your legs. Coming from Stuttgart with a WC it was like being hit on the head with a sledge hammer, a huge shock to the system.

That nice observant obedient school kid quickly became disillusioned, scared, and longed for his family. Needless to say, for me learning anything in school was difficult, and even though some people were quite nice to me, others were not... (*None of the Kids in Kuernbach had to spend nearly every night in a cellar in darkness with sometimes just a candle or two, neither did they experience any Air Raids as I did in Stuttgart.*)

With Onkel August, my favourite uncle.

Even the local barber, who was also a farmer, pretended to slip with his scissors and cut my ears every time I was sent to have a haircut, and then laughed when I was in pain. One day the same prick came back from his field with a wagon pulled by two cows and laden full of hay. While I was walking on the other side of the street early one evening he got his whip and hit me with the leather strap around my right knee. I screamed with pain and hid between two buildings so no one could see me crying.

Of course if I told anybody that I got bullied in school or by the barber they would say, "It serves you right, you must have been a bad boy".

I could tell of many more incidents like that, but people say with a bit of a laugh, "let bygones be bygones."

That may be fine, but I will never forget.

After some time living with Aunty Frieda and Uncle Gottlieb I was taken to Tante Mina (*Frieda's twin sister*) who was married to August Eigenmann who became one of my favourite Uncles. Onkel August had a *'Stage Coach'*, yes like in the Wild West, only without tomahawk throwing Indians. He would take people and postal goods to the railway 5 Km away to *Flehingen* because *Kuernbach* never had a railway connection. Little Fritzle was allowed to accompany him early in the mornings.

We had to get up at 4 am and I have never forgotten the fantastic breakfast we had. Aunty Mina was already down at the pen where she had milked the goats. She warmed up the milk and put pieces of her homemade bread in to it and it was absolutely delicious. One must remember, by the end of 1944 Germany was just about on its knees, and food was hard to come by. Even in the country we started to feel the pinch. About 4.30 am uncle August (*all the kids loved him*) and I walked about half a Kilometre to the middle of the village where the horses and the coach were kept. I never forget the names of the two horses, one a silver female *Lotte* and a brown male *Max*. On the way to the railway station Uncle August often sang a song, which went like this:

"*HEB am GAUL dor SCHWANZ hoch ond guck am henda nei, do liggd a GOLDNER APFEL dren ond der isch DEI.*" which in English would translate as: "Lift the horses' tails up and have a look inside, there rests a golden apple and it is yours to take".

I had a great time with my uncle and being with him made me feel safe and protected.

Anita and Fritzle in Stuttgart

Not that much later I got the news that our home in Stuttgart had been totally destroyed. It was the 14th of October 1944. There was this huge air strike and it destroyed just about everything. Lucky Mum and Heinz were in Backnang and Dad was in Loerrach near the Swiss border to finish of his REFA course which he and another college student were studying for Mahle, their employer. Had they been in Stuttgart it would have been the end of them.

A few weeks earlier my uncle Paul Habrik who married mum's older sister Anni got bombed out so they moved with their Daughters Anita, who was my age, and the younger twins Karin and Ilse who were two years older than my brother Heinz, to Kuernbach and into Grandma's house.

Heinz, Karin, Fritzle, and Ilse in Kuernbach.

Early Journeys

A couple of weeks later they took me to Stuttgart in a friend's old delivery truck to have a look at what was left of our apartment house. There was absolutely nothing left. We found an undamaged orange drinking glass and kept it for years as a reminder of a very bad time.

Stuttgart was flattened because it was a big industrial city, and the bombs were still coming. Just after we left to make our way back to Kuernbach as quick as possible, the air raid sirens were already telling people to take shelter.

A few weeks later our 'Backnang Oma' found a little two bedroom apartment in the top level of a two storey house for us, on the bottom lived Mrs Schenk who lost her husband in Russia, and so we moved into Nr.9 Zwieschenaeckerle Backnang.

It was the end of November 1944 and it started to become very cold. Mum told me years later that all we had when we moved to Backnang was 50 Kg of briquettes and 50Kg of potatoes to keep a family of 4 alive.

She would always get tears in her eyes remembering those times. Unbelievably, the radio still told us how good our soldiers were doing, even though most of the people were starving. We lived on daily rations which we got with the ration coupons every family was handed once a week.

The Glasbrenner family in 1943 in Stuttgart. Dad, Mum, Fritzle, Heinzle.

Now for the sore point... I had to go back to another School. My school time in Kuernbach was next to nil and home work was not important because after school us kids had to work in the fields with the 'Harvest and Grape stamping'. Grapes where harvested by adults and we kids had to trample them in big vats with our bare feet. After moving to Backnang it took till mid-December before I was enrolled in my third School. (Mind you I was only 8 years old.)

One morning I happened to look out of our lounge room window up and down the street. I noticed this young blond kid coming down the hill (*Zwieschenaeckerle* was built on a small hill) with a fancy leather school back-pack that had an image of little red riding hood and the big bad wolf on it, going to school. It annoyed me, and maybe I was a bit jealous, so I spat down at him.

He looked up, waving a fist threateningly and yelled, "If I ever catch you I'll break your neck."

I guessed that he was maybe one year older than me. Well, on the way back from school the same thing happened again, the fist was made and my neck was going to be broken. One would think that guy would walk on the other side of the street, no he just had to walk under our window, Knowing I would be there waiting to spit on him.

The inevitable confrontation happened when I had to go to the corner shop to get some milk, only it didn't turn out as I expected. Turning the corner there he was, ready and waiting to break my neck. We stood glaring at each other, each determined not to give way.

After a few minutes of sizing each other up, he finally made a fist, shook it at me and said, "If you spit at me again, I'll break your neck." Then he turned around the corner and strutted up the hill as if he just won a big battle.

That felt good, even though nothing happened.

In Middle School where I was enrolled I had to make new friends and I did. Sitting next to a kid called Juergen Bittelmann we became a good friend for a while. His parents came from Berlin as refugees bringing along him and his Sister. Juergen did not live far from us so it was just natural that we became friends. That was also the time when I met Theo Guth, and Rolf Muenzing among others.

After the Christmas Holidays we went back to school in January 1945. The first weeks in the New Year went well in school, then *the shit hit the fan*. The war intensified and the Allied Soldiers came closer and closer. The air raids even hit Backnang and the British fighter planes were shooting at everything that moved. Many stories were told by my friends who had close encounters when the bullets hit the ground missing them by only a few centimetres.

I also had a bad experience with one of those fighter planes. It was in the middle of April 1944 on a sunny morning. There was no school anymore because the end of the war was near. Sirens where blasting, warning people to find shelter, enemy planes were on their way.

Stupidly not bothering to seek shelter I stood and looked out the windows at the deserted streets thinking how peaceful it all looked. All of a bloody sudden this little plane came over the hill with an incredibly loud noise and flew straight towards me. It fired a salvo of bullets which hit the window frame 30 centimetres from where I was standing, I nearly crapped in my pants. I was too stunned to move.

At the last instant it pulled up and roared over the top of the house making the window rattle violently.

I can still see the pilot's smiling face to this day!

One day mum decided we should travel to Kuernbach to get some food supplies because in the country things were not quite as bad as in the city. Kuernbach was only 60 Km away, but it took a long time to get there. Trains were still running, but intermittently.

Backnang was built on several hills and wherever you walked it was either up or down. Mum and I left one morning carrying a basket to be fuelled with some food. We walked down Zwieschenaeckerle turned into Gartenstrasse to Sulzbacherstrasse and through town then up the hill to the railway station. Firstly we had to travel to Marbach am Neckar and there we caught a train to Laufen am Neckar.

In those days the trains were still pulled by steam locomotives. In Laufen we had to wait for the little train which supplied all the villages along the 25 Km long Zaber Creek route. The tracks where only about 75cm wide and the train had only three wagons, one for passengers and two for goods. It travelled through little villages like Meimsheim, Frauenzimmern, Gueglingen, Pfaffenhofen, and Zaberfeld to Leonbronn where it finished. From there we had a 5Km walk through the forest to reach Kuernbach. It would have taken us maybe two to three hours to get there. It was great to see all the relatives and some school friends. We stayed a few days and then made our way back to Backnang with full baskets of bread, sausages, fruit and some smoked beef. After the long walk back to the train station through the forest accompanied by some friends we caught the little train back to Laufen.

About 10 Km before reaching Laufen we got hit by a totally unexpected air raid. Travelling as fast as it could to reach a tunnel 2 Km ahead, the little train was hit by bullets from all sides. Fortunately no one was injured before we finally reached the tunnel where we could wait safely until the raid was over. Completely shaken we finally continued on to Laufen. It was nightfall and we were utterly exhausted when we arrived back home.

With no more school, kids were roaming the streets. Dad, still doing his studies in Loerrach, was on his way back to Stuttgart, while Mum was in Backnang looking after Heinz and me.

At half past four in the morning on the 19th of April the SS dynamited Backnang's two bridges which led over our river Murr to make it hard for the Allies to follow them. What a joke!

On the 20th of April on Adolf Hitler's birthday the War in Backnang was over. At 10 am some of us kids where standing on Sulzbacher Strasse watching the American tanks and soldiers with machine guns entering Backnang. It was quite a picture. Instead of Swastika Flags in windows of houses to celebrate Adolf's birthday as we had to do before, there were now white bed sheets hanging out indicating our surrender.

Dad just made it back two nights before otherwise he would have been stuck somewhere on the way. The Americans took over our school and some of the factories to make them into living quarters for their troops. A severe curfew was established with no one allowed on the Street, except for one hour in the morning and one in the afternoon, to get fresh water at one of the wells.

The American Government was looking for Interpreters and naturally Dad and a couple of other men got the job. Captain Watson, God bless his Soul, was in charge of the whole Backnanger Region and Dad became his personal Interpreter. This turned out to be a God-send for us. Dad was the only one to walk the streets, with his armband on. Now and again we were invited to eat in the soldiers' canteen, which was very quickly established. Sometimes we received a care packet, a parcel from Dad's sister in Philadelphia containing coffee, soap, cigarettes and a few other goodies. Every time one of those packets arrived it felt like Xmas.

Early Journeys

(*Aunt Maria and Uncle Pete, also sent parcels to their other relatives, God bless them.*)

There was no school and a few weeks later when the war came to an end in Berlin the curfew was lifted and people were allowed on the street during day time again.

Mum helped the American soldiers with their washing and got paid in tinned food, soap, cigarettes, plus lollies or chewing gum for us. Bleichwiese, a big market place in the middle of town next to the river Murr was used by the Americans to park their trucks, jeeps, tanks, and a lot of their war machinery. It took Juergen my Berliner and I not long to find out where all the goodies were hidden in the glove boxes of their trucks.

Each truck had two or three day's rations consisting of a packet of dried biscuits, a tin of backed beans, a small packet of jam, three cigarettes, a small packet of matches and sometimes a tin of sardines in their glove compartment. We needed them badly. We had to wait till dusk to sneak past the sentries and then crawl under the trucks not to be spotted. Opening the doors of the trucks was always a bit of a problem because we had to climb up to get to the door handle. Sometimes we managed to get away with two or three rations and had to sneak back home because we still could not be seen on the streets at night.

There was no School for the whole year of 1945. On the 18th of June I was 9 years old and by that time learning to survive on the streets was important. We spend a lot of time with the Americans stealing whatever we got our hands on. Sometimes we got caught and copped a boot up the arse. (All in a day's work).

In 1946 we started school again but only two or three times a week. Sometimes only a half day.

Germany was a total mess; the destruction of the country was indescribable. Food was hard to get and people took some of their belongings, clothes, bicycles, cutlery, etc. if it had not been destroyed, to farmers, in exchange for a bit of flour, eggs, or some meat, that is if they had any. I became aware how the Black Market started. It was sheer chaos. I can remember some elderly people saying that Dwight Eisenhower wanted to eliminate the whole German Race. Whether he was fair dinkum or not I can't verify. Never-the-less the Americans started the Marshall Plan to supply food to the Schools called *Schulspeissung*. It was a great relief to get some warm food in our stomachs. It was also a relief for our parents, one mouth less to feed. Nearly all of us looked like the starving African children you can see in refugee camps — you could play on our ribs like on the keyboard of a piano.

By 1946 everyone picked up the cigarette butts which the US Soldiers threw half-finished on to the streets, and you had to be quick to get hold of a butt *which we called kippe or hugo*, because there were always several people trying to get them first. Some of us had already started smoking secretly. We had to be aware of adults; if we were caught we would definitely get a swift kick up the backside.

By the time I was 11, I was very switched on, not in school but on the street. As soon as I spotted a soldier smoking, I followed him, with a few others who were after the same butt. One had to be very quick or you missed out. I was very fast then and I was able to read the soldier's moves. If he held his cigarette a certain way I knew exactly to which side he would flick it, and I also could tell when he made his last draw, and by the time he did I was already jumping towards it and was able to snatch a couple of quick draws before the stronger kids took it off me.

Sometimes Juergen and I shared some of our loot with a few of our class mates, not the cigarettes, but the baked beans and other goodies One day Late 1947 Juergen informed me that his Parents had decided to go back to Berlin with the whole family. That was bad news for both of us, but there was nothing we could do about it.

It was the time also when some of our Soldiers returned from prison camps in France and England (*Russia kept them for many more years*). They certainly did not look as bad as the ones who had to work in Siberia. The clean-up had started. Every German who was able to work did so and soon men went back to some of the jobs which they did before. Industry started up again in factories which were still under repair but no one cared. The main objective was to rebuild Germany and put food on the table again. AEG, a big Electrical Company came to Backnang employing lots of people. Some of the Leather Factories, for which Backnang was famous, started up again. Dad was up-graded. He was put in charge of all the big Companies and controlled their finances. Dad became known in very high places, but had a lot of responsibilities to be fair to all.

It was the End of 1947, Juergen and his family had gone back to Berlin to live. It was a very sad goodbye, because we knew we would probably never see each other again.

Forty years later on a visit to Backnang I got on to his 93 year old Father, (*I got his telephone number through Theo's sister in law Ursel who worked in a Government Office and searched for him*) who was still living in Berlin. He told me that Juergen had died two years earlier in Braunschweig where he was running a Pub.

I would have loved to have seen him again!

Dad was a clever hard working man and a good father always providing for his family as much as the times would allow, and of course Mum and Dad were always talking and thinking of America and how much easier life had been there. They were a bit morbid and disillusioned about the war and the destruction it had caused. But in time they adjusted to the different way of life in Germany, and just got on with it.

Every one in the family, especially Dad, thought I should go to High School, (the school Dad had originally graduated from) except me.

I did not want to change schools again. I had had enough and wanted to stay with my friends. I was promised a new bicycle if I would change. I did not want or need a new bike. I had one which I had re-built from an old frame I happened to come across.

Any how I had no choice, when the day came to do an entrance exam, I deliberately made a lot of mistakes in the hope they would not take me. But I did not count on that stupid Mrs Brown, who was our teacher and lived not far from us and who knew Dad well. She corrected all my mistakes and I passed. What a letdown, being pulled away from my school mates for the third time and taken somewhere I did not want to go. It broke my spirit. Just because Dad went to the same School when he was a young boy and did well shouldn't mean that I should go too. I know they wanted the best for me, but in hindsight it was very wrong.

Again I had to make new class mates and I was not very happy the way things were developing. Needless to say I lasted only 9 months before every one realised, high school was not for me. I was happy about that and looked forward to be with my mates again. It felt like I got hit on the head with a cricket bat when I realised they put me a class below and not with my mates at all.

Well, I was just on 12 years old and this was the 5th school I had to attend and to make new mates again. Lucky, Ernst Kloepfer who lived around the corner from us was already one of my mates and I was sitting next to him so I could look at his school work and copy it.

If one did something wrong, the teacher still gave you a few lashes across your bum or 5 hits with a stick across an open hand. Not being the bravest I copped it several times, and that in front of all the girls who were part of our class. I was fed up with it and during one lunch time I sneaked back in to the class room, grabbed the bloody cane and threw it out the window.

After lunch the teacher was looking for it, and offered 20 pfennig to anyone who would find it. I held up my hand and told him that I saw something looking like a cane near some bushes when I was down the school yard. He sent me down to fetch it, thanked me and gave me the 20 pfennig.

1949 school group: Fritzle is the top left...

In 1948, Germany changed the currency from the Reich Mark to the Deutsche Mark and before one could say *"Jack Robinson"* the shops were chock a block full to the brim with goods. There had been nothing available before the change, and after it, you could get just about anything you wanted.

Early Journeys

Through some connections our parents were able to rent the bottom part of a house in a little no-through road called *zum Plattenwald* (later *Fritz Haeuser Street.*) A little further up the hill and practically right next to us lived my arch enemy, who a few years earlier wanted to break my neck. His name was Hans Kretschmer and as it turned out he was 13 months older than me. What can I say? When you're young, things are quickly forgotten. We became best of mates.

And now every time we go to Germany we call in and have a good feed and a taste of his best wine with him and his wife Nada, talking about old times. They even visit us in Australia.

Just around the corner lived Theo Guth, Guenter Schad, Ernst Kloepfer, and opposite us Rolf Layer. On the other side of the house lived the Adlung family. Their oldest son was Manfred who is still a friend today. It was also the time when I decided that I would like a sand castle. Rolf Layer who lived across the road had one in their back yard. As a matter of fact, Rolf had just about everything. His father was a well-to-do business man who owned his two-family house and Rolf was their only son. Rolf was two years older than me and all the kids were a bit jealous of him because he had so much more than us. Any how it was relatively easy for me to get my castle.

All I had to do was to get some boards nail them together and there you go! I got myself a bucket from the Neighbour's shed and waited until it got dark. I snuck across and looked in Layer's window and as expected they were having dinner. Looking around the neighbourhood to make sure that no one was watching I started working. I made numerous trips back and forth to fill my boards. I was very happy having my own sand castle and I must say I slept very well that night.

Next morning I got up before breakfast to have a look at the hard work I did the night before and was extremely happy with the result. I was not very happy when I got home from school and saw Rolf waiting for me outside our gate. He belted shit out of me and made me carry all the sand back to his place.

What a letdown. Here I was the proud owner of a sand castle for one night, and how hard did I work for it! I thought I deserved better. During that evening while taking so many buckets of sand I had left a trail which I could not see in the darkness. Rolf followed the trail right to my place. The hiding I got from Rolf was not forgotten and I swore I would get even one day.

By that time Germany started to become a Nation again.

We were still occupied but things where looking up. Dad finished what he meant to do and started a new job at AEG (*Allgemeine Elecktrizitaet Gesellschaft*) where he worked in the tool making division which after a couple of years he was in charge of.

Then the rot set in. Our mother got very ill; contracting Polio and there was no penicillin to treat her with. I will always remember a couple of American first aid soldiers carrying her to a makeshift ambulance. I can still see the big wound on her spine when they carried her out of the room. They took her straight to the hospital. Why our Mother should be hit with such a terrible illness was and is a mystery. Mum was a tall beautiful women and one would never have thought that she would get sick.

From the waist down she was totally paralysed, and for a whole year she had to lay on her back, unable to move. It was a bad time and very hard for Dad. To make it a bit easier Heinz was taken to Kuernbach to Grandma where Uncle Paul, Aunty Annie and our cousins Annita, Karin and Ilse also lived. That was good because he never would never be as lonely as I was some years before.

Grandma (Dad's Mother) lived with us to look after me while Dad was at work and did the cooking during the time Mum spent in hospital. We were also a bit lucky because the top storey of the little house was occupied by Mrs Gretel Seitz and her two sons. Ulrich (the same age as my brother) and Joachim a couple of year's younger. Gretel lost her husband in the war. He was a Paratrooper and got killed in action. Gretel was a super organiser, good looking with a Marilyn Monroe Body. She went off to the Farmers to get food for all of us. She would take some of her husband's clothes and never came back empty handed, but then who could refuse Gretel?

Sometimes I was allowed to come along on my bike (she had one also) and was astonished to watch how she operated. She would show a farmer a pair of trouser or a shirt, and after she got what she wanted put the shirt or trousers back in the basket, give the farmer a kiss on his cheek and bid good bye; I guess she just had that extra bit of charm.

On holidays or long weekends I would jump on my bike and ride to Kuernbach 65 Km from home to visit Heinz and all the others. Heinz had settled in without problems. He started school and did quite well. By that time of course there were no more Nazi teachers and life had a new purpose. I also had a few friends there and all the relatives wanted to see Irma's young Fritzle. A visit to uncle August and aunty Mina was always a highlight.

Grandma Backnang (the other one was always Grandma Kuernbach) was a beautiful elderly Lady who helped where help was needed. Her husband died when my dad was eighteen. Dad was already on his way to Bremen where he was supposed to board a ship to America. He had to return to be at the funeral and had to board the next available ship.

Grandma Backnang was born in the Siegelsberg part of Murrhart where her parents owned a sawmill. Maria Nusskern had two younger brothers Gottlieb and Gottlob. When she was 19 or 20 she met the young Gottlieb Glasbrenner who she fell in love with. Her father was not happy with Maria's choice because he worked for the railways as a Kramper. (A Kramper was a guy in charge of a certain length of railway track and had to control all the bolts and made sure they fastened the tracks securely). He was sure his Maria could do much better.

But when the time came for them to get married he told her that he would not come to the wedding otherwise the Devil would get him. He sat in the park waiting until they were married because he was frightened of the Devil. Never the less, he paid for everything and all went well. They moved to Murrhart where Lotte was borne in 1905 then Maria in 1907 and in 1910 our Dad Friedrich Gottlieb Glasbrenner was born.

When Grandma came to look after me she was getting on and I could wrap her around my finger. Dad did very well at AEG and loved his work. Eventually he got himself a little motor bike (called Express) with pedals to start it. It had two forward gears and for a while I could keep up with him on my bike. What a let down from the cars he owned in America (Ford Dodge and Buick).

That was about the time I started to wag school.

There was an old empty house next to where Theo lived where we created our Hideout and only a few of us knew where it was. We cleaned one of the rooms as good as we could and made it our meeting place.

In the mornings I left home after breakfast to go to school and once I got to the corner made a right turn to go to our hideout. One thing I got hooked on was reading. I must have read most of Karl May's adventure books and I loved all the Wild West stories which were available in book stores. When I got home from 'school', Grandma would ask how the day was and whether I had any homework. I always said I did it in school.

Naturally the wagging came to an abrupt end when two policemen turned up and took me back to school. The teacher felt sorry for me because Mum was in hospital paralysed with Polio. Of course Dad was with her every day after work, which meant I had practically no one who really looked after me and I could roam the streets as much as I liked. I visited Mum every second day and assured her that all was well. Back at School I talked my good friend Ernst to do my homework for me. Ernst did it for a while, but eventually he got sick of it and it took me all my persuasion to keep him doing it. Years later we still laughed about it.

Dad never punished me much. He was a good Father who went through hard times to look after his family. Every time I did something wrong or someone complained about me I always talked my way out of it. Dad would say, "*I could find an excuse quicker than a mouse a hole*".

Now and again I got a slap behind the ear, except one time. Dad was never late for work, I mean NEVER, whether the sun was shining or a there was half a metre of snow. When he could not ride his little motorbike he walked.

One evening in summer Hans and I decided to borrow his bike. We waited until dusk and snuck in to the little shed where Dad kept the bike and wheeled it out ever so quietly and pushed it against the back neighbour's fence. We had a difficult task ahead of us because the fence was about one and half meters high and the bike was very heavy. Iit was one of the first bikes ever built with a steel frame, and it was Dad's pride and joy. When we finally got it over the fence we had to be careful not to make too much noise going through the neighbour's property. At last on the other street we pushed it along a bit further before jumping on it to start it. Hans being a year older was handling it ok while I was on the back.

We were having a great time riding and enjoying it and covered quite a few Km around the area when suddenly the bloody chain broke. What a disaster. We didn't know what to do. First we had to push the bike back home and lift it over the fence again, then we put it back in the shed where we found a torch and some wire. With a pair of pliers we managed to wire the chain together again. I didn't sleep too well that night and got up pretty early to be dressed and ready to bolt before Dad got on his bike.

I told Grandma that I had to go to school a bit earlier because of some excursions.

I left and went to the opposite neighbour's property where I hid and waited for Dad to get on his bike. Twenty minutes later I saw him coming out of the house to get his bike. Once he was on the street he sat in the saddle and let it roll down the little hill to start. Well, he didn't go 10 metres before the chain busted. He stopped got off the bike and looked what was wrong and sure enough found the problem straight away. When he found the piece of wire he put two and two together.

He pushed the bike back into the shed, took the chain off, went back to the house, got cleaned up and came out the house to walk to work. As I watched him coming out I could see that he was not a happy man. His face was a reddish colour and he was muttering to himself. I knew it had been a wise move to leave early, but the day was not over. In hindsight we should have just left the bike without using the wire to try and fix it.

He would have thought it just happened and if he questioned me about it I surely could have talked my way out of it. I went to school thinking all day about what was going to happen later on. I knew when Dad was coming from hospital so I had time to speak to Hans about it. Hans had to be careful that his Father didn't get wind of it because his Dad was much stricter than mine. Herr Kretschmer did find out about it and Hans had to clean the whole family's shoes (His Mum, Dad, older brother and older twin sisters) every Sunday for three months.

Dad finally came home after being with Mum and somehow had mellowed a bit and the bad belting I expected turned out to be a half a dozen hits on my arse. Mind you they still hurt.

Dad told me in later years that it wasn't so much wiring the chain together; it was because he was late for work.

Not long after that episode I decided I had to have a rabbit and with some of my mates help we built a small rabbit house. I must add that just about every one at that time had rabbits because meat was hard to come by and on special occasions a roasted rabbit went down very well.

As it happened I finished up with a little white Angora rabbit with red eyes and we had lots of fun with him but, he had to be fed and rabbits eat grass and hay! Sometime later I had to find a simpler way of getting fodder than going to the paddocks with a basket to collect grass. Next door Mr Adlung had about 40 rabbits and plenty of grass and hay and that of course suited me just fine! Twice or three times a week I waited for nightfall, then climbed over the back fence and snuck in to his shed behind the rabbit house and helped myself with a few heaps of hay and grass; problem solved.

After a while Mr Adlung got suspicious of me because he realised that his hard come by fodder went down quicker than possible. He knew I had a rabbit and he did not like me too much because he caught me a couple of times pinching some of his Strawberries and Apples. Mr Adlung was a very hard working man, but had the misfortune of getting his arm caught in a machine which tore off his left arm just below the elbow. He received a false arm with a hook on the end of it and that did not stop him from doing what he did before. One had to watch that bloody hook; it became a dangerous weapon if one came too close to it. Fortunately for me I was a fast runner and my feet got me out of danger many times.

I can't remember the exact time but I had not forgotten the hiding I received from Rolf about the sand castle. It must have been around the time when mum was getting better. I still remember the time when I got to hospital to visit her everyone was excited because mum could move her big toe. I was delighted because I knew mum would win the fight and probably walk again. She fought really hard and we could see the progress she was making. She was looked after very well in hospital as much as the times allowed then. Mum was brought home nearly one year later and was looked after by Grandma, Gretel and the rest of us.

Back to the rabbit; it became too hot for me to keep pinching fodder from Mr Adlung and I could see how he searched the ground to find any trace of someone dropping some evidence, so here was my revenge!

Late one evening I jumped the fence, grabbed an arm full of hay and dropped very tiny bundles from his shed every couple of meters around his house and down to his front gate, then across the street after opening Rolf's gate. I dropped more hay down the side of Layer's house towards their rabbit house where I made sure I dropped some hay right in front of it.

Getting up early in the morning, (I had picked a Friday evening) I kept watch through our front window for Mr Adlung to appear and sure enough, I did not have to wait long before he came around the corner of his house with a satisfactory little smile on his face, following the traces of hay, obviously thinking they would lead straight in to our front gate and to my rabbit.

I raced to the back of our house, jumped through the back window, snuck around the corner and watched him, great disbelief on his face, marching across the street to disappear into Layer's back yard.

The whole of the Layer family appeared and standing by our front gate where I couldn't be seen I witnessed the commotion and heard every word they yelled at each other. The layers found it hard to convince Mr

Adlung of their innocence. The proof was there on the ground in front of their eyes.

I never told Rolf I had done it, but years later I told Manfred Adlung's oldest son, my good friend to this day.

Looking back I most probably had the easiest upbringing. I had much more time on the street than all my other friends. Most of their parents had gardens to take care of. Theo didn't have it as easy as me. Every time some of us called on him to play football or go on a bike ride, he either had to clean the rabbit house or go to their garden which was about 2 Km from home and full of fruit trees which had to be looked after. The grass had to be cut and taken back for the rabbits. Often, if I had time I would go and help him with his chores.

We all smoked except Guenter Schad because he had something wrong with his lungs.

The house where we lived in was a two family home where Mum Dad and I lived on the bottom. Heinz was still in Kuernbach, Grandma lived about 2 km away, Frau Seitz with her two sons on top and under the roof (in the loft) was a little room which was mine.

In those days kids played on the street and we all were friends in our neighbourhood. Playing football in the evenings became a bit of a problem because one of the neighbours a couple of houses around the corner was not happy with us making any noise and having fun. That man was not liked by anyone and his kids had nothing in common with us. They were shit frightened of their father. He was a real Hitler man during the war.

Anyhow Hans and I thought it was time to teach this prick a lesson. We watched his house one evening and waited until he finished supper and sat down to relax with a book or something. The two of us decided not to have a crap for a whole day and ate plenty of green apples. When nightfall came and the street was deserted we opened the front gate of this prick's house, went up the three steps to his front door, dropped our pants and planted a couple of the most beautiful turds approximately 25 cm long with as good a diameter as anyone has ever seen, right outside his door. It was something to be proud of. We had to hurry because we did not want to be caught. We pulled our pants up and got ready to move, but before we did we rang the doorbell real hard and then closed his front gate, ran across the street, jumped in to his opposite neighbour's yard and hid behind some bushes.

We didn't have to wait long before his front door light came on and the door opened. We could see his silhouette against the back light from his hallway. Of course he did not see anyone so he stepped forward to look around and that was it. He totally squashed and demolished our beautiful turds with his house shoes. I cannot repeat the language which followed; I think he would have killed us in rage. Hans and I didn't hang around any longer and made our way along the street where some of the older kids where still playing football under the street light. We joined in the game so we had an alibi.

It did not take long before that idiot came along the street towards us in a pair of walking shoes. He was still in a rage but there were too many of us and he couldn't do a thing. He might have had his suspicion about who it was but he never found out. Naturally we had to tell the other kids what had happened because they knew we were the culprits coming from his way a short time before. When we told them what happened they could not play anymore football because they pissed themselves laughing, slapping us on the shoulders and were so happy we did what we did because no one liked him. I slept good that night, dreaming about the good way we got rid of those enormous turds.

Mittelschule 1950. I am in front of the teacher, right edge of picture. Theo is next to me. Both of us are wearing leather shorts and jackets.

In 1949 Hans was lucky to get an apprentice ship at Kaelble the big Motor Company in Backnang as a machine mechanic where our father got his trade so many years before.

Mum made good progress with her illness and she was able to move around the house slowly, and with Gretel's help life became easier. Grandma only came once a week to help with the washing and cleaning.

I still went to school for another year and did reasonably well.

In 1950 another blow came. Even though it was still hard to get an apprenticeship they got one for me. I had to become a Toolmaker. I didn't like that at all, but what could I do? I was just 15 at the time and the apprenticeship became available because one apprentice had left and I took his place. I was chosen because Mr Martin who was in charge of all personnel at AEG, knew my father well. The big problem was, there were 60 new apprentices and they all started 4 months before me and I had to catch up to the others which was for me impossible. I should have stayed in school for another 9 months and started a year later, that would have been the right move. In the beginning I tried hard to catch up, starting to file steel until I had blisters on the palms of my hands. I earned 10 Marks a week and out of that Mum kept 8 for housekeeping and that left me with 2 Marks for smokes and drinks; not much at all. About two months earlier Theo was able to get an apprenticeship across the road in a leather factory as a clerk and we caught up with each other nearly every day.

By that time the Americans had left and all the factories were occupied by the original owners and were flat out doing what they used to do. Restaurants and Pubs started to do well again, and so did the shops because people earned money and there was no shortage of work.

Everyone had a job by this time. Every weekend festivals started by the Fire Department, the Musical Society, or they were sponsored by the Council. On Saturdays there was always dancing in town halls or some hotels. One did not have to go far to have a great time. Around Backnang there would have been a dozen or so small villages and one of them would have a festival going with the local brass band providing the entertainment.

Life started to be fun, except for one thing, my work. The Guy who was in charge of all the apprentices, (by that time AEG had over two thousand employees) had something against me. If I did the slightest thing wrong, like making the smallest mistake I would get a slap across the ears so hard that it made me see all the stars in heaven at once. I was not the only one who copped it. A few others got whacked also, but Rolf who was two years ahead of me and I myself felt his hands nearly every day. Most of the Kids were scared of him, even his own kids at home. Talk about a bad human being; he was an Arsehole of the first degree.

I never knew why he had such a great dislike for me. Maybe he had a grudge against my dad because he was doing so well. There was no way I could catch up to the others and after some months I started to become very sad about work and it dawned on me that it was not the right for me to be there. A few years later my brother Heinz did his apprenticeship as an Electro Mechanic and had absolutely no problems and passed with flying colours. They were different times then.

Konne, Fritz, (me) and Theo with our bikes on a trip to Bodensee, 1949.

Early Journeys

I became more interested in riding on our bikes at weekends and holidays with Theo and Konne. We wanted to know what was beyond Backnang. At first we made small tours to Kuernbach or to Stuttgart, later on we started to go as far as Black Forrest, or followed the Neckar River to the almighty Rein River. We loved the adventure and could not get to enough places to see and meet and hear the stories of people we would meet on our trips.

We had met Uli a couple of years earlier because his father was a gardener and had a big market-gardening lot which belonged to the leather factory where Uli's father worked and most of the garden produce was meant for the canteen which the factory ran for their employees. Uli was two years older than me and started an apprenticeship as a fine sheet metal mechanic (panel beater) in Backnang. Uli's older brother Alfred had to work with his father who wanted him to become a gardener which he was not too happy about. Alfred was built like a brick dunny and was as strong as an ox. He was also good looking and according to our mother who said if she was 18 she would have married him on the spot.

Konne, Fritz and Theo on another trip in 1949, at Burgruine Hohentwiel.

Alfred and I got on fantastic, every time I was around at lunch time he would give me 50 Pfennig and send me down town to pick him up some lunch which consisted always of a bread roll and 100 gram of leberkaes (*meatloaf*). On the way back I would get my pocket knife out (*every kid had a pocket knife*) and cut my 10% of the meatloaf as my reward. Many times in later life we still talk and laugh about it. Alfred became a very successful builder and business man. Mr Bauer started a retail stand at the local marked on Wednesdays and Saturdays and Uli had to work there before he started his apprenticeship. Sometimes I helped out and got paid for it. Now and again Uli would also join us on some of our bike tours.

The 2 Marks I had a week was hardly enough to go around. With Beer Festivals every weekend we had to look for other means to keep ourselves afloat. Next to smoking we also started to get the taste for beer, except for Theo who did not like alcohol and only drank Coca Cola. He never had much time for beer fests.

I also had other friends who were in the same boat as me financially, in other words we had to look after ourselves. I never forgot and I think the whole of Backnang has never forgotten because in later years every one heard the tale of the missing sausages (*hot dogs*).

One Saturday evening at a big Fest at Bleichwiese organised by the fire brigade we were thirsty and hungry. We had a really good thing going. If some guy ordered a pint of beer, one of us would stand next to him and ask him a couple of questions and as soon as he turned sideways, another mate would quickly grab the guy's stein and swallow some of his beer while he answered the question, and by the time he turned and lifted his glass it was half empty and wondered what the hell happened. We never got caught except once, when Adolf and I decided to go and ride our bikes to Lake Ebni one rainy Saturday evening.

For some reason I was not allowed to leave home so I told my parents I would go to bed. I jumped out the window, grabbed my bike and met Adolf who was waiting around the corner. At the Festival we repeated the same thing, but Adolf was not quick enough and got caught. I had to step back a few meters because the bloke pulled his leg back and kicked Adolf in the arse with such power that he fell and skidded in the mud on his belly for at least five meters. What a mess!

Back to the Fest in Backnang; we were starving and looking for something to eat. The Brass Band was in full swing the people were happy and the sausages and meatloaves smelled great. The sausages were served with a bread roll and some mustard on a small cardboard plate. A sausage, referred to as a *rote*, was loved by all. The cost of a *rote* was 50 Pfennig and came only one way, heated in hot water in a huge copper kettle.

I had 50 Pfennig but that was all I had on me and I wasn't prepared to spend it on food. And then I couldn't believe my luck.

There was Mrs Schad, the mother of Guenter. *Guenter later, along with our other friends, Herman Foell and Horst Phitzenmaier, committed themselves to migrate to Australia where they worked for several years. They left Germany before we did, and were already established in Melbourne when we arrived.*

What I saw made my heart jump faster and soothed the hunger pains in my stomach. Every time someone ordered a *rote*, Mrs Schad or another women had to walk several meters to the back wall were the kettle with hot water was standing full of sausages, and taking one she walked back to the customer. It was a huge tent, holding at least two thousand people and the kettle stood right in front where two sections of the tent were held together with strong leather straps. I pointed out to a couple of mates that I had in mind to grab myself a sausage, after which it would be their turn.

Konne leaned on the counter to watch while Karl and Erwin followed me around the corner to the back part of the tent. We had to be careful not to be seen. Looking through an opening on the tent I watched Mrs Schad walk away with a rote on a plate and that was the moment for me to act. As soon as I put my arm through the opening I could see Konne waving his hand to a couple of mates. He then left the counter from where he held watch. I put my hand in the hot water and grabbed a sausage.

I could not believe what happened next.

Someone up there really thought I wasn't a bad guy after all and thought he would present me with more than one because I was hungry. Yep they were tied together and you had to cut each individual sausage off with a knife. I was pulling and each time one sausage came through the hole over the leather strap it made some kind of a plopping noise.

I pulled and pulled and they kept coming. Through the opening I could see Mrs Schad coming for another one. When she saw the sausages disappearing through the hole in the tent with that plopping noise she dropped her plate and knife, threw her hands up in the air yelling, "my sausages, my sausages, someone is taking my sausages."

God bless her she was a good woman. After several more pulls the last one came through the hole, my mates and I had rings of hot sausages hanging around our necks. There must have been close to fifty of them.

Konne and two more mates came sneaking around the corner and each of us cut a few off with one of our pocket knives and then made our way along our river Murr and ate as fast as we could because there was a big commotion inside the tent.

Everyone wanted to know what happened hoping there was maybe a murder or something exiting. What a letdown when they found out that someone had pinched a string of snags.

Still, we had to disperse quickly because we could hear the police sirens coming through town to search for the culprits. By the time they got there we were all back in the tent from different entrances and the proof was in our stomachs. I must have eaten at least four of them.

On looking cautiously around the corner we saw Mrs Schad warming up another batch, so no harm done!

Time went by, the beatings got worse and my dislike for work accelerated. There was no way I could ever catch up to the others.

Our bike tours became longer and further from home. Sometimes we got as far as the Swiss or Austrian Border. At that time one still had to have a Visa to get in to those countries. Never having much money we had to find ways to survive. In the early fifties there wasn't much traffic, the roads were not bad and new trucks and cars were being built. The West German Industrial Revolution had begun. Farmers were happy to extend their hospitality and let us sleep in the barn on the hay with breakfast on the house. Most Farmers and their families were happy to hear the stories of our travels. At that time there weren't many cyclists or back packers travelling and it was still a novelty for farmers or others to get to know people from other towns or states.

It wasn't long before it all changed because a few idiots smoked in the farmer's hay sheds which was a definite no-no. Some sheds burned down with a big loss to the farmers. They closed shop and thanks to those idiots the good times were gone.

Konne learned to become a Stonemason and got his apprenticeship with Mr Wenzler who had the Tombstone business next to the Cemetery in Backnang. Konne was one year older than Theo and I. On our tours he was always the strongest one on the bikes. He could pedal faster than us, which is why he always left last.

When we were hungry the three of us would go to a restaurant

Ready to leave for my confirmation.

(*wirtschaft*) and order something cheap to eat, mostly sausages or scrambled eggs.

After finishing our meal Theo and I would pretend to go to the toilet, then sneak through the back door, jump on our bikes and ride hell for leather out of town! Several kilometres later we saw Konne pedalling furiously to catch up with us, happy to get away without paying the Bill.

March 26 1950 was a big day. Theo and I had our Confirmation in the Presbyterian Church in Backnang. All kids in Germany looked forward to their Confirmation Day. We had to assemble in Church at ten in the morning and most of the boys had stomach rumbles because we all had to recite a verse from the Bible. But it went well and we could not wait to get home to open our presents and go to a restaurant for a good meal and coffee with cakes. We made sure that several of our relatives and friends were also invited because it meant lots more presents.

After confirmation at the Presbytarian Church in 1950, Fritz and Theo immaculately dressed for the occasion.

During the year of 1950, through our father's connections we were able to acquire an apartment in a new family block built by AEG for their workers. Situated on the other side of town, it was a great relief to live in a modern place with excellent facilities. The street, Im Benzwasen, was not new to me. Dad's other sister Aunty Lotte, Uncle Eugen Deess, and family lived there.

*Members of the Backnanger Cycle club in 1952.
Theo is on one end while I am on the other.*

I had joined the Backnanger Cycling Club with Konne and Theo trying to become good cyclists. Wednesdays and Saturdays we trained and Sundays we took part in road races. One Sunday, we took part in a road race in Schweikheim, (15 km from Backnang). Theo and I started in B Class and we did very well, always in front. At the last kilometre there was a good rider called Hans about 500 Meters ahead of Theo, running second with me close behind. Lucky for us, Hans punctured a tyre with 400 Meters to the finish line and started running towards the finish to win the race. Naturally Theo and I gave it all we had and passed Hans about 50 meters before the line. Results in the newspaper next day had Theo Guth first, Fritz Glasbrenner second and Hans Steiger Third.

It was quite some time later that we told people there was only the three of us in the Race. Years later we heard that Hans Steiger drowned while trying to swim across the Rhine River I guess the current was to strong.

It was in the spring of 1952 that Theo and I decided to plan our next big adventure. Just the thought of getting away from my daily routine was exciting. I would literally do anything to escape the bullying that went on at work. Every time we got together we talked about our coming big adventure, and after a few weeks we decided we would go to South Africa on our bikes. They were of course our only means of transport.

After we knew where we were going the planning didn't get easier; it became very intense. We weren't 16 years old at the time and needed to get passports and other documents, immunisations, health certificates and visas. We never told anyone about our plans. They had to be totally secret.

Getting our passports was relative easy, we told our parents that we would like to go across the border in to Austria on our next holiday and they signed all the necessary papers. After getting our photos taken we went to the Town Hall, paid the DM 10 cost and in a couple of weeks we had our passports, issued on the 19th of March 1952 and send to us by mail. In those days passports were only valid for two years with a three year extension.

The next hurdle to jump was traveling to Stuttgart to get the Austrian Visa which took three days, and once we got that we showed it to our parents and a few friends telling them we intended to cycle to Austria. As soon as people knew that, we didn't show anybody our passports anymore. After that it was easy to sneak in to Stuttgart and get the Swiss and Italian visas.

On the 18th of June I had my 16th birthday and the time for our departure got closer. We still had lots of things to take care of. Road maps to be purchased and hidden. Theo got a transistorised travel radio. Our tent from previous trips was still okay; sleeping bags and cooking utensils we also had. Our Bikes were in perfect order and we were just about ready to hit the Road.

Theo had no problems getting his holidays but I had difficulties in obtaining mine because the shithead Aprentice Teacher did not want me to go on a little adventure. Actually he couldn't stop me from taking my annual leave, but instead of three weeks which I should have got, he only allowed me two. It really didn't matter because I knew I wouldn't be coming back again.

Theo, Konne and I still took part in some Criterions to keep fit, but we had to act as if we were looking forward to our trip through the Austrian border. Even Konne our closest friend did not suspect anything.

Criterion bike racing in Backnang 1952.

Chapter Two

On the 19 of July early in the morning we got on our way, just like all the other tours we had made previously.

I was a bit worried about our cash situation; I think we had about 15DM each in our pockets and 10DM stashed away for an absolute emergency. We thought that would see us through to South Africa.

It was a great feeling to be cycling away from Backnang into an unknown adventure, to be going to strange countries and meeting different people with different languages and customs.

I was a fresh 16 year old and Theo was still 15 for another couple of months.

We stopped outside Backnang and had one cigarette between us and decided to bypass Stuttgart and turn south via Goeppingen to Ulm. Just after Ulm after riding all day we found a friendly Farmer who let as stay in his barn and invited us for Vesper (Dinner) with his family.

Next morning after an early breakfast and a few sandwiches prepared by the Farmer's wife we bid them goodbye and hit the road again heading towards Sigmaringen where we put up our tent in the evening.

In the morning we finished our last sandwiches for breakfast and after sharing a cigarette we jumped on our bikes to see if we could get as far as the Swiss boarder past Singen. We managed to get to a little town — I think it was called Stein — very close to Switzerland and started to put up our tent.

Discovering we were almost out of smokes, I walked a short distance to a small shop. I entered the well-stocked shop and waited to get served, but it took several minutes after ringing the bell a couple of times before an elderly lady came along the corridor to serve me. I asked for a small pack of cigarettes (*in those days one could get a pack of three*).

After buying a packet I ran back to Theo and told him to pack up again, which we did and rode our bikes back to the same shop. We took our sleeping-bag bags, had a look around to make sure the coast was clear and went quietly into the shop and filled the bags with all kind of tinned food, biscuits, dried bread, a few packets of cigarettes and some fruit. We filled both bags to the brim and Theo walked out with them just before the old lady waddled out again to serve me.

I don't think she even recognised me so I just asked for a box of matches and left. Outside we jumped on our bikes and rode as fast as we could to the border station where we put up our tent and took stock of what we had got away with. To our surprise it was a lot, and in the morning we had great difficulty getting everything packed.

It was the 24th of July. We crossed the border into Switzerland, our first country outside Germany, and made our way toward Zurich, where we arrived just before dark.

Coming from a destroyed Germany to Switzerland was an eye opener. We could not get over how clean everything was. Zurich was at that time the cleanest city we ever saw. Pushing our heavily loaded bikes through the centre of town, looking at the funny trams, we were approached by a good looking middle aged woman who asked where we came from, wondering what we were doing at this time of day.

In those days we were still an attraction because there were not many cyclists on the roads, especially as young as us. She asked if we had some place to stay. When we told her we were looking for a park to put up our tent she offered to let us stay the night at her apartment just around the corner. We kindly accepted her offer and followed her to the house where she lived. Our bikes were locked in a store room and after grabbing our overnight bags we followed her upstairs to the second story. It was very comfortable and she offered us the guestroom for the night.

Theo and I just could not believe what was happening to us. Talk about Swiss hospitality…this lovely woman prepared us a sensational dinner and later she wanted to know all about our lives and adventures. She would have listened to us all evening, wanting to know about the war and the bombings, which she had never experienced.

As we wanted to have an early start in the morning, we promised her we would call in on the way back to talk more about what happened to us. Unfortunately things did not turn out that way. We did not mention to her that we were going to Africa and were running away from home. Before going to bed she gave us a pair of pyjamas each and took our dirty clothes to be washed over night. Needless to say we slept like 'Angels in Heaven'.

Around seven in the morning she woke us up to have a shower and to our surprise our clothes were washed and ironed, and on the sofa next to our beds. After a glorious breakfast, we felt reborn and could not thank that great woman enough for what she did for us. To this day we have not forgotten her hospitality and have loved Zurich ever since.

After packing our still fully laden bikes, she gave us a hug and we waved goodbye, and on a beautiful sunny morning at about 9 am we rode off, heading towards Luzern on the Vierwaldstaetter Lake.

We travelled along The Lake of Zurich but often had to push our bikes because the road went uphill towards the Alps. The scenery was like something out of a picture book; in front of us those huge mountains and behind us in the valley, Zurich with its beautiful lake glistening in the sunshine.

It was very slow going and after passing Horgen und Zug we stopped just after Schwyz and put up our tent just off the road near a little creek with very cold but crystal clear water. I dare say, we did not sleep as comfortably as the night before. Nevertheless we were used to sleeping on hard ground, and had done it many times on previous trips. Early next morning we got on our way, but the going was tougher; most of the day we had to push upwards, with very hard pedalling, but we made headway. We passed Altdorf, a few smaller villages and in late afternoon reached Andermatt.

We were pretty well stuffed by the time we got to rest in our tent. Next morning we found out that we could only travel through the St Gotthard Tunnel by a little train to reach the other side of the mountains, a big relief because we would nver have been able to pedal over those mountains. At the train station we asked what we had to do to obtain the cheapest fare. Again we were in luck! The two Guys behind the counter charged us the children's fares and let our bikes go free.

On top of that we had only half an hour to wait before the train left and took us as far as Bellinzona. By the time we hit the road again it was early afternoon with glorious sunshine.

Feeling really good we travelled downhill all the way to the Swiss/Italian Border. No hard pedalling this time...

The customs officer looked at us with a fair bit of curiosity. At that time there were not many cyclists on the road, let alone anyone as young as us. He stamped our passports without looking in our luggage and waved us on.

And we were in ITALY...

If only THEY could see us now.

I felt like waving my arms in a wild happy salute to all those left behind who had to work.

One thing was for sure, Theo and I would have been the first ones from Backnang to make it this far on a bike, just seven years after the end of the war.

It was fantastic to descend down the alpine road enjoying the beautiful sunshine with not a cloud in the sky. Wherever we looked there was ripe fruit growing in orchards, especially peaches, apples and pears.

When we felt we weren't being watched we helped ourselves, stocking up with some delicious fruit.

Needless to say that our German language did not get us very far, but with hand signs and our dictionary we could make ourselves understood. On the border we had changed half of our Deutsch Marks, which only gave us a handful of Lire. Actually we did not need much because we still had lots of tinned food, *and fruit was free.* Every time we came through a village we asked where we could buy *pane*. Instantly there was someone eager to take us to a bakery where we purchased a loaf of bread which more often than not we got as a present. People were very curious about us and wanted to know what we were doing in their country and what our future plans were. We told them that we only knew about Italy from school and learned what a beautiful country it was. We wanted to see for ourselves so we could tell our people of the wonderful hospitality we experienced when we get back home. (We became quite entrepreneurial; not bad for two young cycling friends).

I think we got as far as Como and found a great spot to put up our tent right next to the lake.

It had been a long day, so we looked forward to a good night's sleep. It was still too warm to sleep in our sleeping bags so we lay just on top of them and found out next morning that during the night we had lots of visitors, mosquitos... Every bit of bare skin was red with mosquito bites.

Oh well, it's all part of camping.

Just before midday next morning, heading towards Milano, disaster struck. We had made good headway, because it was all slightly downhill going away from the Alps. Theo was ahead of me and must have been looking at the scenery when he hit a small pothole. He nearly lost balance and I could not work out why he kept going from one side of the road to the other.

When I caught up to him I saw the damage. Through pressure on his handlebar the left side had broken off right on top of the upright.

He could only steer with his right arm, and though wobbling from side to side he managed to come to a stop. How lucky was he? Only his cycling skills saved him from having a bad fall and injuries.

We were about 20 km short of Milano in the middle of nowhere and Theo could not ride his bike steering with one arm. What could we do?

We looked around and saw a farmhouse not far from the road. It was surrounded by lots of fruit trees and vegetable gardens. Getting closer to the main house a couple of dogs came running towards us barking, making a hell of a racket. They ran straight towards us, but were wagging their tails so we knew they would not harm us. The front door opened and a big man, a woman and a couple of kids walked towards us, greeting Theo and me with '*bon giorno*' and a big smile. We reciprocated the greeting, and after showing the man Theo's broken handlebar he nodded his head and gave a hand sign to follow him inside the house.

Once again we couldn't get over the hospitality.

As soon as we sat down his wife, full of smiles, started to put some bread, cheese, ham, boiled eggs and other goodies on the table. By that time it was early in the afternoon and we were quite hungry. Theo did not drink alcohol so he was served a glass of orange juice while I enjoyed a glass of white wine with our hosts. We found out that the wine and food were all home grown produce. Afterwards we had some coffee in small cups which we found to be bitter, not what we were used to.

Our host saw that we were a bit worried about Theo's bike and indicated to us to follow him outside. He took Theo's bike and pushed it towards a shed, which was his workshop full of tools and all kinds of spare parts. After shifting a few old pieces of materials he came back with a rusty old bicycle and started to pull the handlebar off, which took some doing.

We could not believe our eyes when we saw this old thing he was going to put on Theo's new bike. After he mounted all the parts back together it certainly did not look too good. I wish to this day I had a picture of it. Once the rusty old handlebar had been fitted Theo took the bike for a spin and to his surprise it handled just as good as before. We could get on our way again and thought we would purchase a new handlebar in Milano, but we never did. By the time our host finished with the repairs it was late in the afternoon. We had a clean-up and were preparing to leave when our good man suggested that we stay overnight in his house.

Why leave when one gets an offer like that?

Naturally we accepted.

We enjoyed some more glorious food. Theo missed out a bit because he can't eat cheese, but I made up for it. After dinner and some more Vino we had a great time trying to make ourselves under stood, which we did with the help of a dictionary. Later on we were shown in to a small room with a sofa and a single bed to spend the night. Being the oldest I slept in the bed. How wonderful these people were. I can't praise them enough.

In the morning they had breakfast ready and on top of it the wife made us a parcel with bread, smoked meat, cheese and tomatoes, which lasted us for a couple of days. It was still reasonably early and after a few hugs and some *Arivederchies* we finally got on our bikes and hit the road again.

If Theo had not broken his handlebar we would never have met these lovely people.

Milano was a big city and the road led us right through the centre. We had to be extremely careful because the traffic was chaotic… not what we were used to. There were Lambrettas (*motor scooters*) swerving in and out coming dangerously close to our bikes, cars honking horns, and people all over the place trying to dash across the road without being hit by a car or a motor scooter. It was a relief when we got to the outskirts and back into the country again.

The further we came away from the Alps the warmer it got and we loved it. We really felt free and didn't have a worry in the world. We by passed Pavia and found a place to camp a couple of kilometres before Voghera. Next day we arrived in Genoa, another chaotic city, and we were glad to get out of it.

Once we were out of Genoa we saw the mighty Mediterranean and what a sight it was. I could hardly believe my eyes at the extent of it. This was the first time I had ever saw such a big expanse of water. We got as far as Rapallo where we camped next to a fruit orchard.

We were up bright and early the next morning, and after passing Chiavary we travelled most of the day with hardly a stop until setting up camp a bit beyond La Spetzia. All day the Mediterranean stretched away to the far horizon. Cool breezes off the sea kept us refreshed as we rode.

The sun was still shining once the tent was up near a beach, I could no longer control my urge to go for a swim.

"I'm going for a swim," I told him. I knew Theo had never learned to swim because his father always made him work in their big garden or cleaning out the rabbit stalls next to the house. "Keep an eye on our stuff, okay?"

I changed into my swim wear walked across the road, ran over warm sand, and jumped in to the beautiful crystal clear water.

I immediately stood up spluttering, spitting water out.

What a shock ! The bloody water was full of salt.

I got out as fast as I could, ran back to the camp.

"The bloody water is full of salt," I told Theo. "I'll never go swimming in the ocean again!"

Back home our friends and I had learned how to swim in our little river Murr or in the public swimming pool and knew the ocean only from picture books. It never occurred to me that it would be salty.

I found a nearby fresh water drain and washed the salt off my body.

The next day we passed Carrara, Massa, Viareggio and finished up in Pisa where we visited the leaning Tower. We didn't want to miss the chance to climb to the top. Over the next two days we passed Cascina, San Miniato and Empoli to get to Florence, from where we cycled south towards Rome.

Why we did not take the road along the Coast but went inland to Rome is still a mystery to me to this day.

Asking Theo about it recently he reckoned that we wanted to get away from home the fastest way possible and the inland roads were better to ride along.

It was great travelling in this new environment. We got fitter by the day and enjoyed the hospitality along the way. We could not believe the abundance of fruit and vegetables, peaches, oranges, melons, grapes and so on.

It was hard cycling because it was hot and there was not a cloud in the sky. Even at night time it was too warm to put up our tent. We just put the canvas on the ground with our sleeping bags on top. We still had plenty of food and water, but our money started to run low.

It took a few more days through this beautiful countryside before we saw Lago di Bolsena. Rome was only another day away.

Travelling through Rome in 1952 was already a nightmare, especially on a bike. Traffic was horrendous. We rode past the Colosseum and had a glimpse of the Vatican, but sightseeing was not on our minds, because if we wanted to go anywhere one of us had to watch out for our bikes and luggage. The Italians were very hospitable towards us. However in big Cities we still had to be careful of thieves.

Once we got through Rome and were on the way to Naples, we stopped at a roadside restaurant where we sat under a shady terrace and sipped a cool Coca Cola while listening to Theo's transistor radio. We felt absolutely great.

Needless to say, we soon had a small crowd of people watching and listening to the music. They had never seen a portable radio before and were amazed at what they were seeing. The owner of the Restaurant joined us to see what the commotion was all about and invited us for another drink. He was surprised to see two young German Cycling Adventurers in his tavern.

He spoke to us in reasonable German and wanted to know if we were interested in selling the Radio.

At first Theo would not have a bar of it, but knowing that we were very short of money he finally agreed to sell his beloved radio. To our surprise, we made a great sale. The owner paid us much more than what Theo had paid for it in Germany. On top of it he invited us for dinner and we could spend the night in a spare room at his house; what a deal.

Next morning after breakfast and a big farewell from his family, we set of for Naples. We were convinced that he paid us more, because he was happy to have us as Guests and to hear about our adventures.

The more we travelled south the hotter it got. Our skin got browner and my hair blonder. The shortest way to Naples was along the highway, but it was not so pretty as riding along the coastline. It must have taken us three or four days to get to Naples, and I must say from what we saw it certainly wasn't to die for! It would be an interesting city to explore today, but at that time, like most big cities we encountered, we were more than happy to get through them as quickly as possible,

Sometimes it was hard to ride because the countryside we passed through was very hilly. It just wasn't downhill all the time. Also because of the heat, sleeping in our tent became a definite no. We would spread it on the ground to keep away any bugs and used our sleeping bags on top.

From Naples we went to Sorrento and then over the peninsular to Salerno, where I would have had plenty of possibilities to go swimming but I had had enough of salty water from my experience in La Spezia.

From Salerno we travelled along the coastline via Agropoli, Sapri, Scalea, Amantea, Pizzo, Palmi, south towards Reggio Calabria from where we were able to catch a ferry to Messina in Sicily. I can't remember how many days it took us from Naples to Reggio but I know we travelled along some beautiful coastlines and had to master some winding and very steep roads.

As soon as we jumped on our bikes in Sicily, we knew we were the first from Backnang who made it this far after the war, quite an achievement for a couple of young fellows like us.

We still had some money left, but thought we'd better not to waste too much time in one place. Messina was hot, like the rest of southern Italy. Towards Venetico Marina it was hard going. The road was not the best and went over very mountainous terrain. We were fortunate in meeting a nice family who gave us a lift most of the way towards Falcone in their ancient little truck, and thus avoided the worst of the mountainous roads.

As on the mainland the people of Sicily were very hospitable, maybe even more so. In every little village or small town we rode through, they would look and stare at us as if we came from another Planet. Some of them quite often rode their rusty old bikes next to us, just to keep us company and we did not mind at all because sometimes one or the other of them gave us cool drinks or even some bread with cheese.

In Falcone we were advised to go the longer way along the coast towards Cefalu because it was easier to ride our bikes beside the sea instead the shorter but very hilly and winding road through the mountains. I can't remember all the little towns and fishing villages we passed through except some of the bigger ones like, Locanda, Mongiove, Acquedolci, Caronia, Milianni and Cefalu.

When we passed through it, Cefalu was a small town living mostly from fishing. Vineyards and fruit farms were in abundance.

Sitting under the shade outside a small tavern sipping a coke and eating some portions of pasta, next to the fisherman's wharf in front of the usual inquisitive crowd of people, we reminisced of home and wondered how our Parents took to the fact that we had not returned from what they thought was a short trip Austria. We were more than four weeks overdue. I didn't care about work because as far as I was concerned I knew where I would rather be. I couldn't help wondering what Mum and Dad would be thinking.

Would they have reported us missing to the police?

As we were talking, we noticed this guy who looked a bit like Tarzan walking towards us with a backpack containing diving gear over his shoulder and a spear gun in his hand. He asked in an Austrian accent if he could sit with us.

As it turned out, he was born and grew up in Vienna. His name was Rudolph Watschinger and I must say he looked extremely fit, like a smaller version of Arnold Schwarzenegger. Rudolph was 19 years old and fascinated with the Oceans. He worked in Vienna, saved his money, learned Italian and set out on his diving adventure in Sicily. We liked him and had a great time exchanging stories. Rudolph told us he could not believe his eyes when he looked at the mob of people and saw our bikes. He had to investigate. Then he saw the two of us sitting under the shade smoking cigarettes and was astonished what the two of us had achieved at our age. We told him about our plan to go to Africa and he just looked at us, shaking his head in disbelief.

We put up camp for a couple of days between some disused fishing boats and Rudolph decided to stay with us. We were quite happy with that. We watched him spearing fish and selling them to a few Restaurants where he earned good money for his catch. Rudolph had been in Cefalu for a couple of weeks before us and knew the town and some of the people fairly well. His well-spoken Italian helped him a lot. Needless to say, we had mastered quite a few words ourselves by then.

Rudolph intended to stay a few days longer and then hitchhike along the coast to Palermo. After two days of rest, we got on to our bikes to continue on our journey. We had made arrangements with Rudolph to meet him somewhere at the fisherman's wharf in Palermo in approximately one week's time.

Once again riding next to the azure blue Mediterranean and through unspoiled small fishing villages was a pleasure beyond description.

I can't remember how long it took us to get to Palermo, but when we arrived at the fisherman's wharf late in the afternoon Rudolph came running towards us with a big grin on his face and after a big hello, he guided us to an old disused fisherman's shack which he got on to the day before.

Rudolph had been in Palermo already for two days and was not sure if we would make it. He told us he would have waited for another three more days and if we didn't show up he would have continued along the coast. We were mighty glad to see him again because by that time we were running desperately short of cash.

Rudolph invited us to a small tavern for a bite to eat. It was full of fisherman smoking, drinking and most likely talking about the price of last night's catch. They all wished us *bon giorno* and invited us for a drink. Rudolph and I enjoyed a glass of wine, while Theo had his usual Cola. We had a great evening and didn't give a thought to the next day. We were treated like Royalty and loved it.

We were very happy when we walked back to the shack. It must have been close to midnight by the time we laid in our makeshift beds using some old fishing nets as mattresses with our sleeping bags on top. It was very smelly and hot which made it hard to go to sleep even with the door and some tiny windows open.

Next morning with a heavy head we had our usual breakfast (some bread and plenty of fruit) and talked about our next move. Our idea to go to Africa, tickled Rudolph's fancy, He would like to join us, but how? After breakfast Theo and I rode our bikes in to the centre of Palermo to change our last ten Marks which we had kept in reserve for emergencies.

A guy noticed us in front of a Bank and offered to exchang the ten Marks for more than we could get inside. We weren't sure at first but after thiunking about how much more he would give us we agreed.

Back with Rudolph we talked about Africa and the best way to get there. We finally came to the decision to go by boat, nothing big, but a small sailing or fishing boat. We asked a few fishermen if there are any boats for sale and sure enough one of them knew someone not far from us who had one which could suit us. When we met the guy, it turned out we knew him from the night before in the tavern. It was already getting dark so he told us to meet him in the morning when he came back from fishing. We were excited about this and talked all night about the big adventure which lay in front of us.

We were there early next morning to meet with him but we had to wait until he sold his catch. We walked around a lot of boats of various sizes until he stopped in front of an approximately 7 Meter long clinker boat anchored in shallow water. Not knowing anything about boats, Theo and I left it up to Rudolph to do the inspection. We climbed on board and it seemed to be very stable, not like the small rowing boats we were used to paddling along the Murr. It had a small storage room in the bow which would come in handy for our luggage. Further back was a wooden board (seat) and then came a mast with one sail. About a metre back from the mast was another board in front of the tiller. According to Rudolph the boat was pretty sound and the fisherman told him he was selling it because it was too small for him. Apparently he had almost finished building his new one. Rudolph started a debate with the fisherman which took a fair while. Finally he came over to us and explained that he was arguing about the price. We told the Fisherman we would have some lunch and be back later on in the morning. Well that was that. We were not sure what we could do at that point.

How could we buy a Boat and how would that get us to Africa?

Rudolph had a certain amount of money, but we had none left!

But we had our bikes.

After some arguing between us about what we should do, we decided that we had no choice. We had to sell our bikes.

At sundown the three of us went over to the tavern where they knew us and asked the owner if he knew of someone who would like to buy our bikes, someone who would give us a fair price for them.

Next morning after a bit of breakfast, two Men came to our hut and told us they heard we wanted to sell our bikes. No problem we said and wheeled them out. They gave them a good look over. We had cleaned them the night before and they looked spotless. We got the impression that they liked what they saw. Naturally being Italians they wanted to bargain, but Rudolph laughed at their offer and sent them away.

"We'll sell them to someone in town," he told them.

We didn't have to wait long before they came back. With a show of reluctance they paid us what we had asked. The sale was done and to our sorrow the bikes which brought us all the way to Sicily were going to keep some young Sicilians happy.

As soon as the deal was done and we had the money we went straight down to buy our boat from the fisherman, who was waiting for us. He took all his belongings out of the boat and gave it a once over. After we paid him we found that we had some money left over which made us very happy.

The Harbourmaster signed over the necessary papers for us as the new owners, and officially we had a boat. Rudolph had to take a few sailing lessons and had to sit in an office to answer a few questions about buoys, ship's channels and so on. This took all day, after which he had a piece of paper to say he was allowed to skipper our Boat.

I didn't know what the future would bring. Our bikes where gone, but now we had our own 'BOAT'.

The ever present onlookers watched as Rudolf checked out our boat...

With heaps of onlookers we loaded the items we kept, our sleeping bags, knives, forks, dinner plates, spoons etcetera. While Rudolph did his courses, Theo and I went to a nearby shop and bought a big 20 litre glass bottle for fresh water with cork strips on the outside to protect the glass, a cooking pot and some extra eating plates for Rudolph. We needed matches and of course tobacco and papers so we could roll our own smokes. We bought those as well as some loaves of bread and fruit. We put everything in a basket, which we also purchased. The little store room in the bow was lockable which was handy, because too many eyes were watching.

What can I say? What lay ahead of us?

Would we reach Africa in our boat?

We had been studying maps of the coast and the shortest way to get to Tunis. The decision was made to sail as far as Marsala and from there to Pandelleria, an Island owned by Italy but close to Tunisia.

Early next morning after a big breakfast and '*Arrievederdchies*' to some of the people we got to know, we set sail.

I was on the tiller while Rudolph handled the sail and Theo stowed some of the gear away. Sailing inside Palermo's Harbour with a good breeze behind us pushing our little boat (I can't remember if it had a Name) towards the open Sea was up to that point the most exciting moment of my life. I couldn't help yelling out with excitement,

"AFRICA HERE WE COME!"

There were big smiles all around.

For a while we thought we were the greatest seamen under the sun, until we reached the end of the breakwater, where disaster struck.

We had no trouble inside the harbour, but as soon as we got outside we hit a wind change which turned the boat sideways into the waves and nearly tipped us over.

Quick thinking Rudolph dropped the sail and the boat righted itself. I glanced forward to Theo and he did not look happy. He was terrified. I thought he had '*crapped his daks*'. He told me later that he thought this was the end because he could not swim.

Rudolph gripped the oars and rowed over the next few waves into calmer waters with me hanging on to the tiller. About a Kilometre out into the open sea we decided that for us sailing would be too dangerous, rowing would be much safer. We folded the sail, packed it in the bow and tried to lift the mast out of its mount. It wasn't easy because the bolts were rusted into the wood. But once we got it done we threw it into the sea.

The boat was wide enough for two to sit next to each other in comfort rowing with one oar each while one remained on the tiller. Rudolph and I had no problem rowing and Theo picked it up very quickly. It could have been disastrous had we turned over and lost the lot. Our passports would have gone and all our belongings. The absolute worst of it would have been Theo; he could not swim and would surely have drowned.

We rowed north along the coast and the going was relatively easy. We had water, plenty of fruit, some cheese and bread, but the sun was merciless. We put towels around our heads and that gave us some relief.

After several hours of rowing we turned towards land and anchored in shallow water on a sandy beach. We were still close to Palermo but at least we had gotten over our early scare and were starting to get used to our boat. Rudolph showed me how to use a mask and snorkel, and how to propel myself under water with fins and this was my first experience of putting my head underwater and actually seeing another world.

I shall never forget my first dive. Now I didn't mind that the water was salty. It was only about two meters deep and the first thing I did was swallow a lot of salt water. I stood up spluttering and choking while Theo laughed his head off. But once I got used to the technique of clearing the snorkel I fell in love with the whole idea of it.

There were people on the beach enjoying a great day swimming and fishing. Rudolph grabbed a small basket and filled it with sea urchins for which he had quickly dived and gathered. He sold them to a couple of guys on the beach for a small amount of Lire. Theo and I could not believe that anyone would want to eat those spiny creatures, let alone pay for them, but we felt good because here was an opportunity to make some money; diving for urchins and spearing fish, and then selling them to people onshore.

Our first night we spent on the beach sleeping on the sand which was okay, even though two of us would have had room on the floor of the boat.

Next morning a completely new life started for Theo and me. As 'Landlubbers' we were not accustomed to life on the high seas but we made a go of it. Anyhow we had no other choice. Everything we had was in this boat.

We had more or less left part of civilisation and had started rowing north along the coast. Who would have thought that we could change from cycling to rowing our own *'sea-going boat'*? No one! Not even we could have imagined it a couple of weeks ago.

It wasn't easy going. It was much harder to row a boat than it was to ride a bike, but we made headway. We rowed along some spectacular country, passed many beautiful tiny inlets and sometimes we saw a little farm house on land. When one of us felt tired he would change position with the one on the tiller.

The coastline was rocky with many small bays to anchor and camp in overnight. We didn't have a worry in the world. It was warm and the sea was relatively calm. We watched Rudolph spearing fish, which in those days was quite easy. In later years when big trawlers and long-liners overfished the oceans, the Mediterranean suffered immensely.

While Rudolph fished, Theo and I collected driftwood which was in abundance and started a fire on the rocks. We filled our pot with sea water and by the time Rudolph came back with a few fish he had speared we had boiling water. We didn't clean the fish, we just threw them one after another in the pot and waited a few minutes, and while we started eating the first one off the bones we boiled the next one and the next one...

What a life!

We slept on some sandy patches between the rocks under billions of stars. At day break we finished off some of the left over fish, threw our leftovers for the crabs.

Back in the water and we were ready for another day's rowing.

Before we departed Theo and I grabbed one of our baskets and climbed up to the top of the rocks and observed the farmer and his wife walking their donkey out to work on the field. When they were a fair distance away, we walked to the house and knocked on the door just to make sure there was no one inside. After a few knocks we entered and walked straight in to the kitchen were we found some bread, cheese and plenty of fruit.

Filling our basket quickly we left the house and made our way back to the cliff, where we found it a bit difficult climbing down to the water. Rudolph had the boat ready and after we stored our fresh provisions on board we rowed away as fast as we could.

When Mr 'farmer' and his wife got home they would have scratched their heads and wondered if there was any thing missing, because we didn't leave a mess and only took a little bit of everything.

We had no problem finding fresh water; there were rock pools all over the place. We had no means to measure how far we travelled in a day, but then we couldn't have cared less. As long as we kept moving that was fine.

We rowed past Mondello towards Faro di Capo Gallo-Cape Gallo Lighthouse. Occasionally we met some Fisherman setting their nets for the next morning's catch and their surprise was understandable, meeting up with us young guys rowing towards them for a big "*Bongiorno Amici*".

The camaraderie of those fishermen was second to none. Here we were sitting on the high seas getting advice about the weather and at which bay to anchor overnight and of course with them sharing their food and drink with us. A couple of times they even gave us some wine which made us pretty drowsy in the heat.

Sometimes we finished up in a small inlet where there were some fishermen's huts with people mending nets and some houses nearby. People came running from everywhere trying to help us anchor our 'BOAT' and touching us to see if we were real. Several times we stayed for a couple of days to rest and enjoy the hospitality. That was when Rudolph swam out to a reef and speared some fish which the people paid us for. I did my bit and dived for Urchins which the people opened, gave them a quick rinse in the sea, scooped out the gonads and down the hatch they went.

Once we passed Cape Gallo we rowed towards Isol Delle Femmine and on to Punta Raisi, where today the Palermo Airport is situated. After Terrasini we attempted to cross the Gulfo Del Castelamare to Castelamare. At one time we were a hell of a long way from land and it was the only time where we had to row through the night. Dark as it was we had to navigate as best as possible, using the light from coastal villages along the way. Having arrived in Castelamare we created great interest amongst the locals. Even the only policeman came running to see what the commotion was all about. He found it necessary to check our passports to feel important. Much to everyone's surprise they could not comprehend the manner in which we landed on their shore. Later we found out we were the first Germans to visit them after the Second World War.

Having spent a couple of days resting and enjoying the Hospitality we moved on towards Scopello and San Vito lo Capo. I can't remember how long it took us to reach Marsala.

Today when I look at the map of Sicily I realise what a mammoth task we achieved at the time. Just thinking about it still runs cold shivers down my back. The danger we put ourselves into could have turned out quite different. I remember one afternoon Rudolph standing on a reef holding the boat for Theo and I to step on to the rocks, which was alright for me, being only to waist depth.

As soon as Theo jumped out he disappeared because next to me the reef had finished and he found himself in deep water. I dived under and grabbed him by his hair and pulled him up holding on to the side of the boat. He was coughing and spluttering because he had gulped so much water. He didn't look very happy.

Eventually we reached Trapani a bigger industrial town with an important deep water port. We still did a fair bit of diving, and selling fish and urchins is what kept us afloat so to speak. By the time we reached Marsala we asked some fishermen, what our chances would be to row to Africa, and they all came to the immediate conclusion that it would be suicidal.

The only way to get there would be on a cargo ship.

We made enquiries about selling our '*Home*' and the costing for the three of us on freighters to Tunisia. We couldn't believe how quick we got rid of our 'BOAT'. When word got out we had three different Fishermen and a private guy bidding for it, and we finished up with the private guy giving us considerably more than what we paid for it in Palermo.

Everything just snowballed. Within a few days and full of expectations we boarded a big freighter to Tunis. We had just enough money to pay for our passage and enjoyed living like kings.

What a difference between our past three months on the road and at sea. We had a beautiful cabin with a separate toilet and shower plus clean comfortable bunks. Breakfast, lunch and dinner were included, and needless to say we stuffed ourselves with all the 'Goodies'. Rudolph and I ate everything but Theo was a very selective eater. For instance he would not eat cheese, onions or olives, nor did he drink wine. Rudolph and I made up for it, except for the olives which we could not stomach either.

Today we can't live without them.

On the way we stopped at the Island of Pantelleria (which is closer to Africa but belongs to Italy) for a couple of days unloading and loading. We had a great time and really got on very well with the crew. They loved us and could not do enough to make us feel at home. I remember Pantelleria for the size of the white grapes, I'd never seen anything like them before.

Finally… AFRICA!

The coast shimmered in the harsh sunlight as we approached.

We made it! We were about to arrive in Africa.

Chapter Three

When we docked at Tunis we bid everyone on the freighter goodbye and stepped on to Terra Firma, and for us, a new continent.

What now?

Somehow the excitement of arriving on the African continent diminished and we stood there on the docks wondering what to do next.

We were in a very strange land, where mostly French was spoken. We only had a few *Lire* in our pockets which wouldn't go far at all.

Our belongings were what we had on; shorts, singlet, runners, and our passports in our pockets. Somehow we made it into town, all the while wondering what our future would hold.

Walking along a busy street where People looked curiously at us, we spotted a sign in several different languages: '**Foreign Legion**'.

We looked at each other, looked again at the sign… and thought spontaneously 'Well why not?'

We were in front of an old colonial three storey building and as we walked towards the entrance a guard wearing a French uniform with a rifle strapped around his shoulder gave us a salute and opened the door to let us inside.

There were quite a few miserable characters sitting in a big room like a hospital waiting room. They all had a number in their hands and were waiting to be called up. We also had to take a number and wait to be called. After about an hour having been served some coffee, it was our turn.

We were led in to a room where we were welcomed by an officer who had a couple of stripes on his jacket. After enquiring where we were from and why we wanted to join the Legion he informed us that it was against French rules to take anyone under the age of 18.

What a disappointment for Theo and myself.

Now what do we do?

Rudolph had no problem he was three years older and built like Tarzan. It was quite emotional saying goodbye to Rudolph with whom we had shared such big adventures. We wished each other all the best for our futures and promised to keep in touch where ever we might be.

It was 40 years later that we found out Rudolph was living in French Guyana, but that's another story.

Out on the street again without Rudolf, we made up a story that we had been robbed of all our belongings, mainly our money. We made our way to another building further down the road where a sign announced **Gendarmerie.**

With our story embedded in our brains we went inside.

There were two officers standing behind a desk and of course they couldn't understand a word we were saying. We mentioned the word Allemagne and one of them went upstairs, we assumed to get someone who could understand us. It wasn't long before he came back with a guy in civilian clothes, a suit and tie. He took us up two stories, opened a door to an office where in big letters was written INTERPOL He made us sit in front of a huge desk.

He went outside and came back about 15 minutes later with a couple of folders under his arm and another guy also in civilian clothes, who spoke perfect German.

They studied our passports and then he asked lots of questions about how and why we came to Tunis.

We told him about our ride on bikes through Switzerland, Italy, then rowing our boat to Marsala. Every so often we stopped so he could translate it to the other guy who just kept shaking his head. After telling them about the arrival on the freighter and being robbed, they opened the folders and glancing over we could see that a picture of us was in each one of them. According to the officer, Interpol had been on the lookout for us for the last couple of months.

Our parents had gone to the local police in Backnang and the detectives there had contacted Interpol who in turn traced our steps through the border crossings in Switzerland and Italy.

According to those guys, the Captain of the freighter should not have brought us to Tunis, because we did not have a French Visa.

Well so much for Africa!

We were put in a room with a couple of bunks, reading material and a toilet, where they kept us overnight. The door wasn't locked, but there was nowhere for us to go anyway, especially without any money.

Early Journeys

We never mentioned Rudolph because we didn't want them to search for him. We were given some food, which was reasonable even for Theo's standard.

Next morning after breakfast we were taken back to the wharf in a police car by three policemen and the guy who spoke German.

The same freighter that we had arrived on was still there.

It was ready to leave but the Captain had been ordered to wait until we were on board again, which made the Captain very unhappy because he lost valuable time and on top of that he would not get paid for taking us back because we had no money for the return passage. He made us stay on deck in the heat and wouldn't give us any food or water.

Getting out of the harbour in Tunis took some time. The breakwater protecting the harbour must have been 3 or 4 km long. About two hours after leaving Tunis and the breakwater far behind us the Freighter came to a halt and we could see the Captain looking at us with a very unhappy face.

Half hour after we had stopped a police boat came racing towards us. It stopped beside the freighter and one of the policemen climbed up the rope ladder and onto the deck. Seeing us watching he beckoned us over and handed us our passports which they had forgotten to return to us in their haste to have us returned to Italy.

After that he waved to the Captain and scrambled back down the rope ladder to the speedboat. Moments later the freighter's propeller started churning the water and the ship began to move again. Very soon it got dark and thanks to the crew who welcomed us back we didn't suffer too much except for sleeping on ropes coiled on the deck.

In the morning the freighter stopped again in Pandelleria and looking at the eyes and gestures of the Captain we thought he was going to leave us on the Island. He didn't, and we stayed on board until we docked in Marsala later that afternoon.

We were greeted by three policemen who guided us to a police van and they took us to Palermo. The Captain of the freighter must have known about this, otherwise we would have been stuck in Pantelleria.

Once back in Palermo we stopped at police headquarters where we were interviewed again and put into a holding cell overnight. Next morning we were taken to a Youth Remand Centre where all the young criminals were held.

What an experience! We suffered a pretty tough three days at the remand centre. The food was lousy, some of the kids wanted to fight and we had to go to church where the Wardens hit us behind our knees because we would not kneel and pray.

On the second day one of the kids tried to shove an onion in Theo's mouth, which made him furious. Theo stepped back one pace and when the kid followed, Theo king hit the kid on his jaw and he went out cold. I had no idea Theo could do such a thing. He must have really hated onions! The other kids were going to gang up on us, but thought twice about it when they saw what happened to their mate. After that the wardens separated us from the other inmates.

Early on the third day, I think it was a Monday; two policemen picked us up and drove us back to the police station. After receiving some breakfast they escorted us to the train station where they handcuffed each of us to a policeman who led us to a waiting train. We had our own cabin and we found it silly to be still cuffed since there was no way of escape. Anyhow, the two cops were okay and quite talkative. One of them could speak a bit of German and he told us they were taking us to Rome.

What an unjust World. How could this have happened to us?

At the start we were on our way to Africa, full of expectations, happily riding our Bikes, and now we were cuffed to a cop and on the way back.

I don't remember how long it took to get back to Messina, but it was evening when we reached the ferry to Reggio. Our cops became very friendly and shared their food and orange juice with us. Going to the toilet would have been funny if we felt like laughing. After opening the toilet door he would take off the cuffs and guard the door until one was finished then put them back on again.

We travelled through the night, stopping at a couple of bigger towns and after an uncomfortable night we reached Naples. Once we reached Rome another police car was waiting and it took us to their station where we met up with a man and a woman from the German embassy. They asked us lots of questions, took some notes and left with our passports.

Our two escorts shook hands with us said *Chao* and disappeared.

JAIL! This one was for real!

Two cops and a driver took us in one of their lock up vans not too far from the station to a big old bluestone building. There were guards everywhere and we were led through some thick walled doors.

No one was smiling and it looked frightening. We were escorted upstairs towards a long corridor. Half way down they opened a door which led in to a small room. The only furniture was a wooden table and one chair. A male and a female warden made us undo our belts and then also our shoe laces. By that time we felt like actual criminals. Surely we could have been treated a bit better.

No bloody way: after a body search we were taken to the back of the prison and put in to a small cell. By that time it was late afternoon and our stomachs demanded food.

The cell had two bunks one on top of the other, a little wash basin and a drum with a wooden lid as a toilet. After about an hour, talking about our plight and what was going to happen to us in the future, the door opened and a guard passed us a couple of plates of food.

Both plates had the same; two bread rolls, some fruit and a round carton which looked like cheese. We were hungry and whacked in to the rolls and I started to open the little box. Theo got angry and passed the 'cheese' to me and ate his rolls with fruit. Well, it wasn't cheese at all it was chocolate. Needless to say I didn't tell him and ate mine quickly with one roll, but he became suspicious. He noticed the dark colour and the different aroma and he wanted his back. He called me a few not so nice words and told me that a true friend wouldn't do such a thing. He really rubbed it in. Anyhow, it would have served him right if he didn't get his chocolate back because he was such a finicky eater.

After the sleepless night on the train we were very tired and slept reasonable well, Theo in the top Bunk. Very early next morning we washed as much as possible and were served coffee and some kind of porridge. At about 8am the door opened and were led down stairs and given our belt and shoe laces back. The two embassy people from the day before were waiting for us and gave us our passports back and some Lire. They told us two policemen would escort us on the train to the Austrian border.

"Nothing to it," we told them. "We are used being in police custody on trains,"

They wished us a good Journey, said, *"Alles Gute"* and left.

Well, we were not alone.

There was another guy standing nearby, smiling at us. He was tall about 190cm, very slim and about 25 Years old. He wore a trench coat, which didn't reach to his knees, long black trousers which hadn't been washed for a long time and badly worn shoes. He was a real hobo, but had a warm smile. It turned out that the police got hold of him after he tramped as far as the outskirts of Rome. They got hold of him and contacted the German Embassy. Hartmann, I forgot his first name, was three days in prison, because he came from East Germany and the Embassy had problems sorting out his papers.

Thank God we got out of that miserable place. We never wanted to see another one like that from the inside.

Here we go again, I thought.

This time there were three of us with two cops escorting us. To our surprise we weren't cuffed this time.

It was a fast train which only stopped a couple of times before a longer stop in Florence. By the time we reached Milano we had to leave this train and had to walk to the police station just around the corner where the policemen greeting us were relatively friendly. Our two escorts left to spend a night in a hotel and we had the dubious luxury of sleeping in the holding cells.

I can't say a bad word about Italian police; they were all very friendly to us and were always very polite.

We had a wash and then they allowed us to sit with them and share their food. The cells were unlocked and we could use the bathroom at our leisure. In the morning after a quick bite to eat and some coffee the same two policemen who escorted us from Rome picked us up again and led us to the railway station to take us to the Austrian border.

By this time we got to know Hartmann pretty well. Apparently he left the east for a better life and with no other means of transport, started to walk to find some place better in the west. He relied on handouts from people and slept on farms where he sometimes got odd jobs helping out.

After a year tramping through Austria, he finished up in Rome where his journey came to an end.

The train from Milan to Como was a smaller local one which stopped at every little town and village. It seemed to take for ever. Theo and I found ourselves getting colder the further north we went. In Como the temperature was still bearable, but the closer we got to the Alps we could feel the cold creeping into our bones. We were still only dressed in singlets and shorts.

According to my passport, the border crossing into Austria was called Kiefersfelden and by the time we got through customs it was cold and late afternoon.

Once we were through the border the two policemen who escorted us waved goodbye, and we were on our own.

Hartmann, being streetwise told us not to worry, "we shall organise some clothing shortly."

Not far ahead of us we saw a small township with the usual Church Spire towering above the houses. Hartmann aimed straight for it with us in tow. Several people we passed had to look at us twice; they were all dressed in heavy winter clothes while we were in singlets and shorts.

When we got close to the Church, we saw a house with a big garden next to it with several pine trees growing in it. Coming closer we noticed this little man with a long white beard, wearing a big black headpiece and a long black robe reaching to the ground. He was slowly walking along the side of the house facing the trees. After a few steps he turned around to face us and we saw that he was smoking the biggest pipe I have ever seen and when I say big, I mean huge.

Hartmann opened the little gate and walked towards the Priest followed by Theo while I held the gate open. Hartmann had to walk about five meters towards that little man along a narrow path. Once in front of him he unexpectedly fell to his knees and said, "*Hochwuerden wir haben Hunger.*" "Your Holiness we Are Starving."

I was still holding the little gate open but when I saw the very tall Hartmann falling to his knees in front of this orthodox looking small man I could hardly stop myself from laughing out loud. Lucky for me, I was still holding the gate pretending to close it and straining my stomach muscles, laughing quietly into by then the dark Street. Over many years when I had to laugh about something real funny I still get the picture in my mind of what transpired that evening. Not in animosity towards the priest or the Catholic Church. The scene to a sixteen year old was just unreal. Later I asked Theo how he managed and he it had been the same for him because it was so unexpected.

The priest held his pipe in one hand and helped Hartmann up with the other. After greeting Theo and me he led us behind the house towards a large building which we had not seen from the street.

It turned out to be a Convent. The priest opened a big solid door and we found ourselves in a warm room with a few nuns doing chores. They all looked at us bewildered and wondered what their "*Boss*" brought along. The three of us must have looked a pretty sad lot, dirty, cold and hungry. The priest left us with one of the nuns, who turned out to be the Mother Superior. She gave some orders and in no time we were led into a large beautiful aromatic kitchen.

Mother Superior asked us to sit behind a long wooden table. We were served us some herbal tea which started to warm us up a little. We didn't have to wait long before a couple of nuns put three big plates of scrambled eggs and slices of freshly baked bread in front of us. Who would have expected this, only two hours ago?

After our bellies were full, the nuns wanted to hear all about our adventures and we certainly entertained them for a couple of hours. We didn't tell them that we were sent home by Interpol. Eventually they showed us where we could sleep overnight. Theo and I were taken to a small bedroom with two beds, plain bedding, all clean and very comfortable. Through a side door there was a bathroom with a bathtub filling with hot water and a WC. I thought we were in Heaven. Hartmann got a room further down along the corridor with the same treatment.

After taking a bath each and putting on pyjamas which were lying on our beds, we hit the sack and had one of our best night's sleep ever.

Next Morning we were woken by Hartmann, who had a bundle of clothes under his arms. He was up earlier and some of the nuns gave them to him for us to try on. Theo put on a pair of trousers which fitted okay, a thick sweater which was a bit too big and a kind of a jacket which made him look like John Dillinger. I didn't do much better, but beggars can't choose. After some oats in warm milk and a couple of fried eggs each for breakfast, we were ready to hit the road again.

His Holiness came over to say goodbye and all of them wished us well. All the Lire we had left we put on the big table because we had no need for them anymore. Mother Superior put a few Schillings in Theo's hand which we gladly welcomed.

We walked to the next village, and then through a few more until we came to a small town. There were still plenty of apples and pears hanging on some trees by the roadside so we picked and ate them.

In the middle of this town, situated on the way to St Anton, Hartmann walked straight to a good looking bakery and proceeded to open the shop door.

We asked him, "What's on your mind?"

"Are you hungry or not?" he asked, and walked in with us following.

Inside the bakery an elderly, friendly lady asked if she could help us. Hartmann put on a sad face and told her we had no money left and had to find our way back home to East Germany, that we had nothing to eat. The lady did not hesitate; she grabbed a '*Sackel*' (paper bag), turned around and filled it with six bread rolls. She handed it to Hartmann, wished us all the best and started to serve another Customer who came in after us.

Outside, Hartmann gave Theo and me two rolls each, but as soon as we were about to bite into one of them he stopped us.

"What's wrong?" Theo asked.

"We are *not* eating these rolls *dry*," he said.

Three doors further on, there was a butcher shop. Hartmann handed us his rolls and marched straight in. A little while later he came back out with another paper bag in his hand. A little down the footpath he opened the bag and God behold, he pulled out two small sausages, one Salami and one Liverwurst.

We were speechless…

The Rest of the way was relatively smooth. We got several lifts with trucks and a couple of nights we slept in a friendly farmer's haystack and the rest towards Bregenz we travelled on trains. When we took a train in one village, we stayed on it only until we saw a Ticket Inspector getting on. We would immediately get off and wait for another.

We finally finished up in Bregenz and had no trouble crossing the border into Germany. We got a lift along Lake Konstanz (Bodensee) to Lindau were Theo knew someone who put us up for the night in their garage.

Next Morning we had to say goodbye to Hartmann ,which was again very difficult for the three of us. We never saw each other again.

We had to go north towards Stuttgart and Hartmann to the East. I shall never forget him.

Years later when Theo came back from Australia, Hartmann did write to him and told him that he had Heart Problems and didn't think he would last much longer. Every couple of months Theo sent him some Money to help him a bit financially, but after a few months the last money he sent came back.

Theo and I finished up getting a lift in a BMW all the way to Stuttgart and the guy even dropped us in front of Gretel's house. Gretel had by now married Victor Gradel and moved to Stuttgart where they bought a lovely house. You should have seen Gretel's face when she opened the front door and saw us standing there. She thought we were ghosts!

Gretel, along with all the rest of the family, was still under the impression that we are missing. She quickly made us some sandwiches, while we answered most of her questions.

After that, everything went pretty fast. Victor came home from work and couldn't believe it when he saw the two of us. Gretel cooked an evening meal for her family. She had two boys, Uli and Juergen. After dinner she made up two beds and not long after we got in and fell asleep.

Just before midnight, we had a rude awakening.

The light was switched on and in front of us stood Mr Guth, Theo's father, my Dad and Uncle Paul, staring at us with stern faces.

After we went to bed, Gretel ran down several streets to the Habrik's home and informed them that we were there. Uncle Paul decided to walk to the railway station and caught a train to Backnang while Gretel came back home. After reaching Backnang Uncle Paul walked to my Mum and Dad's apartment and filled them in on what had transpired.

The shock was enormous! They had not expected to hear from us ever again. The surprise was even bigger when they heard that we were healthy and fit.

Dad and Uncle Paul walked to the Guth's house about 3Km away and informed Theo's parents, who suffered the same shock. They decided not to waste any time and left for Stuttgart straight away, because Herr Guth had a car.

They got us out of the beds and bundled us in to the car. Uncle Paul was given a lift back to his place and we carried on to Backnang.

Theo's Dad dropped us off at our home, and then went on to their place.

And that was the end of our adventures, but only for the time being…

Theo with Konne circa 1954…

Chapter Four

The whole family was happy to see us back in one piece and were astonished to hear how far we had travelled. It must have been two in the morning before we went to bed. There was no way of sleeping in because the neighbours started to knock on the front door to say hello. The news that we are back again travelled fast and all wanted to hear our story. Some of our friends turned up and I had to repeat myself many times.

On one hand I was glad to be home because of Mum and Dad, but on the other hand I was sad because I missed the Adventure.

The day after we had to go to the Police Station in Backnang for an Interview with Mr Noller and Mr Krimmer, the two detectives who got in touch with Interpol to report us missing.

I felt really down. Here I was, with no bike and no money. and with winter approaching I had to walk wherever I went.

The detectives didn't look too happy when I entered the room. After saying hello they asked me to sit in front of them at a big desk. They wanted to know why we ran away from home. I told them that I wanted to see other countries. I never mentioned the real reason about HR, my apprentice teacher.

Their expressions changed for the better the longer they questioned me. They were impressed and smiled appreciatively when I told them about being sent back handcuffed to a Policeman. They must have filled several pages of a big note book. The said that it all had been taped and a copy would be sent to Interpol.

After about three hours I was allowed to leave. Before leaving they told me they "don't want to see me anymore under such circumstances."

Little did I know that Detective Noller's son Walter who learned his trade as a toolmaker next to me migrated to Australia and we are in touch to this day. Detective Krimmer's daughter Lore married our best friend Konne. What a weird World!

Exiting the building I saw Theo walking (also bike less) towards me. He also had to be at the Police Station for questioning. This was the first time after returning home that we had seen each other. He told me that in the coming week he had to start work at his old place to finish his apprenticeship.

Walking back home through Backnang, I was stopped and greeted by several young people I knew. They also wanted to know about our Adventure. However some elderly women I knew walked straight past me as if I didn't exist. For a while we weren't very popular. But as time went by people had more important things on their minds.

When I got back home Dad had returned from work with the news that I had be at AEG, where I had spent the last 1½ years, to see 'HR' on Saturday morning at 10am. That wasn't really what I wanted, but I had no bike, no money and no choice.

Come Saturday morning I fronted up with mixed feelings. AEG had about three thousand employees and the apprentice floor was on the top level of the building and everyone was working a 48 hour week.

All eyes were on me because nearly everyone knew of our episode. There were about sixty apprentices on that floor and work stopped when I walked in. HR greeted me with a sour face and took me behind a partition to interrogate me without being seen by the others.

Well, he certainly got stuck in to me with questions. The more I told him the more his face reddened because he did not want to believe we got as far as Tunisia. He wanted me to describe the harbour of Tunis, which I did.

I must have moved my hands the wrong way to express myself and for some reason he didn't like the movement because next thing I knew he slapped me across the face, knocking me completely off the chair.

"You're a lying dog," he snarled.

As soon as I got up from the floor he started to belt the living daylight out of me. Somehow I managed to escape the worst of the blows and ran out the door and along the corridor, down the staircase and didn't stop until I was outside of the factory. What a swine!

I ran the three kilometres back home and told Mum what happened.

"I don't want to go back there ever again!"

Dad was still at work and didn't know what was going on. I really didn't want him to know more than was absolutely necessary. Dad, who had a much better position than HR, was told by his Boss that I should go back to finish my trade because at that time it was important.

Early Journeys

After the belting I received that day. I knew inside myself I would not last. The following Monday with my heart full of dread I went back to work.

Winter was approaching and walking to work at 6.30am was tough. I had no hope of catching up to the others and the odd slap behind the ears, more often than the others did nothing to encourage me. It was a relief when after a couple of months I was sent to the heart of the tool-making division one story below (*Werkzeugbau*) where I was supposed to learn and work on different machines. I liked it there because I got on with the tradesmen who taught me very well. Being away from HR was great and for awhile I didn't mind going to work. The only drawback was, on weekends. We had to fill in our *Berichtsheft* (Report book) and had to hand it in upstairs for corrections every Monday morning. Tuesdays we (Siegfried and I) had to go to *Gewerbeschule* (Trade school) to another Factory, *Karl Kaelble* where my Father learned his trade years earlier, to learn how to develop drawing tools on paper.

Being in the second year I got 20 Marks a month, a big help. On Saturdays, after work we went to the local baths '*Hallenbad*' to have a swim and a shower to get rid of all the dirt we accumulated during the week. The baths were situated near the Abattoirs not far from work. The little pool was only about 5 by 5 meters and about 2 meters deep. If there were any more than ten people in it, one could hardly move. The water was warm but greenish in colour and the smell of urine wafted above it. I could not stay in for long. There were six showers and everyone washed everyone's back. After we got out nice and clean, we were ready to go to the local dance hall in the hope of meeting with our mates and some of the Ladies. During lunch time I still caught up with Theo at the local Grill, Sausage and Alcohol Stand.

Theo was always having a coke and me a Fanta. Theo's father was an insurance broker and Theo delivered papers and parcels for him after work. Theo must have had more money in his pockets than me because he kept paying the bills.

Everyone looked forward to Christmas and a few days off. By that time Germany was well on its way to prosperity. Everyone had work and the rebuilding was in full swing. It was a time when Germany imported lots of so called 'Guest Workers' from Italy, Spain and Yugoslavia. One day at the Grill Stand Theo told me that he put a DM 10 deposit on a new bike which he had to pay off in one year.

On the weekend I walked to his place and he showed me his brand new *Meister* bike. It had 3 gears, was painted green and looked fantastic. It was a great help for him and made it so much easier to deliver his father's documents. He had 10 monthly payments to make to pay for it. Christmas brought some nice presents and even a bit of money for me to save for another bike. New Year's Eve I celebrated with my friends at the Citizen Hall in Backnang and said good bye to 1952.

It had certainly been a memorable year.

Theo with his new Meister Bike ready to deliver a document.

1953 started off with lots of snow and walking to work was hard. I had to walk 3 Km each way and the mornings were freezing. Work was tough, but I tried my best to catch up to the others. By the time we spent on our journey to Tunisia they were 6 month ahead of me, never the less I still learned a lot because at the tool shop they helped me as much as they could.

Springtime arrived and I had saved enough money to put a deposit on another bike made by a cycle manufacturer EHB '*Emil Hahn Backnang*'. It was a beauty, jet black and it had three gears.

I was finally mobile again.

Konne, Theo and I were still members of the Cycling Club and as springtime approached we started training again. Konne purchased a racing bike which had wooden rims. Wednesday's after work and on Saturday afternoon we would go training with some of the club members. The starting point was mostly from Bleichwiese and we cycled via Sulzbach to Murrhart from there over the mountains via Sechselberg back to Backnang. Our normal training run was between 40 to 50 K's.

Some Sunday's we would take part in races around a few of the smaller towns in the area. Theo and I had turns with Konne's Racing Bike, because we were in B class, and then Konne took over being in A class.

It was about that time when we heard that two Australian Pro Cyclists were in town, staying with the local Idler family (Butschers) in Backnang.

When we first saw them we were surprised that they were '*White*'.

None of us had learned much about Australia in school. We thought there were only Aboriginies and Kangaroos living there.

Their names were John Tressidder and Frank Brazier. Both of them soon became the 'Toast of Backnang'. John and Frank were 20 years old, and boy could they handle a bike. I remember the first Criterion in Backnang where John and Frank took part and I was also in the race because A and B classes were together.

After being lapped about 8 times John won the Race by a mile, with Frank a close second.

John Tressidor after winning the race in Backnang in 1953

We had the good fortune to take part in a few more races with them with the same results.

At that time I was not able to talk to them, firstly because they could not speak German, and secondly they would not waste their time with a little '*Shit kicker*' like me. John became German Road Champion and raced all over Europe and Frank evetualy went back to Melbourne to take part in the 1956 Olympic Games.

Neither John nor I knew then that thirty-five years later we would became the best of friends when our paths crossed again in Melbourne. Forty years later we even had our picture in the Backnang paper and the story of our lives.

In 2010 John and I were inducted into the 'Cycling Hall of Fame' on the same day!

On long weekends and holidays we still did some cycling tours around the country, not so much with Theo, he still had to work in the Garden and at home looking after their domestic rabbits. Uli had joined us by that time. Usually there were six or seven of us and we had lots of fun. In June I had my 17th Birthday and had almost completed two years of my apprentice ship, still with the occasional bashings from HR.

In September when Theo was 17, he got special permission through his company to get a limited driving licence (20 Km around Backnang). Working for a Tannery they always had to take their finnished product to the Railway Station for delivery to their customers by horse and cart. By car it was so much quicker and cleaner, one could tell the German Industrial Revolution had started.

At that time Theo would have been the youngest guy to be able to drive a motor car on the road, it was great!

On weekends he used to pick me up in his dad's VW Beetle and we drove around town and made sure everyone could see us, especially the Girls. On little country roads Theo let me have a go driving the car and I did rather well at it. I was still very much into cycling with Konne and some of our other mates. Theo became too busy at work helping his Dad with the Insurance and looking after the big garden.

I didn't mind working in the tool making section, until one Monday morning when I was summoned upstairs to the apprentice level. HR was sitting behind his desk and I could see he had my report book in front of him. On one of the pages I had under lined a drawing of a tool with a straight line instead of a broken one. He got up from his chair put down the report book and started to slap me around my face and then again proceeded to belt the living daylight out of me in front of all the other boys. Finally he kicked me up the backside and threw me out the door. Some of the boys told me later he made them stand around in a circle and said in a stern voice, "If you make mistakes like he did the same thing will happen to you."

When I got back to the toolshop and walked to the machine I was working on, the tradesmen could not believe what they saw. I was gone only about twenty minutes looking great and now I was a piece of pulp. My face was swollen, my nose was bleeding and some of my ribs were sore. It was too much for some of the guys who were teaching me.

"We'll fix that prick," they said. HR was not very well liked by them either.

I think it was Heinz Z who went over to the offices to report the incident to Mr Hoffman who was in charge of the whole Apprentice section and more. He could not believe his eyes when he saw me and found out what happened. He told me to stay put and left very angrily.

I didn't have to wait long before I was summoned to the Director's office. The Director's name was Dr. Wudke. He knew me because I helped to do some electrical work on the new house he was building. I knocked on the door and his secretary led me in to a room where several men, including Mr Martin the personnel manager, and to my annoyance, my dad were standing. All of them wanted to hear my story after which they called for HR to come down. As he entered the director's office I could see his face change the moment he saw all those men and me standing there. He had no idea why he had to come to see the director.

Dr. Wudke made him look at me. "If you ever he hit one of the company's apprentices again you will be immediately sacked," he told him. He didn't need to say anyhting else. His tone of voice indicated there would be no arguments.

That sounded good to me!

I am sure if it had been one of the others he would have been thrown out straight away, but because it was me who had been sent back from Sicily they gave him half a chance.

Back at the Toolworks I had to tell everybody about the outcome and they were all delighted.

HR was not a happy man though; he could no longer hurt anyone.

The Apprentices were happy about the outcome and in their eyes I was a bit of a hero.

As winter started to approach, wine and beer festivals were in full swing, and we had a great time. Riding my bike to work every day and still training twice a week made me very fit. One day Theo came up with an idea to make some spare cash on the side. He got in touch with a shoe factory which sent him their catalogue and gave him a concession to sell the shoes around our area.

It seemed to be a good thing at the time, starting our own business. We only managed sell 10 pairs of shoes to some of our friends and that was it. Selling shoes was much harder than we expected and the commission was hardly enough to pay for our smokes. We called it quits. So much for our first Business Enterprise!

On New Year's Eve, about ten of us celebrated in Grossaspach in a Pub and welcomed 1954 with much anticipation of excitement to come.

I was close to the end of my third year as a Toolmaker and my time was running out being taught in the machine section after which I had to go back upstairs to work with the other Apprentices.

I certainly didn't look forward being close to HR again. One morning I must have had a grin on my face which he wasn't too happy about. Had it been a few months earlier I would have copped a good belting but those times were in the past.

He got up from behind his desk and asked me, "What the hell are you smiling about?".

I must have given him an answer he did not like. He was convinced I had been grinning at him.

Well I couldn't believe what was coming!

He walked away and came back with a piece of round steel about 20 cm long and about 8 cm in diameter. He handed it to me and ordered me "to file it in to a square of 2 by 2cm".

"That's a stupid punishment. I've done nothing to deserve this."

I could see his face getting red. "Do you refuse to do what I order?"

"Yes! I am not stupid," I told him.

He raced out the Door and we all waited with dread. About half an hour later he came back with Mr Hoffmann, a couple of other men and again with my Dad (I hated it). He had told them that I wouldn't do what he asked, and they wanted to know why I refused the work I was supposed to do. I showed them the piece of steel and told them this was a rediculous order for a guy in his third year. They debated for a while without me hearing what was said then my Dad came over and told me to make a bit of a start. I could see he wasn't too happy about HR either.

I put the piece of steel in the vice, grabbed a big file and started with HR watching. After a while, he left to do his morning rounds through the factory to check on the other apprentices who were working in different sections. We knew he would be gone for at least two hours.

I took the piece of steel and gave it to one of the fellows who worked on the Milling machine and asked him to take about 10 mm off the top and some off the side to make it look square. It only took 10 minutes to do while another of the guys stood guard by the door to make sure we didn't get an unpleasant surprise. When that was done I put the steel back in the vice at my workbench and filed over the top of the marks which the machine left.

Once the marks were gone I hit my hands on the workbench a few times to make them look red and rubbed a bit of the file shavings on them. Then we waited!

As soon as HR walked back through the door I started filing to break into a bit of a sweat. He walked right up to me, but when he saw the metal in the vice he told me to stop and step aside. He opened the vice and took out the piece of steel, looked at it in disbelief and told me to show him my hands.

Very proud of himself he walked by all the fellows and pointed to the piece of steel he held and told them if they didn't behave, the same would happen to them!

I don't think he ever found out how I had done the job because all the guys were frightened of him and kept their mouths shut. It didn't stop us all from having a big laugh behind his back though.

In March 1954 I heard that the owner of the local Quarry which was only 3 Km from where we lived, was looking for a young switched on Boy to help in his office. Writing out dockets and loading trucks with different grades of crushed rocks.

The next day after I finished work I cycled to the Quarry and met Mr Seybold the owner. He was shorter than me but carried quite a bit of weight. He wore an old hat and very dusty overalls. He told me he liked to work below to make sure everything ran smoothly, which was why he needed someone to work in the office. He showed me through his very dusty office while explaining what had to be done.

"Are you interested?"

"That's why I'm here. But I'm still working as an apprentice at AEG. I know I won't pass the exam because I missed so much time while away.

So I have been thinking about leaving."

"Why don't you take a few days to think about it," Mr Seybold suggested.

I had already made up my mind that this would be the job for me, but I said I would think about it, which seemed to make him happy.

"Good, let me know when you are ready."

That evening after dinner I told mum and dad where I have been and what I had done. Neither of them were too happy about their son working in a Quarry, but the way they looked at each other told me they had suspected I would do something like that. They knew that AEG was not the place for me, that I was not meant to be a toolmaker.

After work on Saturday dad came with me to have a look at what would be my new job. I introduced him to Mr Seybold and while I looked around the Quarry they had a long talk. Finally they decided that I would start on a Monday in two weeks' time.

The pleasure was all mine! On the Monday morning when I turned up for work I immediately left my work place without asking HR for permission. I marched straight past his desk without giving him a glance and walked through the door towards Mr Martin's personnel offices. After a few minutes of waiting his secretary led me into his office. He was rather sad when I told him I was leaving, but he accepted my resignation and wished me all the best.

On my way back to my work place I went by the machine works and told all the fellows who taught me during the past year what happened. The surprise was not welcomed because they all liked me and I had made good friends. I must have been there for over two hours before I got back and HR was not there.

"He's out someplace looking for you," The guys told me.

I filled them in with what I had done and most of them agreed with me getting another job. Finally HR came storming in and walked straight towards me. He was furious, upset that I had given my notice to his superiors instead of going through him.

This was music to my ears!

I stared at him until he ran out of steam and when he finally had shut up I said, "I only talk to people who count."

I turned my back on him and walked across the floor to bid all the other apprentices goodbye. After that I went home.

For the rest of the week and the following one I took my holidays, which I was entitled to, and I never set foot in to that place again.

On the Monday morning I arrived at the Quarry at 7am to start work. The crushers were ready to be started and Mr Seybold was already waiting for me to show me what to do. From the start we got on very well. I must have made a good impression on him. I found out he lived in Fellbach, was married but had no children. My working hours were from 7am to 5pm with one hour for lunch, if we had time.

The best thing was I didn't have to work on Saturdays and earned DM.50.00 clear for starters. I loved the job!

It wasn't hard work but I had to be on the go all the time. Every time a tip truck would arrive he drove straight under the Silos. I had to climb on the back of it and open down gates with different crushed rocks, from big ones for road base, down to small ones for concrete and cement dust. It only took a few minutes to fill a truck then I had to write out a docket and hand it to the driver. Once one was done, the next one was already waiting to be loaded.

I could handle everything with ease and loved meeting all the different people. After a few days Mr Seybold spent most of his time down in the Quarry and left me in charge in the Office. I had to answer the phone, give out quotes and charge farmers and the public cash for their purchases. I got on well with the 'Truckies' and sometimes when it was a bit quiet they would spend a while talking to me in my 'office'.

Next to the office was a storage shed only half full with spare parts. After about 3 weeks Mr Seybold asked me to get in touch with *WULLE*, a Brewery in Stuttgart to see if they were interested in supplying Beer to us. The following Monday a Wulle truck arrived delivering a Refrigerator stocked full with beer bottles and a couple of full crates, which all went into the storage shed. Mr Seybold told me that I could sell the beer and make 10 Pfennig profit on each bottle I sold. Some of the drivers got one free and Mr Seybold paid for that one.

What a life! Here I was with a great job selling my own *Grog*. I was only seventeen, and absolutely loved it!

Theo had finished his apprenticeship and was looking for another job. His office manager had retired and didn't get on with the new one, so he gave them his notice.

"Why don't you come and talk to Mr Seybold at the quarry?" I told him. "He's looking for someone to operate a small front end loader. It can't be too hard to drive one of those."

"I can do that," Theo said with absolute confidence.

He came, had a look, talked to Mr Seybold and was hired on the spot.

It was great having Theo working with me. He had to work harder but got paid more than I did.

Talking to the Truckies was great. They told me to get a truck license. Driving trucks I could make a lot of money. I spoke to Theo about it and we decided to go to a driving school to do a class 2 license which would allow driving motorcycles up to 250cc, motorcars and all trucks.

I was looking forward to my 18th birthday in another couple of months. Twice a week in the evenings we had theoretical classes, and when suitable also driving lessons. I could practice on a spare truck parked at the Quarry when I wasn't busy. Some of the truckies helped me with the road rules and the answers to the questions I had to learn for the test.

Hermann, Fritz, and Uli, all grown up and smoking before a night out at a Gasthaus...

Friday the 18th of June 1954 was my 18th Birthday.

When I arrived at work MS handed me an envelope with DM 100.00 in it. I nearly fell backwards because that much I didn't expect. At midday he came back in to the office and told me I could take the rest of the day off, which was GREAT. I couldn't wait to get home to tell mum about the present I got from MS. and have my first legal cigarette in front of her. After some lunch, a wash and clean clothes, I jumped on my bike and rode downtown to meet up with some of our mates to have a drink for my special day. Pubs (*Wirtschaft* or *Gasthaus*) in Backnang which we most frequented were The Rose, The Engel, Waldhorn or the Baeren. This particular evening we did the lot!

Cycling home at midnight was extremely difficult; it felt as someone was trying to keep pushing me off my bike.

The next day as always this time of the year the sun was shining at her best. Mum and dad arranged a party for me in our little garden behind the house. We invited the relatives and some of my friends and I must say I felt great.

It gave me a lot of pleasure to walk through town with a smoke in my mouth making sure that everyone could see I was an Adult!

In the middle of 1954 Uli and Konne decided to do a big cycling tour through France, Portugal and Spain as far as Gibraltar, and then back home via Belgium Holland. They were gone for 4 months.

All was well I loved my job, made some extra money selling beer and the day of our driving exams came closer. At that time we were hooked on going to the movies. Backnang had three movie theatres, the Upper Town, the Under Town and the Bali. Our heroes were James Stewart, Garry Cooper, John Wayne, Errol Flynn, James Cagney, and James Mason. That was reason enough to wag our theoretical lessons and go to the movies. Naturally we were warned if we kept wagging we might fail, but we thought we knew better!

It was about the middle of September when we had our exams. There were about 20 of us going for different licenses. We had two Government License Testers from Stuttgart to do the tests and they were tough!

We had no problems doing the practical in the morning but the theoretical in the afternoon was a different story. We were asked a lot of questions. When it was my turn to answer I couldn't explain how air brakes function on trucks. He wanted to know how they worked from the compressor near the engine to the brake drums. I had a bit of an idea but it was not to his satisfaction. He bid me goodbye and told me I'll see him next time.

What a letdown, what a shame! I walked out of the building down the stairs towards Stuttgarter Strasse when I heard a door closing behind me. It was an 82 year old farmer who also failed his test. All he wanted was a license to drive his tractor to his fields. What was I going to do? Here is, to me an old man who wanted to work in his fields and me wanting to drive big Interstate Trucks and we both failed.

I was talking to the farmer when I heard a whistle. Looking up I saw Theo walking out of the building towards us with a shy grin in his face.

He had also failed! Was I happy about that! The three of us were the only ones who failed.

We decided not to tell anyone wanting to keep it a secret as long as possible. When we turned up at work next morning we were met with raucous laughter. The bastards already knew. That was it, no more wagging.

On the 24th of September was Theo's 18th Birthday and he got an unrestricted car license. The next time we repeated the truck driver's licence exam it went without a problem and on the 20th of December we got our big license.

Theo left the Quarry and got a job as a truck driver at a Cider Factory in Winnenden, not far from us. His route took him mainly to Berlin. He was away for four to five days at a time. His wage was very good and they (there were always two drivers) also got a living away allowance. After about three weeks at his job he told me that 'Hummel,' the owner of the Company was looking for another driver and he had told him that he might have someone suitable.

Theo and me with the other drivers of the Hummel Cider trucks.

Early Journeys

In January the Quarry had closed for a month because there was no road construction in winter. Most of us had to take our holidays so the timing was perfect. I was happy to take on another job instead of sitting around at home. The next morning after Theo had told me about the job I introduced myself to the owner of the cider factory who was a big man living in Stuttgart. He suggested while I still had some time off to take a shorter run with one of the other drivers to see if I would like it. It was arranged for me to do a two day trip with a very funny guy and we had a ball. After discussing wages and allowances I told him I would start as soon as I could finish at the Quarry.

On the first of February I told Mr Seybold about my plans and he wasn't very happy to see me go. However, the next day he told me he had a nephew who just finished school who would take over when I left.

It felt sad to leave a job I had grown into, but the new adventure to meet other people and see new places was something I looked forward to.

I started in mid-February 1955, the coldest part of winter. I had to travel about 3 Km further to get to work but I didn't mind. The Factory was big and warm and smelled of fermented fruit. Most of it was bought from local Farmers. Their main product was Apple Cider which was delivered in one litre bottles all over Germany. The first few days I had to work in the Factory to familiarise myself with the products and get to know the workers. There where big cellars with huge barrels full of freshly pressed Apples ready to be bottled and labelled. Their Brand Name was *NATURELLA*.

After a week one of the Drivers fell off a ladder at home, broke a leg and was unable to work for at least three months. I had to replace him straight away. That happened on a Monday and after loading the truck and trailer I was told to be ready at 4 am next morning. I told mum and dad that I would be away for about three days and they wished me good luck with my new venture.

It was bitterly cold riding my bike to work at that time in the morning, but I was there on time to start. I was driver number two and had to get experience. I won't forget that first trip on the Autobahn to Koln, it was tough. We arrived late afternoon at our first customer ready for unloading next morning. We went to a pub to have for dinner but had to wait a long time to be served. We had picked the wrong time! It was Carnival time and Rhinlanders celebrated more than at any other part of

Germany. Sleeping in the truck wasn't too bad; but of course the number one driver slept in the sleeping cabin and I slept cramped on the front seat.

Early in the morning the gates to the warehouse opened and we were greeted by an elderly man in overalls. He turned out to be the owner of the place and told us he was the only one to help us unload. His other workers were too crook to work because of the celebrations. Hearing that, we felt sick ourselves.

We backed the trailer up to a loading ramp and started. There were no forklifts and we had to unload with hand trollies stacked up with four crates on top of each other. We pushed them to the end of the building. It was lunchtime by the time we had finished. The owner was a great guy who worked very hard to get the job done. He took us to a nearby pub for a big lunch which we appreciated. He told us we could leave the trailer in his yard to make it easier for us to drive to our next customer. By the time we got there it was just after 3 pm but to our dismay we were told the warehouse was closed in the afternoons while the Carnival was on. Damn! Nothing we could do but wait until the next day.

Nearby was a service station specialising in big trucks and their drivers. After having a shower we relaxed in the restaurant with a beautiful famous *KOELSCH* beer while waiting for dinner.

The next morning we were there early waiting for the gates to open. This time we had to unload the lot ourselves because there was only one woman in the office to do the paper work and keep an eye on us. This was very insulting and we made sure we got away with two bottles of the best whisky in the place. We didn't even feel guilty. At midday we drove back to our first customer to collect our trailer and to our surprise he invited us for lunch again. Thank Heavens for lovely people.

Later in the afternoon we left Koln and headed for the Autobahn Stuttgart/Munchen towards home. That's where I took over. I felt like *'a pig in shit'* sitting behind the wheel driving this huge truck (a120 Bussing). It wasn't easy because in those days there was no power steering nor synchronised clutch. Changing gears required pressing the clutch pedal twice. Halfway home we stopped at an autobahn resting place to spend the night. We could have made it home but getting there before midnight meant we would lose one day's living away allowance. After a good meal we went back to the truck to sleep.

I must point out work had not finished. In winter all trucks' radiators had to be drained because of freezing temperatures and topped up in freezing mornings with the engine running. Things were much harder in those '*good old days*'.

After breakfast we made our way back to the factory with me behind the wheel. Except for the cold and doing the unloading ourselves, I liked the job. By the time our truck was unloaded another one arrived, coming from Munich. In the Office I was told that Theo and his driver were only one hour away. I decided to wait for him. By the time we cycled back home it was nearly dark. It was seldom that we had to work on weekends except for urgent deliveries and if we did we got paid extra.

Twice I had to go to Berlin with Theo and his number one driver to help out. What an experience that was, travelling through the eastern part of Germany without permission to stop. Berlin was still very much demolished but restorations had already started. Berlin was very exciting and I finished up doing two more trips with Theo and Otto.

Lots of times when we were together we made plans on how to get rich. The latest plan was to purchase a Grill and Alcohol Stand on a railway station, then slowly to purchase one after another all over Germany. It was the middle of May when we actually bought a removable small shop. Waiting for a suitable site, we had it moved to Theo's garden and looked forward to selling our first sausages.

And then came a huge disappointment: to have a business in Germany, you had to be 21 years of age. We each asked our parents if they would be willing to go to court and sign a guarantee for us to finance the business. They wouldn't do it. The reason was very simple; if things didn't go to plan they would be responsible. So soon after the war, dad had other things on his mind and I didn't blame him.

We had the stand but we would have to wait two years to start. I remember very clearly on a hot Sunday in the beginning of June when the two of us walked down Stuttgarter Strasse towards the town centre, Theo stopped turned towards me and said, "let's go to Australia, I heard there is an Olympiad next year."

Just like that out of the blue.

I stared at him, looked in his eyes, and saw that he was very serious.

"Are you out of your mind?" I said.

I knew where Australia was but had no idea about Melbourne.

"The Olympic Games are going to be in Melbourne," he said, "next year. I know some friends from our neighbourhood living there. What about we visit them. We could stay with them while we are there."

"How in God's name are you intending to get there?" I asked him.

"By bicycle, how else? What other way to we have of getting there?"

"We should plan to leave in September." He said, a big grin lighting up his face.

I laughed out loud.

"And how long do you think it will take to get there?"

"A bit less than a year. If we stay there a year we will only be gone two years."

"You are out of your mind, crazy."

Never the less the seed was sown!

From that day onwards all we only talked about and planned for was what would be our greatest adventure; from Backnang to Melbourne by Bike.

We kept this mostly to ourselves, and spoke only to a few of our mates about it. Naturally they also thought we were nuts.

One of our mates, we called him King; wanted to join us and we agreed thinking it was better if there were three of us rather than two. King was a bit of a lady's man and was always chasing girls. There was nothing wrong with that except he never had time for our project.

Near my 19th birthday we met a few mates in town and amongst them standing next to his bike was Uli. He lived about 15 Km away from Backnang. After a few cigarettes we went across the road to the *Engel* (The Angel Pub) for a drink. It was there that Uli happened to mention he had in mind to cycle to Australia with one of his mates Juhl Goetz. You could have knocked us over with a feather duster! It's really weird how different people come up with the same idea more or less simultaneously.

We told him we had been thinking the exact same thing. We told him about our plans and it was decided that the three of us would meet on the following weekend to discuss the idea.

Work was great and driving big semitrailers was fun. But I felt sad knowing that in the near future I would be leaving. Was this going to be a huge mistake? On the other hand I could not resist the temptation for the greatest adventure of my life.

Having been friends with Uli for such a long time we knew each other well. Theo and I decided Uli should join us and we would forget about any others.

We did this and became a fully hands-on-team. There was a lot of planning to do and little time to do it. We made a list of all the things to do and it grew bigger by the day. We had special saddle bags made by our local boot maker and my mother knitted us a beautiful black jumper on her machine (God bless her). Someone else made us an emblem out of white cotton with Germany written in black on it.

Road maps had to be organised which wasn't easy. Spare parts for our bikes had to be bought and two sets of tyres each. A three man tent and sleeping bags were on the list plus pots, pans, plates, cups and cutlery, all of which cost lots of money, and we were running very short.

Uli's older brother had demolished an old leather factory and told us there were heaps of old copper pipes lying around. One evening the three of us went to this place situated next to the river Murr with some torches. Theo kept watch while Uli and I climbed a fence and searched for the copper. The pipes were about two meters in length 20 cm in diameter and weighed about 20 Kg each. We managed to lift five pipes over the fence to Theo, then we carried them over to the river bank were we sunk them in to the water. The tops of the pipes were covered with some grass and after a slap on our shoulders we went home.

One of our friends' fathers was a dealer in scrap metal and Uli knew him well. He offered to pay us for the pipes but he could take them only at night. We sold him five loads over the next three months and did very well. Theo bought himself another transistor radio; he loved his music.

Our plan was to leave early in October but time was running out fast because we were still working. It was difficult to get all the things done. Theo's father's garage was the place where we stored all the gear. The 24th of September was Theo's 19th birthday and we still had a lot of things to do. Visas for Yugoslavia, Greece, Turkey and Syria had to be organised clothes had to be packed etc.

Theo showed us an advertisement from the Stuttgarter newspaper. A Greek company was purchasing old second hand trucks to be delivered to Greece and they were looking for drivers with truck license endorsements. We left it with Theo to get in touch with them to find out what was involved. Someone who spoke good German told him that two trucks were to be driven to Salonika in two weeks' time.

Theo told them we would be interested but unfortunately we would not be ready by then. He was told that on the 20th of December there would be another two to be delivered. He told them we would be ready by then.

I didn't know about Uli and Theo, but I had this queasy feeling in my gut not knowing what I had let myself into.

We told our parents we had the possibility to drive a couple of trucks to Greece and being paid a good sum as well. They weren't too happy about the Idea and it took a lot of persuasion, but eventually they gave their blessings.

That was it! From now on we told everyone we would go to Greece.

Money was still a problem but of course selling the copper had helped a lot. At the end of October I gave notice at work and Theo did the same.

We told them about delivering two trucks to Greece, and if the job was still vacant we would be back by the end of January. We finished a week before Christmas and so did Uli.

Every day from then on we packed and went through our list in detail to make sure that nothing was forgotten and having been on long trips before helped a lot.

Two days before leaving we got dressed and called our friend Helmut Schweda. Helmut was the local photographer and a good one too. He took the last photo of us with Backnang behind us. He told us he would wait a few weeks until he heard from us and then put it in the newspaper with a bit of a story.

Uli and Theo each had DM.60.00 saved and I had only 40.00. It wouldn't have mattered because we expected some pay in Salonika. At home I came across my brother's bank book with some of his savings in it. I took it to the Bank and collected 20 Marks so then I also had 60. I said to myself, Heinz one day I will pay you back with Interest... which I did.

On the 19th of December I said goodbye to my parents and brother, not realising that it would be thirteen years before we would see each other again. We slept that night at Theo's place for a very early start next morning.

What will the future bring? was the last thing I thought that night before falling asleep.

Early Journeys

Me, with Mum and Dad and my brother Heinz a couple of months before leaving for Australia. This was the last family photo taken in Germany until I returned with my wife and son David thirteen years later... in January 1969.

*The three of us dressed to leave:
the photo Helmut Schweda took two nights before we left.
He later used this image in a story he publisherd about us
in the Backnang Newspaper.*

Part Two
The Big Adventure

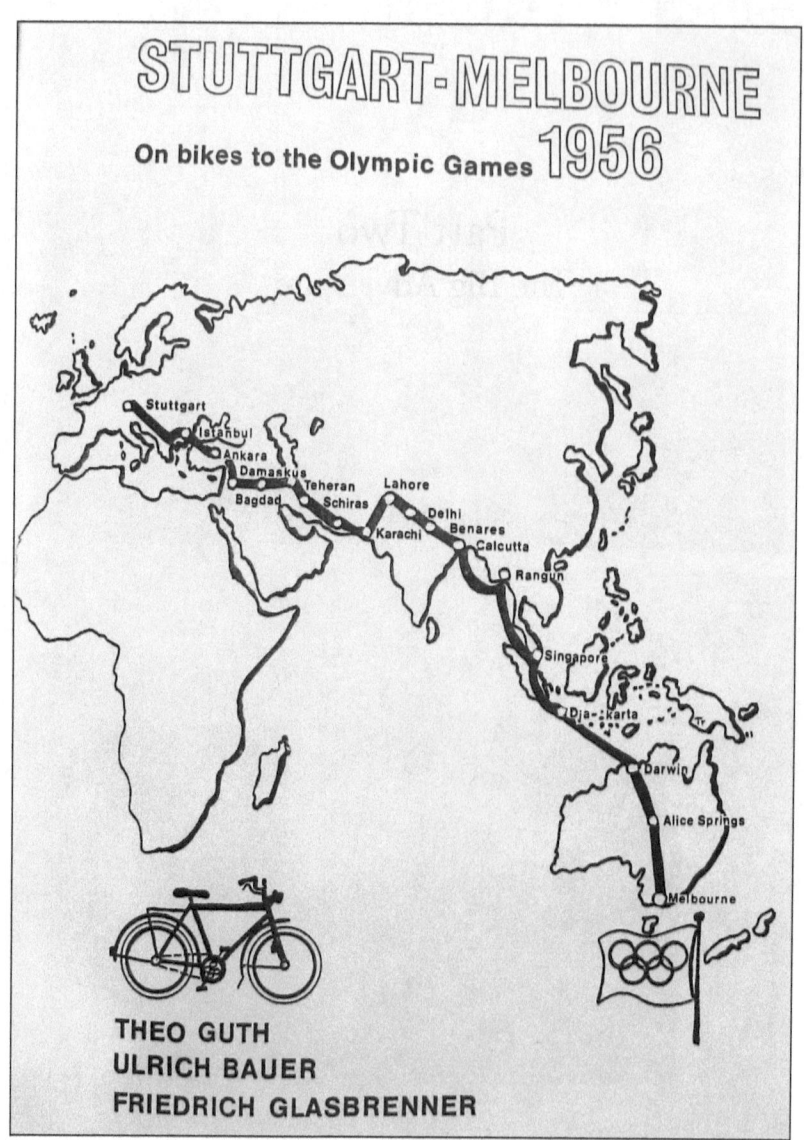

Chapter Five

On Tuesday the 20th December 1955 at 4am we turned our back on Backnang and headed for Stuttgart.

On the outskirts of Backnang we chanced upon one of our school friends out early on her way to work. She was surprised to see us with our loaded bikes.

"What in God's name are you doing at this early hour?" She asked.

Uli with his usual dry humour replied, "Just exploring the surroundings."

She gave us a weird look before moving on.

She was the last Backnanger we saw.

It had been snowing during the night and the roads were covered with a light dusting of snow and some ice slick. This made pedalling bikes very difficult, especially with each of us having 100 Kg plus of luggage.

Ten Kilometres from Stuttgart near Sindelfingen, the Greek truck drivers were waiting for us at the truck depot, biting their fingernails in the hope that we would not leave them in the lurch. But because of the horribly bad weather we took a lot longer to get there than we had anticipated. It must have been well after 9 am when we finally arrived.

They were happy to see us and we instantly liked these guys.

But our smiles turned to a grimaces of horror when we saw the trucks their boss had purchased. One was a 'M.A.N' goods carrier, the other a Mercedes tip truck. Both of them were built during the early war years and had done a lot of work. The tyers were virtually bald and the seat in the cabin was badly worn, even the windscreen was scratched.

We were told they had Government papers which allowed them to travel only on Bundesstrassen, not on the Autobahn.

"Is good, yes?" one of the Greek drivers asked.

"Just beautiful," Theo said sarcastically.

After loading our bikes and luggage on the back of the trucks, we were invited into a small dining area beside the office for a good hearty breakfast and then we hit the road.

It turned out that neither of the two Greek drivers were much good so it was up to Theo and me to do most of the driving. I was driving the M.A.N with Uli and one of the Greeks (whose names I have forgotten) next to me because our cabin was bigger. Theo was with the other in the 'Merc'.

They told us the reason they got the job to deliver the trucks was because both of them spoke some German. We had no worries about food. They filled a whole wooden box with loaves of bread, butter, different cheeses, tinned fish, dried beef and heaps of bottled water. There was no way we would starve.

Here we go again, I thought to myself; *Travelling into the unknown.* What lay ahead remained to be seen.

Leaving Stuttgart behind, we travelled through Ulm towards Munich. Theo was leading. Not being able to drive on the Autobahn we were forced to use old country roads and highways which made the journey a lot longer having to drive through every little town on the way.

Munich itself was catastrophic and I had to watch out not to lose the Merc in front of us. These blasted trucks were built during the war when power steering and power brakes hadn't even been thought of. We had to double clutch every time we changed up or down a gear, and to slow down we had to drop to a lower gear before applying the brakes. To turn left or right we had to pull a switch and an indicator arm would come out the side next to the door. To keep the water temperature at a certain level we had to keep an eye on a gauge mounted on the dashboard. A canvas roller in front of the radiator had to be pulled up or down manually from the inside of the cabin. It was tough. Today's truck drivers don't know how fortunate they are with the luxurious vehicles they have now.

I was exhausted after the first hundred or so kilometres, and we still had to go all the way through Austria and Yugoslavia to get to Greece…

We passed Rosenheim and headed towards Salzburg. Just before the Austrian Border we stopped at a Trucking Hotel Service Station to spend our first night since leaving home. The three of us got a room with three beds and the Greeks had the room next to us. After a meal and a couple of drinks we studied our road maps to plan the route for the next day.

Utterly exhausted I slept like a log. It had been such a very long day!

Early next morning after breakfast and refuelling our trucks we headed for the Austrian border. With a last glance and a casual backward wave we left Germany behind.

The traffic in Austria wasn't too bad and we made good headway, passing Salzburg on route to St Wolfgang beside their beautiful lake. The roads were good but wet. A fine drizzle made driving quite difficult, and the bald tyres didn't help either. We were heading towards Graz but had to survive the Poetschen Pass first.

The Alps in front of us, white with snow, majestic, ruggedly beautiful were awesome. Knowing we had to get over them sent cold shivers down my spine.

Climbing Poetchen Pass was probably the hardest drive I ever did. By the time we were a quarter of the way up it started snowing and our trucks started slipping all over the place. Not far in front of us was a snowplough shovelling snow aside to keep the road clean. We stayed behind it for a while before it pulled off and stopped in a parking zone to let the banked up traffic behind it pass.

The steepest part of the Pass had a 17% grade with lots of curves. Half way up Theo's truck had a puncture on the right hand front wheel. Now that was a bummer! It could not have happened at a worse place.

Imagine changing a tyre in those conditions! It was extremely cold, and wet with sleet, with traffic bumper to bumper, on-coming as well as behind us. It took over an hour before we had that wheel changed and not one car or truck could get past. What a mess!

Finally we reached the top and found a place where we could stop to let the banked up traffic go by. It was a good time to have a rest and some lunch before attempting the descent.

Going down was horrendous, much more dangerous than coming up. We had to stay in second gear and sometimes in first gear to slow us enough to use the brakes which we had to do constantly while trying not to slide all over the road. I was glad Uli sat next to me and kept his eyes open. After an eternity we reached the bottom and all of us sighed with relief. It was a drive I would never want to do again.

It was still cold but it had stopped snowing and visibility had improved. We bypassed Graz and headed south towards the Yugoslavian Border. Just before crossing over we stopped in a small town where we got a very good dinner and a couple of rooms for the night. At breakfast we filled our stomachs because we knew from then on we would be getting food which we were not accustomed to.

Crossing the border was not so easy. We would be going through a Communist country ruled with an iron fist by Field Marshall Tito. At that time Yugoslavia was made up of Slovenia, Croatia, Serbia, Bosnia, Herzegovina, Montenegro, Macedonia and part of Albania. The customs officers, who looked more like soldiers, searched through our trucks, but did not touch our luggage. They obviously did not like the Greeks much and spent a lot of time studying their passports. It seemed to take forever before all of us got our passports stamped, after which we were allowed to proceed into Yugoslavia.

At the border between Austria and Yugoslavia.

Theo and me with one of the Greek drivers checking our bikes after Yugoslavian Customs inspection.

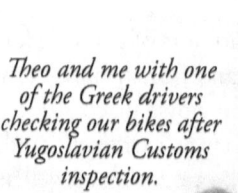

The Big Adventure

Driving along roads so iced up they looked like frozen rivers.

Leaving the border we went through a small town called Maribor and were taken back in time. It was like Germany a hundred years ago. The roads were not maintained and neither were the houses, and people were poorly dressed. Driving was hazardous because we had to dodge countless horse or cow drawn trailers. We headed towards Zagreb, passing through many sad looking villages and a couple of small Towns.

Everything seemed grey and miserable and I caught myself thinking, *I should have stayed home*. But we were already here so I had to make the best of it.

It was cold and wet and the iced up road was very slippery. Just before a village not far from Zagreb I lost steering control slid off the road with the front wheels stuck in a ditch.

I put it in to reverse but the wheels spun uselessly unable to grip the slippery surface. We had no hope getting out by ourselves. I got out of the truck to assess the damage and overcome with rage I furiously kicked the tyres. Under the circumstances I could do nothing about it.

Theo who was driving ahead of me must have seen what happened because he was already backing up towards us. Of course traffic on both side of the road had stopped with onlookers all around us making it hard for Theo to back his Truck into position. Once he got close enough he put a chain around his bumper bar and hook onto ours.

Some of the onlookers helped to push and with me in reverse, Theo started to pull. Being slippery made it difficult but we succeeded in getting the truck back on the road. The whole operation took us a couple of hours during which we caused traffic to bank up for miles.

Back on the road finally, it was a struggle to drive through the chaos.

Some of the locals studying the wheel marks we left in the ditch.

The Big Adventure

Taking a lunch break beside the road, closer to Belgrade where it was warm enogh not to have any snow.

Driving towards Belgrade was a little better because the main road had been maintained more than some of the others we had travelled on.

Belgrade, the Capitol, was nothing much to write home about: Lots and lots of high rise apartment buildings all the same grey colour, the same design, the same height, and there were endless rows of them. How anyone knew where they lived was a mystery to me since there was little to distinguish one building from another. Just looking at them made me feel depressed.

After another long day we finally got as far as Skopje late in the evening. We stopped outside a service Station which was closed for the night (they all closed for the night). We parked our trucks and prepared dinner from our supplies which we still had plenty of. After that we got our blankets and tried to get some sleep sitting up in the cabin. It was an uncomfortable night and we were happy to see the service station opening early in the morning. After refuelling, the service attendant made us some hot coffee and let us use the toilet facilities. Then we hit the road on our last stretch to Salonika.

The weather had improved considerably and got better the further south we travelled. It was still cold, but no more rain the sun started to show itself. We had come through some rugged but interesting country. Wherever we stopped the people had smiles on their faces and were very friendly towards us. We still had to conquer several mountains but the road had dried up which made driving a lot easier.

When we finally arrived in Thessaloniki it was a late afternoon. This time the Greek drivers managed the trucks and they knew where they were going. We stopped in the middle of the city next to a hotel where we were met by an elderly lady who spoke fluent German. She told us that we were to spend the night in this hotel all paid for by her. She handed us DM. 200 and about 20 Marks in Drachma for our work, more than we expected. We thanked her very much for her generosity.

We unloaded our bikes and luggage and the rest of our belongings. After a few hugs and well-wishes from our Greek friends they jumped back into their trucks and with a last wave drove off.

We never saw them again.

The waterfront at Thessaloniki - Greece.

The Big Adventure

The beautiful waterfront walk, Thessaloniki

It was the 24th of December and we were on our own in a very foreign country. Suddenly I felt homesick and somehow wished I had stayed in Backnang. Later on when I mentioned to Theo and Uli how I felt, they told me they had the same feeling. Perhaps it was because it was Christmas Eve and we were a long way from home and everthing familiar.

The hotel wasn't five stars, but by our standards it was pretty good. We checked in and were given a big room with three beds. There was also a security room in the basement for our bikes. After a hot shower and a change of clothes we asked at the reception where we could get something to eat. They recommended a nice little restaurant across the street.

When we entered every one stopped talking. They looked at us as if we were from Mars. There were smiles all round when they found out we were Germans. There was a Christmas tree in the restaurant and Christmas Carols as background music. One of the waiters, a young friendly guy who spoke a bit of German and a few words of English handed us the menu. It was all in Greek and we had no idea what to order.

After some difficulties we managed to order a chicken soup, followed by pieces of grilled lamb. We also ordered some Greek white wine.

When the soup arrived we thought they were trying to poison us, it was sour. We called the waiter and when he came over I asked, "What's wrong with the soup?"

He looked perplexed.

"Has it gone off?"
It took a moment before he understood what I meant.
"It is a Greek delicacy," he told us, "made from fresh lemons and egg white."

The only thing we understood was lemon. That explained the sour taste. Theo refused to eat his and passed it across the table for Uli and me to finish. Once you got used to the taste it wasn't too bad at all.

When the wine was served we got a double shock; it tasted dreadful!

It was called *Retzina* and it tasted like boiled wood mixed with a dash of bitumen, even though it was a white wine and looked perfectly normal. We had expected it to taste like some of the German wines we knew back home.

Theo laughed and saluted us with his glass of coke.

When the lamb was served we got a nice surprise, it tasted really good and sipping the retzina after each bite of lamb wasn't too bad after all especially once the alcohol took effect.

We became friendly with the young waiter who was happy to practice his German in front of his Boss and customers. Being Christmas next day the restaurant would be closed until after the New Year and our waiter (Spiro?) was going home to his family, catching a bus early the next morning.

We told him of our plan to cycle to Australia and he invited us to stay with him and his family in Kavalla on the Aegean Sea, half way from Salonika to the Turkish Border. We asked for the bill and to our surprise we didn't have to pay for the soup, nor the retzina. Spiro wrote his address on a piece of paper and when we got up to leave every one wished us luck on our journey. What a hard day it had been and what a pleasant Christmas Eve we experienced.

We slept like rocks and greeted Christmas Day in a cheerful mood. Sitting around the breakfast table at the hotel we studied our road map and worked out the best route for the day. Our bikes were ready, just a few minor adjustments with the luggage. We bid the hotel staff goodbye, after they pointed us in the right direction.

Back on our bikes again we felt great. Christmas day was on a Sunday. With very little traffic on the road we decided to have a look at the harbour which was only one block from our hotel. It was a wonderful scene, cold but the sun was shining and people were everywhere either going to church or coming and enjoying the beautiful day. After taking some photographs we headed east.

Unfortunately we had to cycle through the whole city to reach the road to Kavalla. The road was dry and it wasn't too cold. It was after midday when we reached the outskirts of Salonika and the open road leading east. Uli was leading with Theo at the rear. Every village or small town we came through people looked at us with big eyes and when we stopped they stood around us all smiling.

We made good headway. Very little traffic and lots of waves from drivers in cars and trucks. We must have travelled for about 50 or 60 km when we arrived at a lake. We decided to look for a sheltered place to set up camp. We didn't have to look long to find a spot not that far from the road but surrounded by trees and bushes.

Uli and I erected our tent while Theo collected wood to make a small fire. We still had some tins of fish, pressed meat and some beans from Germany which we had not used. At breakfast earlier at the hotel we were given some bread, smoked meat and some fruit, with compliments from the hotel staff along with their wishes for a safe trip.

Tent up with sleeping bags in place, fire going, preparing dinner didn't take long. Sitting around the fire, eating and listening to Theo's radio was great. We all felt that we had achieved something special. We were well and truly on our way to Australia and the Olympic Games.

After locking our bikes together we put some more wood on the fire and hit the sack! This was our first night in the tent since we left and it was better than we expected. We had plenty of room and I slept surprisingly well. So did the others.

Early the next morning we woke to the sound of bells which seemed to be all around us. As we opened the tent we saw that we had company. We were surrounded by a flock of funny looking sheep, accompanied by several boys two of whom were riding donkeys.

Theo and me riding donkeys in the herd of sheep

The sheep had longer heads and different fur to ours back home. The boys looked at us as if we were from outer space but with big smiles on their faces. We greeted and invited them for a bit of breakfast which we were going to prepare but they shook their heads pointing to their tummies that they had eaten already.

They stayed with us while we packed. After cleaning our campsite and covering the ashes to kill what was left of the fire we were ready to leave. But before leaving we asked the boys if we could sit on their donkeys to take some photos and they agreed happily.

Theo and me in the donkey cart.

It was still early, the sun was shining and we covered a fair distance by midday. Cycling through many villages we found every shop closed because of Christmas but some service stations had opened where we could buy drinks, smokes, and refill our drinking bottles mounted on front of the handle bars. By 2 or 3 o clock in the afternoon we reached the outskirts of Kavalla. We showed the address to some people on the footpath. They pointed straight ahead and indicated with their fingers that we had 3 to 4 Km to go.

As we rode along we could see the Aegean Sea sparkling in the sun.
It felt great to be alive.

The Big Adventure

Along the road to Kavalla...

When we got to the centre of town we asked again and to our surprise we were only 500 meters away from our destination.

It was about 3pm by the time we saw Spiro and met his family. They lived in a house next to the railway station where his dad and one of his brothers worked. Spiro was so happy to see us. He wasn't sure whether we would hold to our promise to call by. He ushered us inside to meet the rest of his family.

We didn't have to wait long before Spiro's mother and sister brought a big platter of sliced bread, goat cheese, sausages, olives and a variety of fruit. Next to the house was a small lawn suitable to erect our tent.

Opposite the house were some disused railway tracks where children were playing. Spiro and some of his friends brought along loads of wood to make a fire for a grill later that evening in our honour.

Never in our wildest imaginings could we have expected to be treated so wonderfully. It was like we were Royalty.

Erecting our tent took some time. Everybody wanted to help, and they got in each other's way, but we got it sorted eventually.

What a great evening it turned out to be. The fire was lit and blazing, garden lights glowed creating a romantic atmosphere. Some neighbours came over with arms full of food. There were heaps of meats for the grill, lamb chops, beef, pork and even some goat. Bowls full of salad and lots of Retzina to wash it all down. What a feast!

There would have been close to 30 people sitting around us when an elderly man started to play a fiddle. What a shock to the system. He produced the most awful sound. I had never heard anything as bad as that before. But it seemed the guests loved it. They started clapping and some got up to dance.

Theo and I could hardly stand it. We crawled back into the tent and pissed ourselves laughing, we couldn't help it.

"Hey you bloody idiots," Uli called out. "Behave yourselves. You are embarrassing us."

We had never heard Greek music before. All we knew was German, Italian and some American music. Because it was so weird it seemed bad to us. We watched the dancing and after a few more glasses of retzina even the music didn't seemed to get better. Or was it because we were becoming accustomed to it? I think the retzina definitely helped.

It was one of our best and happyiest evenings. I had no idea at that time how accustomed I would later become to love everything about Greece and her traditions, but that evening taught me a big lesson, never to ridicule another country's way of life, and to learn more about them.

Fritz and Theo with Spiro in the middle in Kavalla.

The Big Adventure

It was tough leaving next morning. The whole family wanted us to stay longer, but we had to hit the road. We had a long way to go and if we stayed too long in anyone place we would never get to our destination in time for the Olympic Games.

After lots of handshakes, cuddles and best wishes, we finally got away just before midday. All the neighbours and friends of Spiro came to wave us goodbye. Spiro had tears in his eyes and held us in his arms for a while. Wow! Greek hospitality was unbelievable.

Spiro and his family in Kavalla watching us leave.

We told them we would keep in touch but unfortunately we lost their address. We never did see them again. Thirty years later when I returned to Greece with Theo, my brother Heinz and our wives Zara, Ilse and Sybille we tried to locate them, but Kavalla had grown tenfold and had had changed so much nothing was recognizable. Not having their names or an address, we had no hope of finding them.

To this day I still think about that family and their friends, especially when I listen to Greek music.

With Uli leading the way it wasn't long before we left Kavalla behind. We headed northeast towards Xanthi, but the going was hard. We rode into hilly countryside and the alcohol and food from the night before didn't help Uli and me. Theo was fine because he drank only fruit juices. But once the alcohol had worked its way out of our systems we made good distance. Before nightfall we found a secluded campsite and lit our usual fire. We had no problem with food. Spiro's mum had packed us a big food parcel which would last a couple of days (God bless her). Reminiscing about the past and making plans for the next day we crawled in to the tent and instantly fell asleep.

Next day was up and down hills with a stiff cold breeze blowing side on making hard riding. Until now we had spent very little of our precious money, buying only smokes and drinks. Travelling through several villages we arrived at Xanthi a small town where we stopped at a little restaurant for some coffee and a couple of smokes.

It didn't matter where we stopped we always drew a crowd and were welcomed by friendly people. A few kilometres past Xanthi we camped, lit a fire, had a bite to eat and unwound listening to Theo's radio. The next two days the road wound through some big mountains and it took us another two days to get to the Turkish border. It was about midday on Saturday the 31st of December when we arrived at the Greek/Turkish Border near Edirne (Turkey).

It was cold and overcast with not much movement, just a few trucks at customs. Waiting behind some trucks we were spotted by a couple of Custom Officers. They beckoned to us and we followed them to a small office. When we told them our plan was to cycle to Australia they begged us to stay in Greece and not go through Turkey.

"Why?" we asked innocently.

"The Turks are bad people. You won't be safe over there."

They seemed worried that something might happen to us.

"Well just have to take that risk," we told them, maintaining suitably worried expressions. "There's no other option but to travel through Turkey."

"Perhaps we should share a coffee together before you cross over."

One of the officers served us tiny cups of thick black coffee while the other stamped our passports. When we had finished the coffee they both wished us good luck.

It wasn't a pleasant ride in no-man's land towards Turkey. We were sad leaving Greece behind where we had such fond memories. It took us about twenty minutes to cross the empty barren stretch of land between the two borders.

The Turkish Customs post looked much the same as the Greek one had. There were trucks and cars lined up waiting to pass through to head into Greece. I could see a couple of rough looking soldiers standing there watching us as we approached and was not looking forward to meeting these dangerous people.

To our incredible surprise we were welcomed with open arms by the Turkish Customs Officers.

"Are you all okay?' one asked.

And when we nodded assent they told us that we were lucky people to get away from those thieving Greeks.

We looked at each other and couldn't help smiling.

Not knowing much about World Politics at that time, we definitely got the message that the Greeks and the Turks didn't like each other. We didn't mention that we had had such a good time while in Greece.

"We're just happy to be here in a safe country," I managed to tell them without smiling or bursting into laughter.

They liked that and ten minutes later we had a hot glass of tea in our hand. Our passports were stamped and they gave each of us a four week transit Visa. Before we got on our way the Chief Officer asked if we wanted to change some German Marks, telling us he would give us the best exchange rate. We took the offer and I think we changed about 100.00 DM. for Turkish Lira.

Now we were in Turkey, a new frontier for us! After a few handshakes and well wishes we jumped on our bikes and hit the road. We made it through Edirne and found a nice place next to a creek to set up camp.

It was New Year's Eve and very cold, but having a small camp fire was okay. Before we left Germany Theo had written to the Stuttgarter Radio Station asking them to play the song *Heimat Deine Sterne* on New Year's Eve.

After erecting our tent and preparing some dinner we spent New Year's Eve far from home, cosy in our tent, listening to Theo's radio. What a surprise we had about 10 pm when we heard the voice of the announcer from Stuttgarter Rundfunk, saying that he would play the request of a Herrn Theo Guth, *Heimat Deine Sterne*.

Hearing that song made us feel terribly sad. It made us realize just how far away from home we had come. With each of us feeling homesick we didn't sleep too well that night.

New Year's Day 1956. We crawled out of the tent shivering. It was a very cold morning. Wondering what the future would bring, we quickly packed and loaded our gear and jumped on our bikes once again. Riding hard was the best way to keep warm.

From Edirne we headed southeast towards Corlu and the Sea of Marmara. It wasn't easy going and we were happy to reach the water after about two days of hard cycling. We were lucky with the weather, still cold but the sun was shining and the roads were not too bad. Riding alongside of the Sea was beautiful and brought back memories of Italy three years earlier.

Turkey was different to Greece, we didn't see many women and the food was new to us. We created huge commotions wherever we stopped whenever we passed through or stopped in small towns.

Theo and Uli (back towards the camera) surrounded by onlookers as we passed through a small town.

In the begining we had problems with ordering a meal in an eating place unless there was someone who could speak a little German or a few words in English. The patrons in these restaurants were always all men. There was never a woman in sight. Alcohol was not served, only tea coffee or fruit juices. Most of the time we walked straight in to the kitchen and lifted the lids on pots cooking on the stove to see what was cooking, after which we indicated to the cook what we wanted. Uli and I had no difficulties in choosing food, but Theo, far too fussy for his own good, always found it hard to get something to his liking.

Further along the way in bigger cities, in larger restaurants he would always order 'Omlette Natuer' while shaking his fingers to indicate no, and pointing towards onions.

Everything was new to us; the music that played nonstop wherever we rode through a village or town was even stranger than the Greek music we heard in Kavalla. The voice of the Muezin calling the faithful to prayer from the Minarets of the Mosques was particularly strange to our ears. Women on the street were covered in black with a Burka over their head and a companied mostly by a man or children. We never saw them alone.

In Toilets we had problems because they had no seats, only two steps for the feet with a hole in the middle. To have a crap one had to bend down on knees and hover over the hole. Mounted next on the wall was a short water hose which one turned on to wash one's bum, supposedly with the left hand. Those toilets were definitely not made for reading a newspaper!

When we arrived at the European side of Istanbul we saw the Hilton Hotel and headed straight for it. Why? To head for their proper toilets of course, to have a decent crap and a good clean-up. It took some time because only one of us could go at a time because the other two had to look after the bikes. We were newly born after cleaning up at the Hilton. We then looked for a small hotel near the harbour not far from where the Ferry docked to leave for the other side of Istanbul. It was a one star hotel and cheap. By that time we were running low on cash and didn't want to change more German Marks on this side.

Istambul and the Hagia Sophia can be seen above the city skyline.

It was a great sight crossing the Bosporus. We were really impressed with the size of the two Istanbul's and the beautiful Mosques with many other great buildings. We were surrounded by curios people; some even took pictures of us. As soon as the Ferry docked, we got off and were approached by two guys who introduced themselves as Hussein and Ahmed. It turned out that Hussein, a smallish sort of a guy, was an assistant Director for a film company. They both spoke some German and some English. Somehow they knew we were on this Ferry and they came to welcome us to their city. They asked us the usual questions, where from and where too. Both of them were impressed by our adventure and offered to show us around the city. They insisted on us being their guests for a couple of days.

It sounded a bit fishy to us. We discussed the situation and decided to trust them. We figured if anything happened there were three of us against two of them so we should be okay.

They led the way along the footpath; the road was near impossible to manoeuvre. Traffic was 'choc a bloc' with all kind of wheels, big trucks, small trucks, cars, scooters, rickshaws and cycles. We must have walked for close to an hour before we stopped in front of a medium size apartment block, opposite a big school campus.

It turned out that Ahmed was a Teacher at that school and the apartments belonged to the school. Hussein, being a friend of Ahmed was able to rent the apartment next to his. Luck was with us again. Hussein would stay with Ahmed and let us lodge in his apartment. It was on the first floor but it didn't matter, carrying our bikes and luggage up the stairs we had enough helpers. The apartments were well appointed with two bedrooms, a living room, kitchenette and a bathroom with shower and of course the typical hole in the floor toilet. They told us to settle in and they would come back an hour later to take us for coffee.

What was happening? We could not work it out, how could two strange men invite us to their home when they actually knew nothing about us?

We were sure they had a hidden agenda and we were going to keep our eyes open. After freshening up, and sorting our luggage on the floor, Hussein and Ahmed knocked on the door. They brought another guy with them and told us he was also a teacher and wanted to meet us. I have forgotten his name but he spoke reasonably good German and had been there once. They carried a small basked full of fruit, two bottles of orange juice and some bread.

The Big Adventure

After consuming some of the goodies we sat around on the floor, telling them about ourselves and our future plans to reach Australia. By that time they wanted to show us a bit of their city and take us out for coffee. We still couldn't work out their agenda.

We were in a Muslim country and we had noticed that younger and elderly men walking along the footpath were often holding hands. Because we didn't see many women with uncovered faces, we assumed they were all homosexuals. There were women in public but they were mainly Christians, or they had other religions. It was late in the afternoon, by the time we had coffee and more conversations. There wasn't much time left to do more sightseeing. Anyhow by the time we got back we were exhausted. They bid us good night and arranged to show us around the whole day tomorrow. After a visit to the 'hole in the floor' and a quick shower we slept great. This was the first time we slept in a bed in Turkey.

After some breakfast with fruit, orange juice and a flat type of bread which looked like stale pancakes we heard a knock on the door. All three of them with big smiles on their faces greeted us like old friends.

We were ready for another day. Yesterday we had asked them whether they knew how to find the Australian Embassy in Istanbul. Hussein told us the High Commission is not far from here and we would go there first. We passed some magnificent old buildings and some very old Mosques and it wasn't long before we entered an office building with a sign telling us the Australian High Commission was on the third floor.

We were greeted by a very attractive Lady, who to our dismay informed us that she could not help us here. To arrange for a visitor visa for Australia, we would have to visit the Embassy in Ankara when we get there.

So much for that! But we still had a long way to travel and time was on our side. Our new friends led us to a huge Mosque, called Hagia Sophia. Three years earlier in Milano, Florence and Rome Theo and I saw some magnificent buildings. Hagia Sophia wasn't just grand, it was absolutely magnificent. We had never been in a Mosque before and we had to take our shoes off and put them next to a thousand other pairs. It was overwhelming. How could anyone build something like that so many centuriess ago!

There were hundreds of worshipers praying on their knees reading the Qur'an (Koran) and we were careful not to make any noise. This was something special.

Coming back outside and searching for our shoes, we had a problem finding them. Others had piled theirs on top of ours and it took a while before we found them. After moving shoes all over the place in search of our own we couldn't wonder what problems worshipers inside would have when they came back out and went to put on their shoes. We left before anyone else came out.

Over a cup of coffee in a little cafe Ahmed mentioned that we should visit the Bazaar, supposedly the biggest in the world. Another eye opener! We never saw so much life in one place — one shop next to the other and a thousand different ones. Hussein told us to watch our pockets because there are thieves here. We couldn't walk five metres before being accosted by a money exchanger offering us good rates for our German Marks. We found out that we could have gotten four times as much here as we did at the border. No wonder the officers where we crossed the border offered us cups of tea. They made a good profit by exchanging our money. The Greeks had warned us before crossing over to be careful. Now I knew what they had been talking about.

We could hardly move along without getting pestered but suddenly I had a great idea about how to make up for it.

After watching how carpets were made, admiring the gold and coppersmiths, and looking at all the different spices we started to get tired legs. We had been walking everywhere. At a food place Hussein ordered some of that round bread filled with roast lamb, onions (not for Theo) and some salad. It tasted good especially with fresh fruit juice. After that we called it quits.

On the way home Ahmed told us they had a surprise for us to heal our sore legs. It wasn't long before they stopped in front of an old building with steam coming out of some side windows. Entering through a door we were confronted by half naked men, wearing only towels around their waists. They told us we were in an '*Amman*' a Steam Bath, and to strip off.

Aha! Here we go. We were in a 'poofter's club.' This was their Agenda!

No wonder they were always smiling.

For the moment we played along and stripped off. All the while searching for a weapon we could use. Uli said there were a couple of chairs in a corner which we could demolish. Using the legs of them we would be able to defend ourselves and do some damage. Some guy led us to a room full of steam and made us lay naked on our tummy on a hot concrete slab on the floor. Another guy was waiting with a bucket of hot water and some kind of rubber steam hose. On one hand he had a glove looking like it was made of sand paper, (we were later told it was made of shark skin). Then he started!

I saw stars. Shit, this guy is ripping off my whole skin. I was in pain and the hot steam and water didn't help either.

Next thing I felt his arms around my legs and whoosh, I was lying on my back and he worked on my chest and down to my feet. Then I got washed down with warm water which felt great. He made me stand up and rubbed me down with a soft dry towel. He gave me another towel for my waist and I was led out a door into a room with four beds in it. He gestured for me to lay on one of them. Uli who just came in was asked to use the other one.

"We better be careful and watch our Backs," he said half joking.

At that moment Theo entered the room and seeing us on the beds looked like he was about to panic. He searched around for a weapon to hit the next guy entering the room if he so much looked as if he would make advances.

We were struck dumb when two guys entered each carrying a big plate laden with fresh orange juice and huge slices off watermelons.

What is this? we asked ourselves, as we sipped the orange juice and ate some watermelon. We were still not sure whether everything was above board. Twenty minutes later our friends opened the door and asked how we felt? We assured them we felt newly born and great. They smiled and asked us to get dressed because they wanted to take us for dinner. Because they knew we were leaving in the morning they wanted to celebrate our friendship.

How bloody wrong can one get! Here we thought we were surrounded by a group of 'poofters'. But it turned out our 'friends' became real friends and their Hospitality came from the bottom of their Heart!

Theo and myself with our new friend Hussein (next to me) and his teachers sharing interesting Turkish food.

We had a great evening the six of us. The Restaurant was in a better hotel and the food was delicious. I think this was the first time Theo was served with his 'Omlette Natuer' with many more to come in future.

Hussein told us his greatest wish was to live in Germany. His wish came true when he got a job in Köln as a teacher three years later. He visited our parents several times and still had the postcard we sent him I think from Karachi.

We had another good night's sleep and felt great in the morning. We packed our gear, cleaned the place a bit, before our friends arrived with some breakfast. With their help we carried everything down stairs to the front and packed our bikes. One more look at our road map and with directions from our friends we gave them a big hug and thanked them very much. After about 100 meters we turned around and saw them still waving with lots of other people next to them also waving. We waved back before we turned round the next corner on our way.

But before we left, we had one last mission to complete. We crossed a few streets and then turned back to the Bazaar. I still don't know why I brought along some of my Grandmother's *Inflation* money (Reichsmark) but it turned out to be a wise move. At the Bazaar Theo stayed with our bikes, whilst Uli and I entered the market. I can't remember whether I had a ten or twenty thousand Mark notes on me. They were worthless even before the change to the new Deutsch Mark, and weren't even worth the paper they were printed on now. It wasn't long before we were approached by a money changer.

"Deutsch Mark please. Deutsch Mark good exchange," he said.

We ignored this one and went further into the marketplace.

One elderly guy coming towards us with a bundle of notes in his hand wouldn't go away. In exasperation I showed him the Reichsmark notes and his eyes widened. He told us he would look after us well. Obviously he didn't know the difference between the old German money and the new DM. I looked at Uli and he smiled and nodded. We bargained a bit to make it look good, until finally he agreed to pay us the equivalent to about 300 DM for the worthless Reichsmark note. After counting the money into our hands he turned around quickly and disappeared into the crowd. I would have loved to have seen the expression on his face when he found we had conned him instead of the other way around.

Uli and I quickly made our way back to Theo. Jumping back on our bikes we took only a few seconds to get away from the Bazaar, and we were on our way, leaving Istanbul behind us.

Getting out of Istanbul was difficult because of traffic. We had to be careful avoiding cars, trucks, small carts being pulled by donkeys and people all over the roads. It was late afternoon by the time we had reached the outskirts. Although it was time to look for a place to stay for the night, there was no way to put up our tent with so many people still around.

We stopped at a small hotel where we were able to stay overnight. It wasn't much but the people were very friendly and couldn't do enough for us. Next morning after an early breakfast consisting of tea, bread and fruit, we headed towards Koerfez in the direction to Ankara. It was cold and overcast but no rain. With Uli in front Theo in the middle with me behind, we made good headway and covered a fair distance getting in to the countryside. Over laden trucks and bad driving was always a problem but funny enough we saw only minor accidents.

It had to happen; Uli punctured a tyre on a straight stretch of road.

We didn't mind because we could pause for a bite to eat and relax while he fixed his tyre.

Uli preparing to fix the first of many punctures.

We soon left behind the Sea of Marmara and headed east. All along the way through Turkey we had to conquer countless steep hills and high mountain routes. Some of the mountains were still covered with snow and it wasn't pleasant sleeping in a tent under those conditions.

I remember one night high up in a forest after putting up our tent and making a fire to prepare some food, we roped our bikes together (as we always did) and climbed into our sleeping bags.

It must have been after midnight when we were woken by noises outside. There were rattles on our bikes and we heard snuffling and heavy breathing around the tent.

"Did you hear that," Theo whispered in the dark.

"Do you think someone is trying to steal our bikes?" I asked.

" We should go out and have a look," Uli said.

Theo and I immediately decided Uli should be the one to have a look.

"Why the hell should I go outside and not one of you?"

"Because you are the oldest and it is your duty to do so," Theo said.

After a few swear words Uli finally opened the front zipper of the tent and looked outside. We stayed behind looking over his shoulders. The fire was still glowing red and beyond it all we we saw were shadows in the distance. There were a couple of glowing eyes under the darkness of a tree, but they disappeared so quickly we couldn't tell whether we saw them or only imagined it.

Theo cautiously stepped outside and threw some more wood on the hot ashes which started the fire going again. As soon as the flames lit up the area close to the tent we saw paw prints around our campsite.

"Just some dogs looking for food," Theo suggested.

We couldn't go back to sleep for the rest of the night and next morning we discovered paw prints everywhere.

"There must have been a whole pack of dogs," Uli said as he stared at the paw prints all around the tent.

We were told later by locals in the next town that there were packs of Wolves roaming the mountains; that it was very dangerous to camp out like we had been doing.

We made sure from then on whenever we put up our tent we would try not to camp high up. Whenever we came through a bigger town like Ismit, Adapazari, Bolu, Gerade, Yazikoey, Siphalier and Sincan, we always tried to find accommodation in a small hotel. Quite often we enjoyed the hospitality of some farmers where we were able to put up our tent next to their house.

The Big Adventure

A couple of days before Ankara, we passed a lone cyclist on the road who looked like a German.

He was! His name was Hans Killian and he lived near Mosbach on the Neckar only about 80 Km from Backnang. Hans told us he wanted to see a bit of the world and had jumped on his bike to see how far he could get. Well, we understood that all right. He had got as far as we had., and that was a hell of a distance from Germany.

After a long talk and a few smokes, we decided he could ride with us for a while. Hans wasn't a bad bloke and we were pleased to have him along for company. He had his own little tent and had no problem keeping pace with us.

When we reached Ankara we were spotted by a Newspaper man who took some Photographs of us and invited us to his office nearby. After some tea and the usual bread with fruit, he wrote down our story so far. He and his colleges where quite impressed with our achievements.

They were even more impressed when they found out we were cycling to Australia. They invited us to stay for a couple of days as their guests, which we gladly accepted and they put us up nearby at a nice clean hotel. After a warm shower and feeling great, we were invited for dinner at a small restaurant.

Our conversation was mainly in German. It was surprising how many spoke German or English. The article in the newspaper would appear in the paper in two days. They offered to show us around Ankara, which is the Capital, and of course we accepted. Ankara was not as cosmopolitan as Istanbul but it was full of old buildings and Mosques with lots of trees and parks.

The next day one of them walked us to the Australian Embassy to find out about our Visas. Once again it was without success. We were told that we would have to show them a certain amount of traveller cheques or a return ship passage to leave Australia before they could grant us an entry visa.

We didn't have anywhere near enough money and certainly didn't have a ship's ticket. That was really disappointing! But we were determined that it wouldn't stop us from continuing our journey.

Next morning we were presented with a couple of newspapers with our article in it. The picture looked great but the text was in Turkish.

We had in mind of reaching karagedik but got away late, because we had to bid farewell and thank people for their kind hospitality.

Bisikletle dünya turuna çıkan dört Alman genci dün matbaamıza gelerek bizleri ziyaret etmiştir. Bisikletli turistler Adana yoluyla Hindistan'a gideceklir.

We headed south and got as far as a town called Goelbasi where we found a small hotel. To our pleasant surprise the owner came towards us with the newspaper in his hands showing us the article which he read in the morning.

How about that, we were Famous!

He gave us two rooms (Uli with Hans, Theo and I) and then we were invited for dinner.

All the way through Turkey the same thing happened every time we ate in restaurants. We would walk straight into the kitchen and lift the lids off pot after pot. If we saw something we thought was edible we would then show the cook what we wanted. It was always hilarious for the waiters and patrons to watch us march in to the kitchen. Needless to say we always had smiling faces around us and everyone wanted to shake our hands. Most of the people were poor but they all worked and didn't look undernourished.

We had a good night's sleep and got away early. We rode through Karagedik, Kocayala, and camped just past Karahamzali. The weather was still cold but the further south we cycled the warmer it became. Continuing on we rode along the edge of a big lake (Lake Tuz) passing Sereflikochisar. Asipinar and Aksaray where we made camp outside the town near a small river.

We still had plenty of very hilly roads to travel but it was dry, so we pushed on as hard as we could.

It was almost an obsession; keep going…keep going… until exhaustion forced us to stop. Sometimes we copped south westerly winds and rain which was the downside of cycling. Being wet and cold with no way of warming up made us so miserable we couldn't help having doubts, and in those dark moments we would stare at each other and wonder; *What the Hell are we doing?*

After riding almost non-stop all day we were absolutely knackered. It was dark and cold and we couldn't find a suitable place to set up the tent. Finally, somewhere near Ulucista, we spotted a light inside what looked like a service station. It was locked but we knew someone was in there. We knocked hard on the front door and a guy partially opened it. He stared suspiciously at us.

He said something in a tone that seemed annoyed. We didn't understand but presumed was like: "What the Hell do you want at this time of the night?"

With hand gestures, a bit of miming, and speaking slowly in German we got across the message that we wanted to put our tent up beside his service station so we could sleep. We also pointed to our water bottles, upended them to show they were empty and mimed drinking.

He finally understood when he saw our bikes. He opened the door wide and gestered for us to come inside where he lived in one room next to a small kitchen. "No hotel" was the only thing we understood out of what he told us. He pointed towards a small room and indicated we could sleep there for the night.

In the room was one tiny table, two chairs, a small wardrobe and a double bunk bed of which the bottom one was his.

To this very day it was the worst night I ever had and the others felt the same. Nothing bad to say about the fellow, he was just a poor service station attendant who felt he had to help. We shared some food we still had and some smokes. Then came the hard part; all four of us had to climb into our sleeping bags and help each other up on to the top bunk. Sitting next to each other with our knees bent and feet hanging over the edge was shear torture. After half an hour our legs cramped and there was nowhere to move.

It was a very long night and we were happy when daylight started and we got down and could move our sore bones and stiff muscles. As soon as we used the toilet (the usual hole in the ground) and had some tea we gave the guy some money which he did not want to take but it made him smile from ear to ear then we took off.

We have never forgotten that night and often talked about it whenever we got together. I think that lovely man never forgot us either.

That day we made it to the outskirts of Adana even though we were pretty stuffed from the night before. We found a nice secluded place in what must have been an orange grove that was ideal to put up our tents. The air smelled of oranges and we got a sniff of sea air from the eastern Mediterranean again. Very nice after the dry dusty air of the desert inland. We couldn't see the sea because Adana was too far inland.

After a good night's sleep we woke up to the beautiful air and rode in to Adana. We stopped in the middle of town and leaned the bikes against the front of a small restaurant where we had breakfast. It didn't take long before we were surrounded by onlookers asking all kind of questions.

...having a break in the middle of Adana

This time it was relatively easy because we could show them the newspaper article which some of them could read and tell the others. Word spread fast and soon we had an invitation from the local sports club to stay over night and meet some of their Sportsmen (no women). This was again very welcome because we didn't have to look somewhere for a camping spot.

We liked Adana, lovely people great weather and near the Mediterranean with a good fishing fleet that used several rivers to access the Sea. The island of Cyprus was not far off the coast in the bay at the end of this part of the Mediterranean. We felt that Adana was more prosperous than many of the other towns we came through. People dressed better, the streets were clean and buildings being renovated.

The Sports Club where we were led to was only a few years old and had a football oval surrounded by an athletic track. Inside the club house there was a canteen next to a gymnasium full of sporting equipment. On the other side there was a hostel for some of the sports men from other towns who trained here.

Our bikes were pushed into the Hostel and leaned together in front of our beds which were next to each other. After a clean-up we were asked to join some of the men for lunch in the canteen. The food was excellent and we could pick what we wanted from several different pots being prepared by a couple of cooks. This was good living and we loved it. Later in the afternoon we walked over to the gym and were surprised how many young and elderly men were using the equipment. Someone asked us if we would like to do a bit of exercise on some of the machines.

We looked at each other. "Why not?" we thought. After all our bike riding we were very fit.

What a stupid mistake that was.

After an hour doing push ups, lifting weights and running around the oval, we were stuffed. We did exercises which we were not used to that had nothing to do with riding a bike. We certainly suffered for it next day! We slept like rocks but woke up with stiff muscles and ached all over. We could barely move as we crawled out of bed and stood beside our bikes.

"That will teach us for showing off to those guys at the gym," Uli said. We had to laugh at that. "Never again," Theo said, which was exactly what I was thinking.

After moving around, stretching and washing up we didn't feel too bad. We packed our gear and went down for breakfast after which we headed out onto the road again, riding slowly until the stiffness had disappeared. A few cyclists escorted us out of town along the road towards Iskenderun.

The road was reasonable but narrow and we had to ride carefully to dodge traffic. We passed through small villages where we were greeted firstly by barking dogs running after us and heaps of kids running beside trying to keep pace. We still had some smaller hills to climb but as soon as we got closer to the sea the land flattened out. We passed vineyards and fruit orchids with farmers selling their produce beside the road.

A couple of kilometres before a small town called Yeniyurt we found a secluded spot to camp. We felt great because the temperature was warmer and we only had to make a small fire to heat some tinned food. The reception on Theo's Radio was very good but we only got Turkish language and music, but we didn't mind. In the morning we could take our time because we only had 30 km to travel to get to Iskenderun.

We arrived there just after midday and rode straight in to the centre of town. We could definitely smell the sea air here. Iskenderun lies in the gulf of Alexandretta which is as far as the Mediterranean reaches.

We asked where we could find a Hotel and someone pointed across to the other side of the street; that was easy! The only thing was, it happened to be about the best one in town. We asked about the price of two rooms and it was okay except it was a lot for us. By that time our finances had lowered considerably and we had to be careful not to overspend. On the other hand we had to spend most of the Turkish money left because the next day we would be in Syria.

The Hotel was great and it was good to have a shower and a shave. Later, walking through town, we were surprised how busy it was with many cafes and different stalls everywhere.

In one of the shops we noticed a money changer who changed some of our German Marks for Syrian Pounds. Walking past a fruit stall we purchased a drink of orange juice, which was made from fresh oranges.

It was quite funny because the guy only had two glasses to drink out of. He had a small press were he inserted half an orange which he then pressed the juice in to a small container underneath. He then took the orange skin and wiped the inside of a glass, pressed another two oranges and filled the glass and that was it. When finished he took the empty one and repeated the process for the next person. The juice was fantastic and we often had it the same way as we travelled. With only about 50 Ks to reach the border we had time to get more provisions and fill our water bottles.

We bid Iskenderun and the Mediterranean good bye and headed south east towards Syria. Kavalcik was the last of Turkey's villages before the border and being afternoon we decided to put up camp and cross the next day.

When we arrived at the check point we got some bad news. Hannes was not allowed into Syria because he had problems with his passport.

How could this have happened?

We liked the idea of him to travelling with us. He had become a good friend and we felt he was a part of the team.

"Don't worry about it," he said. "I'll sort it out in Istambul and catch up to you later."

We gave him what was left of our Tutkish money, and each in turn hugged him and wished him all the best.

He never did catch up to, and years later we discovered Hanness had gone back to Backnang where he got a job with Uli's brother Alfred who had a building company. We visited hin 48 years later in Mosbach where he had married and created a huge plant nursery.

Sometimes when I look at how much we carried on our bikes, I wonder how we managed to pedal enough to even move them... Uli's bike is the one in the middle with the thin tyres.

Chapter Six

Syria here we come!

Uli of course stated *"So jetzt gemer ens Siirische nei"*, Friends now we are entering Syria!

We already missed Hannes but we had to move on because we felt we had to get as far away from Germany as possible. Our finances had started to shrink and we didn't know how to replenish them. We still believed that when we ran out of money the German Government would send us back like before. This was one of the reasons that compelled us to push on as far as we could. We also wanted to be able to tell everyone we had got further than before, much further. Three years earlier we had been under-age and they had to send us back. Now we were considered adults, so it was unlikely they would send us back.

But we weren't sure, so to be safe we kept going.

Leaving the Border it got warmer by the hour as we travelled inland.

The road was narrow but well maintained. It wasn't easy going because there were huge trucks laden with more than double the recommended weight, some with people sitting on top, continuously driving past us. Lots of American cars too, Fords, Buicks, Dodges, Cadillacs, Chevrolets, etc. forced us to stay in single file along the very edge of the pavement.

The wind blew from the north/east, not hard but enough to put a slight film of fine sand on the road. About 20 km from Aleppo just off the road we spotted a fruit and vegetable stall with a big truck parked next to it.

We stopped and couldn't believe our eye's, it was a *"KAELBLE"*, one of those trucks built in Backnang during the war. Later it was bought by a Syrian trucking company and it was still in reasonable condition.

We talked to the driver who had stopped for some fruit and drink and told him where we came from. He happened to be a partner of the company and had been to Backnang, but had purchased the truck in Stuttgart along with several others. I had a few pictures of the trucks Theo and I had been driving back home to show him. I don't know why I took them with me but they turned out to be very handy.

He asked what we were doing and where we were going and when we told him his eyes lit up. He insisted we put our bikes on the truck and come with him to the depot in Aleppo.

Easier said than done… It took a lot of lifting and shifting things to get our bikes safely roped on top. The driver's cabin was cramped with the three of us squeezed in with the driver. On top of that it was a hair raising trip. This driver must have thought he was *"Juan Manuel Fangio"*. He only knew one speed, full throttle. Not even going around curves did he ease off. All the other drivers did the same which no doubt explained the reason we saw many overturned cars and trucks along the roadside.

It was a relief when he had to slow down at the outskirts of Aleppo (Halab) which is Syria's largest city. There was no way he could drive fast through streets crowded with foot traffic, donkey drawn carts, bicycles, cars, busses and trucks of all sizes, mostly overloaded, or packed with people so tight some hung out of the doors.

It seemed a long time before we finally halted in a big yard full of trucks, delivery vans and cars. The driver begged us to follow him into a double storey office building next to a big mechanical workshop. We were introduced to several people even to a couple of women, surprise-surprise! In no time did we get hot tea and fruit with some fresh juices.

Then came the usual questions from where were we going and what we had been doing in Germany etc. They found it hard to comprehend that the three of us wanted to cycle to Australia with little finances. We didn't let on that we were just about on our last legs. Some of the men unloaded our bikes. When we were asked where we would stay overnight, we asked them if we could find a place to erect our tent not too far from the city. They deliberated for a while then asked us to have some more tea and to stay for a short while.

An hour went by when the driver and several others came through the door holding it open for smallish older man with long hair and beard.

They all bowed their head when he passed by them and we did the same when he walked straight towards us and shook our hands. We were introduced and told his name was Abdullah the head Mullah of a nearby

Mosque. Apparently they had called him over and told him about us in the hope that he might be able to help.

Abdullah is standing between Theo and Uli in the entrance to the Mosque. The other man on the right was the one who transalted from German for us.

Abdullah's Mosque.

And help he did!!!

Hundreds of times in later years we would remember Abdullah.

At his Mosque they had condominiums for Students studying the Koran. Abdullah asked us to follow him and we said goodbye to our hosts with big handshakes and waves.

We followed Abdullah along the footpath pushing our bikes behind him. Every one we passed bowed their head and we recognised very quickly how important he was. A few blocks down the road we saw this big Mosque which Abdullah steered us towards. There was a building next to it a couple of stories high where he led us.

We could hardly move because we were surrounded by people who wanted to see and touch us young sportsmen. We were led into a room with six bunks plus a desk and a sink with running cold water. We looked at each other as if to say "Why us? How could we be so lucky?"

We were left alone for a while to adjust ourselves to the new surroundings. With our bikes leaning against one wall we unpacked some of our luggage. It wasn't long before Abdullah returned and greeted us as if he had known us for years. He bade us to follow him and he led us over to the Mosque. After taking our shoes off we entered this great hall which was four or five hundred years old. we couldn't help marveling at the beautiful mosaics and architecture those tradesmen performed so long ago. The building was superb. We followed Abdullah past a big hall full of worshippers kneeling on mats and praying.

Through a side door we entered Abdullah's quarters. We couldn't believe our eyes when we walked into a huge near empty room. The floor was covered with handmade carpets, most likely many years old, some maybe hundreds of years old. There would have been two or three layers of them. On the floor the middle of all the rugs was a big square wooden board covered with many plates with different kinds of food. Abdullah introduced us to two, also robed men. One of them taught English and the other German and French.

We were invited to join them for dinner, which we accepted gladly because we had not eaten much during the day. We had to sit on the carpets next to the board because there were no chairs. (People all over the Orient and Asia sat on the floor). The food was great. Even Theo found something he liked. There was plenty of flat bread, pieces of chicken, lots of lamb and a big bowl of olives and steamed rice. One of them passed us some kind of cloth to wipe our hands because there were no knives, forks or spoons. We had to tear a piece off the bread and filled it with some of the goodies. "Olives" what a surprise! The last time Theo and I ate olives was in Sicily with those fishermen and we nearly chocked! Abdullah had a big bowl of them. Uli wacked in to them and told us to try some. I had a taste and found them quite tasty but Theo would have no bar of it. We couldn't believe our luck. In the morning we were in Turkey waving goodbye to Hannes and now this magnificent feast!

We couldn't get over how friendly our acceptance by these generous people was, even though we were Christians. Abdullah understood and spoke some German. He also spoke fluent French and English and with the others who translated we had a great evening, talking about our future plans.

The English teacher suggested we should go to a photo shop to have our picture taken and get about 200 postcards made to sell. That would have been a great idea if we had the money to pay for it. But the seed was sown, we had to sell something. Before we went back to our room, Abdullah offered to show us around Aleppo the next day to meet some good people.

As soon as we got back Uli and I had the same thought. Theo's Radio!

When we mentioned it to him that he should sell it, he told us to get stuffed!

"Why should I always sell my Radio? I did it in Italy and now you want me to sell this one also".

"If we could get enough for it, we might be able to finance the postcards?"

It took some time for him to realise the potential of getting maybe as far as Damascus or even Baghdad.

"I'll think about it," he said grudgingly.

We knew then he had agreed, but didn't want to admit it straight away. We had the room for ourselves and slept well.

As promised the night before, Abdullah knocked on the door next morning ready to take us out to see the town. He was accompanied by two young men carrying a pot of tea, some bread and fruit for our breakfast. We showed him Theo's Radio which we had decided to sell and told him that we would like to get those postcards done.

He came back an hour later and we followed him down the street where everyone we passed waved and bowed. He led us straight in to a Bazaar and passing some shops stopped in front of one selling electrical goods. He called for the owner and showed him the radio. In less than two minutes we had more money than what Theo had paid for it. Such was the power of Abdullah, no bargaining. He told them to give us a good price and that is what they did.

After leaving the Bazaar we crossed the road and walked to a photography shop and Abdullah told the owner what we had in mind. I forgot how much he wanted to supply 200 Postcards, but we would still have some money left over. We were asked to come in the afternoon to have our picture taken. It wasn't easy, first we had to go back and pack our bikes, cleaned-up a bit before pushing them down the street to the shop.

One thing we did not anticipate was that we had to carry our gear two stories up to a studio. It took the three of us quite some time and we were exhausted by the time it was done.

The photographer took several different shots and ten minutes later we carried our gear back down again. That's all it took, ten minutes. He told us the postcards would be ready the next morning.

Arriving back at the Mosque Abdullah waited with some lunch. He told us with a big grin on his face, that we were invited by a very rich man and his family to visit their house in the evening. Abdullah, the German teacher and the three of us were picked up in a big chauffer driven car and taken several Kilometres out of town to an enormous house surrounded

The Big Adventure

by a wall. Guards stood by the gate.

Inside, we drove past a small lake with a row of date-palm trees lining the road. We looked at one another, "Christ, where are we?"

We were greeted by a uniformed man and led in to a room totally carpeted with little furniture except several cushions in a big ring. A door opened and a well-dressed tall man entered, holding a young boy with one hand and a younger girl with the other. He greeted Abdullah like an old friend. He also knew the teacher. We were introduced and welcomed with big handshakes.

There was no two ways about it, this guy was important. The way he looked into your eyes and the way he spoke, you just knew whatever he commanded was done instantly. We were asked to sit on the cushions and were served the usual glass of tea by a couple of servants. Abdullah had told him already about our great adventure and he was very eager to hear from each of us, again where from and where to.

He had been to Germany several times before, spoke reasonable German and what he missed the teacher translated. He (I call him He because I have forgotten his name) told us that he bought a Mercedes in Stuttgart and he was pleased to hear that we came from there. He wanted to know about our schooling, our apprenticeship and what gave us the idea to start such a venture. He and the others listened while we told them about ourselves and our journey so far. He was all ears and could hardly believe our plan to get to the Olympics in Melbourne.

We must have talked for close on two hours, when He, Abdullah and the teacher excused themselves and walked to the other side of the room. They spread a small carpet on the floor, knelt down and started praying without taking any notice of us. This was new to us. We had seen worshipers and people praying before in Mosques but never in a private house.

Uli motioned us to be quite and we just sat there in awe and waited for them to finish. It didn't take that long before they got up, rolled the little carpets together and bid us to enter another room.

A great surprise awaited us there! In the middle of this big room was a table laden with some of the most exotic foods we had ever seen, a table set for at least a dozen or more persons to gorge themselves.

Much to our surprise we saw a bottle of Arak and Uli and I had some of it. There were so many things on the table, different dips, flat bread, lamb, beef, chicken pieces, a bowl of olives, steamed vegetables and even pieces of fish. Lots of stuff we had never seen nor eaten before.

We couldn't get over the variety of the fruit. What an evening! It turned out to be. The hospitality of those wonderful people will stay with us for the rest of our lives.

We must have thanked our host many times over and told him we would keep in touch. We sent postcards from several countries and one from Melbourne but sadly never got a reply.

Next morning Abdullah told us that he had word our postcards were ready to be picked up. We had a quick breakfast and started walking to the photographer's shop. Just before the photo shop on the other side of the street we passed a small cafe and tea house with tables on the footpath, full of people enjoying a break. Uli stopped and pointed to one of the tables where someone was waving to us, beckoning for us to come over.

We did and two European guys stood up as we approached. They asking us if we were Germans. We told them we were and they answered in clear German, telling us they were from Hannover. One of them might have been fifty or so while younger one looked a bit older than Uli. The older one had had his left arm shot and amputated during the war. He wore a prosthesis from the elbow down with the hand covered in a black glove. His name was Albert. I can't remember the younger one's name. After we introduced ourselves they invited us to have some tea and smoke a Hooka (Water pipe). We had seen them in Turkey but never had the chance to use one.

Albert had been an Officer during the war and a true SS man. He told us he did some work for the Syrian Government, working for the Army as an advisor. The younger guy was his nephew who was visiting him for a few weeks. They couldn't believe that we are here on bikes and what we planned on doing.

Smoking the Water pipe was great fun and we had some good laughs around the table, while a lot of people watched us. We had two pipes, both with three long hoses and each had a mouth piece on the end. The pipes consisted of a water bowl holding a container on top filled with glowing tobacco. You had to draw hard to get the smoke through the water and into the lungs. It didn't taste bad, better than I had expected, and was probably much healthier than cigarettes. At several other tables people smoked the same. There were water pipes everywhere.

We told both fellows we had to go to pick up some pictures and we would join them again shortly.

As soon as we entered the shop, the teacher greeted us and said he was sent by Abdullah to translate and to make sure we had no problems. We received four small boxes containing 50 cards each.

Looking at the postcards we were more than pleased, what a great job.

We asked the teacher if he could write something in Arabic about us and our Adventure.

"I would be happy to," he said, and got a pen and paper to write down a few points about us. "In Syria, and in fact in most Arab speaking countries, being a High school Student is highly esteemed."

We asked him to write that Uli was studying to become a designer in the Metal Industry and Sport. Theo Studied Business Management in the Auto Industry and I studied inventing tools for different applications. My sport was of course cycling and my ambition was to become a professional Cyclist.

"Don't forget to put down that we are on our way to the Olympics, to be held in Melbourne, Australia, and that we would like to help finance our journey through these cards. Thank you for your help."

He wrote that and we thanked him, adding that we would see him at the Mosque later. We paid the shop owner the money for the postcards and thanked him for the great work.

Across the road, Albert and nephew were waiting for us with a few plates of tasty dips and flat bread. To our pleasant surprise Uli and I each given a bottle of French beer. I handed Albert and nephew a postcard, the first ones we gave away. The idea of having a postcard of ourselves seemed to impress them.

They ordered another pipe, but before it came I stood up and said, "I'll be back in a minute."

I grabbed a couple of postcards and walked across the street. We had noticed a big car dealer with several American cars in the showroom and I went straight for it.

I didn't exactly know what I was doing; I think the beer had gone slightly to my head. I walked up a couple of steps and opened the show room door, to be greeted by a well-dressed gentleman with "how do you do?"

I told him I was German and showed him the written card. He read it and indicated for me to follow him. He led me in to an Office where another well dressed gentleman was sitting behind a desk. A small boy played on the floor. I assumed this was the boss and his kid. The salesman handed him the postcard which he turned over and read. I certainly didn't expect what came next: He stood up and shook my hand, gave the card to his son and opened a draw on his desk. He took out a note, handed it over and wished me good luck.

I walked out the door as quick as I could and went back to the others.

"Guess what just happened?"

When they said nothing but simply looked up at me I told them what I did. "the man in the office gave the card with the writing on the back to a kid."

"Are you nuts? What did you do that for?"

I reached in to my pocket, pulled out the note and said "I got this for it."

I looked at it properly as I showed them.

"Holy shit!" I saw it was a Syrian 5 Pound note; the equivalent of 50 Deutsch Marks. I had just stuffed it in my pocket without really looking at it.

5 Pounds for one card, we could not believe our luck.

Albert said, "The cards are great, but you should consider getting a big note book to let people you meet write in it with some photos together."

What a brilliant idea!

Advice taken, we said goodbye and arranged to meet here again next morning. On our way back to the Mosque we passed through the Bazaar and spotted a book store. In no time we found what we were looking for, a very thick A4 size notebook. We also purchased a small tube of glue. With our pictures and the blank book we walked back to be greeted by Abdullah and the others. We told them about meeting a couple of Germans and my episode with the card; they loved it.

Our new book was ideal, it was big enough but still easy to carry packed away. On the first page we glued one of our post cards and one of Aleppo, with Germany to Melbourne written underneath, and below that each of us had a passport photo glued to the bottom of the page. It looked good already!

We showed it to Abdullah and asked him, "Is it possible to meet the Lord Mayor of Aleppo and get him to write in to our book?"

"I will see."

Next Morning we had an appointment at the Town Hall. Unfortunately the *Big Man* was away but the Deputy Mayor wrote in our book and got a letter typed to recommend us to the Mayor in Homs.

We had the teacher with us to translate and through him we thanked the Deputy Mayor and gave him one of our cards.

On the way back we also thanked the teacher and told him we would see him later at the Mosque. It was late morning and we wanted to meet up with Albert and nephew. We walked to the cafe but they were not there. After ordering another water pipe we waited for a couple of hours-but they didn't turn up. We never saw them again!

Back at the Mosque we asked Abdullah if we could stay one more day because we wanted to see if we could sell more postcards. He said we could stay as long as we wanted.

Next morning we covered some distance searching for more car yards which we visited with similar success. We didn't get another 5 Pound note though, but still finished up with over 12 Pounds from 3 car yards and one other office we called in.

We had to pinch ourselves about our good fortune. Maybe *ALLAH* was on good terms with us?

At the Mosque later we told Abdullah that we planned to leave the next morning. He told us he was sad to see us leave but understood.

It was time to write back home and tell them that we were okay and were planning to leave Aleppo for Homs. We also posted one of our Postcards home and wondered what they would think about it. After another great meal with Abdulla and friends, we also felt sad to be leaving.

We had our bikes packed and ready to hit the road early in the morning. At breakfast the teacher wrote on the back of another card what he had previously done before on the one I had given away. We handed a couple of cards to Abdullah so he would remember us. We knew we wouldn't see these beautiful people again, but promised that we would somehow keep in touch to tell them how we were.

We did send a couple of postcards along the way but never got a reply. Regardless, we will never forget them.

It took several hours to get to the outskirts of Aleppo where we waved goodbye to a beautiful and hospitable City.

We were heading south towards Homs, the third largest City in Syria.

Homs was half way from Aleppo to Damascus, and although the main highway going south to the capital was wider than other roads we had travelled on, the traffic was still as confused and chaotic as ever. It must have taken us at least two hours to do the forty kilometres to Idlip, a small village where we stopped for lunch.

All along the road were countless small farms with date palms, fruit trees and flocks of sheep. Just past Ariah, another village, we found a place off the road to put up our tent.

Immediately Theo started complaining about not having his radio.

"But look what it got us," Uli and I reminded him.

We waved the valuable Syrian pound notes in his face, and he shut up about the radio. In fact he never mentioned it again.

A couple of days later we reached Hims in the afternoon. This was an old city full of Mosques and historic buildings. Every small town and village we passed had its own Mosque. Riding into the centre of town we found the Town Hall and right next to it was a hotel. I stayed with the bikes smiling at the onlookers that always surrounded us whereever we stopped while Theo and Uli went inside to ask about prices.

They came back with a couple of guys in hotel uniforms to help with our luggage and the bikes. They had shown our postcard with the writing on the back to the reception and got a big cut on the bill and an invite for dinner at the restaurant. Another unexpected surprise!

We had a room for three, with a bath, but the toilet was still a hole in the floor. After settling in we decided to have a stroll through town. We walked past the market, admiring this lovely place with its lovely public gardens full of palm trees.

When we got back, we cleaned-up and were ready for dinner. Being early was good because we got a table with not many onlookers and didn't have to wait long before we were served. By then we had no more problems with eating by hand and quite enjoyed it. Again we got the usual small plates with dips, marinated cheese and this time some small sticks with pieces of lamb, onions, beef, capsicum and chicken grilled over a fire. By the time we finished the dining room was packed and we had lots of questions to answer because it wasn't every day three German cyclists were guests at the hotel. We finished with a water pipe before bidding every one good night.

What a great feeling to have a bath! After bathing and shaving we slept like logs. In the morning we asked the manager if he would allow us to stay a bit longer because we had some business to do at the Town Hall… "No problem, you are our guests."

With our book under my arm and some cards in our pockets we entered the Town Hall. A uniformed guard sat behind a desk, looking bewildered when he saw us walking towards him. We showed him our card and the envelope we got from Aleppo. He made a phone call and motioned us to follow him upstairs. Three stories up he knocked on a door and let us through.

Two guys stood up and led us through another door where we were greeted by a well-dressed man in a western style suit and two others in Arabic clothes. The man in the suit turned out to be the Lord Mayor; the others were business people.

We handed the Mayor the envelope with one of our cards and handed one card each to the others. Within two minutes we had a glass of tea in our hands. With some German and English we managed to spend an hour answering their questions. We asked the Mayor to write a few words in our book. He did this with enthusiasm and put his official stamp underneath and signed it.

He and the others wished us all the best and a wonderful safe journey through Syria. On leaving his office he handed Uli a piece of paper which he was to show someone one story below. We thanked them and mentioned that we loved Syria and of course Hims.

One story down we walked in to a room which reminded us of a bank with several counters. Looking at the note we noticed the number 3 and 25 written in Arabic. (By then we had learned about money and numbers.) We couldn't believe our eyes and walked straight up to one of the Tellers. He glanced at the note then at us and spoke a few words with the one next to him and handed us 25 pounds which was more than we expected.

But Uli frowned, looked at the teller, held his hand out and asked for the note back. He pointed to the number three on it and showed this to the teller. The teller just stared at him as if he didn't understand. Uli mimicked going back upstairs to the Mayor's office. The teller blushed and quickly pulled out his cash drawer again and handed us another 50 pounds.

75 Pounds richer! We nearly jumped for joy.

But we restrained ourselves and quietly left the building.

We couldn't believe our good fortune as we walked across the street where we noticed a few modern office buildings. Walking in to the best looking one of them and showing the man on the front door our card, he led us in to a very plush office.

What can I say, it happened again. The guy behind his desk dressed in Arabic robes with thick golden chains on his arm greeted us with a welcome smile. After reading our card he showed it to another man dressed the same and asked us a few questions. He then pulled out a 10 Pound note and so did the other. With big smiles on our faces and lots of thankyous we left.

95 Pounds in one morning was an absolute fortune for us.

We walked back to the Hotel, asked the manager to write in our book and paid our small bill. Before we left we got an invite for lunch and some fruit on the way.

That was HOMS!

We were so happy the 50 kilometres we did that afternoon were as easy as...

Who in Allah's name would have thought that we were able make that much money? What a great idea the book and the postcards were, and we had to thank Abdullah and the one armed man Albert for that.

It did take a lot of front to meet and get to know important people, and by this time we had lost any timidity we had before. We had to be bold in order to survive.

We still had a long way to go...

We didn't need to light a fire because the further south we went the warmer it got. We erected our tent under some palm trees and slept well. We hit the road early because we wanted to get to Damascus later in the afternoon and had to ride through a small town 10 kilometres before, called Duma. Damascus was buzzing like a bees nest and the streets were choc-o-bloc with traffic and donkey drawn trailers, and push bikes.

There were a lot of heavily laden Camels on the road, which didn't help the congestion.

"Here I am," I was thinking, "a few years back I couldn't get enough adventure books to read, especially the ones written by Karl May (one of Germany's most successful Authors) who wrote 6 books about Istanbul, Aleppo, Damascus and Baghdad, and now, less than a year later, I am seeing these places myself."

There were an incredible amount of passenger busses fully laden with people and animals. How they got through the bikes and carts and camels and pedestrians was simply amazing.

As in Aleppo and Homs, Damascus was very old and full of history.

Towards the city centre we passed several small hotels and stopped in front of one near to the middle of town. This time Uli stayed with the bikes whilst Theo and I walked to the reception. Again we showed them our card and were asked what they could do for us. There was no problem getting a three bed room with space enough for our bikes.

The cost was very low considering it was so close to the Centre of town. After settling in, we went for a walk to explore the city. We passed innumerable shops and small markets, and the streets were lined with big date palms. Further along we came to a huge bus depot with hundreds of busses coming and going. People were yelling and gesturing to people to catch busses to Aleppo, Homs and even to Beirut. We picked a nice cafe, ordered our usual Water pipe and some dips and we enjoyed the life around us.

A couple of tables close by we noticed three young men, about our age looking at us and we could see them debating about who we were. They wore some kind of a uniform suggesting that they were students from a higher School or University. We had just finished our meal and drawing on the pipe, when all three of them walked over and asked if they could sit with us. They introduced themselves and we found out they studied at the University. They were wondering who we were and where we were from.

We told them our names and where we came from and handed them a postcard for them to read. They were fluent in English and French with one of them quite good in German. They invited us for tea and another water pipe which we gladly accepted. They were impressed and couldn't hear enough about our adventures. They were astonished that young guys the same age as them, with little finances to their name, would start a journey like this. They liked it when we told them of our plans to study after we got back to Germany again.

We told them we'd had a hard day and wanted to go back to the hotel, but they didn't want to hear about it. By that time they had ordered more food and drinks, which we welcomed. It started to get dark and we thanked them for saying hello to us but it was time to get back. They even walked back with us and asked if we would mind meeting their teacher the next morning.

"We don't mind at all, but not too early." Uli suggested

At the reception we were greeted by the owner of the hotel, who was waiting to meet us and wished us a good stay in his hotel. They told us if we had any clothes to be washed, they had a laundry and would do them during the night. That was just what we needed.

Another bath again! It felt good to get all that grit and dust off our bodies. After that we enjoyed a good night's sleep. Just after breakfast next morning we had just written a couple of postcards and a letter to send home, when we were told people were waiting for us at the reception. Sure enough, there were two of the guys from yesterday with another elderly man in Arabic clothes. We shook hands and the elderly man was introduced as their teacher.

They asked us if we could come with them to visit their College and meet some of the students. We told them to give us 10 minutes to get our gear in order. Our washing was laid out on our beds and it didn't take long to pack and get ready. At the reception we asked if we could leave our bikes in the room for a few hours. "No problem," the man at reception said. "The room will be locked." We took our book, passports, some cards and our money. Out front they waited for us next to two parked American cars driven by chauffeurs.

It was only a short drive, maybe five blocks and down a couple of side streets. We arrived at a huge College (or University) building surrounded by a big wall with manned gates in front. The whole establishment smelled of money. There were manicured lawns, flowering bushes and palm trees everywhere. The building was modern and relatively new with white marble staircases and statues. We were led in to a big room,

The Big Adventure

like an Auditorium and could not believe what we saw. There must have been over 100 Students sitting around in a big circle with several empty chairs in front of them. They had been briefed about us and apparently were looking forward to asking us lots of questions. Beside each chair was a small table full of fresh fruit and juices.

This was new to us and we had some difficulties adjusting to speaking in front of so many students and their teachers. We each were introduced as German Students who were cycling to Australia and had made it as far as Damascus. We felt a bit awkward in the beginning, but after a while we felt good answering all their questions. Whatever one of us couldn't answer the other two would jump in. I found it hilarious sitting in front of all these people lecturing them when only a few short years ago I was in school myself and came home after exams with unsatisfactory results. After a couple of hours we were asked to join them for lunch in their canteen, which we accepted.

One of the Principals wrote in our book and someone handed Theo an envelope which he told to open back at our hotel.

We had to shake many hands and all of them wished us the best on our future travels. They wanted to drive us back but we declined because we wanted to walk and see the sights of Damascus.

There were people everywhere, lots of stalls on the footpath and shop keepers running towards us trying to sell their wares. We walked past a big Hospital with several advertisements glued to the walls inviting people to donate blood. The writing was in various languages telling people they would get paid for donating blood.

We looked at each other.

"Should we give it a go?" Theo asked.

"Why not?" Uli and I answered almost simultaneously.

We entered and walked up to a big counter and told someone we saw the ads on the street and we would like to sell some of our blood.

They told us we would get 25 Pounds each if our blood was suitable, plus a free meal.

We were led into a very clean room and someone shoved a needle into our arm to take a sample to be tested. After about half an hour the results came back positive for Uli and Theo but they didn't need mine, they had plenty of it. I was told that I would miss out on a meal and had to wait for two hours out on the street.

"No way," Uli told them, "If he won't get any of the meal we all will leave."

They agreed quickly and Uli and Theo were taken in to a room where more men were on drips.

I can't remember how long I waited and how much blood they took but eventually they came out not looking the worse for wear. Another 50 Pounds, what a pity they didn't take mine.

By that time it was late in the afternoon. We'd had plenty to eat and were looking forward to a water pipe and some coffee at our hotel. We asked at the reception if we could stay for two more nights and they told us it would be a pleasure for them to have us.

We couldn't wait. We had to open the envelope from the University.

Theo took it ever so slowly out of his side pocket and looked at it from side to side with a grin on his face taking his time.

"If you take any longer I'll kick you in the arse," Uli told him impatiently, with me pretending to hold him back.

We just could not believe what we saw. We were expecting a written thank you letter, but not the three 50 pound notes inside the letter thanking us on behalf of the College for the great Interview and talk with the students and teachers. We were rich!

We had to find the Australian Embassy the next day and decided to call by the University to thank them once more.

We asked the hotel manager if he could find the address for the Embassy and to tell the taxi driver to take us there, which he was delighted to do.

We drove past the University and decided to drop in on the way back. A couple of blocks further on the cabbie stopped in front of a multi-story building and pointed to an office. We couldn't miss it; there were different Embassies on most of the floors.

The Australian was on the third floor, easy to find.

We didn't get our visa, again being asked to show sufficient money for our passage to leave Australia, which was very disappointing. Without a visa we wouldn't be allowed to enter the country. One of the officials told us the best way would be if we could show at any Embassy about 500 American Dollars each and there should be no problem.

We didn't take a taxi back because we had plenty of time and we wanted to call in at the University. But first we walked over to a Bazaar and looked for a money changer which there were plenty of. We changed 100 Syrian Pounds for US Dollars (I can't remember how many we got) and we bought a leather pouch with a strap to hang around the neck so the pouch could sit on the chest underneath the clothes. I was selected as treasurer. We also brought some Iraqi money and found out the Iraqi Dinar was worth more than the Syrian Pound. On the way back we called into four more big offices to tell our story and collected another 25 Pounds.

At the University we were told there were exams and the teachers were busy so we left a thank you note for them. Just before our hotel we stopped at the previous cafe and had a water pipe and some food.

Our spirits were high; we had a lot to look forward to!

We had found a way to prop up our finances. Even if we never made it to Australia, we would be further away from home than anyone else our age from our town had ever achieved. A lot of our mates had ridden bikes to various parts of Europe. Konne had even gone as far as Portugal, but no one had ever come as far as we had, and we weren't even half way to where we wanted to go. I felt real proud of that.

Back at the hotel we packed our bikes to have an early start in the morning and after having one more bath we went to bed. We knew that from Damascus to Baghdad was a long ride, over six hundred kilometres and most of it was desert to ride through.

We left early enough but it still took us a couple of hours to ride back the 10 km back to Duma where we had to take the road to the border with Iraq. We stopped for some juice and stocked up with water, dried bread, tinned fish and fruit. We were told there wouldn't be anywhere to get food before the border.

After another 40 km we put up camp not far from the road and had a reasonably good sleep, but not as good as the hotel. We were now in the Syrian Desert and the ground was hard with no grass or leaves to lie on. It was still another 100 km to the border and we wanted to get there next day. We rode dead east on a still slightly sand covered road.

Next to the road was a big oil pipeline which came through from Baghdad to Damascus. It was late afternoon and we still had to ride another 20 km to the border but it was hard going and we stopped for the night by the road.

It didn't take long to the border the next morning. Actually there were three borders in one Syria, Trans-Jordan and Iraq. Talk about busy; there were busses, trucks, cars and even a caravan with camels. There were a few mud houses with offices and some shops, also a couple of service stations for fuel and repairs.

Like before, all eyes were on us as we pushed our bikes towards a building with a big sign Pass Control standing next to it. A man in uniform with a gun on his side waved us inside. We pointed to our bikes that one of us had to watch over them, no problem he said, he would watch them himself. This time we were greeted by a women dressed in a black robe with her hair covered by a scarf. We handed her our passports and showed her our card which she read and passed it to another female officer next to her. In no time everyone in the room knew who we were and where we were going. Our passports were stamped and a transit visa through Iraq was stamped and signed.

We were told that over the next 300 km we would be unable to get food or water and to make sure we had enough to last until we got close to Baghdad. They also told us we could not get lost because the pipeline was always next to the road and every 80 km there was a sentry post with security guards.

All we had to do was 'follow the pipeline'.

Dry and dusty Duma... a small square on the edge of the town.

The Big Adventure

Chapter Seven

We waved goodbye to Syria and its wonderful people, as we rode into the desert. We will never forget you!

We still had half a day left and covered a fair distance before we made camp. After leaving the border we passed a Camel Caravan only about 500 meters from the road and sometime later we saw another one further in the distance. We certainly knew we were far from home.

Had we gone only 10 K's further the night before we could have camped near the first guard house and had some company. We stopped and showed one of the guards our card and with a big smile were offered tea and fruit. They told us we should try and make it to the next Post.

That seemed a good idea so we started immediately. There was a slight breeze blowing all the time against us which made it hard to ride and the traffic passing blew fine sand in to our faces.

Getting closer to the next post we saw a couple off soldiers waving, they were actually waiting for us. The guys from the previous Post had rung them and told them who we were. They indicated to us that we could erect our tent right under the pipeline, which we did because the ground was nice and even. Unfortunately neither of them could speak much English, but after the tent was up they served us a water pipe and some tea. We got on like a house on fire.

Same thing happened next day. We passed another three Caravans, two in the distance, but one of them rested just close to the road. We stopped, put our bikes together and walked over. There were about 20 Camels with fully packed sacks one on each side. There were men, women and children all sitting in the sand having some kind of meal. One of the guys kept waving to us to come and join them. They looked different to the people we met so far. Their faces were hard as if chiselled out of stone and their eyes seemed to look right into one's soul. They pointed to our bikes looking bewildered. Theo handed them our card and one of them read it out loud in a beautiful kind of voice. Suddenly there were smiles and handshakes all round. We were handed some water melon, dried bread and some kind of milk which Theo had no bar of. He stayed with his water melon. I felt as if I was living inside my Adventure books from Karl May's *'Durch die Wueste'*.

Unfortunately we couldn't stay too long because we still had to travel a fair distance to reach the next guard house. They were a great bunch of people. They kept waving until we were out of sight.

By late afternoon we reached the next Post and again they knew we were coming. These guards had to patrol and guard the pipeline half way either side of the post for a week at the time before being relieved. Once again we slept under the pipeline in relative comfort. This one was our last guard house before we hit civilization again.

Al Ramadi was about 70 K's of travelling and we arrived mid-afternoon, to be greeted by a bunch of barking dogs. It was a big village built adjacent to the road with some shops, a service station a couple of cafes and a police station. We stopped in front of the police station and left our bikes leaning against the mud wall. By that time a crowd had gathered around us. I suppose they were wondering why someone was stupid enough to cycle through the dessert. It didn't take long before two policemen came through a door to see what the commotion was all about.

One of them stepped in front of us and asked for passports which we handed to him. We saw straight away that he could not decipher the visas but he could look at the photos. To show how important he was he spoke to us in a loud voice in Arabic which we couldn't understand. At the same time he kept glancing at the crowd to see if they were taking notice of him.

We handed him our card on which the teacher in Aleppo had written about us in Arabic, and his face brightened when he discovered what we were up to. He passed the card to the other policeman and informed the crowd all about us. They were all happy when they found out we were German students and some of them even shook our hands and touched us. We indicated to the police that we would like to put our bikes in their office to keep safe while we had a bite to eat next door. Through our gestures and by moving one bike towards the front door they finally understood what we wanted and were happy to oblige. By that time we were pretty hungry and the little restaurant looked after us with plates of grilled pieces of lamb, rice and fruit. While we ate everyone in the street had eyes on us and followed our every move.

We had to hurry because it was getting dark and we had to find a place to camp. Back at the Police Station we asked were we could find a suitable place to erect our tent to stay the night.

Before they could answer I noticed an open door with two open cells, empty except for two bunks in each. I pointed them out to Uli and Theo who had the same thought as me. We asked the two policemen through gesturing and miming if we could sleep in there. Once they realized what we were asking they laughed raucously. ,I suppose they never had anyone willingly want to stay in their prison!

Well, this was a first one for us too, but we had a place for the night which we agreed was as safe as you could get. It wasn't exactly the Hilton Hotel, but beggars don't choose. We each had a bunk and slept soundly even though the mattresses were smelly and dirty.

Next morning we invited the two policemen for a small breakfast before they changed shift. We handed them one of our postcards, thanked them very much and jumped on our bikes and off we went.

Al Fallujah another small town on the Euphrates River only about 50 K's away would be our next stop. The scenery changed rapidly the closer we came to the river. Little farms with date palms surrounding small mud houses and the desert turning into fertile soil. Most of those farms had small water channels dug through their land, irrigating their crops. We passed some stalls again next to the road with lovely fruit and dried dates which we found to be delicious. We stopped at quite a few off them because it was always a good excuse for a pause and a cigarette.

Standing on the shoreline of the mighty Euphrates was like a dream to me. We walked with our bikes slowly across the big bridge leading in to Al Fallujah, only stopping for Uli to take some pictures. We never imagined there could be so many palm trees, they were everywhere. Apparently Iraq was one of the biggest exporters of dates in the world. Like Al Ramadi, the streets were choked with people and traffic and we had to be careful not to have an accident. This place was different to the last one; there was no sand and the people seemed to be more prosperous. It just shows what a river can do!

We had to walk with our bikes to be safe, but it wasn't far to the town centre. There were shops and cafes on both sides of the street and all seemed to be doing great business. We spotted a bigger cafe with several vacant tables. We leaned our bikes against the wall and pulled the tables and chairs next to them. This was done with every eye in the place watching what we were doing, but by this time we were used to it.

Three people approached. One of them with a few words of English asked what we wanted and where we came from.

Again we handed him our card to read and watched the transformation when they all read it. They took the card inside and within a minute came back accompanied by an elderly gentleman dressed in fine Arabic clothes. He spoke English and welcomed us with a big smile. (Between the three of us we had learned a few words every day and when we didn't know a word we searched in our small dictionary and found what we wanted.) It didn't take long to be served with food and drink. By that time every spare seat was taken, with us being the focal point. The elderly gentleman joined us for a water pipe after we had finished eating and he wanted to know about our travels. Every time we answered a question he translated to some of the other people around, who nodded, oohed and ahhed appreciatively. We told them we would like to be with them longer but we wanted to be in Baghdad some time the next day. They wished us a safe journey and some of them wanted to shake our hands. Once again we didn't have to pay anything, compliments of the manager.

With big smiles all round we departed. We had to walk a fair distance before it was safe to ride again. By that time it was late in the afternoon and we only covered another 10K's, not as much as we had hoped, but I was getting dark and so we looked for a spot to camp surrounded by date palms. There would be no rush in the morning and we could take our time to cover the last 40 or so kilometres into Baghdad.

The road was still busy but easy to ride on. Lots of stalls lined the road on both sides, but the closer we got to Baghdad the busier they became and the traffic on foot and on wheels got heavier making our riding more difficult.

A few kilometres before Baghdad we were passed by five cyclists on racing bikes dressed in cycling gear. They shot past us as if we were standing still. They must have wondered what we were doing, because 100 meters or so in front they stopped and waited for us by the roadside.

We stopped and the elderly one asked where we came from, when we told him from Germany his face lit up and he spoke to us in reasonable German and told us that he had studied for some time in Tuebingen.

What a surprise! We were told they belonged to the Adhamiyah Sporting Club and were all members of the cycling section. They had just about finished their training run with another 10 K's to go when they saw us. After telling them that we had no plans yet to stay anywhere in Baghdad we were asked to follow them to their club where we could have some food. Naturally we accepted. It wasn't long before we crossed the second biggest river in Iraq, the Tigris.

Baghdad was another magical City!
Here I was thinking about Ali Baba and his seven thieves and looking around for a Magic Carpet flying over our heads. What was happening to me?

The cyclist's took us along side roads with not much traffic, too narrow for big trucks or busses so it was easy going. We passed a lot of old buildings and beautiful Mosques, we even spotted a Church. Before long we came to a better looking suburb with nicer houses and lovely gardens. We also noticed big office blocks and several car dealers, worth visiting.

A few minutes later we stopped in front of a big sporting complex. We rode through a huge iron gate and stopped in front of some buildings adjacent to a large sporting ground for all kinds of sports with a soccer and cricket pitch in the middle. We were led inside whilst some of the guys pushed our bikes next to us past a big Gym and entered a food hall. We were served drinks and some food with probably 20 sportsmen around us.

Uli, Fred and Theo with members of the Adhamiyah sports club.

I was wondering what they thought of us, the way we looked. One must remember we hadn't had a bath since Damascus and couldn't do much washing and cleaning since then. By now we were pretty smelly and rough looking. The guy who spoke German (he wasn't the only one, there were a few more) asked us if we would like to stay with them for a few days next door where they had rooms for athletes from out of town.

We told them we would take their offer and thanked them very much.

We told them that we would like to stay a few days so we could go to the Australian Embassy, and as well to see some of their city.

We also told them we would like to visit King Faisal.

They burst out laughing at this while shaking heads and saying "*Nein, nein* ... No no."

There were plenty of different rooms, just like a good hotel. Someone led us in to a big room with four beds and plenty of space for the bikes. A few doors away was a huge shower room with toilets opposite. Everything was spotless and we were looking forward to a shower and a shave.

Adhamiyah is one of the cities of greater Baghdad. It is one of the affluent parts where all the Politicians and Industrialists live. There are beautiful homes, lovely gardens and well maintained streets lined with the ubiquitous date palms.

We slept well and early in the morning joined some of the guys for a few exercises and were hungry for breakfast which we enjoyed. Somebody told us he knew where the Australian Embassy was and offered to take us there.

We were taken by car and driven to another part of Baghdad, passing other Embassies and many office buildings.

Again it was the old story about how much money we had and they wouldn't be able to give us a visa, but wished us good luck. By this time we were no longer disappointed but were expecting exactly that response.

The car had waited for us and the two fellows asked if we would like to see a bit of Baghdad on the way back.

"*Aber naturlich,*" (Of course) we said, "If you have time."

"Do you know where King Faisal lives?" Theo asked.

"Everyone knows where The King lives. We'll take you there so you can see it."

The King's Palace was only about five kilometres from Adhamiyah near the Tigris. After passing more Mosques, monuments, and shops with people everywhere, we came to a huge roundabout. There must have been five or six busy streets leading in to it. We headed straight for a

The Palace of King Faisal.

Watching a motorcade going to the Palace.

large parking area from where we could see the Palace. It was surrounded by a high stone wall secured with big iron gates with sentries on each side.

By the time we got back to the club we knew it would take us not more than 30 minutes by bike to get to the Palace.

After lunch we were asked if it was possible for us to visit a school next door to tell some of the students about our adventures. Naturally we said we would be delighted.

There weren't just some as we were told, but close to 100, and not just students; there were also teachers and some of the athletes from the club. We could see that it was a well to do school. (It turned out to be a private school.) There were a lot of students including Africans and Europeans. whose parents quite likely were doing business in Iraq. It was surprising for us to see different religions learning in one school together.

We gave a talk similar to what we did in Damascus and after a couple of hours we got handshakes and pats on our shoulders. Later when we were by ourselves we decided to jump on our bikes and ride over to the Palace to familiarise ourselves with the route. Again we passed many nice office buildings and pointed to some which we should visit next day. On the way back we stopped at a small cafe for a water pipe and some coffee. We didn't want them in the club to know that we smoked.

The next morning as soon as we had finished breakfast we took our book and some cards, jumped on our bikes and headed for the Palace. On the way we stopped near some offices to see if we could make some money. Because of the many people one of us had to stay with the bikes at all times. Theo and Uli walked into a building with several occupants whilst I kept watch. They seemed to take a long time. I smoked two ciga-

A street in Baghdad.

rettes and was beginning to think something was wrong, when they came out of the building with big smiles on their faces.

No wonder it took so long, they had visited four different offices and sold three cards, and two Directors wrote in our book. I had a hard time believing that they managed to collect 60 Dinars. It was a small fortune!

Two hundred meters further on we stopped again in front of a big building. because they did so well I told them they should try again while I stayed with the bikes.

They made 50 Dinars this time but got a letter to visit another company just past the Palace.

We finally crossed the big roundabout and stopped before the big Iron Gate and walked towards the Soldiers. We showed them our card and with a short gesture with his rifle one of them told us to stay where

Fritz standing in front of the monument to King Faisal.

we were. The other guard took our card and stepped inside the guard house and we could see he was on the phone. It wasn't long before we saw a big car driving from the palace towards us. Three men got out. They certainly looked official in their beautifully pressed uniforms with stars on their shoulders. After saluting one of the guards handed the first one our card and after reading it he passed it to the others. They had a small conversation between themselves, then one of them turned towards us and asked us in reasonable German, "What do you want?"

"We would like to meet King Faisal because we love Iraq and want to meet the great King."

After giving us an odd look he turned and spoke again to the other two for a few minutes. Turning back to us he said, "The King is very busy and it would be near impossible to see him." He paused a moment then added, "Why don't you wait here in the guardhouse and have a cup of tea? I will go back and show the King's uncle Abdullah, your card."

(Abdullah was also the Kings Advisor).

Nearly one hour went by and we started to become impatient, and fidgety because we wanted to go and make more *Wages*.

"Maybe this wasn't such a good idea," Theo mumbled, but before we could answer we saw the big car coming towards us again.

"Gentleman," the officer said, "The King is very busy, but after reading your card he became interested in your adventure and would like to meet with you at 10 am in the morning."

JUST LIKE THAT!

We couldn't believe it.

We thanked them very much, shook hands while smiling from ear to ear. Then they got back in their vehicle and left us standing there.

Just past the Palace we stopped at a small restaurant and had a coffee and some fruit. We had to get our thoughts together before we visited the next office. We only had to ride one block past the roundabout where the monument to King Faisal on horseback stood with pride before we reached the building to show the letter they had been given earlier.

Because Uli and Theo received it we decided they should go up again. What a success they made this time! Apparently they had to go to the top floor and when they entered the guy who wrote the letter earlier greeted them with a big smile on his face. When they told him that we just came from the Palace and were going to meet The King in the morning, they were totally surprised. The reason I had to wait so long before they got back was because the boss had sent a couple of personnel to some of the floors underneath and next thing his office was full of people who wanted to hear our story. I waited close to two hours before they came down followed by a few people who also wanted to meet me. After a lot of well wishes we finally got back on our bikes again.

When they told me how much they got I was dumfounded.
130 Dinars!
This was unbelievable. Australia was beginning to become a reality.

By the time we got back some of the students were waiting for us to join them for dinner. We had made 240 Dinars plus we had arranged a meeting with The King; no one could imagine how we felt! At dinner we told them who we were going to meet the next morning. They looked at us as if we were ghosts. They didn't believe us. None of them had ever met The King. No one they knew had ever met The King. But a couple of them had seen him at a Parade. We were still so excited that night it took a long time to fall asleep.

At 9 o clock in the morning we jumped on our bikes and headed for the Palace. Half an hour later we were told by the guards at the front gate to ride along the entrance road to the Palace.

What a great place, the Palace was surrounded by beautiful gardens, huge palms and exotic fruit trees with flowers everywhere. We stopped between two guard houses in front of this great building. One officer asked if he could inspect our passports which we obliged. He gestured to a couple of guards to look after our bikes and asked us to follow him. A uniformed guard opened a big iron door and we followed along a magnificent corridor with so many paintings on the walls we couldn't count them, and ornate vases on top of gold filigree handcrafted tables. A big door was opened and we were led into a room where several officers and a couple of European style dressed men were standing around a big table.

The King was standing in front of a huge desk with his Uncle next to him. As we entered he walked towards us and shook our hands. He was only two years older than me.

The King and his uncle were dressed in tailored suits, also the other two. One man was dressed in Arabic clothes looking like a Sheik, which we were told he was. On the wall behind the King's desk was a huge painting of Gutzy the first King of Iraq and next to it the young King Faisal.

The room was half filled with smoke. Everyone had a cigarette in their hand except the Sheik who had a water pipe in front of him. After introducing ourselves the King's Uncle offered us a cigarette, which we gladly accepted. Theo showed them our book and The King signed the postcard of us which we had glued onto the first page. We answered lots of questions, but a few times the German speaking officer had to translate. Someone took a couple of photos but it hardly registered, the excitement was too great.

We must have been with them for close to a half an hour when The King walked back to his desk and came back with three tins of Players cigarettes. He handed one to each of us, shook our hand once more and wished us all the best for our journey. We handed him two of our cards thanked them all, and after some bowing, were led out towards our bikes.

We were just about to mount our bikes when one of the two plain clothed guys from the King's office walked towards us. We wondered what he wanted and to our surprise he invited us for dinner that same evening.

No problem we said happily. He would pick us up at seven in front of the club house. When we stopped at the first Guard house, there was a small entourage of cyclists waiting to ride with us back to the club.

Apparently they had followed us because they could not believe that we were actually going to meet their King. They had to see it with their own eyes. There were questions all round but we told them we would answer them back at the club.

We felt like Kings ourselves when we got back and walked in to the canteen. There would have been at least 50 or more people including some women standing around waiting for us. We told them that the King offered us a cigarette and showed them the tin of Players which contained 50 cigarettes, with the King's emblem on every one. They also wanted to see the King's signature in our book. It was then that it occurred to me that Uli never took one photo.

"How come you never took any photos?" I asked him. "Normally you never stop taking photos."

He looked sheepish. "With all the commotion I forgot I had the camera with me."

We mentioned to them that an official had invited us for dinner at 7pm. One of the cyclists asked if it was the guy who was talking to us in front of the Palace and we said yes. He told us the man was a Minister in Parliament and was well known.

We wanted to hit the road again next morning but decided to pack a parcel each to send back home. The weather was warmer and we didn't

The Big Adventure

need to carry all the heavy clothes with us. When we told the people that we would need three cardboard boxes sure enough we had them a couple of hours later and were able to sort out what we didn't need. By 6pm the parcels were packed and we could get ready for dinner.

At exactly 7pm a big black Mercedes stopped in front of the club driven by a uniformed chauffer. The Minister stepped out greeted us and the club members who kept us company. We jumped in the back seat feeling like Royalty ourselves.

It must have been one of the better restaurants in town because everyone, women and men, were dressed immaculately, except us!

Needless to say, all eyes were on us. Not just because of the way we were dressed, people wondered who the Minister introduced as his guests. We were led to a big round table where eight people including two ladies were already seated. When we approached they all stood up to greet the Minister and us. Each of us had to sit between other guests and the Minister told them all our names and showed them our card. How about that! the same card which was shown to the King in the morning.

We were asked if we wanted something to drink, perhaps some beer. Uli and I got the beer and Theo asked for fruit juice. I must say we had a great feast, lots of lamb, rice, different vegetables and fruit. Half way through I had to urinate and was shown to the toilet. There were three cubicles, each with that certain hole on the floor and a bucket of water next to it. As I walked in to one of them I couldn't believe my eyes. There was a 5 Dinar note lying on the wet floor. I almost stepped on it.

I picked it up, shoved it in the bucket of water, rinsed it, folded it and put it in my pocket. What a find! I couldn't wait to tell Uli and Theo about my luck but didn't want to tell them in front of everyone.

We never saw anyone pay the bill as we said goodbye but it didn't matter to us anyhow. Theo handed out postcards to the people, who wished us all the best. The chauffer was waiting for us and drove us back to the club. We gave our names and address in Germany to the Minister and asked him if it was possible to find out about the photos which were taken at the palace with The King and us. Maybe someone would be kind enough to send them to our family. He said he would see what he could do. After big handshakes and thanks for a beautiful never to be forgotten evening he pulled out an envelope and handed it to Theo.

He waved to us as the car drove off and we watched until they got out of sight. There were still a handful of people at the club, but we went straight to our room. "You'll never guess what I found in the toilet." I told them.

They looked at me stupidly for a moment then Uli said, "No, what would one find in piss – a block of chocolate?"

Their eyes nearly popped out when I pulled the wet, still smelly 5 Dinar note out of my pocket. I gave it another rinse and put it on a piece of paper to dry out.

But our eyes really popped out after Theo opened the envelope from the Minister. Inside we found 6 brand new 10 Dinar banknotes.

No note, just the money!

We must have jumped 5 meters high with happiness. We had made 300 Dinars including my smelly one in Baghdad so far. Bloody fantastic!

Unfortunately our parents never received those pictures, which was a pity. Three years later in Melbourne I heard to my great sorrow that King Faisal and the whole Royal Family had been assassinated.

To this very day I remember the short time we had with them.

Someone drove us to the main post office next morning so we could send our parcels home. While there we purchased postcards of Baghdad and stamps for Germany. Back at the club we must have written close to 20 postcards between us to our family and friends. Theo also wrote one to our newspaper editor and told him about our meeting with the King. We told everyone if they wanted to write back to us to send it via Poste Restante Teheran in Persia. Teheran would be our next big city.

This time we rode our bikes back to the post office to hand in our cards and to visit a few more offices on the way back to see if we could make a bit more money. We only made another 10 Dinars at one place and headed over to one of the Bazaars to look for a money changer.

There were several of them and we found quickly the one with the best $US Rates. I can't remember the exact amount we got but we changed 250 Dinars for US$ and 10 Dinars for Iranian Rials. I was carrying all the money on my chest. That still left us with about 40 Dinars to use along the way.

Because we were leaving in the morning a big gathering of students wanted to join us for dinner at the canteen to wish us goodbye, but before that we packed our bikes to be ready to go in the morning.

It was arranged that 5 of the cyclist would accompany us to show us the way to Baqubah.

We loved it here, and would gladly have stayed longer, but we had to move on. In the morning after breakfast we thanked everyone a thousand times for their great hospitality and hoped that one day we could meet again. We felt sad as we sat on our bikes ready to leave Adhamiyah with its wonderful people.

After a final wave we hit the road.

With some cyclists in front and a couple behind it was relatively easy to get out of town. A few kilometres out we said goodbye to the fellows who took off along another road to do some training.

And once again, we were on our own.

With less luggage to carry, pedalling was much easier and we certainly covered a good distance before we had lunch and a couple of smokes. (We hadn't smoked any of the kings cigarettes yet.) We were travelling north and the country side was green, full of rice and vegetable fields with date palms everywhere. Lots of stalls along the road made travelling easier. We followed the Tigris north and reached Baqubah mid-afternoon.

Baqubah was an open, rich looking small city with shops and market places along clean streets with nice restaurants on either side. Passing a couple of Mosques we headed straight for the Town Hall surrounded by palms, manicured gardens and lawns. We created quite a stir when we pulled up in front of the steps leading to a big open door into that grand building.

Uli minded the bikes whilst Theo and I equipped with our book and a couple of cards entered. Again we were asked to show our passports to a pair of friendly uniformed guards, before they read our card. One of the guards motioned us to follow him and stopped in front of a door with big Arabic letters stencilled on a copper plaque. The guard knocked on the door, motioned us to wait and with our card in hand entered.

It was a beautiful old building and I had to wonder again how those Architects and Builders many hundreds of years ago with limited tools could create such wonders. There were people coming and going and we got many curious smiles. They must have been wondering what two dusty and not the best dressed Europeans were doing in here. After a short time the door opened and the guard begged us to enter. It was a small room with only one desk and two young guys standing in front greeting us with handshakes. Both were dressed in suits and they spoke fluent English. We were led through another door into a large room where we were greeted by an elderly gentleman dressed in traditional robes. He was holding our card. He must have read it because he told one of the two guys who brought us in to arrange tea for us and gestured for us to take a seat. There were pictures hanging all over the wall of *'our King'* and the Royal Family.

It turned out he was the Mayor of Baqubah and was pleasantly surprised when he found out that we'd had an Audience with King Faisal. He ordered the two guys to send a couple of guards outside to mind our bikes and bring Uli back to his office. After tea was served we must have answered 100 questions about our adventure, our families and Germany.

Once several cups of tea had been consumed we were asked if we had a place to stay for the night. We told him that we were looking for a place to put up our tent. Well, he wouldn't have a bar of it, and spoke to the two guys in Arabic and waved one of them out of the office. Theo had shown him our book where he willingly wrote some sentences and put his official stamp to it.

The other guy turned up again, spoke to the Mayor who then told us to follow that guy. The Mayor got up, shook our hands and said we would see him that night. We thanked him and followed the guy out on to the street. By that time it was late afternoon and we pushed our bikes to follow the guy a couple of blocks down the road. We stopped outside a small three story hotel where people were waiting. They greeted us as if we had been known to them for a long time.

We explained to the Guy, "We have no money to stay in a Hotel. All we want is a place to erect our tent."

"You are guests of Baqubah" he told us. "Do not worry about any cost. He also told us the Mayor would pick us up for dinner at his club after we settled in.

We were shown into a nice room at ground floor with a lock up room next to it for our bikes. We hardly had time to clean up enough to be presentable when someone knocked on the door and told us there was a car waiting to pick us up.

With our driver and his beautiful pontiac car.

The Big Adventure

We grabbed a few cards our book, passports, Uli's camera, one tin of The King's cigarettes and headed for the street. A big American Limousine was parked outside with a smiling, uniformed chauffeur standing next to it. He opened the doors for us told us his name and started the car leaving lots of onlookers behind. It was only a short drive outside Baqubah when we stopped in front of a big iron gate which was opened for us by a guard. On the end of the small road we stopped next to lots of parked cars in front of a well-kept three story English style building. It was surrounded by palm trees adjacent to a small lake.

At the entrance we were greeted by two well-dressed gentleman who asked us to follow them. They lead us through an entrance hall into a big room like a restaurant but with lots of partitions to separate one, two or more tables. We walked past some partitions with whole families having dinner and the women dressed in European clothes and water pipes standing on most tables. Our guides stopped next to a big table, occupied by eight men, two women and a young beautiful, maybe 18 year old young lady. Three of the men were dressed in Arabic robes the others in tailored suits. When they spotted us they stood up and we were greeted by the Mayor, who by now was dressed in a suit, introduced us to his wife who was standing next to him. He then turned to the others who greeted us with big smiles and gestured us to take a seat. The Mayor had our card in front of him, so we assumed he had informed them about us. They all spoke fluent English and one of the Arabic dressed men even spoke good German. It turned out they were all business people with a couple of them in local Government. Later we found out one of them was the chief of police.

The first thing we were served was a glass of Arak (distilled from Anise). Theo declined and had fruit juice. We could see how these people were impressed with us meeting their King and we had to answer lots of questions about how it happened, because not one of them had ever shook hands with Him.

Theo opened the tin of Players and handed each person except the young lady one of the cigarettes. When they saw the King's emblem on them they looked at us as if we had given each of them a big diamond. We were told they would smoke them at home but we knew better, they probably kept it as a souvenir to show others. I wish we still had some today.

The food was served and we were starving. It was similar to the dishes we had with the Minister in Baghdad and to our surprise they all knew him when we told them about that invitation. The gentleman who spoke German asked us if we had ever been hunting.

"Not much chance of that for us in Germany." Uli told him.

"Would you like to go on a hunt? We can arrange for that tomorrow. You would be very welcome."

Both Theo and Uli nodded enthusiastically. "That would be fantastic."

One of the others wanted to show us his factory because he found out that Uli was a sheet metal Specialist and I was a Toolmaker.

"We would be delighted." I said.

We had a terrific evening especially because that young beauty kept smiling at us nonstop. We finished off smoking some water pipes and it was organised that someone would pick us up in the morning.

We thanked them for a wonderful evening , especially the Mayor and his wife for their great hospitality. The same chauffeur took us back to the hotel. We were stuffed! It had been a hard day for us after riding from Baghdad to here and then meeting up with these beautiful people.

I couldn't go to sleep straight away, I had to digest what was happening to us and why? We left Backnang about eight weeks ago not knowing what lay ahead of us. In that time we met University Principals and held talks in front of students. We met and stayed with a high Moslem priest in his Mosque and had an audience with a King.

So far we had covered about two thousand kilometres and tomorrow we are invited to go hunting. We were learning fast how to meet people, rich and poor. We also learnt fast how to sell ourselves.

Before I fell asleep I was thinking, *How long had it been since we knocked off those sausages in the beer tent back home?* It only seemed a few moments ago. It was hard to believe now that we were on our way to Persia.

Uli woke us early next morning. We needed to clean ourselves and have breakfast before going on this hunt. No sooner were we finished when there was a knock on the door. Uli opened it to be greeted by the same chauffeur from the night before. We grabbed our stuff and Theo even pocketed a tin of *Players*, thinking they might be useful like the night before. This time there was no limousine but an open Jeep or Land Rover. After travelling for about 30 minutes on a small road we turned off on to a non-paved but good track. We followed a narrow but fairly fast running channel until we arrived in the middle of a tiny village.of not more than about 20 houses all made of mud bricks, each surrounded by mud walls.

In Baqubah with the Mayor.

With the Baqubah Chief of Police (centre) and members of the hunting party.

The German speaking gent from last night welcomed us and introduced us to a lot of people who wanted to shake hands with us. The chief of police was there and one of the other members of parliament from last night.

We followed a few of the men through a clay path with big walls on each side to a clearing under the palms. There were several tables and lots of chairs all carved of wood. A few men and women attended to a big fire grilling a sheep. On a couple of tables we noticed some bottles of arak which Uli and I accepted when offered, even though it was still early in the morning. A short distance away we saw some beautiful horses and sheep grazing in a big Paddock surrounded by mud walls.

Relaxing and eating before the hunt...

After getting to know some of the people we were asked to follow some of them back to the village to take part in the hunt. We only saw our own car when we arrived but now there were 7 or 8 four wheel drives standing in a row. They were occupied by a driver and another guy holding some guns or a couple of well-groomed dogs. This was excitement in the first degree. We each were asked to hop on to a different vehicle. After a quick check the chief of police raised his hand and we were on our way.

The Big Adventure

...along the clay path with high mud brick walls on either side.

We had been told that the village and all the land around for miles belonged to the German speaking gent and his family. We soon found out how wealthy he was. Following the channel we drove by hundreds of date palms, olive trees and citrus trees. After a while we turned away from the channel and headed into knee high dry grassland which seemed to reach as far as the big mountains in the distance. A short distance travelling through the grass the vehicles stopped and we all got out.

I was handed a gun, which I didn't know how to handle. I had never held a gun in my life before, nor did Uli or Theo. I was told it was a shotgun and shown how to release the safety before shooting. Well here I am standing up to my knees in dry grass rifle in hand shooting at what? We were all motioned to move quietly forward, the excitement really got to me by then. I kept looking around me maybe I could defend myself against an approaching Lion or some other wild and dangerous animal. I didn't have to wait long to get some action.

The Chief gave a sign and the dogs were let loose. They stood there with shotguns pointed to the sky. I was just thinking, my god I hope they don't want to shoot down a plane when the commotion started.

All of a sudden a flock of big birds were flying towards us, scared into flight by the dogs. Everyone was shooting and yelling The dogs were barking and there were dead birds falling from the sky. I lifted my gun, pulled the trigger but nothing happened. I had forgotten to release the safety.

I would have been easy prey if there was a Lion attacking me.

It was all over in a couple of minutes except for the yelling and laughter with the dogs collecting the dead birds. Uli reckoned he shot one and Theo nearly got a small cloud except it was too far away.

We counted over 20 birds, (Uli told us they were Pheasants) and they were carried back to the vehicles by some of the men.

We had to walk a fair distance and the same thing happened again.

Theo and Uli looking for and waiting for something to shoot

The Big Adventure

This time I had the safety off and at the first sign of birds coming I took a shot. When I fired the recoil of the shotgun hit my right shoulder and nearly threw me off balance. It bloody well hurt and I didn't fire another shot. We had one more shooting session and finished up with close to 70 birds.

Well what can I say? This was my only time I ever pulled the trigger on a shotgun. We were gone for about 3 hours but when we got back to the clearing the sheep was ready to be served. It was already on a big table surrounded by pots full of steaming rice and heaps of flat, freshly baked bread. Someone handed us a wet cloth to clean our hands and help ourselves with the food. There were no knives or forks; one had to eat with the right hand because the left one was unclean.

We soon got used to it and got stuck into the food which was absolutely delicious. In Aleppo we had our first invitation where we ate with our hands. But this time we were in the open, standing around a whole grilled sheep with chairs to sit on if needed. Uli and I were offered some English beer which was welcomed, Theo had some tea. What a great day to be a part off. I think the whole village was present enjoying themselves. Everyone wanted to know us, read our card and our book. We had to tell them about Germany, The War and about the rebuilding.

They all wanted to know how we met their King. Theo opened the tin of players and handed all the rest of them to the men who treated them with deep respect. Not one of them lit one. In the meantime we noticed people dunking the birds into hot water to pluck the feathers and cleaning the innards, ready to be grilled later. Water pipes were lit and enjoyed.

Someone asked if we had ever ridden a horse? Uli said yes but Theo and I never had. Asked if we would like to ride Uli said it would be nice. Some of the fellows walked over to the paddock and came back with three beautiful horses and motioned us to jump up on them. We thought they were making fun of us because there were no saddles or reigns. All the horses had was a rope around their neck to guide them.

"How the hell are we going to ride horses without saddles?" I asked Uli.

"No problem," he said, "Watch this." He was handed a rope, put his arm around the horses neck, jumped up threw his right leg over the horse's back and sat up. "How easy was that."

Theo was next but nearly fell backwards and had to be helped by a couple of guys. I didn't even try to jump up and the two fellows helped me get on top. Of course everyone was watching. Uli must have made a wrong move because his horse started to take off with mine and Theo's immediately running behind. I was hanging on for dear life, not knowing what to do with my horse running straight towards a loam hut. I nearly crapped my pants. Just before the hut the horse turned right to follow the others and I flew off directly towards that hut. Lucky for me it wasn't a solid brick wall otherwise my journey would have come to an end at that moment.

I hit the wall side on and hit the dust sliding to the ground. I must have seen a thousand stars and for a few seconds I didn't know where I was. There were people all around me trying to help me to my feet yelling and gesturing. I felt along my body to see if there were any broken bones but everything was okay except for a few scrapes on my left arm and a couple of ribs were aching.

Thanks to ALLAH who must have had his eye on me.

Further along Uli and Theo were halted by a couple of riders who were following us. They jumped off their horses and came running towards me with shock on their faces. I waved to them and someone told them I was ok. Well so much for sitting on a horse. I never got on a horse again after that.

It was about then when we noticed two guys being greeted by the Chief. One of them we knew from the night before who owned the factory for us to visit, the other one we did not know. We were greeted like old friends and were told by the factory owner he felt sorry he couldn't take part in the hunt. The other man was a close relative to the Mayor and was asked to let us know we were invited tomorrow once more for dinner at the club. Yep, what a day!

Sometime later the pheasants were grilled and the feast started again.

After another good meal and some more Arak I didn't feel much pain any more. It was night time when we were taken back to the hotel after shaking hands with everyone and getting patted on our shoulders, with well-wishes from all. The factory owner told us somebody would pick us up mid-morning and the German speaking host told us he would be at the club tomorrow.

Finally we were by ourselves again, talking about our experiences of the day. It took me a while to go to sleep thinking about falling off the horse. It could have been disastrous with me lying in a hospital. Just the thought of it made me shiver. I woke up the next morning with Uli and Theo already dressed sipping tea. They thought to let me sleep in to get over my injuries. I told them I was better, and ready for another day.

The Big Adventure

At 11am the same chauffeur picked us up again and asked me how I felt after falling off the horse and was happy when I told him I was okay. These people were very concerned about my well-being. Not far from town we came to a large factory again surrounded by palms with a few trucks being laden with different types of tin barrels. We were led in to an office by our driver and greeted by the owner. He also was pleased that I was not badly injured. He introduced us to some of his employees and ordered the obligatory glass of tea.

The office was well appointed with photographs of the products they produced hanging on walls. After the tea we followed him along a short corridor into a big factory full of different machines. It was very noisy. The machines were ancient, still driven with leather belts. There were milling machines, lathes, small and big presses, stand-up drilling machines and many others. There were lots of workers who seemed to know what they were doing. Everybody looked up when the Boss walked past entertaining three young Europeans. No doubt they wondered who we were.

Many different containers, drums of all sizes and canisters were being produced. They made big drums for the oil industry (Iraq has lots oil) and smaller drums for the various foods that were exported such as olives, almonds and dates. We were astonished that those old machines still performed well. After an hour of touring the premises we sat back in his office and he asked what we thought. We told him that we were very pleased with his products and his machines, but Uli and I worked on more modern machines. We also told him if in the future he could invest in new automated machines his output would increase many times. He was very impressed with our comments and wanted to know about our apprenticeship, our studies and life in Germany.

He wanted to know if we had girlfriends and if they were German, and we told him we had.

"German women are the best," he said, and asked if we knew any, or had some addresses he could write to. He also told us if we could find him a German wife he would give us 200 date palms, (a small fortune at the time).

"I may have a picture of one," I told him. I could see Theo and Uli looking at me and wondering who I was talking about. What pictures?

"I'll bring it to the club later tonight."

He offered us a good paying job in his factory if we wanted to stay in Baqubah. We told him we would consider it after the Olympic Games.

After a while he led us into another room and to our amazement we were treated to a small but beautiful banquet laid out on a big table. After the lunch he thanked us and was looking forward catching up with us in the evening.

Our driver dropped us back at the hotel and told us he would be there for us in the evening.

I was waiting for it! As soon as we entered our room I was told off.

"You stupid idiot, how could you tell the owner you would show him a picture of a German woman? Are you pulling it out of your arse?"

I smiled, opened my little briefcase and pulled out a few photos which I had brought along. They were pictures of my family and relatives. A couple of them were of my mother in America before she was married and she looked absolutely stunning. I handed them one and said, "that's my sister," laughing out loud.

They looked at me, bewildered for a moment, but then I could see they slowly apprehended what I had in mind.

"All we have to do tonite is give him this picture and write my '*sister's*' name and address on the back, what do you think?"

Uli said, "well you aren't as stupid as you look but you still should be in jail!"

Theo said, "what a great idea, this will work."

We spent the rest of the afternoon relaxing and writing postcards to send home which the hotel Manager offered to post for us. When we arrived at the club the same people were there again with big smiles on their faces they greeted us like heads of states. Uli and I were offered our usual Arak and then the Mayor wanted to know about yesterday's hunt and my fall off the horse.

He was impressed and apologised that he could not have been there to join us. The factory owner pulled me aside, asked, Do you have the picture of the German women," and when I handed it to him his jaw dropped and his eyes nearly popped out when he looked at this beautiful blond, blue eyed women.

"This is my older sister," I told him trying to keep a straight face. "You should write a letter to her in English because she knows that language very well."

He nodded his head, "yes, of course I will," and handed the picture to all of his friends and they each congratulated me and told me that I was very fortunate.

I felt a bit guilty about the whole affair, but then I thought he wouldn't get in touch with mum anyhow.

How wrong I was. He did write a letter to her the following day. Of course I didn't find this out until much later when Mum wrote and told me.

We had another great evening and were told by all that they would be sorry to see us leave in the morning. We thanked them with all our hearts and told them we would never forget Baqubah. We mentioned to them that we would like to reach the Persian border by the next evening and were told by the Chief we should stay in Khanaqin and cross the border the following day.

Back at the hotel we still had enough time to have a shower and pack most of our luggage for an early start in the morning. Had it been up to me I would have stayed a few more days with all the attention we received.

It didn't take long to pack our bikes next morning and with help from the Manager and staff we were ready in no time. Before leaving, the Manager handed Uli an official looking letter which he had been asked to give to us on leaving. Uli asked him where it came from and was told our driver passed it on to him when he dropped us off last night. He told us we were not to open it until we get close to the Border. Theo handed him one of our cards and a couple of the King's cigarettes. With people waving behind us we jumped on our bikes and headed out of town.

Leaving Baqubah was hard to digest; none of us spoke much. The road was good but busy and we had to be careful not to have an accident. It took close to three hours and it was midday before we arrived at Al Miqdadiyah, a village only about 40 km from Baqubah. It had a small market place and a couple of shops. We stopped at one of the two coffee shops and ordered some bread, dips and a water pipe. Having coffee and sucking on the pipe we felt much better and decided to open the envelope even though we still had 60 km to the border. Uli opened it inside his jacket because there were onlookers all around us. He pulled out a letter which was written in English.

It just said, *dear friends, thank you for sharing your adventures with us and we hope that you will reach Melbourne safely, your Iraqi friends.*

Theo and I looked at the note whilst Uli with a huge smile told us he just counted 10 brand new 10 dinar notes but couldn't show us because too many eyes were watching.

We were rich, and did not mind paying for the hotel bill, not that it was very much anyway. Before leaving, Uli and Theo walked over to the small market to buy cigarettes, tinned food, dried bread and fruit.

After a couple of hours of riding we soon realised we could not make it to Khanaqin with at least another 60 km to go. I told them that I needed to take a break. My ribs and the side chafed in the fall off the horse were giving me hell. "Maybe we should look for a camp site and rest."

10 km past the village we found a secluded spot about 200 Meters from the roadsideto put up our tent. We hadn't slept in our tent since before Baghdad and found it difficult sleeping on the ground again after the luxury of sleeping in beds. I found it particularly hard because my ribs and the chafing on my side were hurting a lot.

Nevertheless we had an early start next morning but after an hour Uli had another puncture. his bike had thinner wheels than ours and small stones did more damage to his than to our wheels. Theo and I had a good rest while Uli repaired his puncture.

We arrived in Khanaqin, the last big village before the border by midafternoon. After kicking aside the usual dogs, and followed by some children we stopped in front of the police station. Two uniformed police men opened the door before we even leaned our bikes on the wall. We handed them our passports and our card.

The Big Adventure

Arriving at Khanaqin.

After scrutinising us for a few minutes and looking at our bikes in astonishment, one of them asked us to step inside. They said something to the crowd which instantly dispersed, except for two men watching our bikes. They handed back our passports and asked the usual questions. After inquiring about a hotel we were told there was only one which was a short walk along the road. We thanked them and pushed our bikes in the direction they indicated towards a bigger building we could see with a hotel sign in front.

It was old but clean, and the servants were all dressed in some kind of uniform. We were lucky to get a big enough room for us and the bikes. They told us that being so close to the border the hotel was often booked out. Next to the hotel was a small coffee house where we got some dinner and our pipe, as usual surrounded by onlookers.

Because of the traffic it took us close to an hour next morning to get to the border. We felt sad to be leaving Iraq but had to push on. Showing our passports at the Iraqi check point we were told we couldn't cross because we had overstayed our visa by three days.

"Okay," we said, taking our passports, not wanting to understaand.

We proceeded towards the Persian border but instantly four uniformed soldiers with raised machine guns stopped us.

We couldn't believe it.

We were marched back inside and we pointed to the Persian visa in our passports to the officers. They told us that was okay but we still had to go back to Khanaqin for the police to sort it out. We told them we didn't want to go back there because we just came from there. We showed them our card and our book with the King's signature but they still insisted.

What a bummer!

They told us we could leave the bikes with them and catch one of the busses coming through the border. We waited for an hour before we could board a fully laden bus travelling as far as Baghdad. We grabbed our book and papers and then climbed onto the roof with several other passengers, holding on for our lives. What a crazy ride! Several times we almost fell off, but we made it.

In Khanaqin we walked straight into the police station to the surprise of the two policemen from the day before. We managed to tell them what happened and were told we had to go to Baqubah to the big station, there they would be able to help us. That of course was not on!

The Big Adventure

We showed them where the Mayor and the Chief had written in our book and asked them to ring one of them. They tried a while to make sense at the Police station in Baqubah and finally got the Chief on the line. He of course was worried about us and Uli explained to him what happened. He said to give him half an hour and we should be okay. He spoke to the Khanaqin police men for a few minutes and then wished as good luck again.

Apparently the police were told to write a letter for each of us to hand over at the border. We were served some tea while we waited for the letters. We each got the letter, put it into our passports, and thanked the police very much for their help.

After having a bite to eat at the coffee shop from the night before we wondered how we could get back. Opposite the coffee shop was a parking place for trucks and busses. There were also three horse drawn passenger coaches parked behind each other. We walked across the road but there was no truck or bus leaving for the border at the time. The only way was using one of the coaches but none of them had any drivers.

We climbed in the first one hoping the driver would spot us, but no one came.

After a while Uli got the shits and climbed on to the driver's seat and grabbed the reins. With a big *hoi hee* the horse started to move onto the road.

Suddenly there was a huge commotion behind us with people running from everywhere gesturing for us to stop. Within a few seconds a little guy jumped up next to Uli and grabbed the reins to stop the horse.

After a few angry exchanges Uli managed to calm the guy down. Uli asked him if he could take us to the border. He heasitated but after Uli promised him a good Baksheesh he smiled and said yes.

It was late in the afternoon when we finally got back to the border. We paid the coach man with all the small money we had plus a one dinar note and he was as happy as Larry.

We had no more problems at the check point. The officers kept the reports the police had written and we were allowed to leave.

And so with much relief we crossed the border and were in Persia.

Riding through no man's land between the border crossings Uli in his usual wisecracking way said, "*Buaba jedsd geamer ens Persische nei*"

"Boys now we are off to Persia".

Taking a well earned rest after travelling along a stony unmarked road in Persia.

The Big Adventure

Chapter Eight

Check Points are always very busy and we had to wait sometime before it was our turn to show our passports and had someone look at our luggage. One guy even opened our saddlebags which we never experienced before.

There were some women working in the office wearing no headgear at all. It was unusual because we had not seen women working anywhere like that in Iraq. We showed one of the officers our card but he only looked at the picture. He ignored the written note on the back. Our passports were stamped and they waved us on without another glance.

Feeling uneasy with the strange reception we wasted no time in jumping on our bikes and pedalling away as fast as we could.

We headed northeast towards Qasr-e Shirin about 40Ks further on. The road was reasonable but busy, so we had to take care. After about 20 km we saw a small space between some bushes and decided to camp there for the night. It was getting late and we were tired. Going through border checks certainly sucks the energy out of you. We pushed our bikes off the road and put up our tent. Back to sleeping on hard ground, and our first night sleeping on mother earth in another Country so far from home was quite creepy. We still had about 20 km to reach Quasr-e Shirin our first town in Persia.

It was different to where we came from last. The houses were similar, a few stone buildings and a Mosque were the same, but the people seemed different. They were dressed differently to the previous countries, but were still as inquisitive as before. We stopped in the town centre in front of some dilapidated shops and eating places.

We had hardly got off our bikes before we were surrounded by a group of men and lots of kids. They stared at us as if we had just fallen out of the sky.

Because of the commotion two uniformed policemen came running towards us, yelling at the crowd to disperse so they could find out what had happened. They looked at us as if we were ghosts.

"Passports," one of them demanded.

To show off in front of the crowd we made a grand gesture of digging them out of our pockets and handing them to the police.

They looked through them, flipping the pages, pretending that they could understand what was written in them.

We also showed one of them one of our cards, but it was obvious he could not read the back of it judging by the way he turned it around so the writing was upside down. He glanced at us then started looking into the crowd. He waved to a well dressed man who was walking towards us and showed him the card with the Syrian writing on it. After reading it the man translated it to the two cops and told the bystanders we were from Germany, that we were cyclists and had ridden all the way from Stuttgart to here.

Everyone stared at us with big eyes and open mouths. Most of them knew Germany only by name and because of the past war. The guy introduced himself and invited us into a small shop for some coffee, which we gladly accepted after one of the policemen assured the guy he would watch out for our bikes.

The man must have been fairly well known; the shopkeeper made a fuss about asking what he wanted. After he ordered some food; the usual dried, flat bread and some boiled meat as well as the coffee, he told us he had printing companies in Iraq and Syria and was in the middle of establishing one here in Persia. Most of his printing machines came from England but he had already ordered a German one. We were very happy to hear what he had to say as we ate the food and sipped the coffee. As soon as this was finished we were served a white, shaky, milky substance in a small clay pot.

"Maast," the man said as the clay pots were placed in front of us. He smiled encouragingly.

Having no idea what it was we looked at each other and decided that Uli should try it first. He did and we could see in his eyes his approval. I tried it and found it surprisingly tasty. It was like a mixture of buttermilk and yoghurt and we had it many more times later as we were riding through Persia. The Gentleman ordered some more bread, meat and fruit and had it made into a parcel and handed it to Uli. "For later" he said.

Our thanks were effusive as we told him we appreciated his hospitality and would remember him. Back outside again we were surrounded by kids wanting to touch us. The policemen pushed them back so we could get on our bikes. They stood to attention and saluted us as we started to ride along the street. With a big wave back to them we headed out of town, towards Eslamabad about 70 km ahead.

We were heading in an easterly direction and ahead of us in the far distance was a big mountain range. It was hard to tell how far away it was because with the air so clear as it was here distance is deceiving. They were snow capped and looked very cold. We remained silent as we rode. All you could hear was the sound of our wheels on the pavement and heavy breathing as we sucked in the dry air. Uli didn't feel inspired to make any wise cracks; we only concentrated on pedalling. Sooner or later we would have to cross those mountains. It was cold on the road but still not too bad to travel. The thought of how much colder it was going to be in those mountains was a daunting prospect, but there was no way around them.

Ten kilometres before Eslamabad we camped next to a fast running icy creek. It was too cold to sleep much and we made an early start. It seemed only a few minutes before we entered Eslamabad where we stopped for some breakfast. We wanted to make Bakhtaran later in the day.

It was hard going. There was a slight but cold head wind coming from the mountains. The road was not bad but there was a lot of traffic, lots of over-laden trucks and busses that caused smaller vehicles to bunch up. On bikes we could weave our way in between the bigger trucks and busses but it slowed us down.

We got into Bakhtaran late afternoon and headed straight for the Town centre. As soon as we halted people surrounded us asking all sorts of things we couldn't understand, and of course a couple of policemen would inevitably appear from the crowd and demand to see our Passports.

All through Persia wherever we stopped we had to show our Passports. We soon got used to it and even had some harmless fun with some of the policemen in small towns. Sometimes we handed them over upside down. They would always study them for a few minutes before handing them back with a stern face. We knew they could not make head or tail of it, but it looked good for the onlookers and made them feel important.

We mentioned *Hotel* to the cops and they motioned us to follow them. They stopped in front of a big building with a sign in Persian meaning Hotel. Uli and Theo stepped inside while I watched the bikes with the cops.

The Hotel wasn't too bad, but the best thing was, we didn't get ripped off and the people were very friendly. Theo showed the Manager our book and some pictures about our travel so far and in no time were we led to a big room on the ground floor, big enough for the three of us and the bikes. There was even a separate toilet, a hole in the floor, and a sink with fresh, cold tap water in the room. After a good wash we entered the dining room which was packed, most likely because of us. Inspecting the cooking pots in the kitchen and selecting some food, we were then seated with the manager and a few other gents. Some of the patrons were dressed in suits, but most wore traditional robes. Some of the guests spoke English and wanted to know all about us. Happy to oblige we told them of our journey up to the moment we had arrived in this town and where we intended to go next.

"It's uphill all the way to Kangavar' we were told. "...and it would be very cold. By the time you get to Hamadan there will be snow." Having said that they waited for our response but when we didn't say anything one of them added, "You will find it difficult riding bikes as far as Teheran."

"Germans are tough and used to the cold," Uli said.

What a lot of crap, I thought, but Theo and I nodded in agreement.

We started early next morning. After the Manager wrote in our book about our visit, we were told that we were guests of the Hotel and they wished us all the best on our way.

This was it! Our cards did not seem to work much in Persia, but our book seemed to do the trick! We thanked the manager and his staff with big handshakes and smiles all round, then we hit the road again and waved Bakhtaran good bye.

They were right, the road went upwards!

Worse still, the weather started to turn sour. It got colder by the hour with an icy wind blowing down from the snow capped mountains ahead. We couldn't make it as far as Kangavar and were forced to put up our tent some twenty kilometres before. It was a miserable cold night! The icy wind never let up and there was not enough shelter to light a fire. We shivered all night desperate for daybreak to come so we could jump back on our bikes. Once we got going we would warm up.

In Kangavar we stopped at a Bazaar to buy some provisions and then kept going towards Hamadan. It started to get windier the closer we got to Hamadan which was much higher up than Kangavar. To our deep dismay it started to snow. It was not very heavy at first, but got more and more as we were climbing. We were miserable, utterly exhausted and very unhappy when we erected our tent for another freezing night.

When we got up next morning everything was white. It was difficult to fold our tent, it was covered in snow and the canvas seemed as stiff as wood. No one spoke. Each of us had the same thought, what the bloody hell are we doing here?

Back on the road we found it almost impossible to ride our bikes and the going was very slow. Many times we had to push and it was late afternoon before we reached Hamadan, which while not covered in snow because it had melted away, was still a very cold looking place.

Looking along the street we could clearly see the snow covered mountains through which we would soon have to travel.

Hamadan was a bigger Town with a big bazaar, shops and some manufacturing Industry. Towards the town centre we noticed a large truck and bus depot with lots of busy people moving around. We headed straight

The very cold main street of Hamadan the evening we arrived.

towards it. We pushed our bikes towards what looked like an office. We wanted to find out about the roads leading north.

I stayed with the bikes surrounded by the usual inquisitive crowd, whilst Uli and Theo entered the office. They were told, Qazvin near the Caspian Sea was impassable by bike. The only way for us to get there was by Bus. Even as far as Karaj the roads where iced up. It was suggested that the best thing for us to do was to take one of their busses to the depot in Teheran which was a two day trip.

They had a bus leaving early in the morning and we were offered a bunk each to stay overnight at the back of their depot. There was no real choice so Uli and Theo accepted and were pleasantly surprised when the cost of the tickets for the three of us was a lot cheaper than we expected.

We were taken into a big hall with a big hot stove in the middle, surrounded by plenty of wooden bunks, most already occupied by travellers. It was fantastic to feel warm again. We hadn't realised just how cold it had been outside until we got into that bunk room. We chained our bikes together; rolled out our sleeping bags on top of the bunks we had selected, brushed our teeth and almost immediately fell asleep.

We woke up long before the bus was due to depart because of the commotion. People were yelling and doing stuff outside, and other travellers were moving about and packing gear to load up on the bus.

It never stopped snowing during the night and the whole town was white. Two men indicated that we should follow them towards a bus. One of them was the driver, the other a helper. We could hardly believe what we saw! They stopped in front of a very old fully laden Chevrolet Bus chock-a-bloc full with passengers and their luggage.

Turning to the bus driver Theo asked "How in the hell are you going to fit the three of us and our bikes on board?"

"No problem," he said. "Take the luggage off your bikes first."

We did as he asked.

He called a few more helpers and in no time our bikes were lifted right up on top of the other luggage on the roof of the bus. Our saddlebags were also stowed on the roof, tied down and covered with a large tarpaulin.

The bus would have been much older than the MAN or Merc, which we chauffeured to Greece. We had a quick walk around the bus to inspect the tyres and were not too happy with what we saw. In Germany this bus would never be allowed on the road!

Behind the driver was one empty seat, for two people, but the three

With our bikes stowed safely on top of the bus, we couldn't wait to get going. It was so cold... We didn't have clothes for this kind of weather.

of us had to squeeze in to it. No wonder the price was cheap. It was very early and cold when we left Hamadan and headed north through the mountains. Following lots of over laden trucks busses and cars, the going was extremely slow and averaged not more than about 40 km an hour: still it was much better than we would have been able to do pedalling our bikes. Apart from that it would have been too damned cold and miserable to be exposed on bikes anyway.

Every couple of hours we stopped at a roadhouse to use the toilets and buy some tucker and have a smoke. It took close to ten hours to cover the two hundred or so kilometres to Quazvin. When we arrived at the depot everybody was happy but didn't look forward to the same kind of journey again the next day. All the passengers were put up exactly like the night before.

I must add, our bus was only about a 20 seater like they were at that time, not like the double deckers which we have today. Leaving Quazvin early the next morning gave us no chance to see much of the town except through the windscreen behind the driver. Looking at our map we saw that we were the closest to the Caspian Sea that we would ever get.

The snow had stopped and the road rapidly became slushy. We now travelled in a south easterly direction, and slightly downwards. After a few hours we had descended enough for the roads to get clearer and the driving better. Eventually we got out of the mountains and into open country. By early afternoon when we stopped at a roadhouse for some food and smokes in a small town called Karaj, we noticed the road was nice and dry.

We asked the driver about the condition of the road as far as Teheran.

"It's only 50 Km to go," he told us, and when he saw us looking at the road which was perfect and dry, he added, "You paid until Teheran. If you want to get off here it would be too difficult to get all your gear off the bus at this spot."

He knew how uncomfortably the three of us had been cramped together on one small seat barely big enough for two people. "It's only a few more hours and we are there."

"We might as well stay on the bus," I said.

"Yeah," Theo agreed. "This way when we get to Teheran it would still at daytime."

We arrived at the Teheran bus depot in the middle of the city early afternoon. Once our bikes were unloaded we asked where we could find a cheap hotel and were pointed to a triple storey building down a ways but across the road. Theo waited with the bikes while Uli and I walked over to find out the cost. We stepped over a couple off open water drains where people were washing themselves in grubby water. We found those drains alongside footpaths all over Teheran. The smell that wafted up as we passed made us block our noses.

"What a lovely *au de colon*," Uli said as we stepped over the wide drain.

I had to laugh at that. Uli was always making jokes.

The hotel was called *Johana New World Hotel*, and it badly needed a facelift. The painted adobe facade seemed to be crumbling away as we watched it.

"I hope the rooms inside are better than the outside looks," I mumbled as we walked through the front door.

Inside the foyer was quite clean and looked much better than we might have expected. We were greeted by two men in traditional robes. They introduced themselves as Ismail and Ahmed. They told us with a touch of pride that they were the owners of the hotel. We told them who we were, what we were doing, and showed them our book as we asked about the rooms.

"We have just the room," Ismail said, beaming at us.

"With three beds, on the first floor," Ahmed added.

We smiled back and Uli asked if there was somewhere we could store our bikes.

Ismail immediately took Uli to see a store room behind the lobby, while I went upstairs to see the room. I'd seen better, but it seemed okay and the price was reasonable, so we booked it for a few days.

Back outside we found Theo waiting patiently, surrounded by onlookers who crowded too close for comfort. He was worried that some of the kids would pinch some of our gear. We quickly grabbed our bikes and crossed over the street with a small trail of kids behind us. They stayed outside as we went into the hotel.

The room on the first floor had no running water and the beds had been slept in but not changed. We could tell because the blankets were only straightened.

"What do you think?" I asked Theo who hadn't seen the room until now.

He looked at the remade beds, walked around a bit sniffing the air, and then said, "It'll do. Better than sleeping on the ground outside," referring to the freezing nights we had experienced before catching the bus to Tehran.

The room was sparsely furnished with a chair next to each bed, one small wardrobe and a writing desk. A window overlooked the street in front of the hotel, and we saw some of the kids that Theo had attracted were still hanging around. There was a common wash room and a toilet on the floor which was relatively clean.

We splashed some water on our faces to freshen up and then went downstairs to talk to the owners. We were hungry and wanted to know if there was a good place nearby where we could eat. Ismail came to the front door with us, yelled something at the kids still there which made them run away, and then pointed to a place down the road. "They have good food there. When you go in tell them you are staying at this hotel."

"No problem," Uli said. We figured the owners would get a commission for sending customers to the restaurant. That didn't bother us because that is just the way things work. The restaurant was half empty and we were greeted by the owner. We told him who we were, where we stayed and asked him if we could visit his kitchen to pick out some food.

Yes, as usual people stared at us because we were obviously different, but there was no malice, only curiosity, and we had gotten used to that so we took no notice.

"There is no need to go into the kitchen," the owner said. "Do you like steamed rice with beef? It is our specialty."

"We have had it before,' I told him.

"We like it," Uli said.

Theo didn't say anything. He was the one who always wanted to go into the kitchens to see what was cooking before deciding what he could eat. He would reserve judgement until he saw what was served.

The owner nodded and smiled. "You may have had it before, but not like this".

He led us to vacant table and served us some tea. We looked around the room and noticed all the customers were men, not one woman to be seen. A few moments later a waiter served each of us a steaming hot plate of rice. The rice was shaped like a pyramid and surrounded with pieces of marinated grilled beef. The owner followed as soon as the waiter had left the plates of rice, holding three plates with big slices of butter. He placed a piece of butter on each of our flattened top of rice. He sprinkled crushed rock salt and ground pepper over each plate as the butter started to melt right through the rice.

It was a meal fit for a king, and we enjoyed every bit of it. Even Theo was excited.

The owner told us that we were not really in a restaurant but a club and this was their number one meal. "It is called *Celo Kebab*."

After paying for our meal the owner presented us with a small bronze medallion, which I still have today, designating that we were members of the club. Back at the hotel we thanked Ismail and went up to our room for a good night's sleep. Needless to say, we slept in our sleeping bags which we spread on top of the beds.

A loud knock on the door next morning woke us out of a great night's sleep. Uli opened the door and to our surprise it was a smiling Ahmed handing him three small terracotta tubs. He wished us a good morning.

The Big Adventure

"Breakfast" he said, pointing to the tubs. "Maast."

He was gone before Uli could thank him. The little pot was covered with a thin cardboard lid, similar to the old Peters ice cream Dixie. We appreciated this gesture and enjoyed our breakfast. After using the toilets and having a good wash, we were ready to hit the streets of Teheran.

We asked Ismail about the surroundings, especially the Bazaar and the Shah's Palace.

The Bazaar was very close, walking distance, but why did we want to know about the Shah?

"Well" we said, "because we want to meet him and Queen Soraya."

With a big non-believing smile on his face he told us maybe we should go to Parliament House first and enquire about them. We were told it would be best to go by cab.

We grabbed our passports, our travel book, some Postcards, camera and smokes. Ishmael hailed us a cab and told the driver were we wanted to go. He also gave us his address so we could find our way back. Teheran was a big city with wide streets, incredible traffic and people everywhere. We saw big office buildings, American car sales and big luxury hotels. We also saw women who hadn't covered their hair and some of them were even driving cars.

By the time we stopped in front of a big building about 5km from our hotel, it would have taken us at least twenty minutes. Parliament House was a very imposing Building set high with a massive set of steps leading up to it. To gain entry we had to drive through a huge portal manned with two armed soldiers who wanted to see identifications.

We showed them our passports and the cab was allowed to drive us through. On top of the big steps we had to show our passports again, and inside a huge visitor's hall at a reception desk once more. Finally we were asked what we wanted.

We told them, "We want to meet the Shah and Queen Soraya."

The guy choked and we could see that he struggled to suppress a laugh.

It must have been the first time that three not so well dressed guys, asked him if they could see the Shah and Queen. He motioned us to wait and disappeared behind a big door laughing. It took at least fifteen minutes before the door opened and he came out again, followed by a big man in Army Uniform and a beautiful woman dressed in European clothing. The Army guy had lots of Medals hanging on his uniform and we assumed that he was a man of authority.

He wasn't smiling and with a stern expression on his face he asked us in fluent English what we wanted and where we came from.

Theo gave him one of our cards and Uli showed him our book.

We told him that we had arrived in Teheran from Germany on bikes, on the way to the Olympics in Melbourne and his face lit up like sunshine. He asked us to follow him and the woman in to his office, where we were offered chairs in front of his big desk. He and the women were all eyes and ears when Uli went through our book with them and were very pleased when they found out that we'd already had an Audience with King Faisal in Baghdad. The Gentleman introduced himself as a retired General in the Shah's Army and the woman was his Secretary.

It wasn't long before the door opened and a couple of young men entered with cups of tea and very sugary sweets covered with honey. We felt better by the minute and slightly important.

"You have come at just the right time," the General said. "In two days time it will be the Islamic New Year and there will be a holiday. There will also be a celebration at the Shah's Palace with the Shah and Queen Soraya giving out medals honouring people of distinction. I will contact the Minister of Ceremonies at the Palace to see if you can take part in it."

We were speechless. This was unbelievable.

By that time, his Secretary who had left the room earlier, returned with a piece of paper which she handed to the General. The General made a phone call and spoke in Persian. All we could understand were the words Germany and Australia.

He looked very pleased when he hung up and wrote something on the piece of paper.

"It's not as simple as I thought," he said, "because of security, you understand."

I thought it was too good to be likely to happen. But before our hopes were completely dashed he continued. "You will have to go to the Palace tomorrow morning to be interviewed by the Minister of Ceremonies himself."

He asked us where we were staying and told us we only had to travel 30 minutes by cab to the Palace from there. We asked him if he would be so kind to write a few words in our book, which he willingly obliged. He handed us the piece of paper with the time of our appointment, the address and the name of the person we had to see.

It must have been close to an hour when we left the office. The reception guy wasn't smiling anymore, when he saw The General himself

The Big Adventure

opening the door, shaking our hands vigorously and wishing us all the best with our future travels.

Out on the street we jumped in one of the many cabs and told the driver to take us to the Bazaar, which wasn't far from our hotel. On the way we asked the driver if he knew where the Australian Embassy was and he replied that it is in the same Building as the English one, only five minutes from here. Theo told him to take us there first, which he did and told us he would wait. Several buildings which looked like Government offices were occupied by Embassies and well-to-do Businesses.

On the second floor of this building were the English and Australian embassies. We entered and were led to a smaller office, with Australian High Commission written on the door. Two well dressed guys stood up from behind their desks and greeted us with a big hello. We told them who we were and that we were cycling to the Olympics in Melbourne. One of them asked, "Why were you here at this office?"

We explained that we had no visa as yet. We were asked the same questions as before. How much money we had to get out of Australia. We had about US$500 we told him. They told us to wait a moment and disappeared behind a door. A few minutes later they came out and told us the Consul did not approve our visa application and they were sorry, but they wished us good luck.

The cabbie was waiting and took us to the Bazaar. This Bazaar was huge! One of the biggest in the world we were told. The most amazing part of it was that it was carpeted!

Yes carpeted! What was happening? We soon found out that the carpet weavers whose Persian Carpets were the very best, would —after finishing a new one which could take a year or longer to make— put it along the path for people, animals and fully laden goods trailers to be walked and driven on.

When we asked why, they explained the reason was the thousands of different knots the carpets were made with needed to harden. Apparently those carpets are left for months on end before they are cleaned and ready to be sold worldwide for big money!

Being amongst big crowds like this, we had to watch our pockets, not that there was much danger, but pick pockets are everywhere, and being strangers we were obvious targets.

We spent hours looking through the place and were really tired by the time we walked back to our hotel.

Ismail greeted us with a huge smile and wanted to know how we got along.

"We have an interview at the Shah's Palace in the morning."

His eyes and mouth opened when we told him that. He called Ahmed and told him to bring tea and Maast to our room. We managed to write a couple of postcards back home before it was time to walk to our favourite Club. Greeted as if we were old friends we were served hot tea the moment we sat down. We told the owner we were starving and were looking forward to the same great meal again as yesterday. And it was great! We had our book with us to show him what the General had written and Uli gave him one of our cards which he showed to all his other guests.

When we got back to the hotel Ahmed was waiting with some more Maast, Allah blesses him! We asked Ahmed to wake us early because we wanted to be at the Palace by 10am. It had been a long day and we were ready to hit the sack.

We were already awake in the morning, when Ahmed knocked and served us Maast and freshly baked Pita bread. By 9am we were ready to hop in a Taxi after Ismail told the driver where to take us. It took at least 30 minutes before the cab turned in to a beautiful, large Cull de Sac lined with big trees. Every driveway had uniformed Guards in front of big iron gates. The buildings behind them looked huge. As a matter of fact they all looked like Palaces. The driver drove up to the last one and was stopped by two guards. We had to show our passports and our names were recorded, even the cabbie had to show some identification. One of the guards walked in to the guardhouse and we could see him talking on the phone. He came back out and told us we were expected. They talked to the cabbie for a moment and waved him on.

I find it hard to describe what opened up in front of us! We thought King Faisal's Palace was big, but it was nothing compared to this!

We drove up this wide driveway lined with beautiful, manicured bushes and small trees and stopped in front of a long row of steps leading up to the Palace. A uniformed guard opened the cab door and while Uli paid the cabbie Theo and I got out to be greeted by an elderly, clean shaven man, dressed in a suit and tie. There were people all over the place, lots of workers and overseers. They were erecting a big Marquee and the big empty car park in front was laid out with red carpets. The cab was allowed to leave and the three of us were asked to follow our guide up the steps and in to a huge entrance hall. We were led to a big visitors desk were a couple of uniformed Army Officers checked our passports against some documents on their desk.

A moment later, one of the officers led us across the hall to a big ornamental door. He opened it and waved us through. It was a spacious office with many desks occupied by women and men of all ages busy on typewriters. They all stared at us as we were led past them in to another big room. This one only had one desk, but it was a giant one!

A smiling Gentleman in an impeccably fitted black uniform festooned with medals just below the shoulders and two golden stars on the lapels greeted us. He looked great and we knew instantly, that this guy was important. He came around from behind his desk and shook our hands and begged us to sit down. He said a few words to the guide who led us in and closed the door behind him.

*Moushsime,
Grand Master of Ceremonies
for his Majesty
The Shahinshah*

After we introduced ourselves he asked us if we prefer speaking in French, English or even in German which he had mastered quite well.

We told him how we managed to get to Teheran and he was all ears. Theo showed him our book and I gave him one of our cards to read. By the way he looked at the book and the time he took to study it, we knew we made a friend. The door opened and a couple of servants rolled a small table in with tea and little baskets laden with Persian Sweets. Our new friend told us that he had served many years in the Army, starting as a young man in the Shah's Father's Army and had retired after a distinguished career. He was now employed as the Grand Master of Ceremonies to His Majesty the Shahinsha, and was in charge of all festivities in and outside of the Palace.

"You are extremely fortunate to be here at this time," he said, "because of the festivities celebrating the Islamic New Year."

I think it was their Year 1335.

"I am certain that I can manage for you to meet the Shah and Queen Soraya twice. There will be some people meeting privately in the Palace before going outside for the handing out of the medals ceremony. You could join them in the Palace. I will arrange some seats for you in the Marquee as well."

We could hardly believe what we were hearing and were totally elated!

The big day was to be tomorrow, Friday, which was also the Islamic day of worship, like our Sunday.

"Come to this office by 10 am so you can take part as my guests."

How about that for luck? We couldn't have timed our arrival in Tehran any better.

He pushed a button on his desk and the same officer from earlier opened the door. Our friend spoke to him for a moment and told us to follow him. After some handshakes and lots of thanks we were led out of the office towards the big entrance hall. At the visitor's desk we were handed a folder and told to show it at the security gate in the morning. Just about everyone looked at us when we descended the big steps, walking towards the huge gate that opened onto the street. We had been in the Palace for well over an hour by the time we walked down those steps.

A cab took us to the Bazaar for some lunch and a well earned Water Pipe. We were on a high and looking forward to tomorrow. Of course Ismail and Ahmed were waiting for us to hear the latest and were super happy for us about the next day. After writing some more postcards we walked to the main Post Office to post them and collected our mail which we received Poste restante in all the major cities. We always looked forward to mail from home. I had letters from mum and dad, a postcard from grandma and some from our mates telling us how proud they were when they got news about our meeting with King Faisal.

Later at our club having our usual dinner, we had to tell the owner also about visit to the Palace. To our surprise, he asked if we would like some beer, because being a club he was allowed to sell alcohol. Naturally Uli and I said yes but Theo was happy with a Pepsi Cola. No Coca Cola was sold in any of the Arab speaking countries we visited. With Dinner finished, a cold English beer on the table and a water pipe bubbling, we couldn't ask for anything more. When it was time to leave, we only had to pay for our meal. As expected, tubs of Maast were waiting for us at the hotel and Ismail wished us a good night. It was hard for me to fall asleep, thinking about what happened during the day.

Early next morning after a shave and a good wash, we got dressed in our best clothes, including pullovers and jackets because it was still very cold. Laden with camera, our book and some cards we jumped in a cab at 9 am to make sure we were on time.

At the big gate we paid the cab and showed the sentries the forms. With a short salute they motioned us on up to the Palace. The big Marquee, under construction when we were there the day before was now complete and full of flowers. In the middle a couple of huge upholstered chairs were raised on a podium, around which groups of well dressed men were talking. Some wore immaculately clean uniforms covered with medals and stars while others wore European suits. There were only a few women amongst them, beautifully dressed and looking like stars.

As we walked up to the crowd we were spotted by the same Gentleman as yesterday, only today he wore a uniform and not a suit. He greeted us with a smile and led us up the big steps to the Palace entrance. I could feel a thousand eyes staring at my back as we went slowly up those steps. Inside the big hall we walked past the visitor's desk which was surrounded by people filling out some kind of forms. We looked out of place amongst all these people, but one thing was for sure, no one was dressed like us!

We entered a smaller hall, empty except for some chairs against the walls and lots of flower pots in every corner and on each side of the doors. There where statues made of white marble and beautiful paintings decorating every wall. There were ten men in the hall, the special guests, and amongst them was the Grand master. He shook our hands and with a big smile introduced us to the others. He must have told them about us, because they also shook our hands and wished us good luck. He informed us that the Shah and Queen would enter through a side door to greet the special guests and dignitaries in this hall. He told us we would have about twenty minutes with the Shah and Queen and then we would see them again outside under the Marquee. He left us with the others and walked through the side door. While waiting we talked to the others, who were anxious to know about our adventures so far. The wait was just about unbearable not only for us, but also for everybody else. A small gong sounded and the Grand Master opened the door. The Shah and his Queen entered the room.

What a moment! Here we were, three kids from Backnang, in the same room as the Shahinshah Reza Pahlavi and Queen Soraya. We were mesmerised!

Years earlier we had heard on the radio about the fairy tale wedding and every paper had been full of pictures showing the breath-takingly beautiful Princes Soraya. She was born Soraya Esfandiara Bakhtiari in Isfahan to a German mother and Persian noble man. She had been educated in Berlin.

The Shah and Queen Soraya

You could have heard a pin drop when they walked in to the room, followed by the Grand Master. Queen Soraya was dressed in a long black body tight gown reaching up to her neck. She wore black suede gloves and a white cashmere shawl around her shoulders with a hint of a thin necklace around her neck. She was more than beautiful and walked as elegantly as a Gazelle! The Shah was dressed in a dark suit and tie covered by a black overcoat.

The others in the room were known to them and were greeted with handshakes and spoken to individually. Then it was our turn. The Grand Master introduced each of us and we were greeted with a strong handshake from the Shah and the Queen. The Shah spoke to us in English for

Her Imperial Majesty Soraya Pahlavi Empress of Iran

several minutes, and then Queen Soraya spoke to us in fluent German. She wanted to know of many dangers we had experienced and how much hospitality we received in different countries, especially in Persia.

About twenty minutes the Grand Master approached deferentially to suggest it was time to go outside. He led them back to the open door, but not before we received another handshake and good wishes for our journey. The first officer guided us back through the empty entrance hall out to the Marquee were everyone else was waiting for the Royals to turn up. We didn't have to wait too long before they entered through a door leading in to the Marquee where all men saluted as they walked past them. They stepped up to the podium and sat in those big chairs. Our friend spoke into a microphone for quite some time, followed by a Mufti or Mullah with a long beard, wearing Persian robes with turban.

Several soldiers walked in carrying stacks of wooden tablets covered with different medals. The Grand Master walked back to the microphone with a long list of names in his hand. When he read out the first name, the Shah and the Queen got up and stood next to him so they both could present the medals to each recipient. Each recipient received with their medal a hand shake, after which they walked backwards bowing their heads.

The Shah and Queen Soraya entering the courtyard where the medal ceremony took place.

It seemed a very long ceremony, but we were glad that we had the opportunity to see it.

Finally, just when we thought it was all over our names were called out. I couldn't believe it! We did our best to walk up as all the others had done, and once again we shook hands with the Shah and Queen Soraya as we received our medals.

Our medal

The Big Adventure

Who would have thought that? Not in our wildest dreams did we expect anything like this. To this day, I think we are perhaps the only Germans who ever received a medal from the Royals of Persia.

The event came to an end when the Shah and the Queen turned to leave. Once they had gone most of the dignitaries made their way towards the gate and their chauffeur driven cars. Our Officer asked us if it was possible for us to come to the Palace once more tomorrow, because the Grand Master wanted to see us again, being too busy today to say good bye.

We told him of course we would be there in the morning, shook his hand and left to catch a cab.

Wow, what a day! We had achieved something no other German at our age had done before; certainly no one in Backnang or even in Stuttgart.

What would our parents, relatives and friends say now, when they find out?

Back at the hotel Ismail, Ahmed and several other men were waiting to hear the news. Between spoons full of Maast we told them all about what had happened. Ismail had to translate to some of them. They were all ears and when we showed them our medals their eyes popped out. We got pats on our shoulders and handshakes all round.

It had been a long day and we were busting to go to the toilet, with all the happenings we had to hold on. Up in our room we sat on our beds discussing what happened and to our dismay, we discovered that Uli forgot to take pictures of us with the Royals, but he managed to take a few handing out medals.

We had to forgive him because neither Theo nor I had thought about it, the spell was too great. We marched over to our club for a well earned meal and greeted again by the owner, we had to answer lots of questions and he asked Uli if he could show his medal to the other guests which Uli obliged. This time we got the beer and Pepsi before our meal and afterwards some more which we didn't have to pay for, we paid only for the meal.

About 10am next morning we caught a cab to take us to the Palace for the third time. We still had to show our passports at the gate, but with a smile, one of the guards escorted us towards the big steps. The Marquee was already dismantled and workers were rolling up the carpets. At the visitor's desk we were led straight to the big door without having to show our passports again. Walking past all the office people the guide opened the door and we were greeted by our smiling friend. He told us that he had been very busy yesterday, but was also happy that the day went as planned. He also told us that the Queen was astonished that we were so young and had managed to cycle so far. He passed on her hopes that we shall reach Melbourne safely. Uli asked him if it is possible to take a photo of him and Theo asked him to write a few lines in our book, which he obliged with a smile. Tea and Persian sweets were served and we must have been with him close to an hour before he wished us all the best for the rest of our journey.

A knock on the door, an official walked up to our friend, handed him an envelope, turned and left. Theo was handed the envelope and we were told to open it later. I shall never forget the good bye from one of Persia's most influential persons. There were hugs and handshakes all round, as if we had known each other for a long time. We left him one of our signed postcards and promised to write along our way.

We wrote to him from New Delhi and from Melbourne, but we never heard from him again. Years later we were very sad about the news of what had happened by then in Iran.

We walked out of the Palace, smiled at passers-by and went down the big steps. At the gate we were saluted by the guards and we saluted back. Catching a cab we told the driver to take us to the Bazaar for a pipe and some coffee.

Sitting at a table with coffee in front of us we just had to know what was in the envelope.

Theo opened it and took out a cheque. There was also a note written in English telling us the cheque could be changed at any bank or money changer. Uli and Theo walked over to one of the changers nearby whilst I minded the water pipe and looked in our book to see what our friend had written. The page looked very impressive, with his name, signature and a couple of official stamps. They came back, grinning from ear to ear. The cheque was in Tuman, Persian currency and equivalent to 300DM.

We were happy and decided to write more postcards. Theo wrote about our experience with the Royals and our trip so far to the Newspaper back home. Then we thought about Ilse and Karin, my twin cousins having their Confirmation in a few weeks time, perhaps we should buy them a gift. Theo and I searched through some stalls and found two beautiful hand crafted shawls, which we thought would be a great present for the two girls. We had them wrapped in a small box and walked over to the post office to post the lot.

Back at the hotel we showed Ismail and Ahmed the page from the Grand Master and they were deeply impressed. We didn't mention the money, no one needed to know about that.

Up in our room, we started to get our gear packed because we wanted to leave in the morning, to go south towards Qom. We discussed which route to take. We could go east towards Mashhad and through Afghanistan to Kabul, but eventually decided to go south towards the warmth.

The last evening in our club was special, the room was packet. Everyone wanted to look in our book and shake hands; needless to say none of them had ever shaken hands with any of their Royals. We had a few beers and a great meal. The owner and staff were sad to see us leave and we told them that we would tell people throughout Persia and beyond about their great hospitality. No payment for our food and drink was accepted; apparently most of the patrons had chipped in with big smiles. We also felt sad to leave, but we had to move on.

Back at the hotel Ahmed was waiting with some guests and handed us some Maast. They were extremely sorry to see us leave, but understood we had a long way still ahead of us. Packing our bikes next morning took longer than usual because everyone watched and wanted to help. Finally the big moment, saying good bye. Ismail and Ahmed would not accept any money for our stay, telling us they had more people staying at the hotel because of us. We knew that wasn't true but it was nice of him to say so. We hugged both of them, handed them a couple of our cards and shook hands with the others.

Jumping on our bikes and with a final wave backwards we headed south.

We felt pretty morbid riding out of Teheran. It was a wonderful city and it had given us so many memorable moments. The highlight had to be our meeting with the Shah and Queen Soraya. That was something none of us would ever forget.

The riding was difficult because of the traffic and those water canals next to the roads. We had to be careful not to get pushed aside or we could fall into them. In the clear air the snow capped mountains behind the city stood out stark against the sky.

Some 30km out of Teheran we stopped at a small village and had some dips with pita bread and fruit, which this time we actually paid for. Sleeping in our tent again, which we erected not far from the main road created a bit of a problem, because there was no wood for a fire. The land all around was barren, not even small bushes could be seen. And it was very cold, close to zero as night fell.

Frozen stiff next morning, it took longer than usual to pack up and load our bikes because our hands and fingers were numb. At least the sun was shining and it didn't take long to warm up once we got back on the road. It was still busy but nowhere as bad as yesterday. We had to contend with many trucks, busses and cars, but we got plenty of encouraging toots and drivers waved to us as they passed. We even saw a camel caravan way back from the road going slowly in a different direction. As we rode along it got further away until there was only a trail of dust floating in the distant air to indicate where it was. We made good headway and covered a fair distance before stopping at a roadhouse about 50 Km further along.

Late afternoon we found a suitable campsite and erected our tent. Frozen to the marrow again we could hardly wait to hit the road next morning headed for Qom. We couldn't get warm, no matter how hard we peddled. A very cold northerly wind coming straight down off the snow capped mountains behind us helped to push us along and the kilometres flew past. It almost felt as if we were in a bike race. We passed a strange big lake, all white with no water in it. We found out later that it was a salt lake. We didn't reach Qom and had to spend another freezing night in our tent.

One of the many Mosques in the Holy City of Qom

The Big Adventure

Qom, the holy city of Persia was finally ahead of us. There was less traffic than we expected and it wasn't long before we reached the centre of town. Qom was a nice friendly City full of old buildings and many Mosques.

As we rode into the city people everywhere looked at us surprised, but always smiling. The further into the town we got the harder it became. There were people and all kinds of vehicles everywhere all over the roads which made it impossible to ride and we had to get off and push our bikes. There were people walking next to us and kids touching our luggage, we had to be on the lookout in case someone tried to pinch something. I guess all cities are the same. Uli asked a couple of well dressed men to show us the way to the Town hall and Police station.

By the time we reached the Police station four policemen were waiting in front surrounded by people. Word of our arrival had passed along the street so they knew we were coming. After looking through our Passports two of the cops stayed with our bikes and the others begged us to follow them inside to a big office with plenty of different carpets covering the floor. I couldn't help wondering how much one of those carpets would cost in Germany. There were three big desks, a wooden stove and pictures of the Shah and Queen Soraya on every wall. There would have been at least five policemen in the room and two of them spoke very good English. We had to show our Passports once more because they could hardly believe how far we had come.

Uli pointed to the pictures on the wall and told them we had met the Shah and Queen Soraya a week earlier. They looked at Uli then turned to each other speaking rapidly in Persian. They clearly thought we were trying to bullshit them.

"They don't believe us," Theo said. He turned and went back outside to our bikes and fetched our book to show it to them. When they saw the picture of the Grand Master and read what he had written, each one of them shook our hands. But once we showed them our Medals the welcome was complete.

We asked them if there was a cheap hotel close by because we would like to stay a day to look at their beautiful city. When they seemed uncertain Uli mentioned that sometimes we were invited to stay at a police station.

"We don't have much money and we have a very long way to travel. Perhaps you have an unoccupied cell we could sleep in for the night?"

They talked again amongst themselves for a couple of minutes then told us we could stay here also. There were four empty cells and they would be happy to show them to us.

They led us into another big room with six doors, each leading into another small room. Well if these were cells, the prisoners had it relative easy. Instead of bunks there were two lots of six foot by four foot carpet squares three foot high on each side by the wall. A small window up high let in plenty of light, and a small globe on the ceiling and that was it. The two other doors led to a hole-in-the-floor toilet with a full watering can. Next to it was a tiny wash room with a porcelain sink and a small bench next to it. There was only one tap only because there was no hot water. This suited us, especially when we got asked if we would accompany two of them as their guests for dinner.

Our bikes were brought in and stored in one of the cells .Hot tea was served, which went down well. Next thing we heard some kind of chanting from the Minarets of the mosque over the road from the police station and suddenly every policeman unfolded his praying carpet on the floor, kneeled on it and all facing the same direction they started praying. Here we were again, Moslems and Christians in one room as friends. Why is it so much different today?

It wasn't long evening and we had an hour before dinner. Unpacking our sleeping bags and toiletries, we had a good clean up. After three days travelling we were looking forward to a good meal. One block away there were shops, coffee houses and small restaurants. By the time we had reached where we were going at least a dozen men followed us. They all wanted to know who we were and what we were doing. One of the Policemen stayed back a little, to tell them our story.

In the restaurant we asked the owner if they had *Celo Kebab* and with a smile, were told they made the best. Tea was served and we didn't have to wait long before our meals were on the table. To our surprise the two policemen had ordered the same. It was delicious, but not quite as good as the one served at our club in Teheran. Nevertheless we told the owner and our hosts it was the best we had eaten so far. After dinner we were asked if we would like some coffee and a water pipe, which we gladly accepted. We thanked the restaurant owner. It was a short walk to a coffee shop where we enjoyed coffee with sweets and the water pipe. Back at the police station we thanked them all for their hospitality, had a wash and hit the sack, I mean the carpets. What a big day it was and it felt good not to sleep in our tent.

It was barely daybreak when we were woken up with loud chanting from the Minarets calling everyone for morning prayers. I must have slept like a log and would have slept a while longer if there wasn't so much activity in the office already. After freshening up we dressed and stepped in to the office to be greeted by three or four new smiling faces. They pointed to a desk covered with lots of goodies, a big pot of tea and large plate of fresh pita bread for breakfast. There were also boiled eggs some different dips, fruit and to our surprise, about a dozen small clay pots containing our favourite Maast. How about that? This is as good as being in a hotel! The breakfast wasn't only for us, there was enough for everyone in the station.

After Breakfast we were asked what we would like to see and we told them we wouldn't mind visiting the Jamkaran Mosque. We were told in Teheran, that the Shah's father "Reza" drove down from Teheran all by himself and whipped one of the Muftis because he insulted his wife.

"That's right," they said, "and the Muftis have never forgotten and are still angry to this day."

Two of the Policemen were ordered by their Sergeant to guide us around.

Qom was a fascinating city.

We were quite impressed with the architecture of the houses and especially of the different Mosques. After a few hours walking we stopped for coffee and a water pipe. Qom was relatively clean and we enjoyed every moment. Again we were invited for dinner in the evening and it turned out to be the same as the night before. The only exception was the restaurant was full, so full of people wanting to have a look at us that they had to stand outside and look through the window.

After a good night's sleep and another good breakfast in the morning, we were ready to jump on our bikes. Saying goodbye was again very sad, but we learned one thing about Persian Police, they looked after us with great respect and we loved it!

We headed south towards Esfahan. We were hoping to make Kashan, about 80 km away, but got away to late and had to camp about 20 km before. Nothing much happened in Kashan except half way through town we were stopped by police who wanted to see our passports. We were used to this by now and didn't mind telling them our story, as long as they could understand us. We didn't stay long, because we wanted to get as close to Esfahan as possible. It took another day and a half before we got there and finally reached the city were Queen Soraya was born.

Esfahan was big, much busier than Qom. Apparently it was the third largest City in Persia after Mashhad and was the capital many years ago. The road from Qom was extremely dry and dusty with hardly any vegetation other than a few ragged bushes. It was also very windy. After riding through a mountain pass the country changed. As we got closer to Esfahan we noticed a few green trees and we even had to cross a couple of small creeks originating in the mountains. It was a welcomed site, because we could replenish our water bottles and have a bit of a cleanup. At that point the water was still Chrystal clear and cold.

We passed through a couple of small villages where fields of different crops were planted and in a small orchard fruit trees had started to lose their blossoms. We sometimes had problems entering small villages because too many dogs were often the first to greet us, barking and yapping, running along beside us, with some even brave enough to nip at our feet. We had to kick them away to stop them getting under our wheels. People would stop whatever they were doing to stare at us. Sometimes they waved, sometimes they called the dogs off, but usually they did nothing and we never stopped in places like that. Once through the village the dogs would fall away.

The more south we travelled the warmer it became. The nights were still cold, but during the day we didn't need our pullovers anymore. With all the traffic and kids running next to us as we entered the outskirts of Esfahan, it took some time before we reached the city's centre.

We asked again for the police station and headed straight towards it. After showing our passports we asked where we could stay overnight and were told there were some reasonable hotels nearby. One of the officers mentioned that if we would go down a couple of streets and pointed to a big building in the distance. "That," he said, "is the University and they have a hostel for their students, maybe you could stay there?"

"Why not," we said, thanked him and pushed our bikes along the footpath, because riding was near impossible.

Walking up to a big iron gate in front of several three or four storey buildings, two surprised guards approached us and wanted to know where we came from. We told them what we were doing and that the police sent us here to see if we could get some accommodation. One of the guards walked in to his little office and we could see him talking on a phone while the other one told the people who followed us to move on.

We didn't wait long before two very smartly dressed men in European suits stepped out of the nearest building and walked straight towards us. After introductions and handshakes they begged us to follow them towards another building further along. Several younger men followed us, wondering where we came from. We were led into an office where a group of men waited for us to be introduced to them. It turned out that they were all teachers and one of them was the principal of the Uni.

We told them about our journey so far and showed them our book and medals. The surprise was real; we could see it by their smiles, though they conversed in their own language.

"We would be happy for you to stay with us," one of the teachers told us.

It would be a pleasure to show you our city," another said. "And perhaps you could speak to some of our students about your adventures?"

"Of course," we said, "no problem at all".

The Principal himself led the way to a building opposite, followed by some teachers and lots of students. Where had they all come from, I wondered. There was a kitchen- dining room, in front of a gym, a wash room and toilets on the bottom and lots of bedrooms on the higher floors. By then it was getting dark and everybody had dinner. We were served tea and a couple of plates with rice and some kind of stew, which went down well.

There was only one problem, we had to share a room with six other students and they all wanted to hear and get to know about us. It was very late before we got to sleep.

Next morning after breakfast, we were shown around the city. Three limousines were waiting outside, one for each of us. Each one of us had to squeeze onto a front seat, because there were five persons already inside. We certainly saw Esfahan in style.

In the afternoon we were led into a large hall jammed with students and staff. Many students were in traditional dress, while those who were foreign students wore European clothes. We were interviewed by the Principal and a couple of teachers, and then the students were invited to ask questions. And ask questions they did; lots of questions. We must have spoken for hours. Eventually we were served with several cups of tea and had to shake hands with all of them.

There was a big goodbye next morning and the Principal handed Theo a letter for the Principal of the University in Shiraz. We reached Qomsheh late afternoon and headed straight for the police station, where we stayed in a couple of cells again. Early next morning we tried to reach

Abadeh, but it was too hilly and we had to put up the tent with only a couple of hours to go. We stopped at Abadeh only for some lunch and headed straight for Eglidabad, where we stopped again at the police hoping for accommodation. This time because it was a small town, there were no cells, only one room next to their office.

There were two stacks of rectangular carpets about two meters high in the room. "Don't worry," they said, and very quickly converted two stacks into three for us to sleep on.

Better than in our tent, we thought.

The road to Mar Dasht was very hilly and going was slow. Riding and pushing through seemingly endless mountains we came towards some flatter ground which was a tremendous relief. There were some old ruins to the east of us and there were signs pointing to Persepolis. Further on we saw Nomad tents, camels, goats and sheep, grazing in the distance. We stopped at a bus and truck station, got some provisions and put up the tent again soon after. It had gotten warmer by the day and we no longer needed a fire at night.

Earlier we had noticed a couple of police cars, with officers speaking with some of the people, but we didn't know why. Late next morning we spotted a nomad encampment in the distance, not far from the road. It was only about two kilometres away from the road and we thought we should check it out. Getting closer we had kids and dogs running towards us and elderly men and women stood in front of some tents. When we came to a halt in front of them there were no smiles, only unfriendly looks.

A tall elderly man who stood out from the others came towards us with a rifle in his hand. He spoke in broken English and wanted to know where we came from and what brought us here. We told him we were *Aleman*, Germans, going to Australia.

He exclaimed, "You are Aleman, Germans?"

We nodded and said, "all the way from there, on our bikes." It was redundant since we had been seen riding towards the encampment and were now standing beside our bikes.

He turned around and explained to the people standing in front of the tents who we were. Instantly their frowns changed to smiles and we had to shake many hands.

There were a lot of tents, all about the same size except one real big one in the middle, with the others erected around it. The tall man begged us to follow him to the big tent, with all the others behind us. We leaned our bikes together and followed him and a few others inside. It certainly was big! Big enough to hold at least fifty people all seated on the fully carpeted floor. We were seated in the middle with the Chief and a few others opposite us, asking questions. Someone served tea with some Maast and flat-bread. It wasn't long before two young fellows who looked like brothers entered. They looked no older than perhaps 30 years old and seemed very fit. The Chief proudly introduced them as his sons. We were stunned when they greeted us in near perfect German. It turned out that they had studied in Berlin for three years and in London for two years. We had to tell them all about our journey and they translated enthusiastically.

We felt real good about the welcome, especially when we were asked to spend a few days with them. They belonged to the Quashqai, a very powerful tribe of about 300 thousand souls mostly distributed on the western side in Persia. We could see the chief being proud of his sons. While they were speaking to us he looked around at those listening as if to say, *see, sending them away wasn't for nothing*. We loved it and told them we wouldn't mind staying a couple of nights. The sons showed us around the tent village and surroundings, followed by most of the people who didn't want to miss a thing.

There were lots of camels, sheep and goats grazing all around with younger men guarding them. Close by was a small lake, fed by a spring where they got plenty of fresh water. There were some holes in the ground, dug out with the piled dirt next to them and some drums of water. If one had to go to the toilet, one covered the deposit with some dirt and some water. Far distance we could make out a couple of long Caravans trekking in different directions. By that time it was getting on dark and some fires were lit to cook the evening meal.

It was hard to believe what was happening to us again. I said to myself, if only they could see me now, not really sure to whom I was referring.

We sat around the fires eating freshly barbequed meat, bread, vegetables, Maast and after wards watermelon. Then came the water pipes which we appreciated immensely. Our beds were prepared in the big tent, sleeping on top of some carpets. Before wishing us a good night's sleep, the sons asked if we would like to ride on Camels during the day tomorrow. "We would love it," we said as we hit the sack.

Morning came and we had some fun times with the makeshift toilets, but where there is a will there is a way. Everybody wanted to talk to us and after some good breakfast the sons had several camels ready and told us we would visit the other village about 10 km away.

We had never sat on a Camel before. The only advice given was to hang on.

We watched how the others did it and Theo was the next one up. He nearly fell back on the ground, because he did not hang on tight enough. Uli and I had no problem because we did, as instructed. There must have been ten of us riding at a fair trot and it wasn't long before my thighs started to ache. By the time we reached the other village my whole body was aching, but I was not alone; Uli and Theo were sore too. The whole village was waiting for us and we knew that someone had gone early and had informed them about our arrival.

They had some kind of lunch ready and the usual water pipes. The sons translated again and we could see the astonished faces looking at us. We were not looking forward to the ride back, but we had to pretend as if we loved it.

It was late afternoon when we finally got away we were about 4km away from the road when one of the sons suddenly stopped, and so did the rest of us. He said something to his brother next to him and pointed at something in the distance. We couldn't make out anything, but they could. We changed directions and moved towards the spot which grew bigger the closer we came.

The body of a man was lying in the sandy gravel, hardly moving. We jumped off our camels and followed the others to the body. We could see he was barely alive. While the others tended to the man, the three of us collected some of his belongings. Some two hundred meters away we spotted a small back pack and an empty water bottle. A bit further along we came across a photo bag and a wind jacket with passport and different papers stacked in a big wallet.

He was German. His name was Hermann Gluecks from Duisburg and he was a journalist for the news paper there. What the hell was he doing here in practically the middle of the dessert? We could not ask him because he was delirious and couldn't comprehend anything we said. One of the Boys sat on his camel and the others lifted him up, and walking slowly we took quite some time to reach the village.

It was night when we arrived and the whole village wanted to know what happened. We were told if we hadn't found him he would have been dead by morning. They took Hermann into another tent, covered him with blankets and tried to give him warm water and Maast. The chief told us and his sons that during the day they had a visit from the police who were investigating the disappearance of a German tourist. "He has been missing for two days. He was last seen at the truck depot in the evening two days ago trying to get a lift as far as Shiraz, where he was expected."

Aha! We had noticed police at that place and wondered what it was all about.

We looked through his papers and found letters and hand written Articles ready to post to his newspaper. There was a Leica camera with unexposed films and some clothes which must have been hand washed in Esfahan. We showed all of it to the boys and they translated it to the others. Before going to bed we checked on Hermann once more and were told he hadn't moved much, but he had sipped some water and had swallowed a few small spoons of Maast. "We will watch over him during the night," they said.

How the hell can something like this happen? We wondered.

Life was already in full swing when we got up in the morning. Apparently Hermann had a reasonable night and recuperated well. He looked at us bewildered when we walked in and didn't know where we came from. He was sitting up, but we could see that he was still in shock. He was eating some food and Maast, which was a good sign.

It wasn't that long before a couple of police cars drove up to the village. The Chief and sons walked over and spoke to the four officers and pointing to Hermann's tent. They went in to see Hermann and the sons translated the few words Hermann could speak. One of the sons came out and told us that an ambulance was coming later to pick him up and take him to a hospital in Shiraz.

News travels fast in the dessert, without phones. It turned out that early morning the Chief had sent a couple of men on their camels back to the Truck Depot to report finding Hermann to the Police. It was all out of our hands now. The policemen made some notes of Herman's passport and left after shaking hands with the Chief and with us. By midday a big Army type Ambulance arrived. The driver accompanied by a doctor checked out Hermann. The doctor told us later that Hermann was extremely lucky that we found him last night, because he doubted he would have survived the night. Hermann was put on a stretcher and lifted in to the Ambulance bound for Shiraz. He gave us the Address where we could find him and they drove off in a cloud of dust.

We had been thinking about leaving early in the morning the night before, but with this commotion it was past midday so we decided to stay another night. The villagers were happy for us to stay and put on a wonderful meal in the evening. Next morning after many handshakes and best wishes we departed. They had been so welcoming that it was sad to leave, but we had to keep moving.

We stopped in Marv Dasht only long enough for a small meal, a coffee and a water pipe. It was a busy little town with lots of old historic buildings. We found out it had lots of history because Persepolis was nearby.

It didn't take long to find the University when we reached Shiraz late afternoon. At the Guard house we showed them the letter from Esfahan and were led straight to a large office building. The Principal welcomed us and told us he had already been informed from his friend about our arriving. Well, did we expect anything less? We received the same hospitality as in Esfahan. We offered to speak to the students next day and told him that we'd had another big adventure since Esfahan.

By now we were quite accustomed to talking in front of people and answering their questions. They were very surprised when we told everyone about the Quashqai Tribe and saving Hermann Gluecks. We showed the Principle and some teachers the Address of the hospital and they offered to take us there after lunch.

One of the teachers bundled us into a cab and five minutes later we were at the reception, only to be told, Hermann was gone. What a Bummer we thought.

A side door opened and a official looking Gent walked through and informed us what happened. When Hermann was admitted late yesterday, they kept him overnight for observation. Apparently he did real well, started eating, drinking and speaking normally. He was picked up by a well known religious group called Bahais only a couple of hours ago. They were the ones he was to visit in the first place and they had started the police action when he didn't turn up. The official knew where their Temple was and so did the teacher. It was only a few blocks away, so the teacher said we should walk. This way he could show us some of his beautiful city. As usual the road was busy, but we passed several big Gardens with lots of Palms and other flowering bushes. They were well looked after and beautifully maintained. We passed a Bazaar and several coffee shops until the teacher stopped in front of a three story building.

He told us to enter and look for the German tourist inside. He said he could not go inside with us, because it was not a Mosque, but he would wait for us. This building did not look like a Temple to us, but we walked

Taking a break on the way to Shiraz

Looking at Shiraz from one of the many domed rooftops.

Enjoying the hospitality of our friends in Shiraz.

up a few steps and entered. It was just a normal office building with several doors leading to different rooms. We walked up to a reception desk and were greeted by an elderly couple in European clothes with the woman not having her hair covered. After introducing ourselves, we asked them about the German tourist who was supposed to be here. "Mr Gluecks" they said, "yes, he arrived here yesterday. You can find him one story up." The woman showed us the way, knocked on a room and opened the door.

Well, what a surprise. Herman was sitting at a big table with five or six men in front of him, with notebook and pencil in front. They all stood up when we entered and looked at us as if we were ghosts. It took Herman a few seconds before he realised who we were. When he saw us last, he wasn't quite with it, still half dazed.

He walked towards us and took each of us in his arms hugging each of us in turn. The others shook our hands as if we were old friends, even though none of them had seen us before or knew our names.

On the way to the hospital, the paramedics told Hermann that there were three German cyclists with the Nomads and they were the reason he was alive. There were questions from all sides, because Hermann must have told them about his ordeal, but didn't know anything about us. It took sometime before we could introduce ourselves and explain what we were about. We told them we were staying for a couple of days at the

The Big Adventure

University and were going to talk to the students the next morning. We mentioned that we had a teacher waiting in front of the building to take us back to the Uni. We asked Hermann if he would like to join us with the students in the morning. We were certain they would also like to hear his story.

"I would be delighted," he said and gave us another hug before leaving.

We spotted our teacher across the street outside a cafe, having a coffee, a water pipe and madly waving to us. We joined him and could hardly wait for the pipe. He was very happy when he found out that Hermann was also willing to tell the students about his adventures. It was fairly late by the time we got back.

By 10 am next morning we were sitting in front of a totally full house. Hermann had arrived a half hour earlier accompanied by one of the men whom we had met the day before. Finally we heard his story.

Because Hermann was a journalist and sports Editor of the Duisburger Newspaper, they decided he should cover the Melbourne Olympic Games. Hermann was picked because he was young, adventurous and spoke fluent English. When Hermann mentioned to his Peers, that he would like to go over land hitchhiking, they were sceptical. It took some time before they came to the party. Especially when he told them he could write articles, take photographs about his travels and send them back whenever possible. What a great idea his boss said. Money could be transferred to every major city wherever he may be. Hermann left by train to Vienna and started his journey from that beautiful city. Quite remarkably his travels took him nearly along the same route as ours with one exception. He had money and all the necessary Visas.

On his way he visited different sporting clubs and reported about their activities. He travelled mostly on trains and busses and got the occasional lift from cars and trucks. After leaving the sporting club in Esfahan he got a lift as far as the truck station where he had a meal. He had made arrangements to be in Shiraz that evening and the Bahais were waiting for him. Unfortunately there was no bus or truck leaving in the late afternoon. He decided to take his chances on the road. He filled his water bottle and started walking. Plenty of cars passed him but none stopped.

It became dark and he started to get worried, especially when there was no more traffic and he had no torch to see in the dark. Making matters worse, he had no matches to start a fire. Somehow he got off the road and kept walking on top of some soft sandy soil lit only by a few stars. It was getting very cold and he had to keep moving to keep warm. On top of it he started to get scared not knowing where he was. Not having warm winter clothes, only his wind jacket for protection didn't help much. His backpack and camera bag started to get very heavy and wore him down. After some kilometres he stopped behind a small bush to have a rest. He was tired, miserable and very cold and it got colder. When dawn finally arrived he was close to an ice block and could hardly move.

Herman didn't have any food with him, only a water bottle. Travelling on trains, busses or thumbing a ride there were always places to eat. As soon as he could move his body again, he drank some cold water lifted his pack on his back and started walking. He kept the sun on his left, because he knew Shiraz was in a southerly direction. He walked for hours hoping to find a road, a track, or maybe a Caravan. By late afternoon he was totally exhausted.

He knew another night in the open could be the end off him. Before sunset he lay down between two bushes and went to sleep totally stuffed. He must have slept for some time, because when he woke he was in solid pain. He was really frightened, knowing he might not make it through until morning. He kept rubbing his body as much as he could to keep warm and after a few hours, dawn came ever so slowly. He had a drink from his bottle and noticed that that it was nearly empty. With no food and water he knew the end was near. By then the sun started to warm his body enough for him to start walking again. By midday he was dehydrated, having finished his water hours earlier. He started to become delirious and dropped his camera bag, his backpack and then his wind jacket. He walked a few more meters, laid down on his tummy and went to sleep.

This was how we found him a few hours later. The rest we knew.

Hermann was a very good speaker. His English was so much better than ours and being a journalist he had no problem telling his story. The teachers and students were very excited and the handshakes were endless. Hermann also took some photographs of us talking. He informed us that the Bahais are organising a roast lamb on the spit in one of the big Gardens and wanted us to be their guests and stay a couple of nights with them. We mentioned this to the Principle and he was very pleased for us. We packed our bikes and thanked the people for their hospitality and followed Hermann and his companion to the Bahais.

There was plenty of room at the Temple and lots of hands helping us with our gear. We were put in with Hermann and it was only now that we got to know each other properly. He wanted to know all about us and made lots of notes as we spoke. I must say, he picked up surprisingly well, after the ordeal he went through.

Hermann was guest of the Bahais because he already had been in touch with them in Germany. He researched some of the interesting and news worthy people of the countries he was going to visit. He had written to several sporting clubs and different religion nominations and had many addresses to visit people.

It was beautiful and warm walking down the street, following about 10 people towards one of those big gardens. When we arrived, there would have been at least 40 to 50 people, including some women busy arranging tables and chairs for a big feast. They all shook hands with us and as usual we had to answer lots of questions. They had a whole sheep on a spit roasting on a fire place attended by a couple of guys wearing white aprons. Some made salads and others were busy arranging a selection of dips, bread, fruit and sweets. It all smelled fantastic and we were starving. The sheep was taken off the spit and placed on another large table.

Someone handed us a bottle of cool Pepsi Cola and begged us to help ourselves to the food.

Easier said than done. There was no cutlery, and we had to use only the right hand! It was difficult at first, but watching the way the others did it, we soon got the hang of it. You had to tear off a small piece of the bread, hold it between the fingers as you ripped some meat off the cooked sheep. After dunking the whole lot into a dip you just shoved it into your mouth.

We loved it and enjoyed ourselves immensely. Uli and Hermann took photographs. Hermann needed them for his paper. Whilst fruit, sweets and tea were served one of the guys mentioned that they would like to take us to Persepolis in the morning. The ancient city of Persepolis was only about sixty km north/west of Shiraz and two hours by car.

We would be happy to go there and thanked them very much. It was just on dark by the time we got back to the temple and retired to our room. We had lots to talk about, we wanted to know about Hermann's future plans and he wanted to know about ours.

As soon as we finished breakfast the next morning, we boarded a small bus which took us to Persepolis. The bus belonged to the Bahais and one of the guys we met yesterday was driving. We drove about an hour back along the same road which we had done on our bikes and turned at the sign post to Persepolis, which was only a short drive along an unmade road.

What a site! Persepolis was once the capital of Persia, 2500 years ago. It was destroyed by Alexander the Great. It sent shivers down my spine standing in such an old place that had been at its prime, long before Jesus was born. It was Gigantic! Workmen with small shovels were clearing away debris, meticulously unearthing old artefacts. It was easy to imagine how civilised people lived in those days, and having constructed a city like this was amazing. They had no cranes or machines and had to do everything by hand. We walked for hours through only a part of those ruins and saw maybe ten percent of it. I could have stayed there a week and not seen everything. It was well after midday when we boarded the bus to take us back.

We had another great feast in the packed dining room at the Temple. Knowing that we were leaving in the morning, the guy who drove the bus approached us with a Pepsi in his hand. He told us that he was leaving for Esfahan in the morning to pick up supplies. If we wanted, we could travel with him as far as Eglidabad.

"That would be great," we said. It meant that we didn't have to cycle this stretch twice.

We wanted to go straight to Kerman from Shiraz, but to get there we had to go via Yazd. Hermann had arranged to stay with the Qashqais for a few days to thank them and could be dropped off also. Again we had to say goodbye to some wonderful people next morning. The driver knew exactly where to drop Hermann, being very familiar with the Qashqais. And what a huge reception we got when the driver stopped in front of the tent village we had been in only a few days earlier. Just about every one swarmed around us patting us on the back, shaking hands, smiling, laughing... Hermann hugged the Chief and his sons who were so pleased to see him fully recovered. In the blink of an eye food was served as well as Maast so we had to say awhile before hitting the road again.

Herman shook hands and hugged all of us. I swear there were tears in his eyes as he said goodbye. "Good luck. I'll see you in Melbourne, at the Olympics."

Yep we thought, if we can get the bloody visa!

It was late in the Afternoon when once more we arrived in Eglidabad where the driver dropped us in front of our Police Station and wished us well. The police were delighted to have us stay overnight again and looked after us the same way they had before.

It took us about three hard days and two very cold nights sleeping in our tent to reach Yazd in the afternoon of the third day. There we were shown to a house where a German Doctor and his wife lived. Surrounded by the usual noisy onlookers, we knocked on the door. A woman opened up, looked at us and with big eyes closed the door again. We looked at each other shrugged our shoulders and wanted to turn our bikes around to leave. Suddenly the door opened again, this time by a man, and standing behind him was a different women. They both looked at us strangely. They probably thought, "What the hell is going on out there?"

It didn't take long for their faces to light up, when they found out where we came from. They begged us to enter and spoke to the onlookers which dispersed waving.

"What about our bikes?" we asked.

"Bring them inside."

Most of the private houses we'd been invited to all had a closed in court yard with a domed roof over it, with the rest of the house built around it. This was the same. There was a hole in the roof so the smoke from the fire below could escape.

The Doctor, a Surgeon, and his wife, who was a Gynaecologist, were in charge of the Hospital. They came from Köln and were employed by the German Government for a number of years. They had both had just arrived from work and were surprised to hear the knock on the door.

After tea and some food, they wanted to know all about us. They mentioned that about two years earlier they had a German cyclist staying at the hospital for a couple of nights. We asked if his name was Heinz Helfgen. They said yes. Only after we showed them our book and postcard could they believe that we met King Faisal and of course The Shah and Queen Soraya.

The discussion led to our health and they were horrified when they discovered that we had no World Immunisations documents. We wouldn't get far without having proof of being immunised. It was decided, that we should stay as their guests for a couple of nights. The housekeeper who opened the door at first prepared a room for us, adjacent to a bathroom and hard to believe, a European water closet. We could hardly wait to use it and have a hot shower after!

Supper was served on a table, not on the floor. Uli and I were served a cool German beer and Theo his Pepsi. After a good clean up and a big breakfast next morning we accompanied them to the hospital, ten minutes drive in their car.

Journey of a Lifetime

A huge crowd near the entrance to the city of Yazd.

Theo and me with some of our new friends in Yadz.

The Big Adventure

Myself and Theo trying to appear casual in Yadz.

The usual crowd attracted by our arrival.

Yazd was a fairly big town, clean with beautiful Mosques and old buildings. The traffic was choc-o-block as always.

The hospital wasn't huge but was very busy and surprisingly clean. We had to wait for a while in the doctors' canteen, whilst they had to do their routine round visiting patients. He in the male section and She in another building with the women. We were served tea and some small extremely sweet cakes. One of the waiters told us that the Yazd sweets are the best sweets in the whole of Persia and we thought he really meant it!

After an hour or so our Doc came back by himself with three small booklets in his hand. He informed us his wife had to perform an operation on a child. Now he was going to operate on us. Each of us received three or four injections, Cholera, Smallpox, typhoid and one other. Each of them were entered in the documents, signed and stamped by him, after we had written all our particulars in them. He told us that without those documents we would get problems in Pakistan and no way of getting in to India. We couldn't thank him enough and promised to keep in touch.

We did send them a letter from Melbourne and received one back, telling us that their time in Yazd would finish in six months.

Theo and I were sore the next morning. Our arms ached where the vaccination had been inserted and we felt feverish. The doc suggested we stay another day, to monitor us. It was the Smallpox which gave us the problems, but after some extra medicine, we felt much better so we hit the road the following morning.

We had to purchase tinned food in a Bazaar close by, because we were told that the road to Kerman was lonely and tough. Apparently we were not far from the infamous Salt desert of Lut and the road to Kerman ran parallel to it. The road was not bituminized, just graded and one of our worst roads so far. I think it was over 300km to Kerman and very lonely, with only a few poor villages along the way. Even the truck and Bus stations were longer distances apart. The nights were still cold, but as soon as the sun came up it got warm and we could shed some of our clothes.

After a couple of days as we got closer to the desert, cycling started to become very uncomfortable. Apparently the Lut is one of the hottest places on earth and with an easterly wind blowing from the side, our mood wasn't the best.

Kerman was close to the borders of Afghanistan, and Pakistan.

It was the Capital of the South Eastern Provinces. There was a large Army and Police Outpost there as the town was well frequented by smugglers and bandits.

After three days in the saddle we were stuffed, by the time we got there. About one kilometre before the city all traffic in and out had to stop by a boom gate where it was searched by Police and armed Soldiers.

Exactly what we needed! It must have been nearly an hour before it was our turn to be searched. The welcome wasn't very friendly until they looked in our passports and saw that we were Germans. To this day it amazes me how our German nationality opened doors for us. Instantly their attitude changed. They didn't bother to search our luggage and we were told to follow a couple of policemen to a big tent. An imposing man in Army uniform, with medals on his chest, got up behind his desk and greeted us. We told him all about us and he was certainly impressed with our achievement.

Uli went outside to get our book to show him the photo of our Minister, and once he saw the medals from the Shah and Queen Soraya, he was even more impressed. He said something to the two policemen who accompanied us and instantly they disappeared. It wasn't long before we were served bread, dips, fruit and the usual tea. The officer must have noticed that we were extremely tired and made a couple of phone calls. A short time later two soldiers turned up and the officer spoke to them and they saluted. He told us that those two soldiers would drive us to a hotel in town for us to stay. We were guests of the Army and were welcomed in Kerman until we recovered.

By this time it was getting dark as evening descended and we were happy for the accommodation and couldn't wait for a soft bed. The officer said he would like to show us around Kerman next day and would pick us up around lunch time. It wasn't the best hotel in town, but it was like the Hilton to us! The two soldiers dropped us of in their small army truck and some servants were already waiting for us to help with the bikes and luggage.

One big family room on the ground floor was all we needed and without any more to eat we hit the sack. At daybreak Uli woke me with some Maast in his hand for breakfast. Theo was just getting up also and said he was feeling much better. There was a toilet and a wash basin along the corridor, which I quickly visited. I was badly in need of a wash to get rid of the desert salt and dirt. Uli had already enquired about getting some of our well worn clothes cleaned, which had to be done urgently.

As promised, the officer and another younger man picked us up exactly at midday. The young one was his son, about Uli's age and spoke fluent English. They had a big chauffeur driven Buick waiting outside and we felt like Kings. Actually, this was the first time in Persia that we had the pleasure of being driven in a private limousine. Kerman seemed to be more neglected and poorer than Isfahan, Shiraz or Yazd. All the women wore black and were totally covered from head to foot, but the men wore lots of different suits and robes. Every one could tell which tribe the others belonged to. Many heavily armed Soldiers and Police patrolling the streets because, the young son told us, "There's a lot of crime in Kerman with different gangs fighting each other to control the smuggling. Being so close to their neighbours, it was hard to safely guard the borders."

The few Mosques we saw and the Town hall were well looked after, as were some public gardens. The Bazaar was no match to those in the other Cities we had seen, and it smelled different. Apparently lots of opium was smoked in every coffee shop. We also had to watch out for pick pockets. There was only one stall where we could find some postcards and stamps.

We visited a big Mosque where father and son did their prayers amongst hundreds of others, whilst we admired the architecture. After finding our shoes again, we were taken to the centre of town to a classier restaurant for an early dinner. Celo kebab we ordered, to the surprise of our Hosts. We had to tell them all about Teheran and the club where the owner told us that they served the best Celo in Persia, and they smiled at that because everyone maintains that their Celo Kebab is the best. It was getting dark when they dropped at the hotel and our host informed us that he would pick us up in the morning to take us to the outskirt of town. Apparently there was another check point we had to go through in order to leave and he didn't want us to have any problems. Our washing had been done and all we had to do was service our bikes for the next challenge. After writing a few postcards home and Theo a few lines to the Paper, we hit the sack.

Getting out of Kerman was the easiest exit of any city so far. We were escorted by the Army! By the time a small truck covered with a tarpaulin pulled up early morning, we were ready. There were four of them. Our host sat next to the driver and two soldiers jumped from the back to help with our bikes. All wore uniforms and the crowd of onlookers got bigger

Uli and Theo with two of our benefactors in Kerman.

Trying to look relaxed, Theo is leaning against the wall while Hermann is squatting down in front of Uli and me... on the way to Kerman.

by the minute. I guess they all thought we must have done something wrong.

Less than a kilometre past the edge of the town was another boom gate where busses, trucks and cars coming in were being searched. We stopped next to the gate. Our bikes were unloaded. Our Host wished us well and told us to be careful, because the road to Zahedan after Maha was not the best. He handed Uli an envelope with a signed document to show someone if we got into difficulties. What a guy and what about these people? Unreal!

We planned to make Maha after lunch, because it was only about 40km from Kerman. We had barely travelled 10km when Uli had a flat tyre and we had to pull off the road. It would have to be the back one, yeah. We had to unload his luggage to fix the tyre. Uli's bike had thinner rims than ours copped more punctures.

It got hotter by the minute with the sun overhead and there was no shade. But the puncture was fixed and the bike reloaded and off we went again. It was late afternoon when we finally reached Maha, a very small town. We headed straight for the police station.

What a Bummer, no one spoke English, except for one word Passport. We handed them over and Uli opened the envelope and showed one of the policemen the document. As soon as he read it he told his mates and the crowd around us who we were and with expansive gestures he invited us in to the station. They helped us with the bikes and luggage and asked us to sit on a bunk along one wall. Tea was served and within minutes a tribal Chief holding his prayer beads in one hand entered. He spoke fluent English. He asked us the usual questions and translated them. Uli showed them our book and medals and the welcome was sincere.

Sleeping at the police station was no problem but cycling to Bam and on to Zahedan could become a big problem. We had to take the risk we told them, because we had to get to the Olympics and this was the only way to reach Pakistan.

They understood what we had to do, but told us we should go to the Bazaar around the corner to get more provisions because there would be nowhere we could get anything until we got into Pakistan.

It was still daylight when we walked to the Bazaar accompanied by two policemen. We carried our empty sleeping-bag bags and filled them with tinned foods, dried bread, and oranges. We each bought an extra canvas waterbag. Someone mentioned that we should buy a tropical helmet, because the heat could get unbearable. We took their advice and purchased one each and put them on. We burst out laughing when we looked at each other and so did the mob. We looked pretty stupid at first, but it was the best thing we could have bought. This was about the only time we had to spend money in Persia, except the bus fare in Hamadan and a bit in Teheran. We really hung on to our hard earned dollars.

After some bread and fruit for breakfast the next morning we waved good bye to all the well wishers and headed south. We soon discovered the value of our helmets when we reached the open road. For the first time we cycled in shorts and short sleeved shirts.

It was more than 160km to Bam and we had in mind of doing more than half of it today. But with the easterly wind getting stronger and the road near impassable, we couldn't do more than 15 to 20km an hour. We encountered road works every 2 or 3 hours usually with a Grader smoothing the hot desert sand to create the semblance of a road. The road was flat and so was the land, but in the far distance we saw big mountains looming. What bothered us most was the wind, pushing a lot of salty air towards us which made us very thirsty.

We rode for hours without talking very much. My mind was blank as I concentrated on pedalling evenly. And then the inevitable happened. Uli had another puncture!

We were told that on the intersection to Bandar Abbas there was a rest station. We had tried to reach it, but not now. We moved a fair bit off the road to stay the night and whilst Uli fixed his flat, Theo and I erected our tent. By the time we finished there was just enough daylight left to open some tins and eat some bread before it got dark.

We still had to sleep in our sleeping bags because it was very fresh at night. Next morning, Theo and I took some of Uli's luggage to make his bike lighter, hoping that with slightly less weight he would not get any more punctures. 20km further on we came to the roadhouse where we could fill our water bags and rest a little.

Had we turned right we would have finished up in Bandar Abbas on the Persian Gulf. Bandar Abbas was a big port where most of the Persian produce, especially Oil, was shipped across the world.

Had we not bought those helmets I think we would have been in serious trouble from sun stroke. Our caps from back home would not have helped us at all. We reached the mountains and got out of that miserable wind, but we had some climbing to do. The road was better because it had solid foundation. In Bam we again stocked up with supplies because Zahedan was 300Km away and there was virtually nothing until then.

After 10km out of Bam we made camp again. We had seen the old ruins just off the road on top of the hills; great castles made of dried rammed earth bricks maybe 2000 years old. Over the years, whenever we talked about our journey, we regretted not staying an extra day to see

these ruins. Had we visited these ancient ruins, which became a world heritage site, we would have been some of the last international visitors to see them intact. In 1982 or 83 an earthquake destroyed more than eighty percent of them.

We had the road to ourselves except for a few heavily overloaded busses and trucks. Out of the mountains the wind became a problem, because we headed in a north easterly direction. It hit us half front on and it was hot and extremely dry. It sucked the moisture out of us making us feel absolutely miserable and worn out. Funny enough, we were happy when we got into some more mountains, for relief. Just before one of those mountain ranges we came through a small village and did not stop.

Half a dozen vicious dogs snarling and barking ran at us and tried to bite our legs, and then a horde of badly dressed kids ran next to us attempting to grab our luggage. To top it all off, some very agitated men shook their fists at us. We were scared to even think about stopping and pedalled faster so we could get through the village as quick as possible. As tired as we were, our leg muscles worked overtime and carried us out of danger. We couldn't work out what would cause that hostility. Perhaps they'd had bad experiences with strangers? Maybe they were a village of bandits? We just got out of there as quick as possible.

Later, looking at our map we thought we could make Zahedan in three days, but the way we were going we knew an extra day would be needed. We set up camp in the mountains out of the wind. We pushed as hard as we could the next day hoping to reach a road house, but it was too hard and once again, windblown and stuffed, we slept in the open just off the road,. It took another three hours next morning to reach the roadhouse where people stared at us as if we were a kind of desert apparition. We hadn't washed since Mahan and probably did look like ghosts. Except if we had to have a crap we washed our bum with some water, the same way as the locals, using the left hand.

It was nice to relax at the roadhouse with some tea, Pepsi cola and smoking a pipe. Had it not been for the bloody wind blowing sand all over the road we would have made Zahedan by night fall.

Then the same thing happened as yesterday. Riding through another village we again encountered the same hostilities. We rode like hell to get out of there.

A few kilometres later I got one too! I nearly crashed because the front tyre punctured and I almost lost balance. Just what we needed! a flat tyre to be fixed at the mercy of the wind. Luckily it had not happened close to that last village...

There was one more mountain range to conquer before Zahedan. We didn't know then that this would be our last night sleeping in our tent in Persia. We made the mountains next morning and saw Zahedan in the far distance, surrounded by mountains. It was just as well, because we were very low on water and looking forward to a good clean up.

Again we encountered a boom gate and passport control. We didn't mind, because there was someone there who could speak English. We were treated as we had been in Kerman, especially after we showed them the document from the Army Officer who had been so kind to us. After the customary tea we asked for directions to the police station. We would have been offered a lift, but it was only about 3km to travel. One of the policemen jumped into a jeep and we followed him into town.

We still had to travel slowly because of people all over the place. The street was not very wide and all the mud brick houses were built along the road with no footpath. Eventually the road got wider and the houses more modern with shops and coffee houses. There were more police present in the station than in other towns, maybe because of being so close to the borders of Pakistan and Afghanistan. Two or three of them spoke English and translated our story to the others. We asked about a hotel and our route to Quetta next day.

There were only three hotels in Zahedan and all of them very busy. They offered to find out which one would have vacancies for three nights. No we said, "We only want to stay one night and get going next morning".

It was then that they informed us that we had to travel by train —the train which goes all the way from Zahedan to Quetta in Pakistan— because, "going by road is far too dangerous."

Only about twenty cars are allowed into the Baluchistan province, which extends from Persia into Pakistan, at any one time, and those had to be escorted by police. The train only ran once a week on a Wednesday.

Well, so much for that! We would have to follow their advice, and take the train.

They quickly found a room for us in a hotel not far from the station and after thanking them for their assistance, one of the English speaking officers escorted us there.

Two blocks past the town square was the hotel, if one would call it that!

It certainly was a very old double story building, erected from handmade packed earth bricks. There was a small foyer with one desk, but a couple of men were already waiting for us at the front to help us. They had been informed by the police that we were on the way there. The hotel was bigger inside than we expected and fairly cool because of the bricks.

We asked the officer if he could find out the cost for three nights and were pleasantly surprised at the price.

"If we had not arranged it from the police station you would pay double the price, or more, if you could get a room."

We told him we would come to the station tomorrow and thank them once more.

The room was quite big, with three bunks and enough room for our bikes. One of the personnel spoke English and he showed us where we could wash and where the toilets were. If we needed anything, "just come to the front desk," he said.

We headed for the washroom, stripped off and soaped ourselves from head to toe. After rinsing off we put on clean shorts and tee-shirts. Even as tired as we were, we felt newly born. There was a jug of drinking water in the room. We opened two cans of fish and had that with some bread for dinner and then hit the sack. It was supposed to be a three star hotel, but although that seemed dubious, to us it was heavenly, much better than our tent or sleeping in police cells. There was a small dining room where we had some breakfast, which was included in the price. At the desk we handed them our dirty clothes and there was no problem getting them washed for the next day. We also asked where we would find the train station.

Zahedan was not a big city, but it was still a fair walk to reach the station on the outskirts of town. There seemed to be more life than in Kerman and it was more cosmopolitan. We saw people from Pakistan as well as Afghanistan, even people from India. The police had warned us to be careful of pickpockets and not to be enticed by anyone to step into back alleys. There were lots of bandits and smugglers in town. We were also told not to smoke pipes unless in public places.

The railway station was something to write home about, not like ours in Backnang. It wasn't big, a couple of small buildings surrounded by an open space with one track leading east towards Pakistan. There were people all over the place trying to enter one of these buildings to get tickets to wherever they needed to go. There were whole families resting in makeshift shelters, screaming kids and covered women holding and feeding babies. There seemed to be as many beggars as there were people wanting to buy tickets, and they pestered everyone. There was no way we could stand in this queue, which was really a mob rather than queue, to get tickets, nor could we find out how much it cost.

We decided to go back to the police station. They welcomed us with tea and sweets and wanted to know how we liked Zahedan and the hotel. "Great," we said enthusiastically, and thanked them once more for looking after us, "but now we have a problem." There was no way for us to find out the cost of the train fare, because the queue was enormous and nobody spoke English. Of course we told them we were short of money and had to save as much as possible.

"You we should visit the Mayor at the city hall," one of them suggested. "Maybe he could help?"

The Town hall was only across the square and was the highest building in town so one of them walked over to inform the Mayor about us.

"We have to get our book and a couple of cards first," Theo told them. "We will be there within an hour."

Walking was tough in Zahedan; every few meters, someone wanted to us sell something, opium, gold, or they wanted to entice you into one of those opium dens. Beggars also followed us asking non-stop to give them some money. We ignored them and kept our hands in our pockets where our passports and wallets were.

Exactly after an hour later we walked into the town hall and were greeted by the same officer and a couple of middle aged, bearded, long robed men. They looked fearsome, but had smiles on their faces when they greeted us. They both spoke English and asked us to follow them after they shook hands with our officer who left.

At the end of a short corridor one of them opened a door for us to enter. It was a big office occupied by two men standing in front of a huge desk, scrutinising us as if they were expecting the Shah himself. One was dressed like the other two, long robe, black beard and head covered with a silk scarf .The other one was clean shaven in a blue immaculate uniform with lots of medals on his shoulders and chest. They spoke English and the uniformed one even spoke reasonable German. They knew a bit about us from the police, though we still had to introduce ourselves and tell them about our travel so far.

All four, listened intensively and were totally surprised when they found out how we met the Royals. We showed them our book the medals and handed them a card. We had them shaking their heads and now and again we got a tap on the shoulder. It wasn't long before Tea and some food was served. The uniformed guy was a high ranking officer in the air force, in charge of it and civil airports. The other one was the chief minister of Zahedan and the surrounding province. The reason, that the uniformed one spoke German was because he spent one year studying with the German Air force near Frankfurt.

We had a great time with those people and finally one of them asked what they could do for us. Theo told them about our problem at the railway station not being able to get a ticket. Then he (Theo) let go and told them that we are also in financial trouble, because we had spent too much of our reserves in Persia. Naturally they wanted to know why this was the case. Theo told them that in Persia people couldn't read the Arabic writing on the back of our cards, plus there were not enough newspapers that could pay for our story. Finally he told them if it wasn't for the great hospitality of the Persian people he doubted that we would have reached Zahedan.

I can't remember if I shed a tear or not, but as it turned out Theo was totally convincing. The four of them spoke for a few minutes in their own language and nodding their heads we were told not to worry, everything will be taken care of next day. One of the guys we met first asked if they could invite us to their club for dinner, which we happily agreed to. After some vigorous handshakes and thankyous we left. A driver was going to pick us up from the hotel later on. We walked out as if in a trance, not believing what happened.

"Like they say, open your mouth and tell people who you are and what you did. Luck will come your way". All my life have I done just that!

We walked across the square and entered the police station to tell them the outcome and they were very pleased. At the hotel our clothes had been cleaned, ironed and laid out on one of the beds. We had time to relax for a while before being picked up and could discuss our good fortune so far. Uli and I congratulated Theo for the superb way he told those men about our problems. We had just enough time to write a few postcards for home before there was a knock on the door. It was the same policeman who walked us to the town hall earlier on. Apparently he was told to escort us to the club, which was a ten minute walk from our hotel.

Behind the Town hall was a small park, surrounded by some Villa type buildings, old, majestic and well looked after. It certainly was the more exclusive part of Zahedan. Our policeman friend walked towards one of those Villas which had an armed guard in front of the entrance. After saluting to our escort and us he opened a big door and waved us in. We entered a large foyer and were greeted by one of the bearded men from the Chief's office. He exchanged a few words with our friend and shook hands with him. We thanked him and told him we would call at the station in the morning.

The Big Adventure

There were lots of different nationalities, men and women dressed in their native costumes. We stuck out like "Dog Balls" in our Knickerbockers and runners. Just about everybody glanced at us and wondered from where the heck we came. The bearded one led us into a big dining room where most of the tables were occupied. The Air force Officer we met earlier got up from one of the tables and walked towards us. He was not in uniform but wore a beautiful tailored suit, white shirt and tie. He greeted us like old friends and led us to their table where we were introduced to two beautiful women and another two men.

One of the men was the other bearded one from the office, the other one was European. It turned out that the women and the other man were English. They were in Zahedan to visit the women's sister, who was married to the Air force Officer. All eyes were on us, but we were used to that and took little notice.

The English couple were fascinated by us and our story and were astonished to hear that we met King Faisal as well as the Persian Royals. Tea and different dips were served and someone asked us if we had a special wish for dinner. We told them our favourite meal in Persia was Celo Kebab which we had first tasted in Teheran. I must say the Celo Kebab here was just as good as our first one back in Tehran and we got stuck into it as if it was our last one. We didn't realise at the time that it was our last one!

It was another successful evening and it was late by the time we had to say good bye and thank everyone. We were escorted by all of them to the front door and they wished us luck. How they did it I still don't know, but by the security guard a policeman waited to guide us back to our hotel.

One of the bearded men asked us if it was possible for us to be at the town hall by ten in the morning. We asked why and were told the Chief would like to farewell us. "We would love to be there and to meet him once more."

It was really good to have a police escort to the hotel at that time of night. We would have been pestered by all those drug dealers and pickpockets otherwise.

With all that excitement and a full belly of food it took some time to fall asleep. Early next morning we walked straight to the police station to have breakfast with the officers and to tell them about last night. At 10 am we stepped into the Chief Ministers office and were greeted by at least 5 or 6 more well-dressed men in different robes all wanting to meet us and shake hands with us. About two hours later we walked out of the

Town hall with smiles from ear to ear. The chief minister had written a few words in our book, while the others watched. Uli took some pictures, I was handed what looked to be Railway tickets, and Theo received an open envelope. We were told that those tickets would take us as far as Quetta and the money Theo was holding was Pakistani currency.

We couldn't thank them enough and shook hands all-round and promised to write when we reached Melbourne. We felt like celebrating and stopped in the main street for a water pipe and fruit juice. Eyes were all on us and we felt like we were sitting on needles, anxious to count the money in Theo's pocket! But we didn't want to do anything like that in public. As soon as we got back to the hotel we discovered different notes in Pakistani money. Uli said if we could change it in Teheran we would get around three hundred US Dollars.

It was like winning a lottery! We wrote a few more postcards home and took them to the Police station for them to post for us. We also wanted to spend more time with them, because they were great. We told them all about this morning, the people we met and showed them the tickets, but did not mention the money.

Why the train didn't get away before two in the afternoon was not surprising. It was like a circus, with all the yelling, screaming and pushing people around. Children were crying, dogs barked, and luggage was thrown in through open windows. Sheep, goats, rabbits in cages and chickens with legs bound together with string were mostly guarded by women and young boys.

The smell was horrendous! It was very warm and we only wore shorts singlet and open short sleeve shirt. Our financial pouch was secured behind my belt and our passports we had in our pockets. We did have another two very pleasant surprises in the morning.

After our clean up in the morning and some breakfast came the first one. We had just packed and were helped by the staff, when about five of the policemen entered. They told us the bill for the hotel was paid by all at the police station. We didn't know what to say. That had been totally unexpected.

The second one was that two of them were to accompany us to make sure we got away okay. They made sure our bikes and luggage were stored in a secure goods wagon at the far end of the train. We took our important stuff in our sleeping bags and we always had our book, some cards and our medals by our side. Because of the police we were placed in the

Standing with our travelling companion beside the train that took us from Persia into Pakistan, just beyond the Pakistan border.

Hermann met us again at Galangur when the train stopped. It was certainly a surprise.
He had travelled in a convoy with a group of soldiers and he interviewed many local tribespeople for the newspaper he worked for in Germany.
He boarded the train with us and came all the way to Quetta. In Quetta, he went straight to his newspaper contacts and left us to find our own accommodation.

first wagon behind the steam locomotive.

It was a long train and absolutely packed, with people hanging out of the doors.

We also noticed a single wagon in front of the engine and thought it was empty. We found out later it was laden with building materials. We noticed the policemen talking to the locomotive driver and some of the personnel, pointing towards us.

Finally the whistle blew and we were on our way. We waved back until Zahedan was out of sight. The train headed towards big mountains in a north easterly direction.

You can't imagine the noise from the people and animals in the overcrowded carriages, plus the smell and high humidity without having experienced it. It was a blessing that all the windows were open, but some had no glass at all. There were no seats, just two bunks opposite each other seating two adult persons. We had to share one with a young man dressed in what looked like a night gown and certainly in need of a clean.

During a stop, taking a break on the wagon in front of the locomotive.

The Big Adventure

He was friendly enough, always talking and gesticulating. The only thing was, we couldn't understand a word he said!

Travelling at a low speed the train stopped after about an hour. We had reached the Border.

What a mess! We had never seen anything like it.

Firstly no one was allowed off the train. Each door was guarded by two armed security personnel. A custom officer motioned us to take our belongings and follow him into a small building. Our passports were stamped and then we were taken into another small building to get them stamped again. The first one was still Persia, the next one Pakistan.

At the Pakistani customs, we got a big surprise, they all spoke English! I find it hard to describe the surroundings outside. There were people everywhere, stalls all over the place with women and kids trying to flog their goods. On the other side off the train track was a whole nomad village with camels everywhere. Beggars pestered us as we walked back to the train. We jumped up on the wagon before the locomotive; we were curious to see what was in it. There were steel girders, bricks, bags of cement and piles of wooden frames stacked neatly on top of each other. The beauty about it was we could easily walk around the pile, two a breast. The top of the pile was covered by tarps, with several of them lying loose on the floor.

We looked at each other and without a word climbed down and walked back to the locomotive. One of the drivers spoke English and when we asked him if we could stay there in front, he smiled, shrugged his shoulders and waved his hand towards it.

What a relief! With the tarps rolled up and our sleeping bags on top, we even could make some kind of sleeping arrangements. While I looked after our belongings, Uli and Theo went shopping. They came back with loads of oranges, dried bread, dates and a few bottles of Pepsi. With the last of our Persian money they brought a whole carton of Lucky Strike cigarettes and what they had left over they gave to some of the beggars.

Three hours after we had stopped the train started up and we left Persia, heading towards a new frontier.

"Pakistan, here we come! Will you be as hospitable as the countries we left behind?"

It was still hot, even with the sun just about to set. With the slight breeze in our face and clean oxygen pushed down our lungs we felt fantastic. I watched the sun dip below the horizon and suddenly it went dark. It was almost like someone had turned off the light switch, but we didn't mind, because there was no pollution and we could nearly reach up and touch the stars. We ate some fruit and bread, pissed over the side and after a couple of smokes tried to go to sleep. What a day this had been. It took me a long time to digest it all, before I finally dozed off.

Some hours later we woke up when the train had stopped at small town. It seemed a lot of people were getting off, and they took their animals with them. Men holding oil lamps walked along the track yelling and gesticulating while it looked like a whole group of women were doing the hard work of controlling the animals. They quickly got clear of the tracks as the train started to move. It didn't stop again until daybreak, this time at a slightly bigger place called Nok Kundy. We climbed down onto a kind of platform and couldn't believe our ears, everybody was speaking English. Everything on sign posts or posters was written in English and underneath in Arabic.

We felt good knowing that we could be understood by most of these people. On one of the buildings was written Toilets and we headed straight for it. The cubicles were fairly clean, because everyone using them used a water hose to clean the hole. There was also a small water fountain were we could wash our hands and face. Nobody took much notice of us; they were too busy doing their own thing. That gave us some peace to have a smoke while we waited for the train to move again. It was still early, but the sun already started to burn down. We made a knot in each corner of our handkerchief and used it as a hat. The fireman in the engine had to work overtime to keep the steam up, because the poor old Locomotive had to slave its heart out to pull the heavily laden train slightly upwards, through some very rugged country. We certainly crossed some wild country. Even the more open plains seemed to have an upward slant. Once or twice we saw a long line of camels in the near distance, a caravan heading more or less in the same direction as the train. Sometimes the line tracked along mountain ridges where far below we saw raging torrents, snow melted rivers. Once we crossed a bridge and there was nothing either side of us. The sides of the train obscured the narrow bridge underneath, and if you looked out the window all you could see was mud coloured raging rapids hundreds of metres below. God help anyone who fell off the train here. There were still people half hanging out of doors. There were even some sitting on the roof guarding their luggage.

We travelled for hours before we stopped again in a huge valley adjacent to a village which looked relatively clean. Entering the valley the train passed through fields of freshly sown vegetables and a multitude of small fruit orchards, with lots of people tending them. Some people got off in this village but lots of wooden crates of dried fruit for the Quetta markets were loaded on.

While this was happening there was plenty of time to chat to the locals and consume some tea. We were also served some dried bread that almost looked like savoury biscuits. We wondered what all the tiny red specks in the centre were. Well we soon found out; one bite and we almost choked. My breath caught in my throat and it felt like something had hit me on the head, but from inside. It took quite a few minutes before I could breathe normally again, before my eyes stopped watering. The red specks were super hot dried Chilli. It took several glasses of water to wash away the burning sensation in my mouth.

Eight years earlier Pakistan because of religious differences, being Muslim, had separated from India which was not. And because there was another large Muslim population on the eastern side of India it too separated. The two became East and West Pakistan, with India in the middle between the two parts. East Pakistan finally became a separate country, Bangladesh. They had been for many centuries a part of India and their cuisine was hot, just like in India: Crikey, we did not expect this.

"We could die of hunger." We told them.

Someone said, "You could stick to fruit, boiled rice and eggs."

"I suppose, "Theo said, "as long as we tell them to ease back with the chilli."

Fifty kilometres along that rich valley we stopped again. More boxes were loaded on and a few relatively clean, middle aged men accompanied the fruit. Travelling through those mountain ranges the temperature dropped quite a bit and we felt comfortable. We had enough food and drink to last till Quetta and thanks to the people in Zahedan, lots of Rupees. The next night we had to sleep inside our sleeping bags, because it became a bit chilly as the train got higher into the mountains. Just before day break when we stopped at Dalbandin, a small town. A lot more people got off and on with much talking and yelling, pushing and shoving; it was almost like a big party, and on top of that it was a great feeling for us to hear so much English being spoken. Not that our English was good, but at least we could understand them. As soon as the sun came up we saw some Minarets in different spots, as well as lots of traffic. ...and the toilets at the station were again not too bad.

There were a couple of Ford Taxies waiting for customers and many rickshaws. To our surprise, there weren't many beggars on the platform. Maybe most of the people had something to do. *Yep, they had something to do all right; trying to sell us just about anything under the sun!*

They pestered us more than the Persians, because most of them spoke English and knew that we could understand them. After some tea, fresh fruit and a water pipe, it was time to get back on the train.

According to our map, we travelled east-north-east along the Afghanistan border at a hair-raising speed of about 40km an hour. The train travelled through the State of Baluchistan, of which Quetta is the Capital. Baluchistan is also the province in Persia just over the border and most people of this area didn't recognize the border which divided them. Perhaps that was one of the reasons there was so much smuggling going on between the two countries.

Out of the mountains it became warmer and we were glad about the nice breeze in front. Before nightfall we had stopped a couple of times at small villages to unload goods. During the night the train stopped once more. We couldn't see much, but the yelling of the workers unloading and loading was deafening. They had to work with oil lamps, held up by elderly men.

The sun was burning down on us, by midday, when we reached a small town called Nushki. Four big trucks were waiting to be loaded with various machines as well as crates of weapons and ammunition. It took hours before we moved again. We had ample time to smoke a couple of pipes, drink a few freshly pressed orange juices and talk to the locals. It was close to midnight by the time we reached Sheikh Wasil, a small place where we stopped only a short time. We were on our last leg to Quetta and were getting tired of train travel. During the night we still moved slower as it climbed uphill. Quetta must be well above sea level

A camel train in Quetta.

The Big Adventure

we assumed. Finally we reached Quetta early in the morning. Embedded in a big mountain range, (at 1500 Meters) it was cooler than we had expected. The sun was shining at its best, but being so high up we had to change into long pants.

Several hours passed before we could get hold of our bikes and luggage, but with help from a couple of train personnel we succeeded. We had to push our bikes into town. Push! that's right! There was no way of riding a bike in this City, walking was faster.

Our first impression of Quetta was favourable. We couldn't judge by the traffic because it was the same as in all the other larger towns and cities. But the whole atmosphere was different to Persia. Somehow it was cleaner; there was no rubbish on the streets and the lovely old buildings were well maintained. The footpath on each side of many streets was covered with stalls selling all kind of goods, mainly vegetables, different fruit and juices. There were also stalls selling dried fruits and hundreds of different spices, most of which we assumed would be super hot, and for us inedible. The smell of the spices and other foods was fantastic, only spoiled sometimes by oil and petrol fumes from the road. The road from the station led right into the middle of the city to a big park surrounded by a huge roundabout. We were told that we would find hotels in all of the streets leading away from the roundabout.

I find it hard to describe the people around us, most of them dressed in different tribal costumes. There wasn't a European women to be seen anywhere. We couldn't work out why women dressed differently? Some wore blue dresses reaching to the floor, with Burkas over their heads. They could see only through small holes or a narrow slit at eye level. Others again wore black. The men also wore different clothes, their heads covered with a kind of turban. Their robes were mostly grey or black. All tribal men grew big beards and carried guns on their shoulders, with awesome looking knives tied to a belt around their waist.

The biggest and most pleasant surprise we encountered was everybody spoke English!

Not long ago, Pakistan was part of India where for many years the British ruled, which of course explained why everyone spoke English as well as their own tribal languages. English was how people from different areas communicated with each other and with foreigners. We felt great! If Pakistan turned out to be as friendly as Persia, we should be relatively safe.

We only had to push our bikes a short distance from the centre, when we spotted a sign reading Hotel in English and Arabic. We headed for it and I waited at the Entrance watching the bikes while Uli and Theo checked out the scene. It took some time before they emerged and I was happy to see them. By this time I was surrounded by a lot of inquisitive people of all ages. I had to answer heaps of questions. They all wanted to know where we came from and where we are headed. Again I couldn't help seeing how friendly they became when I told them we came from Stuttgart in Germany.

Uli and Theo came out and joined me. "The man in the reception told us there was a much cheaper hotel further along the road," Uli said.

"They said we should try there," Theo said.

"It may not be such a nice looking place as this," I said. "Why don't you go inside with our travel book and show it to the manager? Maybe they will give us a discount."

"Brilliant!" they both exclaimed. They both went back inside carrying the book and about five minutes later came back out with big smiles spread across their faces.

"Yes! They dropped the price to the same as the one they said was down the road. Half the price they asked for first."

Well, with that sorted out we had our first stay in Pakistan. We got one room on the ground floor with four beds loaded with blankets. Our bikes were locked in a store room and for our luggage we had plenty of space in our room. It wasn't a huge hotel, but slightly upmarket and very clean. Down the corridor was a big room with toilet cubicles and next to it a room with showers, it seemed only for men. I didn't see anything for women. By the time we unpacked, had shower and shave, the first since Zahedan in Persia, we felt great, but tired. It was now late afternoon and we were quite hungry, having eaten all of our fruit and leftover bread on the train in the morning.

Clean cut and freshly dressed we walked out to inspect the surroundings. It was late afternoon and as the sun started to disappear behind the mountains and it became a little coolish. There were lots of little eating places full of people, but also some better looking Restaurants. We picked one and were welcomed by a man, dressed in European clothes. He led us to an empty table and handed us a well worn menu, which we could read. Of course there was no Celo Kebab, but other rice dishes which seemed okay. A waiter approached and to our surprise asked if we wanted some beer, which Uli and I accepted. Naturally Theo asked for a Pepsi. There were mostly men in the restaurant with just a couple of tables occupied by families. They kept looking at us, but with smiles on their faces.

Uli and I were served English beer which was flat and barely cold. We did not complain and only had the one glass. Theo ordered his Omlette Nature, without onions. Uli and I picked a rice dish with grilled lamb.

And then came the shock! With the first mouth full we nearly choked!

We had never experienced such hot food before, I mean chilli hot!

We called the waiter and he arrived in an instant.

"Are you trying to poison us?' I asked. I was still having trouble catching my breath, and I hadn't even swallowed that first mouthful. I had spat it out into the serviette.

"But the food is perfect," the waiter said. "It is the same everywhere."

"Everywhere?"

"Yes all over Pakistan, India too."

"We'll never get to Melbourne if we have to eat this stuff," Uli said softly to me.

The waiter shook his head, astonished that well travelled gentlemen like us had never eaten food with chilli before.

We would starve to death before even getting into India!

"Could we have some plain steamed rice?" I asked the waiter. "With no chilli, okay?"

"Certainly," he said and headed back towards the kitchen.

"You should order an omelette next time," Theo said. "It tastes quite good and it doesn't have any chilli in it."

The waiter returned within moments with two large bowls of plain steamed rice which we mixed in with our food to dilute it. By the time we had finished we each must have drunk a litre of cold tea. A dish of fresh melons with pieces of orange followed which helped to cool our mouths.

When we got the bill we were surprised to see the two glasses of beer were more than all of the food the three of us had ordered. Even so it was very cheap and we were happy with that. Back at the Hotel we told them of our Hot experience and they grinned from ear to ear. "You should always tell them to put less chilli in your food," the manager said, "or even none, though that may be difficult for them to understand."

We followed his advice for the rest of our journey.

It had been a big day and we were stuffed. The long journey on the train with broken sleep left its mark. Hitting the sack was well earned and almost instantly we were sound asleep.

Waking up after our first night in Quetta. The only way to get around was by rickshaw, wearing our new helmets.

We must have slept for a long time, because the sun was up and the street outside was very noisy. Uli was up, dressed and sipping a glass of hot tea. Theo and I washed, got dressed and did the same. We decided to stay and rest for one more day, before hitting the road again. Breakfast was served in a small but clean dining room. We ordered pita bread with pieces of grilled lamb, but made sure without chili.

We asked about what interesting places there were to see and were told to go to the Information Office just up the next street. There we met a Mr Hajeez Javed, a very friendly uniformed elderly gentleman who was pleased to help us. A few moments later to our surprise, Hermann appeared. How he knew where we were I had no idea. Mr Hajeez was delighted to hear our stories. We showed him our book and he was overjoyed to write a few words in it. He served us tea and told us he would arrange a small taxi bus to drive us around Quetta for a few hours at no cost to us. He suggested we stop at the Bazaar to buy ourselves a tropical helmet, because we would be traveling into very hot weather.

The driver who could speak English was told where to take us and afterwards to bring us back to this Office. Quetta is surrounded by high mountains and in the distance most of them were covered with snow. We passed a couple of Mosques, lots of old Mansions, English style and even a church. The streets were very busy, filled with big American and English cars, heaps of cycles, donkey carts and people carrying big loads on their back. We passed a few nice established parks and lots of houses with beautiful gardens. There were different fruit trees in blossom and we could see the English influence wherever we looked. After an hour or so, the driver stopped in front of the Bazaar and told us to take our time. He pointed to a small parking place where he would wait for us.

The Bazaar was big, but nowhere the size of those in Istanbul or Teheran. People around us were staring and smiling, but we still kept our hands in our pockets; one never knows! It wasn't long before we saw a stall selling hats and headgear, including tropical helmets. It was a bit of a circus trying on different sizes with all the people laughing and gesticulating. Hermann had fun selecting the helmets for us to try on. We had to laugh at ourselves also, because we looked absolutely hilarious with those big helmets on. The shop owner took a marking pen and put our initials on the inside of each helmet. We probably paid too much, but it did seem reasonable for what we got.

Passing a row of stalls, we stopped at a small eating place and ordered some fried veggies, fried rice and pieces of grilled lamb. When we told the waiter to make sure we don't get chilies in our food he looked at us surprised. "We are not used to hot chilies," we told him and he understood. When the food came it was still a bit hot, but healthy. It came on one big tray, served with piles of pita bread and we had to eat like the locals with our hands. After tea and a water pipe we felt blessed.

Our driver was sound asleep by the time we got back to the small bus, but was instantly awake when Uli opened the door. Back at the Information Office, Mr Javed smiled when he saw us with the helmets on our heads. "That is the most practical purchase for your journey ahead. Pakistan and India can be very hot, the sun very intense." He told us while he served us more tea and also mentioned that we should make sure to take plenty of food and water supplies on our way, because we would travel long distances between shops. We thanked Mr. Javed for his hospitality, shook hands, and went outside with Hermann to catch rickshaws back to the hotel. Herman didn't get out but waved goodbye to us before disappearing into the traffic. We wouldn't see him again until we reached Melbourne.

We took the advice given, and with empty sleeping bags under our arms we walked outside to do some shopping. We bought tinned sardines, camp pie, pita bread and plenty of dried fruit, especially apricots and dates. There were tinned baked beans, corn and peas, a carton of American cigarettes to make sure we don't run out of smokes, and packets of matches and batteries for our torches.

Back at the hotel we had a pleasant surprise. Several men were waiting for our return. Amongst them was a reporter from the newspaper and a photographer, who took some photos of us. Hermann had arranged this. The dining room was packed, noisy and full of smoke and everyone wanted to hear our story. The reporter took notes as we told our story and all of them were listening intently. One of them invited us and all the others there for dinner at the hotel later that evening. We never found out who that Gentleman was, but we had a fantastic evening together, and Quetta stayed in my memory to this day!

We still had time tafter dinner to service our bikes and started packing the heavy stuff. We were itching to get on our bikes again, so it wasn't too late when we finally hit the sack, but it took some time to digest what had happened during the day before we fell asleep.

After a good breakfast in the morning we were told that someone from the evening before had organised a small truck to take us out to the open road. To top it all up, the manager of the hotel informed us with a big smile from ear to ear, that we were guests of the Hotel and the news paper and didn't have to pay a single rupee.

Out of town we waved goodbye to the driver of the small truck as he turned around to head back into Quetta. On our bikes again and peddling south, we felt great, but also sad, having to leave this wonderful city and its people behind.

The road was reasonable but very busy and we had to keep eyes and ears alert, especially when riding past fully laden trucks and overloaded busses. We were hoping to make it as far as Mastung, about 50Km south, but with all the extra provisions we had to peddle very hard, especially climbing up steep, winding roads. We made Mastung early afternoon, but did not stop, continuing on towards Khudstar.

We travelled through beautiful valleys and open plains surrounded by massive mountains. Some very fast moving rivers with pristine waters from the snow capped mountains had to be crossed. With about 70 kilometres to Khudstar, we found a secluded spot of the road to put up camp.

All by ourselves once more in the middle of Pakistan we felt as if we were starting all over again. Collecting wood for a small fire was no problem and the tent was up in no time. By the time we boiled some water from the river and heated some tins of food it was dark and cool. Sleeping in our sleeping bags again was a bit uncomfortable, but we quickly got used to it.

It was still chilly when we got up next morning to discover that Uli's bike had a rear puncture. No big problem, whilst Theo and I packed up camp, Uli mended the tyre.

Towards Kalat, 80 kilometres ahead, we came out of the mountains and on to an open plain where the sun started to burn. Our helmets were

The Big Adventure

a Godsend. The wide rim shaded our eyes so we didn't have to squint even though we wore sunglasses. The wind was behind us and we made good headway. Passing through a couple of small villages with truck depots we saw Camel Caravans a good distance off the road. We kept riding until early afternoon and we arrived in a very small place called Kalat. Chasing away dogs and small kids we stopped at the centre to find a place to eat. There were only two places where we saw people sitting outside eating and drinking tea. We picked one and leaned our bikes against the wall so we could keep an eye on them because there was the usual mob watching.

We were served well, especially after we told the waiter we did not want chilli in our food. We were served our beans which we gave them, with some pieces of their lamb and steamed rice. After a water pipe and some tea, we hit the road again and headed towards Khudsdar, 160Ks south. We felt great and having the wind still behind us we didn't stop till late afternoon, to put up camp.

I think this was the last night we slept in our sleeping bags, until we reached Melbourne.

We started to wear shorts and short sleeved shirts because the further south the lower the altitude got and the warmer and more humid it became. We stopped momentarily in a big village called Surab to get some pita bread and a couple of small water melons. We still had lots of tinned food but nothing fresh. 20Km after Surab we made camp off the road again. We slept on top of our sleeping bags with our clothes on.

We arrived at Khudsdar, a small town late the next afternoon and had a big surprise. Riding towards the centre, dodging through the traffic, a big Chevrolet passed us and someone waved and begged us to stop. Two well dressed middle aged gentlemen in suits got out from the back and walked towards us. We had never seen them before, but they greeted us as they would old friends.

We soon found out why. Apparently they had spent a few days on business in Quetta and had read our story in the newspaper. They were surprised that we had gotten this far so soon and wanted us to follow them into town. We followed their chauffeur driven car until they stopped in front of a big building surrounded by groomed gardens. One of the gentlemen turned out to be the Mayer, and the other had big factories making concrete agricultural pipes. They asked to be their guests and would arrange to put us into the Hotel opposite.

How about that! A similar thing happened to us once before where a hotel owner had read our story a few days earlier. By the time we pushed our bikes across the street people were already waiting to take our luggage and our bikes. It was a nice hotel, nowhere as big as in Quetta, but very clean and with lovely personnel. We were given two rooms on ground level, one for Theo with enough room for our bikes and the other for Uli and myself.

The Mayor told us they would like to pick us up as soon as we freshened up, because they would like to show us their town. After a good wash, shave and putting on long trousers, we were soon ready and jumped into a waiting car. The car was driven by the same chauffeur as before. He had been told to show us the nice part of the town and bring us to a certain restaurant afterwards. It turned out to be a very busy and prosperous little place. A big Mosque stood out with lots of worshipers in and outside; we saw a small Bazaar of shops, a fairly large school and many old English mansions. On the outskirts was a small Industrial area with some big brick buildings containing engineering, auto repair and mechanical works to be done. Adjacent to it was a huge place full of concrete pipes, which the driver told us belonged to the other gentleman. It was getting dark when we were dropped off in front of a nice old building next to the Town hall.

We were greeted by a couple of waiters who led us into a dining room full of guests. There were also women there with their hair covered, but looking great. The Mayor came towards us and introduced us to his wife, children and some of the other guests at his big table. The other gentleman was also there smiling as he pointed to his two sons and one daughter. His wife was very attractive also. Naturally they all spoke English and we had no difficulties answering all their questions. It was another successful evening and after Uli let them know that we couldn't have too much chilli, we finished up having a great meal. Before we were escorted to the hotel, the Mayor told us, he and his friend would join us for breakfast at the hotel in the morning.

Like most times when we stayed in a hotel, we never got away early. By the time we sat on our bikes, it was close to midday. One good thing about it, we ate as much as we could fit in to make sure we didn't need anything until the evening. On saying goodbye with many handshakes and well-wishes we finally hit the road. At the breakfast table, the gentleman had informed us that he has another concrete place in Bela and he would ring the manager there to look out for us. We told him that because we got away so late, it would probably take another two days before we got there.

It was harder than we thought. Travelling south we had to put up with a strong westerly, which became very uncomfortable, especially on the open plains. It took us the rest of the day to pass through Wad, a small town 60 kilometres south of Khudsdar. A bit further on we spotted a broken ruin that looked like a disused factory situated next to a small river and out of the wind. It was the best place to erect our tent and make a small fire. We slept well in the tent but woke up early with the heat of the sun. We didn't mind starting early because we wanted to cover a fair distance towards Bela, which was still about 150Km further on. The wind was acceptable, not as bad as the day before. Except for a few smaller mountains to conquer we were in a relatively good mood.

About 40 kilometres on we came to a small village with a Truck and Bus Roadhouse, where we stopped for a bite to eat, but the going got harder the further south we rode. Not because of the busy roads, no, it was because it got hotter as the day progressed! Still, we must have covered close to 100 kilometres before we made camp late afternoon.

By midafternoon the next day after we had stopped at another roadhouse, we arrived at the outskirts of Bela and true to the Gentleman's word; a small pickup truck was waiting for us on the side of the road. Two smiling middle aged men dressed in overalls greeted us and lifted our bikes and luggage on the back of the truck. There was only room for one of us in the cabin so Theo and I jumped on the back and let Uli make friends with the two fellows.

Bela was not as big as Khudsdar but just as busy. It took a long time before we got through town and stopped in what looked like an industrial area. Uli informed us that we were offered the use of a Guest apartment next to the office at the small cement factory in front of us.

Entering the office, a big man dressed in white robes, full headgear (we thought he was a Sheik from a desert tribe) and a long grey beard greeted us as if we were his sons. It turned out, that he was the partner of the nice Gentleman from Khudsdar and was happy to have us as his guests. He led us from the office down the corridor, opened a door and bade us in. What a great surprise again. The room was sparsely furnished but very clean, with two big windows facing towards the big mountains. There were three beds around the room and a small table in front of the window, laden with fruit and flat bread. Another room next to it had two beds with our luggage on top and our bikes leaning against the wall. Further down was a shower room and toilet. "Just what the doctor ordered." Theo said.

The Sheik told us we were welcome to stay and rest for a few days. We thanked him very much for his offer, but had to decline. We told him that we had a long way to travel and we didn't know what lay ahead.

There was a big fan hanging from the ceiling and we had it on low all night otherwise it would have been impossible to sleep with the heat and humidity.

After the morning's prayer, we had breakfast in the Sheik's office. Being at the southern end of town, we hit the open road not long after. We gave the Sheik one of our cards and he in turn gave Uli an envelope and told him to open it during the day. It was something from him and his partner in Khudsar.

It was already getting hot early in the morning. We travelled south through open plains, but mountain ridges on both sides kept the temperature a bit cooler. Karachi was approximately 160km away and we expected to reach there in a couple of days.

Following a swift flowing river south we soon left the mountains behind and hit open plains. Near a small village at a Roadhouse, next to the river we stopped for a meal, followed by a water pipe and to satisfy our curiosity about the envelope.

Uli opened it and what a surprise; 3 brand new $100 American notes inside a folded letter. Actually it was two letters, one for us and the other to a cement company in Hyderabad which was a partner to them.

The letter for us stated that we had been very welcome in Khudsard and Bela. If Allah was willing they hoped that our path would bring us one day to be with them again.

The other letter was a recommendation to the chief of the factory to make us welcome when we get there. This was the second time we had such a surprise, the first one had been at Baqubah.

We felt like dancing, but there were people everywhere and the Roadhouse was packed. I think if we hadn't already come more than 40 kilometres we would have turned around to thank them. When we hit the road again we hardly noticed the heat, we were on a HIGH.

As far as we could see, there was farmland with many small farmhouses not far off the road. Following the river south we eventually stopped next to it under some shady trees and bushes. The river had widened considerably and we were told that we were nearing the open Arabian Sea.

The Big Adventure

We rested for several hours, before setting off again to cover a few more kilometres to bring us closer to Karachi.

We had covered at least 90 kilometres before dark and slept on our un-erected tent half covered by our sleeping bags. Just at daybreak next morning, after a bit of a wash at the river's edge and a bite to eat we hit the road.

We had covered quite a distance before the traffic got so bad that it was difficult to manoeuvre through it. We encountered an astonishing scene, never in our imaginations thought possible; camel, not horse drawn trailers, fully laden with goods filled the streets. Most of them were making their way towards the big city, ever so slowly. We passed donkey drawn small trailers while dodging stray sheep and dogs. By midday the heat was too unbearable to continue so we stopped at a Roadhouse and had a few Pepsis and a couple of pipes to pass the time.

We had thought to make Karachi by evening, but had no hope getting there. We found a small spot under a few trees off the road and had an uncomfortable few hours of sleep. Up Early again next morning we headed south-east towards Karachi. Under normal circumstances we would have covered the 30 Km left into town in well under 2 hours, but not on this jam-packed road.

On the outskirts with about 10 kilometres to the centre, crossing over some water channels for irrigation, we asked for directions. We were told, there was a YMCA not far from the inner city. By noon, the heat was nearly unbearable, but we had no choice but to keep moving on.

Someone told us to take a rickshaw or taxi, as a joke, but it gave us an idea. We stopped and asked one of the rickshaw riders if he knew were the YMCA was located?

"Of course no problem," he said, "not far from the Town hall."

Uli asked him, "Can you drive in front of us to create a space in which we can follow?"

He nodded with a smile and told us how much it would cost.

Uli said it was a bit too much, but we agreed on the price.

"We'll pay half now," Uli said, "And the other half when we get there."

We knew he charged us double, but the amount was very little in the first place, so we were happy to pay. We would have had great difficulties finding our way otherwise, but following him was great. We didn't have to ask every ten minutes which way to go and got there much quicker than it would have taken us on our own. He stopped in front of a big stone building with the letters YMCA written above a huge doorway. Uli paid him and with a grin all over his face he waved us good bye.

Finally we had made it to Karachi! What a great achievement!

We felt so proud of what we had done. Had we really thought it was possible when we were back in Backnang?

I think we did, but there was always the uncertainty of whether in reality it was possible. But we tried never to think of that in the negative, and just kept pushing on to see how far we could get.

We had certainly surprised ourselves; for we were now in Karachi, a very long way from home.

Streets in Karachi. Beggars and homeless speople were a common sight.

Camel drawn wagons were something we had not seen before.

The Big Adventure

Uli and Theo went inside to check if we could stay there while I stayed outside with our bikes. Karachi was a huge metropolis and very busy and smelly. We didn't draw the usual crowd as we did in smaller cities or villages. I guess in such a big place people had too much to worry about themselves to bother standing around and staring at us.

It wasn't long before Uli and Theo came back out with the good news that we could stay there. I was happy to get out of the heat and into the cooler building with its thick walls holding out the worst of the heat. It was a triple story ancient building and it definitely smelled like it, but we certainly didn't care. We were happy to find somewhere to stay!

There was a reception desk with one guy sitting behind it with another talking to Uli. On the ground floor towards the back we were led to a big room with 6 single bunks in it; room for us and the bikes. The bunks only had a single mattress without sheets on them, but that was okay because we covered them with our sleeping bags.

The YMCA was two streets away from the Town hall and the General Post office with all the Embassies nearby. The building was half occupied by students from all over the world involved in Archaeology and History. The cost to stay for a few nights was minimal, but we had to eat outside because there was only a small kitchen to prepare limited amounts of food. The main thing for us was the shower and toilet rooms which we used instantly. It had been a long hard day and we were stuffed! After a small bite to eat we hit the sack and enjoyed a relatively cool night's sleep. Next morning after another shower we got ready to explore Karachi.

With all our important papers, passports and money hidden in pockets around our bodies we walked out into the Oven!

Did I say Oven? Well I meant it!

It was hot and steamy with a strange smell coming from all the car fumes, mixed with all the animal odours and crap in the streets. It didn't take us long to become accustomed to the smell and after a bit we ceased taking any notice of it. We tried to fit in as best we could. Karachi was a fascinating city, the Capitol of Pakistan and one of the most populated cities in the world. Situated on the shore of the Arabian Sea, it has an extremely busy harbour and with a westerly breeze blowing now and again, the city gets well oxygenated with humid sea air. There were people everywhere, footpaths full of stalls selling just about anything, the streets full of trucks, busses, rickshaws, fully laden donkeys, men pushing wheelbarrows and heaps of camel drawn trailers.

We got directions to the Post Office and headed straight for it. We were anxious to get there and were looking forward to receiving our long awaited mail. Finding the poste restante counter took some time because it was as crowded inside as the streets were outside but with people, not animals. We eventually collected our mail and walked back through the crowded streets to the YMCA.

We were very happy about the news from home, from our parents, our friends, and relatives. I even got a letter from my aunt Marie and Uncle Peter from Philadelphia. Apparently our picture with a small paragraph about our travel had been in the Readers Digest. Karl informed us that Konne had left Backnang on his bike to follow us.

We considered if we should wait for him to catch up, but then realised anything could happen and he might never do it, and we would miss getting to Melbourne in time for the Olympic Games. We decided to go on without waiting for him to catch up.

We found out later that he got as far as Baghdad and ran out of money. He worked for 12 months in Basra before turning back.

We took several hours to digest all the news. It was still early afternoon, so we decided to visit the Australian Embassy which was not too far away. It was even hotter by then and we were glad to step into the cooler reception office of the Embassy. They had several ceiling fans circulating the air with big photographs of the Queen and Prince Phillip hanging on the wall. After letting one of the guys know that we wanted a tourist visa for Australia he led us into another empty office and asked us to sit down. Five minutes later a well dressed gentleman entered and introduced himself as assistant to the Ambassador.

He was very interested in our travels and after looking through our book and our cards he thought it was a great achievement. He asked how much money we had in cash and we told him about six hundred US Dollars and some local money. He took our Passports and left the room. We looked at each other smiling hopefully and thought maybe this time we would have no problem getting our visas.

We had to wait quite a while before the door opened and the guy entered with a sad look in his face and told us "no go."

He apologised for the bad news, but could not do anything about it. "If it was up to me..." he started to say but didn't finish.

He had discussed our predicament with the Ambassador, who refused on the grounds that we didn't have US $700.00 each for leaving Australia.

After being on high spirits earlier, we were now down-hearted.

After this let down, we were doubtful if we would make it to Melbourne. At least we knew that we had to get more financial by the time we get to New Delhi where we could try again.

Using a rickshaw was always the best way to get around.

After a bite to eat and a couple of pipes at a nearby eating place we felt better.

By that time we had made our plan to visit some companies which had their offices nearby. We walked back to the post office, bought some postcards, mailing paper and envelopes. Back at the YMCA we sat down to reply to the mail received earlier.

On our ride into town yesterday we had noticed Companies like Siemens, Ford, AEG (where I did my apprenticeship) BP, Dunlop, Philips and others. We were of course hoping to talk some of them into 'donating' or giving us funds to sponsor us on part of the remaining journey. We made a list of the firms we recognised and asked the guy at the YMCA desk if he knew any of them and how far they were from here.

He knew all of them and searched for their addresses in the phone book. After writing each address separately on a sheet of paper, he advised us to use a rickshaw to take us around. By that time it was late afternoon, so we decided to go to work early next morning.

By 9.30am we were ready to visit Siemens, which was first on the list. Getting a rickshaw was easy, because they were all over the place racing each other to get a fare. It was hard to squeeze the three of us into one of them for, but we managed. We only travelled about one kilometre when we stopped in front of a big office block with Siemens written in big letters on top of the building. We paid the Rickshaw guy and told him if he wanted to wait, we wouldn't be too long.

Even though it was early it was already hot and walking in to a fan cooled office felt good. We took our helmets off and introduced ourselves to the guy sitting at the front desk, He was a Pakistani, well dressed in European clothes and very friendly. He made a couple of phone calls, scribbled a few lines on a piece of paper, which he handed to some guy with our card and our book and led us into another room that looked like a conference room with a big round table in the middle and at least 10 or more chairs around it. He begged us to take a seat and ordered some tea for us from a servant who had followed us.

"If you can wait here for a few minutes, someone will be down shortly to see you," he told us. "Please enjoy the tea."

When he left we looked around and found to our surprise large framed photographs of scenes from Germany hanging on the walls. There was Bonn, Berlin, Hamburg, Frankfurt, Muenchen and several more. But of course there was none of Backnang.

We had barely finished looking at the photographs when the tea arrived accompanied by a plate of small cakes. Behind the man with the tea and cakes two Gentleman followed. One with a big black beard was dressed in Arabic clothes, the other, clean shaven, wore a cream suit, black shirt and black bow tie, and was carrying our book and card.

They shook our hands quite animatedly. They had both glanced through our book and wanted to talk about our journey so far. The clean shaven one introduced himself as N.H. Mustafa, the Manager of Siemens Pakistan and the other was his Assistant. Theo as usual went through the book with them, whilst Uli and I answered some of their questions. We were told that for the first three weeks in February they had the Director of Siemens accompanied by three Board members here on a visit. Had we been in Karachi at that time, we would have been able to meet them.

What impressed them the most was our meeting King Faisal in Baghdad and the Shah and Queen Soraya in Iran. They could barely hold back their smiles when we boldly told them that we were going to meet their President Iskander Ali Mirza. There was no doubt in our minds that we would be able to do that.

Eventually they asked us where we were staying and if they could be of any help?

Exactly what we wanted!

Theo explained to them about our difficulties with the Australian Embassies, and not being able to get a visa because of insufficient funds. "We are visiting companies like this, like Siemens, to see if they would be able to sponsor us with a small donation."

"That could be arranged," Mr Mustapha said. "But first we would like to invite you to a restaurant where we can talk some more."

Standing up to move out the room, Uli suddenly stood and pointed at the photographs on the walls. "They are beautiful pictures," he said, "but I am a bit disappointed."

I couldn't believe what I was hearing; I saw the smiles falter on the two company men.

We all stopped walking and looked at him.

With a grin from ear to ear he said, "Why is there no picture of Backnang up there?"

Mr Mustafa laughed. "I don't know that place. But I would be happy to hang a picture on the wall with the others if you could send one to us."

With that settled we headed out for lunch in a place that was very much to our liking; a beautiful upmarket restaurant right next to their office building. We couldn't have found better hosts than these two guys.

We loved the food, (not hot for us) and after lunch we all shared a big pipe with 5 mouth pieces and Turkish coffee. Walking back to the office afterwards we noticed our rickshaw guy was still waiting for us. He waved happily and we waved back.

Back inside the Board room Mr Mustafa wrote in our book in English, and Mr Johw wrote in Urdu as well as Arabic and even translated our names in Arabic. We must have spent a couple of hours there before we started to say goodbye and thanked our hosts for a great day.

"Before you go... hang on a minute," Mr Mustafa said. He walked out the door but was back two Minutes later with an opened envelope for Uli to take out the contents.

I could see Uli's face changing when he pulled out a whole wad of US Dollars.

"Why don't you count it," Mr Mustafa told him.

The notes were $20 and $50 dollar Bills, and in total added up to US$320.

Each of us in turn shook their hands and hugged the two company men. We didn't know what to say for a moment.

Mr Mustafa told us that they sponsored Cricket and Hockey Clubs and it gave them great pleasure to help us out a little also. Well, we couldn't believe our luck. They asked us to visit them once more before we leave, if it was possible and we told them 100%.

We caught our rickshaw back to the YMCA, where Uli paid the fellow a small amount of Annas extra for waiting.

Back in our room we sat on our beds contemplating what had just happened.

Theo said; "Look, even if we don't get the Australian Visa, we should keep going as far as we can. We know how to hold ourselves above water," an odd reference for Theo who actually couldn't swim or hold himself above water.

"Yes," Uli said, "one thing is for sure; nobody from Backnang has ever come so far as us."

"That's for sure. We should keep going on," I agreed.

With the visa problem out of our mind for the moment and a couple of pipes to smoke outside, we felt much better. We decided to visit Philips Electrical of Pakistan LTD., the next morning.

I don't know if the rickshaw guy slept outside all night, but he was there waiting for us the moment we stepped outside. Again he was happy to take us wherever we wanted to go.

The Big Adventure

Philips was in Bunder Road, only a few streets away. The building was a bit disappointing, not half as impressive as the Siemens building. The sign on top was big and we thought it was the Dutch Philips Electronics Company, but it was not.

Nevertheless we walked in to a rather big but half empty office, and greeted the guy at the front desk. This time we weren't given anywhere near hospitality we had received the day before at Siemens. He waved to a guy sitting at another desk by himself who came over and introduced himself as the coordinator and public Officer. He didn't seem too interested in what we had done, but still wrote a message in our book and pulled a handful of notes from a draw and handed them to Uli. He seemed too busy to talk much, because he abruptly shook our hands and wished us good luck. On the way out he called out and told us to visit Eastern Automobiles LTD. not too far up the road. "Maybe they could help you more. They also distribute German cars."

Our rickshaw guy knew where to take us and we got there in less than fifteen minutes. On the way there, Uli had counted the money and it turned out to be Rupees equal to about DM 50.00, Great!

Walking in to the car sales office was like walking into a beehive, with people moving about and chatting to each other. One European dressed guy noticed us and asked if he could help us. Theo told him who we were and what we are about to do. His eyes lit up and told us to stay put he would be back shortly.

We must have looked rather funny standing near the front door, in shorts, short sleeve shirts, half boots and holding our tropical helmets, book and camera. Several women and children walked by looking at us with lovely smiles. We were about to turn around to go back out when the guy arrived and asked us to follow him in to a huge showroom full of brand new cars.

There were all kinds of American cars as well as European cars. In a nearby office we were greeted by about half a dozen differently dressed men. The one in the middle was introduced as Mr I. Balsuren, the General Manager. He greeted us warmly and so did the others.

"Sorry about the delay," he said. "You caught us right in the middle of filming a commercial. The place is a bit chaotic at the moment."

We were told the film crew had gone, but the radio personnel were still here. There was a huge table of different food, hot and cold beverages and lots of fruit. The guy we first spoke to must have told Mr Balsuren a bit about us and it turned out that he was extremely interested in our journey. He closed the office and begged everyone to take a seat, grab a plate and help themselves to the food.

Mr Balsuren was full of smiles, especially when he found out that Backnang was so close to Stuttgart. He had been there several times, doing business with Daimler Benz. There was dead silence when we told our story and then there were questions thrown at us from all sides. The biggest surprise came from the Radio personnel who invited us to their studio next morning for a live interview.

"We are looking for sponsors to help us financially" we made a point of telling everyone. When Mr Balsuren saw what Siemens had written in our book, he wanted to know "How much did they help you with?"

"It was a pleasant surprise but they gave us US$100," Uli told him.

"We can match that."

"Fantastic," Uli said and thanked him very much.

The Radio people were about to leave after asking if we could be at the station by 10am the next morning. They gave us their address. Mr Balsuren wrote in our book, signed it and put the company stamp under it. We shook hands with the rest of the guys and thanked Mr. Balsuren once more for his hospitality. Walking towards the front door there were now only a few people left in that office, quite a change from before.

We had a feeling our rickshaw fellow was waiting and sure enough there he was half on the footpath. Theo and I were happy and patted Uli on the shoulder for telling Mr. Balsuren. Siemens paid us one hundred rather two hundred Dollars. We thought it was very diplomatic of him to do so. We now had quite a substantial sum of Rupees and that meant we didn't have to change any Dollars.

Before going back into the YMCA, Uli showed the rickshaw fellow the address of the Radio station. "I know where it is," he said with absolute surety. "It will take 30 minutes to get there from here."

"Can you be here at 9am tomorrow?" Uli asked him, and gave him some more Annas.

"Of course, I am at your service."

Moving through the traffic next morning was a nightmare and it took close to 45 minutes to get to the station. On the way we passed the Town Hall, which we wanted to visit, to meet the Lord Mayor later in the afternoon. Arriving at the Studio several men greeted us (two of them we knew from the car sales office) and escorted us upstairs into a kitchen and dining room.

"We've scheduled the interview 11:15 but wanted you here earlier for

The Big Adventure

preliminary talks," one of them said. "We need some background material so we know what to ask."

A small breakfast was served and questions were asked and answered while one of the men took notes. The program was scheduled for 45 minutes in one of the soundproof rooms along the corridor.

We mentioned that we passed the Town Hall on the way and wanted to visit the Lord Mayor later and we also wanted to try to meet the President if possible.

"No need to go to the Town Hall," we were told. "The Lord Mayor is in hospital at his home town in Rawalpindi. And President Iskander Mirza is not at Parliament House either. He is at his private residence just outside town."

One of the guys told us that they would be able to help us arrange an audience with him.

That would certainly be fantastic.

The interview went very well and all were pleased with the outcome.

The phones didn't stop ringing all morning but just before we left one of the guys told us a Mr. Bugtani wanted to invite us to his place, called the *Mexicana Bar*, only a few streets away. He had listened to the whole program and wanted to meet us. We shook hands all round and were told as soon as they could get an appointment with the President they would let us know.

We told our rickshaw man that we would walk to the *Mexicana Bar*, but he could pick us up there later. It was a fairly long walk, even taking a short cut through a well groomed park with palm trees and different flowering bushes. People congregated under the trees trying to get a bit of shade. Across the park was a smaller street with old but well looked-after stone buildings and one of them had *Mexican Bar* displayed prominently above the entrance. There were tables and chairs with big umbrellas on the footpath, but without customers because it was too hot. As we entered through the doorway, a tall man immaculately dressed greeted us with a big smile. His head was covered with masses of black hair and he also had a big black moustache. The radio people had already told him that we were on our way to visit him.

We followed him inside past a reception desk into a big dining room full of patrons. Every seat was taken with people having lunch and smoking pipes. There were families with small kids and women with their hair covered, some even with burkas. There was lots of noise and the whole room smelled of food and stale smoke. Walking through another door we went down a couple of flights of stairs into another world!

The big room was fully lit, relatively cool, but beautifully furnished. On one side was a Bar occupied by a barman mixing cocktails and serving drinks. The rest of the room had some large tables with chairs and numerous small ones in front of comfortable looking couches for two. On every wall expensive oil paintings and photographs of important people were hung. The floor was carpeted, except for one big polished wooden square in the middle. We found out later that they had many belly dancers performing and nights were always booked out. One of the big tables was occupied by five gentlemen, three dressed in Arabic clothes, the other two in suits.

Mr Bugtani introduced us to them and begged us to take a seat. The table was already stacked with food and drinks and much to our surprise we were offered some beer which Uli and I accepted happily. By this time we became more fluent in telling our story to so many different people. Every day we learned a few more words and if one of us was lost for one, the others took over, like a well oiled machine! We felt great, being treated so well by people who only knew us through the Radio. Actually there were a couple of reasons for being invited like this. Firstly, Mr Bugtani was a great fan of all sports, especially Cricket and Hockey. Secondly one of his good friends is the Manager of the Pakistani Hockey team and will accompany them to Melbourne's Olympic Games. He wanted us to meet him. Maybe we would catch up with him there?

We told him that our first priority was to meet the President and the Radio people promised to help. No problem he said, he and his friends know lots of influential people in high places who could also help.

Mr Bugtani, mentioned that one of his friends was the General Manager of the Hotel Metropole and he would speak to him this evening about us. After writing in our Book, He invited us to be his guests as long as we stayed in Karachi and he was looking forward to seeing us next day again.

Back at the YMCY again we made plans for the next morning.

AEG (*Allgemeine Elektricitaets-Gesellschaft AG*) got our first visit next morning. Being a German Company, we thought they would welcome us with open arms next morning, but we were wrong. At the front desk we were looked at by a couple of young guys as if we were from another planet.

One of them was Pakistani; the other we saw was German. I dare say, the way we looked they certainly didn't think we were there on business.

The Big Adventure

The German guy opened the front door and told us bluntly in English "You are at the wrong place."

"Not so fast," Uli said in German, "this is no way to greet fellow Germans in a foreign country."

The man was taken aback. He hadn't expected us to be German. He must have thought we were English backpacker tourists.

"We would like to see their boss," Uli said in formal German.

Without a smile the man turned and walked to a door, knocked and stepped inside. A few minutes, he appeared again and without a word he motioned us to follow him. There were two big desks in the room, one occupied by one German looking guy, the other by two Pakistanis dressed in suits. The German, (we soon learned came from Berlin) asked what we wanted and Uli said "just to say hello" and pointing to me he said, "Fritz did his apprenticeship at AEG Backnang."

Suddenly the ice was broken and we were introduced and finally offered some tea and sweets. They were all ears when they found out about us and what our plans where. The man from Berlin had been to the AEG factory in Backnang. He was now stationed in Karachi to connect Germany with Pakistan. They were very impressed when they found out that we had planned to visit President Iskander Mirza and wished us good luck. After writing in our book, we shook hands and bid them goodbye. We purposely didn't mention any financial help, even though they asked if they could help in any way. On the way out we walked straight past the two guys at the front as if they didn't exist.

We couldn't see our Rickshaw, but it didn't matter because five buildings up we noticed a big sign reading GRAX Limited, Electronic Parts Supplier. There were several companies in this building with GRAX being the biggest, holding one complete floor. We always liked the biggest!

Getting out of the heat was also a big relief. Even though it was an English company and with us looking out of the ordinary, the welcome was great. The office was quite large with several tables occupied by Pakistanis all dressed in a uniform with GRAX labelled on their shoulders. After informing the guy on the front desk who we were, he made an intercom call and spoke in Arabic for a couple of minutes. A side door opened and an elderly uniformed gentleman begged us to follow him into a huge warehouse packed with big rolls of wires, cables, electric tools and lots of different machines. Our guide stopped in front of a separate door, knocked, opened it, and indicated we should walk inside. He followed closing the door behind him. A totally different scene opened up in front of us. Firstly, there was hardly any furniture in this big room, except one desk, two couches, plus three little tables with some small stools around them. Two gentlemen stood up from one of the couches and greeted us with handshakes and big smiles. One a Pakistani was dressed like a Sheik, and the other being English, in a suit,. I couldn't believe my eyes; they were smoking at eleven in the morning and drinking strong black coffee. Uli was just about to tell them our names and why we are here when the Sheik said they knew all about us from the radio and Mr Bugtani. They visit the *Mexicana Bar* twice a week and are good friends. The Sheik Mr. Fazul Elahie, was smoking a water pipe and the Englishman, was smoking a huge cigar. They told us we could have either, but we opted for a water pipe.

Well, here we are in what felt like being the world's smallest café, but we could tell big business took place in this room! GRAX Limited, we were told was one of the biggest Electronic Parts supplier, with distribution centres all over the world. Mr Elahie and the English Gent were partners in the Pakistan establishment. They were also Agents for the big German Bayer Pharmaceutical Company, in Leverkusen. Both of them had been to Germany several times and both were extremely impressed how the German People rebuilt their country so quickly after the war.

Theo showed them through our book and let them know that we are looking for Sponsors to finance our journey. Both of them wrote in it and filled a whole page. The Englishman asked us what our plans where for today? Uli told him we had in mind to visit Mr. Bugtani for lunch at the Mexicana Bar, well he said "so are Mr. Elahie and I!" He suggested we should meet there in one hour. "No problem," Uli said, "we shall be there."

We stood up, shook hands and both of them led us to the front door. And he was there, our Rickshaw man! How the hell he knew where we were we would never find out and it didn't matter. He took us straight back to the YMCA so we could freshen up. At the front desk we were informed, that the Radio Station had rung and wanted to get in touch with us. We got the number and walked into our room. We decided to ring the Radio from the *Mexicana Bar*.

"Well meeting these people was great, but we didn't make any wages," was what Theo and I were thinking and said.

"Never mind," Uli said, "we can't win them all."

But we were anxious because we knew we had to raise sufficient to

The Big Adventure

prove to the Australian Government we had funds to support ourselves as well as pay for our future departure from there, or they wouldn't issue us with visas. Why are they so tough?

By the time we got to the Mexicana Bar exactly one hour had passed. One of the waiters led us downstairs into the belly dance room. Mr. Bugtani was already looking after his guests the five Gents from yesterday and our two GRAX friends, and greeted us warmly. There was one new face, the Gentleman who was managing the Pakistani Hockey Team, whom we had yet to meet.

We asked Mr. Bugtani if we could call the Radio Station, because they had left a message for us.

"They already called me so I have some great news for you," he told us excitedly. "You have an appointment with the President at 11 am tomorrow morning!"

Wow! This was fantastic news. Three young fellows dressed in shorts, short sleeve shirts, cycling boots wearing silly tropical helmets and we were going to meet the President of Pakistan!

There were handshakes and smiles all round. Mr. Bugtani and his friends were just as happy as us. Lots of food was placed on the table and half of us were served nice cold beers.

We still had to call and confirm what we were told. We were to be at the Radio Station, just before 10am next morning and somebody from there would take us.

About an hour later, another well dressed Gentleman joined the group and after shaking hands with all of them was introduced to us. He was the Managing Director of the Metropole Hotel, just off Victoria Street. He asked us how long we were going to stay in Karachi and Uli told him maybe another 3 days. He immediately told us we would be welcome to spend that time in his hotel. Naturally, we accepted and somehow knew Mr. Bugtani had something to do with it!

Mr Erweh Mamegh, the manager of the Pakistan Olympic Hockey team was the Managing Director of Woy Hirjina & Co Distilleries (Pak) LTD. He also invited us to his factory and to talk about Melbourne.

Mr.Elahie and his Partner from GRAX shook hands with everybody and wished us all the best and hoped that we get to Melbourne safely. I was the last one the Englishman shook hands with and I felt something getting pushed quietly into my pocket. No one else noticed. The time just flew by and before we knew it, it was late afternoon. We thanked Mr. Bugtani, shook hands with the others and told them we would come by again tomorrow.

We walked back to the YMCA, but I couldn't get there fast enough, holding the piece of paper wrapping in my pocket. Neither Uli nor Theo had a clue about it. They hadn't seen it slipped into my pocket.

We told the fellow on the front desk that we would be moving out the next afternoon, and he said he would be sad to see us go.

In our room I told them "I have a surprise, but I don't know what it is."

"Well," Theo said "what's keeping you? Don't keep us in suspense."

I pulled out the lumpy paper, which turned out to be a thick envelope.

Opening it we discovered three US$100 notes and a short letter from GRAX.

To Fritz Theo and Uli, it stated. It was such a great pleasure to spend most of the day together and we hope this small present for each of you will help on your way. It was signed by both of them!

We were worried earlier that we hadn't made any wages and now look at that! ...and we didn't even have to ask.

We were feeling on top of the world and went out for a couple of pipes. We asked our Rickshaw to come in the morning again to take as to the Radio Station at 9am.

Smoking our pipes and drinking tea, we relaxed and watched the life around us. We were very excited to meet the President the next morning and felt so grateful for the help we received from the various people we visited so far. It took me a long time to fall asleep that night, thinking about the excitement the next day would bring.

Waking up and having a good clean up we decided to wear long pants and short-sleeve shirts in an attempt to appear better dressed. After tea and pieces of bread, we were ready by 9am. On the way out we told the guy that we would be moving out in the afternoon.

It was already hot by the time our rickshaw dropped us at the radio station and it felt good stepping into the cooler building. We knew some of the people and our reporter introduced us to more. We had to travel by car because it would take more than half hour to get there, we were told.

Before getting into a big Ford, Uli asked our rickshaw driver to meet us back at the YMCA mid afternoon, and he was happy to do that.

Even though it was a big Limo, it was still a squeeze with the reporter, cameraman, sound recorder, the three of us and the Driver. We travelled

The Big Adventure

past the harbour and alongside the sea towards the more exclusive parts of Karachi. We couldn't see much of the houses here because they were well hidden behind big mud walls. Some had even sentries by the entrance ways.

Eventually we stopped in front of a huge villa in a cull de sac and parked behind some armoured security vehicles. A couple of uniformed soldiers greeted us and wanted to see our passports, apparently they knew the others. One of them led us through a big iron gate into a beautifully manicured garden towards a huge villa. When I say villa, I really should say small Palace! There were numerous working men doing things about the place. Except for the security guys, everyone was dressed in white, even the gardeners.

It was 5 Minutes to 11 when we were escorted up marble steps and through an enormous entry hall towards the end of a corridor. A wide very high double door was opened for us and we walked into a beautifully furnished room, not exactly like an office, but more like a big entertaining room. Through a wide spread of plate glass window we could see the sea. There were ceiling fans turning slowly, keeping the room at a cooler temperature. Five men immaculately dressed in white greeted us and one of them walked straight towards us and shook our hands.

The man was Iskander Ali Mirza, the First President of Pakistan!

Our Reporter introduced us to The President and to the other official looking gentlemen. The President was a big man, tall, good looking, strong and very friendly.

While Theo showed him through our book, Uli took some photographs and we answered many questions. The President asked several questions about King Faisal and the Shah. Apparently they were in close diplomatic contact with each other, and being borne in India, he also knew the Nehru family quite well.

The President signed our book and so did another gent, who was the Minister of Finance. They all wished us a safe journey. They were also pleased that we had met the manager of the Hockey team that would be going to the Olympics in Melbourne, and hoped we would be able to catch up with them there.

In saying goodbye and shaking hands, we thanked them very much for having us.

We told them Pakistan is a great Country full of lovely, hospitable people and we had made many friends.

It was exactly 12 noon by the time we sat back in the Limo. We had spent just on one hour with the President and his people. Even the reporter was surprised it took so long. The limo dropped us of at the Mexicana Bar and the reporter told us he would join us soon. The same five gentlemen were sitting at the same table again, waiting for us. Mr. Bugtani and the others wanted to know everything that happened. Of course we elaborated as much as possible and they could tell by our excitement how successful it was. Food was dished up, a cold beer for Uli, myself and Theo had his usual Pepsi. The reporter joined us and mentioned that they would get some photos to us within the next couple of days. After a couple of pipes, we had to leave to pack our stuff ready for the move to Metropole hotel. Walking back to the YMCA, was like walking on cloud seven.

Now we had a King, a Shah and a President in our book, who would believe that!

Ligar Sardar Abdul Rab Nishtar with Fred, at the President's residence.

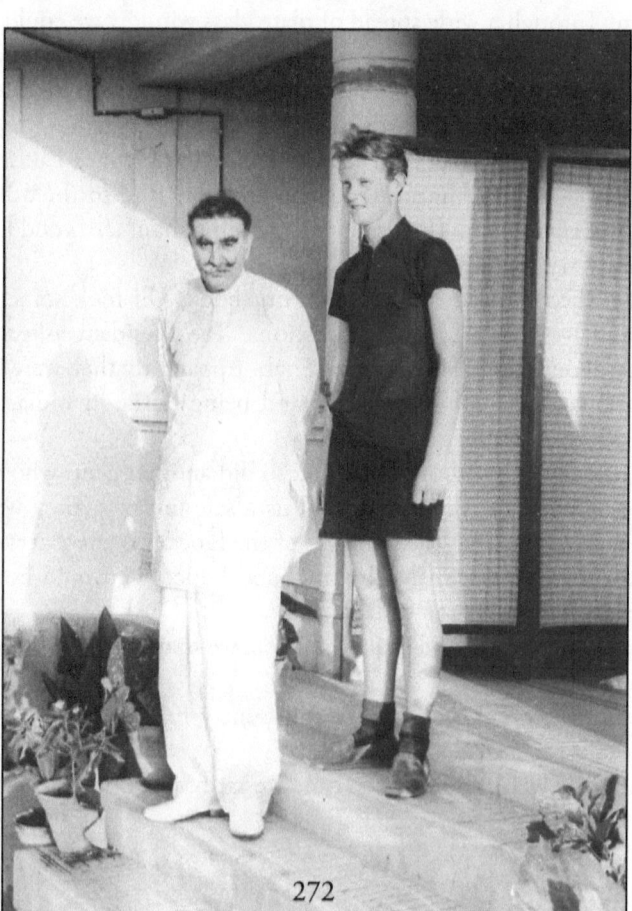

The rickshaw driver was waiting for us when we got back and we asked him if he would do the same as he had done when we first arrived, to open a path through the mad traffic while we rode our bikes along behind him. It would have been impossible to push them through the crowded streets without his help. He happily nodded assent. It was much easier pedalling an empty rickshaw than one with three young men in it, and he got paid the same.

It felt great again to change back into shorts, but packing took longer than normal. I paid our bill at the front desk and thanked them for looking after us. As soon as we were packed he led us on our bikes to the Metropole Hotel. Even with the rickshaw in front of us it was nearly impossible and we ended up walking and pushing our bikes for most of the way.

As we got closer we saw the Metropole ahead on a big intersection and it looked impressive! I am not sure if it was the biggest hotel in Karachi, but it was certainly one of them. A man with a long black beard all dressed in white and wearing a white turban came towards us across the footpath and told us to follow him. I paid our driver handsomely and told him we should be here for a few days. I showed him the address of Woy Hirjina & Co. He knew where it was but suggested it would be better to go by Taxi. "It would take over an hour, and is too hot for rickshaw and for you in rickshaw," he told us.

The bearded man in white took us around the corner to a big car park and a side entrance where two servants were waiting to help with our bikes and luggage. Our bikes were safely put into a lockup room and two doors along the corridor they led us into a family room with our luggage. There were two singles and a double bed, plus a couch and small desk. Best of all, there was a separate room with bath, shower and squat down toilet.

"Anything you need, just tell whoever is at the front entrance."

Uli thank them and gave them a few coins.

"How about that?" we said to each other, "this is more fitting for people who had a meeting with The President earlier on".

We had barely settled in when the Director knocked on the door to check on us. He asked if we are hungry and Uli told him, that we are not. He knew that we had been at the Mexicana Bar and Mr. Bugtani had told him of our meeting with The President.

"We might just walk along the street for something small and a pipe," we said.

"In that case I will see you tomorrow then... Please enjoy your stay in our hotel."

It wasn't so hot by the time we walked outside, but there were lots more people on the footpath and the noise was deafening. We hadn't been to this part of Karachi, even though we were only a couple of kilometres from the YMCA. We passed several very large buildings belonging to large well known companies, and decided that we would visit as many as possible over the next couple of days.

Sleeping in beautifully made up beds was heavenly! We had a quick breakfast in the hotel dining room early in the morning, and ignored being gawked at by several men with families. Outside it was like walking into an oven, it was so hot. No wonder the rickshaw driver didn't want to make a long journey and had recommended taking a taxi. Catching a Taxi was easy; they were all over the place. Uli showed the driver the Address and an hour later we stopped at what looked like an Industrial area, in front of what looked like a big warehouse with a large driveway on one side leading to an extensive loading bay for trucks.

We were expected; the front entrance door opened just as we walked towards it. Two men in Pakistanis attire greeted us with warm handshakes and asked us to follow them. They shut the door quickly behind us to stop the heat getting inside.

Straight away we knew we were in a distillery; the smell of alcohol wafted about, "and this was in Pakistan!"

We hadn't smelled alcohol like this since the time we delivered truckloads of it back in Germany.

Mr Mamegh welcomed us into his office and introduced us to another two gentlemen. They wore sports gear with the Pakistan National Hockey Team, on their chest and back. They looked very athletic and fit, and I guessed around thirty years old. One of them was the coach of the team, the other his assistant. (Theo and Hermann actually met the three of them again at the Olympic Village in Melbourne).

After some tea and listening to our story the athletes wished us good luck and said that they were sorry that we didn't have time to watch some hockey practice. Another Gentleman dressed in a dustcoat entered and Mr Mamegh introduced him as the head spirit maker of the company. They asked if we would like to see the Distillery. We followed them into what looked like a huge laboratory. It was sectioned off with immense glass walls. There were huge copper kettles, steam everywhere and heaps of glass tubes that fed pale liquid into lots of big glass containers stacked in rows and marked with the content and date. In another section we saw different bottles being filled by machines for different customers, but still labelled by hand. They distilled just about everything from Corn; Gin, Whiskey and even rice wine. Apparently they sent their product all over Asia, with the big Hotels being their greatest customers.

I must say it was very impressive for us to be guided through by the big chief himself.

We could see that all the workers wondered who we were!

Back at the office Mr Mamegh filled some small glasses for us to sample some of his product. Uli and I had no problem and downed a few different varieties, but Theo who doesn't touch alcohol had big problems and only managed a few sips to be sociable.

After writing in our book, Mr Mamegh suggested we should have lunch together at the *Mexicana Bar*. What a great idea Uli said and told him it was our plan also. We were driven back with him in his Chauffeur driven Limousine.

As if by magic, the big table was full of steaming and cold dishes with lots of different fruits. There was the usual crowd except for about five or six new faces who we were introduced to. It was great to meet the English man and Mr Elahie from GRAX and to our surprise, also Mr Micloalle from our Hotel. What a lunch we had with all those people! Someone asked how long we were staying in Karachi and Uli mentioned that we were thinking of leaving in a couple of days. Then Mr Bugtani insisted everyone should be here the next evening for a going away party.

Theo told them that we had to leave now to visit a couple of Companies to see if we could get more Sponsors. We thanked Mr Bugtani again and told him, we wouldn't be here for lunch tomorrow, but in the evening.

With a big smile in his face, our driver with his rickshaw was waiting. How he knew we were here I'll never know, but he was here. Uli told him to take us past Siemens, because we promised to see them once more. The same man at the front desk welcomed us and led us straight to the back office to meet Mr Mustafa, Mr Johw and another gent. It was a warm welcome celebrated with coffee and a pipe. They certainly were impressed when they found out, that we did manage to meet President Iskander Mirza and wanted to know all about it. Finally they wished us all the best and we thanked them once more for their hospitality. We also promised them to write and Uli told them we would eventually send them a picture of Backnang to hang on their wall.

By the time we got back to the Hotel we were as hot as, and couldn't wait to get under the shower. By that time it was too late to visit any more companies, so we sat down, wrote a few cards and talked about our travels. Overall it had been a great day.

We took our time at breakfast next morning because there was no meeting up with anyone. Plus we enjoyed looking at and tasting the different foods on the buffet. The Metropole had to look after all their international guests so the variety on the buffet was incredible.

After washing a few clothes we were ready to look for more Sponsors. We visited three more Companies Offices and made slightly over US$100 in Rupees. By the time we got back we were drenched in sweat. Our washing was dry so we packed most of our luggage, to be ready for next morning's departure.

Later in the afternoon our rickshaw took us to the *Mexicana Bar*, but we stopped at the post office to send the postcards and letters we had written. Mr Bugtani, his three regulars and some other well dressed men were already enjoying drinks and smoking pipes. It wasn't long before more guests arrived, with familiar faces amongst them. Our friends from Grax and Mr Mamegh were amongst them and a few minutes later even Mr Micloalle with a couple of others came down the stairs. I reckon there would have been over twenty men sitting around one long table, drinking, smoking and chatting as food and drinks were placed on another table.

What a great evening it turned out to be with all those lovely people. Time just flew and with the eating, drinking, smoking and chatting it was close to midnight by the time we finally got back to the hotel. It had been a great farewell and it must have taken a good half hour to shake hands and receive all the best wishes. Mr Bugtani told us he and a couple of others would come by in the morning to say goodbye.

It was about 10am by the time we had packed and loaded our bikes next morning, before we could go to the dining room for breakfast. Mr Bugtani, his friends and Mr Micloalle were already there and greeted us enthusiastically. While sitting on the breakfast table Mr Bugtani handed Uli an envelope and told him to open it. I could see Uli's hands tremble when he looked inside and pulled out the contents.

Over the last few days Mr Bugtani's friends had donated some money to help us along. They also hoped it might help us with the visas we needed for Australia. Uli counted 12 US$100 notes and an amount of Rupees that looked about the equivalent of US$300.

We were overwhelmed, stunned at their generosity. We had lumps in our throats when we finally said goodbye.

There was also a letter of recommendation to the Principal at the Lahore University from Mr Micloalle who was a friend of his. It was after midday, when we finally pushed our bikes behind our rickshaw which as usual cleared a path for us to follow to the outskirts of Karachi.

And it was hot. It took about an hour to get the 5km to the outskirts of Karachi. We thanked our rickshaw driver for looking after us so well. I paid him handsomely and he couldn't stop shaking our hands. With a last wave to him and a last look back at Karachi, we headed north-east towards Hyderabad our next major stop.

Halfway to a small town called Gharp some 50km ahead, we had to stop for a rest under a row of trees next to a narrow waterway to get some shade. The sun beating down on us and the humidity were incredible.

Hyderabad was approximately 200km ahead and we hoped to make it in two days, but it seemed doubtful the way we are going.

We had to change our rhythm. Instead of riding during the day, we had to start very early in the morning and rest during the day. We were told that it would get even hotter further towards Lahore and India.

Under the trees we stripped off to our undies and enjoyed the warm breeze and soon fell asleep on top of our sleeping bags. An hour or so later I woke up stinging all over I woke up to discover I was as red a s a cooked lobster. Shit! I stood up and looked at Theo and Uli and didn't like what I saw. Their bodies were red too, scorched from the sun. While we were sleeping the sun had crept across and shining intermittently through the gaps in the branches and leaves had been strong enough to hit us with full power. Just what we needed, being sunburnt! We should have known better and cursed ourselves for being so stupid as to let ourselves fall asleep under those trees.

We decided we had to make it to Gharp where perhaps we could get some soothing cream for our skin. We didn't feel like eating, but we drank plenty of water. We had extra water on top of our full Handlebar bottles. It was still daylight when we finally reached Gharb and after asking a couple of people we found a small hotel near the centre of town. We had to have two rooms next to each other with Uli in one, Theo and I in the other because of our bikes. It was still hot, but the ceiling fans gave us some relief. We inquired at the reception about finding a pharmacy in town, but he shook his head.

"In Thatta, the next Town, you could get some medicine," he told us.

It turned out to be a horrible night because we couldn't lie down to sleep. We sat on the edge of the bed, elbow on our knees and head in our hands. With the overhead fan producing a soft movement of air that barely cooled out burning hot bodies. We alternated sitting with walking around the room to loosen up our stiff bones. We hadn't unpacked and after paying our bill at daybreak, we hit the already busy road towards Thatta about 60km ahead.

We were in constant pain, and riding our bikes was sheer agony. On top of all this I had a slow flat on my back wheel. I had to keep stopping to pump it up every fifteen minutes or so until after an hour we reached a roadhouse adjacent to a lake where we could mend it in the shade of a huge tree and have some breakfast. We were a sorry lot indeed. Mending the flat took longer than usual because any movement I made hurt so much. Once the flat was fixed it was harder than ever to keep going, but we still made Thatta before midday.

Finding a hotel, was relatively easy and a good one on top of it. We showed the guy at the reception our blistered skin. He shook his head in astonishment and said, "You should go to the hospital in the next street."

He called a servant over and told him to guide us there immediately. We grabbed our passports and valuables, including our book, and followed him.

Hospital, what Hospital! We were taken to a narrow but long double story building full of sick people where several men and women dressed in white uniforms attended to them. The women had their hair and half their faces covered. It was like a big clinic rather than a hospital. We thanked the fellow who brought us there and walked into a small reception office were one guy looked at Uli's skin and told us to follow him into another room and wait. Two elderly men in western suits greeted us and wanted to know how they could help. Uli again took off his shirt and showed his blistered skin.

Both of them were Surgeons and were wondering what three young Germans were doing here. Uli told them who we were and where we came from. They could hardly believe it. I showed them through our book and when they saw all the people we had met in Pakistan so far, they wanted to know all about us. They wanted to know how we got to meet President Iskander Mirza. Uli pointed to his skin. "You should check our skin first before we start talking about who we have met."

Suddenly they were contrite and one of them instructed us to strip off to our undies (yes they were clean!) because we also had burns on our legs.

One of the doctors opened the door and gave some orders to people outside.

Almost immediately the room was full with younger Interns, holding trays, containing a strange smelling liquid. Our blisters were dried with soft cloths and then soaked with this liquid. The pain was instantly gone and we felt better. After drying off, our skin was covered with a pungent yellow cream, which dissolved into the burnt skin within seconds.

As we were being treated the two surgeons watched and gave orders. We were still sore, but felt 100% better and couldn't thank them enough.

One of the surgeons asked if we were hungry and Uli told them we recently had breakfast. They asked where we are staying and if we would mind for them to invite us for a late lunch. We were happy to do so and told they would be at our hotel within the hour. Apparently they wanted to know more about us and our adventure.

At the reception I was going to pay for helping us, but were handed a small bag with some of the cream for our sunburnt skin and waved goodbye. We felt great, but extremely tired, not having slept much the night before. We had a double room this time and plenty of space for our bikes. By the time we freshened up a bit the two of surgeons were already waiting for us, accompanied by a younger man who greeted us in perfect High German. He had studied at the University in Bremen for over three years and was the nephew of one of the surgeons.

Late lunch was great, sitting in the shade of some large trees in front of a small, but very good eating place. Those three guys couldn't get enough of us and we enjoyed ourselves also. After a couple of hours they excused themselves; they had to get back to the hospital. They wished us all the best, then stood up and left.

Back in our room we rubbed more cream on our burns and decided to go back out again to smoke a pipe. I can't remember the name of that cream but it was fantastic! Later in life, I got sunburnt a couple of times more, but never found a cream as good as this one. It wasn't even dark when went back to our room and hit the sack and fell asleep instantly.

At sunrise we were already riding towards Hyderabad, another 100 Km north. Our burns were still sore, but 100% better than yesterday and after a reasonable good night's sleep we actually felt okay. A couple of hours after leaving we crossed a big river and pulled into a roadhouse for some breakfast. We didn't stop too long; filling up with water and some provisions was quickly done. We wanted to cover as many kilometres as possible before it got too hot.

The big river we crossed was the Indus, which flows through the whole of Pakistan from North to South. I think the Indus is the lifeline of the whole country. A couple of hours later we stopped next to a lake and found a pleasant shady spot to rest during the heat.

Keeping out of the sun was a priority. We had learned our lesson. Uli suggested we go for a swim in the Lake but the edges were overgrown with bushes and bamboo. The water looked inviting and we could have done with a bit of cooling down, but then it was better not to expose our still burnt skin, so we decided a swim was out.

Late in the afternoon when the sun was not so strong we followed the river and stopped for the night a bit south of Hyderabad. Early the next morning we reached the outskirts of town.

A street near the outskirts of Hyderbad.

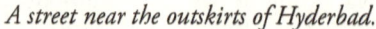

The Big Adventure

We did the same as we had in Karachi. We stopped at the first unoccupied rickshaw and showed the driver the address we had been given for the cement and pipe factory.

He shook his head and looked at us as if we were weird. "It's on the other side of the city, maybe an hour away."

Uli asked if he would guide us.

"You would have to pay double," he said straight up, "because I have to to get back to this side again, after taking you there."

"How much?" Uli asked.

He quoted a price and Uli almost exploded. "That's daylight robbery!"

But the driver was adamant. He wasn't going to budge. Either we paid or we didn't. "If you want to go there..." He left those words hanging in the air and smiled at us.

Uli looked at us, then turned back to the driver and said, "Okay, take us there."

The traffic was as bad as in Karachi if not worse, and I think the driver deserved whatever it was she wanted us to pay. The air so steamy we had difficulty breathing.

To this day I regret that we didn't have film camera or iphones like everyone has today! It must have looked hilarious; a smiling rickshaw driver in front, Uli behind, Theo in the middle and me at the rear, dressed in shorts, short sleeved Hawaiian shirts, sunglasses and tropical helmets, weaving and cursing our way through the traffic on fully laden bikes. What a sight! We went right through the centre of town and finished up in an industrial area off the main road leading north. I paid our guide and thanked him, even though he had over charged us double. It was so little anyhow and he did a great job!

He left us in front of a factory that was at least five times as big as the one in Bela.

We pushed our bikes towards a big gateway with guards on each side shaking our hands. Apparently, we were expected this day or the next. One of them led us to an office building, past heaps of concrete pipes stacked as far as we could see. At the end of the stack nearest us several trucks were having pipes loaded onto them with portable cranes. We were welcomed by at least ten guys and introduced to the lot of them. A couple of times they had calls from Bela wanting to find out if we had arrived.

Next to the office was a double story house built of concrete, their guest house. Aussies would say it looked like a brick shithouse, but upon entering I thought *Wow!* This looks more like a five star hotel.

Everyone wanted to help with our bikes and luggage.

Inside and out of the heat we were amazed how cool it was. This house was really something; two stories, but we only saw the ground level which must have had at least a dozen rooms, a large modern kitchen fit for a small hotel, where a couple of guys were preparing food, and a large dining and lounge room together.

Our bikes were taken to a room near the back and our luggage spread over two big bedrooms, one with a king-size bed the other one had two singles. Finally we were left alone except for one of the guys who stayed behind to tell us, "The Directors and some friends will be joining you for dinner this evening."

I suppose that meant we couldn't really go anywhere, but what the hell… we needed a good rest anyway. Besides it was too damned hot outside and lovely and cool in here.

"There is some food being prepared for you in the kitchen if you want to go there."

It was almost midday and we were hungry! So that sounded good to us.

He pointed to a button next to each door. "If you needed anything, just press that button for service." He then left us to ourselves.

Theo and I decided that Uli should sleep in the room with the king-size bed and the two of us would use the room with the two beds. Checking out Uli's room, we were hit with an unexpected surprise, the adjoining bathroom! Our eyes nearly popped out. We could hardly believe what we saw, a Western toilet! Next to it was a squatting hole-in-the-floor Arabic one, as well as a big bathtub with a shower. Next to our room was another real toilet the same as Uli's. This place was heavenly…

In the kitchen there was a variety of hot food on the table, and plates with cutlery set for three. One of the cooks indicated that we should sit and enjoy the meal. He didn't seem to speak any English but it was clear what he wanted us to do, so we did exactly that.

As soon as we finished lunch, I told my friends "I can't wait to have a civilised crap."

"Me too," both Uli and Theo said almost simultaneously

We all burst out laughing. It was exciting to find ourselves in a place like this, so unexpected.

I think this was the first time I had such a beautiful relaxed crap since Istanbul? It was no fun sitting over a hole in the ground, and that was all we had encountered all along the way until we reached this place.

Uli pressed the button by the door and within a minute a different guy appeared and asked what he could do for us. "Would it be possible to get some clothes washed?" Uli asked.

"Of course," he said, "just put your washing in the basked next to the towel rack and someone will collect it and take care of it."

After a shower and shave we all felt newly born! It was the cleanest we had been for a long time. Writing a letter or two and looking through our roadmaps to plan where we had to go next made the time pass quickly. Our dirty washing was collected and shortly after we had a couple of gentleman dressed in suits, accompanied by one of the earlier guys knock on our doors. Hearty handshakes and introductions over, they led us to the lounge room for afternoon tea and a pipe. They were partners in the company and one was a cousin to the director in Bela, we were told during a pleasant conversation. They had heard some of our story from Bela over the phone, but were very anxious to hear more from us in person. They took our letters to post and said they were looking forward to the evening meal.

It turned out to be another great evening. From our room we could hear the commotion in the kitchen and the smell of exotic herbs filled the house with an enticing aroma.

That evening there were quite a few people waiting for us. Some of them we knew, but the Partners introduced us to the others. Theo had our book to show them while Uli and I answered whatever questions they came up with. The main topic was again President Iskander Mirza, how we got to meet him, as well as how we met the other heads of the different countries we had crossed so far.

Unexpectedly a lot of questions were about Germany and our education. Of course on we elaborated and exaggerated this as much as possible without being unbelievable. As we were talking the kitchen staff had set the big table with a humongous amount of food.

Someone asked how long we would be staying here and Uli told them we wanted to leave in the morning. "No way," the Partners exclaimed, "you must stay a few days, so we can look after you better."

You've done a lot for us already," said Uli, and turning to each of us he then added, "but I think we could stay one more night."

What a wonderful evening it turned out to be. Most of the food tasted great, and some of the dishes had hardly any hot chillies in them.

"I am surprised the dishes don't have hot chillies in them," I said.

"We heard about your experience with hot food in Bela and instructed the chefs to leave out most of the chillies."

"We really appreciate that," Theo said. He was the fussiest of us three and certainly couldn't eat anything that even had a hint of chilli in it.

One of the guys asked how we are financing our trip and Theo told him that we are sponsored by some of the Companies we visited and by speaking to students at Universities, radio interviews and having articles written about us for Newspapers.

One of the Partners told us they would show us through their factory in the morning and take us for lunch in Hyderabad. By the time we finally hit the sack, we were absolutely stuffed! We slept like god in heaven, but I had to get up during the night for a pee. I didn't stand up to pee in the hole, no; I sat on the toilet and had the best relief in ages!

Coffee was served next morning accompanied by soft boiled eggs and the usual flat bread and some fruit. Back in our rooms our clothes had been washed, folded and stacked on our beds. We were certainly being treated like Royalty.

We didn't have to wait long before both Partners arrived to take us to see their factory. It certainly was impressive. It wasn't just one big building, there were several of them adjacent to each other. Before we entered the first one we were given overalls to put on because of the dust. We also got a helmet and facemask, but they didn't have ear plugs!

We entered the first building through a thick steel door and inside the noise was deafening. On one side there were tip trucks unloading gravel onto conveyer belts, leading to big crushers that turned them into grey looking sand. Apparently some distance away, they owned a quarry which crushed big rocks into gravel which was then brought here to be turned into sand. The sand travelled on big conveyers to the second building full of big monstrous tumblers. Some of them turned the sand into fine powder after which it was heated and dried to be turned into cement, while had water and cement added to make concrete. Big trucks periodically were loaded with the mixed concrete which they took to building sites elsewhere. The third building was quieter and not so dusty. There were lots of different forms, made of wood and cement, for moulding and creating all sizes of pipes. Inside the fourth building all sizes of cement tiles and bricks were being moulded. The fifth building was huge; it was a drying and sorting shed where bricks and concrete pipes were sorted into sizes before taken outside for dispatch. It was certainly a massive

The Big Adventure

enterprise. Seeing those giant crushers reminded me of the time I worked in Mr Seybold's quarry. It seemed such a long time ago.

We thanked the Partners. We didn't have to tell them how impressed we were. They could see it in our faces.

They told us that they had help from a pipe company in Melbourne which both of them had visited twice. Without that company's expertise, they wouldn't be so advanced.

Many years later I found out that my wife Zara's uncle Bill worked for UNESCO and had used 'Hume's Pipes' to help Pakistan with the irrigation of their major desert areas. I never had the opportunity to ask Uncle Bill if this was the same company whose people had visited Melbourne, and if this was the company that supplied the pipes locally for the various projects.

After shedding our overalls and masks we walked back to the guesthouse. We were told someone would pick us up in one hour to take us into the city for a special dinner. After being in the dust for some time we wanted to have another quick shower to be more presentable.

A uniform driver of a black limousine collected us and dropped us in the middle of the city in front of a beautiful old English style building of several stories. We were greeted by a well dressed gentleman in a black suit white shirt and wearing a bow tie like Mr Bugtani from the *Mexicana Bar*. He led us up one flight of carpeted stairs to a double glass door leading into an exclusively decorated small restaurant. Most tables were occupied with well dressed men. Even the waiters wore bow ties. All eyes were on us as we were led in to be greeted with big smiles. At the head of the table the two partners greeted us again. The Partners had told the owner of the place about us and he in turn told all the others! This place served international foods and looking at the menu we immediately chose Spaghetti Bolognese. It was delicious, especially since we hadn't had any pasta for months.

Being looked after so well, we were tempted to stay for a week! What a break that would be! They told us that dinner that night back in the guesthouse would be a repeat of the night before so we really looked forward to it. If every day was to be like this, we certainly would be tempted to stay longer, but the road was waiting for us. We still had a long way to go and a certain time limit if we were to reach our objective of arriving in time for the Olympic Games in Melbourne.

The Partners had told us at dinner they would see us in the morning to say goodbye. The next morning someone told us the best way to Sukkur is through Nawabshah. It was very early and we wanted to get away before the day got too hot and unbearable. Uli woke us before daybreak, already showered and dressed. I wanted to sit an extra half hour on the beautiful toilet, because I knew it would be a long time to use another one!

"Come on, move it," Uli called out.

Pumping up our tyres and packing the bikes was routine and didn't take long.

After a short breakfast prepared by one of the cooks we were ready to hit the road. It was daylight by then, and we had just stepped outside with our bikes when the same chauffer driven limousine stopped in front of us and the Partners stepped out. They took each of us in their arms and wished us all the best. At the same time, they handed each of us a sealed envelope. "Something small from all the people you met," they told us.

We really protested, "You have already done so much for us," we said. "You didn't need to do more."

"Just a little to help you along," they said and with another hug each, turned around, climbed back into the Limo and drove off.

Being on the north side of town it was easy to find our way to Nawabshah some 90 kilometres north. Yes we were anxious to open our envelopes but we had to get as many kilometres under our belts as possible before it got to hot. Our sunburn still irritated slightly but it wasn't that bad anymore and riding this time was comfortable because we travelled next to a series of water ways so the road was flat. Even this early there was a lot of traffic but it was easy to get through. We passed countless little farms growing vegetables and fruit. After about three hours of pedalling we had gained perhaps 50 kilometres, and then we had to stop because the bitumen started to melt with the heat from the sun. Just as we stopped at a roadhouse Uli's front tyre blew out. Our tyres were as hard as rocks. We hadn't realised how they could be affected by the heat. We quickly let some air out of the valves so the other tyres wouldn't blow out. Because of his thinner wheels, Uli's tyres punctured blew earlier than ours and more often. We sat in the shade close to the roadhouse and while Uli repaired his burst tyre, Theo and I walked over to get some drinks and fresh fruit.

We couldn't wait any longer, to open our envelopes. Three US $100 Notes were in mine, plus the equivalent of US $100 in Rupees. Theo had exactly the same and so did Uli.

We were dumfounded and couldn't believe our luck.

We were happy and sad at the same time. Happy because this money would get us a long way further and sad because we couldn't hug and thank those people once more. Uli and Theo handed me their Dollars to put in the pouch with the others around my neck, but kept the Rupees.

It got hotter by the minute, but under the big trees it was bearable. Only two of us could go to the roadhouse to get supplies at any one time, one always had to mind the bikes. As it cooled down a bit in the late afternoon we managed another couple of hours of riding and as night started to fall we were only about 10km south of Nawabshah. We found a quiet spot to spread our tent and slept reasonably good, but no comparison as the previous two nights!

We were surprised early next morning by how close we were to Nawabshah. It only took us less than 30 minutes to the outskirts of this small town. We decided not to stop and rode right through it. It was important to cover as much as we could before the heat forced us to stop again. We passed through small villages and lots of farms with land irrigated with water from the channels along the roadside. All the villages had small shops stocked with fruit and groceries. We always made sure we had enough supplies, especially drinking water and fruit. Having those long breaks during the heat was annoying, but we still averaged about 80km a day.

It took about three days to get to Kairpur which we hit early in the morning. We decided not to stop, because Sukkur was only another 40km ahead. Still it took just on an hour to get through town before we reached the main road again. Sweat was pouring off us when we finally made it to the centre of Sukkur. By then it was close to midday and hot and steamy as hell! We picked a good looking Hotel close to the centre were we booked in for two nights. It wasn't as cheap as some of the others, but who cares. We had plenty of Rupees and we desperately needed a shower! On top of it we needed a rest because we were stuffed!

The staff were friendly and helped with our luggage. There was a separate lockup room for our bikes and we got a big room with three single beds. Uli, being the oldest was first to use the bathroom, me second and Theo last. What a relief. We felt much better after that and the ceiling fans did a great job circulating the air pleasantly through the room. Freshly dressed and looking good, but starving because we hadn't eaten since early morning, we could have eaten a horse!

We handed our dirty clothes to a couple of staff at the reception and asked about a good place to eat. Here at the hotel we were told, or two doors to the right of this building is a very good restaurant.

We decided to eat outside to experience the feeling of Sukkur. There weren't too many people walking on the footpath, it was too hot being in the middle of the day. The restaurant was a little up market and fairly occupied. Men dressed in their normal Pakistani dress and the women dressed in black, grey or blue, with their faces covered and their children well behaved. By now we were used to the stares we created as soon as we walked somewhere by ourselves. We ordered meat dishes with rice and vegetables, but told the waiter no chillies. He nodded his head and told us that they often get European guests and they don't like it hot either. Anyhow the food was delicious even though we couldn't tell what kind of meat it was. With our stomachs satisfied, we felt like a well earned pipe. The waiter told us we could sit in the back garden under some shade trees. There were numerous padded chairs under several big trees with men sitting in small groups, talking and smoking pipes. We did the same and also enjoyed some fresh fruit juice.

It wasn't long before the group next to us wanted to know where we came from and asked if we would like to join them for another pipe. It turned out to be a long lunch with lots of tea, some different dips and juices. As always since Karachi, everyone wanted to hear about our meeting with the President and our journey. After three pipes, Uli told them we had to go back to the hotel to rest a bit before we could look at their city. We shook hands and they wished us good luck. Back in the restaurant I was going to pay our bill, only to be told that one of the guys outside had fixed it up already. Back outside again, we thanked them for their kindness and shook hands once more.

We didn't feel like doing anything at all, when we got back to our room. The sun had already disappeared, so we decided to call it quits and rest. It always felt good sleeping in a bed instead on the hard ground on top of our sleeping bags.

After breakfast next morning, we hopped in a rickshaw and told the rider to take us through the city. Sukkur was quite interesting and somehow fascinating. There were new modern buildings and very old double and triple story homes. One could only wonder who the Architects were in those olden days and the tradesmen who accomplished feats like this. We crossed over a few canals and by passed lots of excavation works.

Our rickshaw driver told us they were making huge holding dams for irrigation and in a few years some of the Indus River will be diverted into those dams. We enjoyed our small tour of Sukkur, but after a couple of hours we returned to our hotel, because the heat became too much for us. We had a good lunch in the hotel dining room. Our washing was folded, when we got back to our room, which meant that we could start packing for an early start in the morning. Cleaning and servicing our bikes took a while and warranted another shower afterwards. Later we decided to go next door again for some dips, tea and a couple of pipes. Later when I paid our bill for our stay at the reception, to my surprise it was quite reasonable, even with the great luncheon.

At sunrise next morning we crossed a couple of canals, following on the right side of the Indus north. A couple of hours later we rode through Pano Agil and stopped a short way past it to get out of the heat. Along the Indus we travelled in the State of Sindh and we could see why it was the bread basket of Pakistan. All the way north we passed through green wheat or rice fields and orchards with different fruit. We passed a few big farms with sheep and others with donkeys and goats. We passed a few small villages but made camp just before Ghotki. Sleeping on the hard ground again wasn't pleasurable, but we had rested well in Sukkur.

On the way to Daharki next morning was tough. The wind was blowing very strong from the east out of the Thar Desert on our right and was burning hot. Still we made Daharki and stopped a few kilometres beyond near a roadhouse for the night to where we made camp. With a slight breeze still from the east next morning, we travelled much better than the day before and made camp short of Sadiqabad. The forty kilometres next morning were easy, except for the traffic and we reached Rahim Yar Khan well before midday and booked in to the first hotel we saw. The shower wasn't cold, but felt great and took all the grit off our bodies. Most of these towns were pretty much the same with one or two big Mosque's standing out from the rest of the buildings. At the Bazaar we had some lunch and bought some provisions. Needless to say in those smaller towns and villages we drew big crowds and we had to be careful where we stopped. Sometimes two of us had to watch our bikes whilst only one got some small necessities in a shop. Even though the road was pretty straight, with not many hills it was still tough to dodge all the traffic and animal crap on the hot road.

The sixty kilometres next morning to Khanpur went fairly well, except Uli had another flat tyre. This time we had to fix it next to the road in scorching heat. Still we made it through Khanpur before midday. We stopped not far past at a shady spot next to a small waterway. Before nightfall we had gone another 40 kilometres closer to Bahawal Pur.

Sleeping next to a desert had an advantage; the soil was mixed with sand and soft to lie on. After sleeping one more night on the ground we reached Bahawal Pur late evening next day, completely stuffed. Sleeping in a reasonable hotel is all we wanted and we found one just before town centre. We were now in the State of Punjab and had to camp only one more night next to the road, to hit Multan before midday next day. We rested in a hotel again, stuffed ourselves with good food, drinks and smoked some pipes to get enough energy for the long trip ahead to Lahore next day.

Multan, was another well to do Town like Sukkur. Great old buildings surrounded by manicured gardens and all kind of shops lining the footpath. A rickshaw took us around early evening for about an hour and we were impressed.

Washing clothes in a fountain in Multan.

We made good time early next morning and never stopped until we were well past Khaneval before we rested. It meant that we made Mian Channun by nightfall. Making camp off the road didn't bother us too much because we knew we were staying in another hotel in Sahival the next day.

About 10 kilometres past Chichawatni we rested and made the other 30 to Sahival easy by early evening. The Hotel we found was not far from a Bazaar, which was handy for us to replenish our supplies. Sahival is half way between Multan and Lahore. Studying our roadmap, we realised, that we had a big day in front of us next day to make Pattokoi or even further. At the Bazaar we relaxed with some dinner and a well deserved pipe. Back at the hotel we packed our goodies, had a good shower and it wasn't long before we were out to it!

Yes, it was a hard one next day, but we had some luck from Nature. The wind was blowing from south-west and pushed us along at a good pace. We passed through Okara in record time and had only about 30 kilometres ahead of us to reach Pattoki when we rested under some trees. Even though the wind was very hot we took advantage of it later on and made Pattoki with still another couple of hours daylight ahead. We felt good and decided to push on and camped after a small town called Bhai Pheru. The 50 kilometres early morning were no problem and we finally reached the outskirts of Lahore, long before midday.

Asking a Rickshaw driver to lead us to the University was easy and it took less of an hour to get there. There was a big mob of students and teachers coming towards us as soon as we rode through a huge iron gate towards a big building. As soon as we got off our bikes we were surrounded by dozens of guys young and old, all wearing the same kind of uniform. We could pick out a couple of teachers, because they were dressed in black suits, white shirts and wearing a tie. Everyone wanted to shake hands with us and we didn't know why?

Shit I thought to myself, we are not famous Hockey or Cricket players, but we found out very soon. Apparently, Mr Micloalle from the Metropole Hotel in Karachi had numerous conversation about us with his friend, The Principal, and told him that we would arrive within the next couple of days. Everyone had known about our travels and that we had met their President. They knew we had arrived in Lahore, because someone who had passed us a couple of hours earlier had phoned in.

One of the teachers told us the Principal would be back soon, but left word that we were to be looked after. On each side of the big Administration building, were lots of smaller ones and at the back was a big block of double storeys units surrounded by huge trees giving lots of shade. It was the living quarters of the students, especially for the ones from out of town. This was where two of the teachers led us, followed by most of the students. Everyone wanted to help when we followed our guides towards a couple of rooms on the ground floor. Some of the students even changed places, pushing our bikes behind us. The rooms were simple, but clean. Each of them had three beds, a small wardrobe and a table with a couple of chairs next to it. We noticed some of the boys carried two beds out of the second one to make room for our bikes.

It was certainly more pleasant and much cooler in this building and we were happy to get out of the scorching heat. Most of the students were leaving, but the two teachers showed us where all the commodities were. The bath and shower rooms were just down the corridor and some toilets next to them. There was a big mess hall further down with a very busy kitchen where cooks were preparing good smelling food in big pots.

We were left alone to freshen up and were told that they would come and take us to the Principal in about an hour. The shower felt great, and freshly shaven we felt great, but hungry. We put on clean clothes and waited to meet the Chief. It wasn't long before someone knocked on the door, which Theo opened. One of the teachers from before begged us to follow him. He led us back to the main building and up a big stairway to the next floor. He knocked on a beautifully handcrafted door, with a sign above which read Principal in big letters in English and Arabic. We entered the office and were greeted by a fairly tall man dressed immaculately like the teachers but sporting a silver bow tie and silver handkerchief in his lapel. He looked more like a European, than a Pakistani. (We found out later that his mother was English).

His office was like others we had visited except this one had many sporting pictures, framed Guernseys and awards hanging on the walls. Behind his desk a glass cabinet with lots of trophies inside stood. In the middle of the back wall was a framed picture of The Principal with his arm around Mr Micloalle's shoulder in front of the Hotel Metropole. By this time we and the two teachers were seated, by the desk. It was of no surprise when the door opened and a couple of staff members carried in some wooden trays with lots of dips, flat bread, fruit and a big pot of tea. It turned out that the teachers and Principal hadn't any lunch either. Normally they ate in the mess hall, but decided to have it in the office this time so they could talk to us undisturbed.

It was only a small luncheon because we were to be their guests at the Faletti hotel for dinner in the evening. I commented on the great picture on the back wall of the Metropole hotel. The Principle smiled and told us that Mr Micloalle was one of his closest friends. They grew up together and went to the same schools. They even went through University together. Both of them had been educated in England for several years. Eventually Mr Miclloalle had gone into the hospitality trade while the

The Big Adventure

Principal chose to stay in Education.

Every time he goes to Karachi he stays at his friend's hotel. He has have eaten at the *Mexicana Bar* many times.

It was a lovely afternoon and we found out quite a bit of history about Lahore and surroundings. We weren't asked too many questions because they had heard all about us from his friend and they were hoping we would speak to the students the next morning, to tell them of our journey. "We would be delighted," Theo told him, and asked if we could stay an extra day.

"A whole week if you have the time," was the answer from all three of them. We were informed that both teachers were Vice Principals of the Uni. No wonder we were so well looked after.

It wasn't just a simple dinner that night, it was a feast! Faletti was the biggest and most exclusive hotel in Lahore. The dining room was big and nearly all the tables were occupied. By now we were getting used to big dining rooms and stares from the public when we entered. It felt good to be important. We were seated on a big double table and introduced to several men and their families, including women and a couple of elderly boys. The women had their faces covered but we could still see their beautiful smiling eyes through a square slot in their Burka. One of the teachers told us that twice each year they take their families to England and their wives and daughters dress like English women. Of course after a while there getting used to the free life and English customs it is very hard to get them to come back.

The dinner was great and the evening stuck in my mind for a long time. Lying in bed later it was hard for me to fall asleep. It was hard to digest what happened to me as a nineteen year old boy who all of a sudden started to become an adult. With every new city and country we visited we seemed to become more confident in ourselves regardless of whether we were with rich or poor people.

The Auditorium next morning was packed with teachers, students and staff. We only had barely finished breakfast when we were told that all were assembled. Uli grabbed his camera, Theo some cards and I carried our book. As soon as we entered, everyone stood up clapped and we weren't even embarrassed. We were led onto a stage where our two Head Teachers greeted us and pointed at some chairs next to a small table where we were to sit. Unlike in Damascus, where we had felt very nervous to be confronted by a huge crowd of students, now we were much more experienced and confident. Also by now we had learned a considerable amount of the English and understood most of the questions being asked.

The two teachers were sitting next to us and translated some of the more difficult ones. The Principal sat in the front row with other dignitaries all sporting encouraging smiles of support. One of the teachers introduced us as German students who took a one year leave from our studies to cycle to the Olympiad in Melbourne. We also wanted to meet lots of different people, experience their customs and spread friendship to all the Nations we pass through.

I always felt a bit of a guilty every time our studies were mentioned, because none of us went to Uni. I didn't even finish my trade as a toolmaker but was introduced as an inventor. But then again, as advised back in Aleppo, we had to be students, otherwise we would not have been acknowledged. Many questions were asked and answered plus we had to speak fairly loud to be heard at the back of the hall. The questions came from all over and didn't seem to stop. A lot of students wanted to know about the German school systems, what were the main subjects and what kind of Languages were taught?

Uli answered all of those hard ones, because he was older than us.

Finally everybody wanted to know how we met King Faisal, the Shah with Queen Soraya and a short time ago President Iskander Mirza.

Someone asked, "Was there any special reason to visit all these high level persons?"

"Yes," Uli explained instantly, "because nobody believed, we could!"

There was laughter all-round and Uli even got lots of claps and hands waving!

What a fantastic answer I thought to myself and reached over to shake his hand.

Eventually the Principal came up to us and shook our hands and thanked us on behalf of the Uni for the great knowledge we had passed on to them. We got a standing ovation and everyone wanted to shake hands with us. We made a lot of friends that day and I knew we would be remembered for a long, long time!

After lunch at the mess hall some of the students showed us through the Uni, which took well over an hour. We were surprised how big the place was, with new buildings added, wherever possible. We could tell how excited and proud they were when they led us in to the sporting grounds, past hockey and cricket fields. Inside a large building was a basketball ring, lots of workout apparatuses and in an adjacent hall, even an Olympic pool. They were rapt when we told them that we had met the head of the Pakistani hockey team.

We patted some of them on the shoulder and told them their team would get gold. We did enjoy another lovely evening at the mess hall with a special dinner apparently in our honour. Afterwards, everyone shook hands with us and wished us all the best and may Allah look after us.

The Principal, some teachers and a few students were waiting for us in front of the office next morning to wave goodbye. We asked the Principal to send our fondest regards to Mr. Micloalle and Mr.Bugtani. "Will do," he said and waved farewell.

Someone mentioned that in Amritsar we should go to the hostel, next to the Golden Temple for accommodation.

What a surprise we received when we pushed our bikes through the front gate. On the road outside waiting for us were at least a dozen smiling students with bikes to accompany us to the border, which was halfway to Amritsar.

What a send off! They rode with us for a couple of hours until we got to the last village in Pakistan at the border. After a big goodbye, handshakes and best wishes all round we were by ourselves again.

As soon as they were out of sight we lit our first desperately needed smoke in nearly two days!

The commotion on the border was incredible. It was as if the whole of Pakistan wanted to move to India. By the time we had our passports stamped, which took awhile, because our yellow health booklets were closely examined, we were sweating like pigs.

We were also sad to leave Pakistan behind us! It was a tough country to cycle through, coming close to the freezing Himalayas and then heading south towards the hot tropics.

But what about the hospitality and the beautiful people we met wherever we stopped?

We certainly made a lot of friends and I am sure we left some good impressions behind us!

Entering into India, was something totally new.

We didn't leave only Pakistan behind.

We left all of the Arabic countries which we crossed behind, and now in hindsight I wish all those countries could be the same today as they were then half a century ago.

Journey of a Lifetime

Servicing our bikes the day before heading into India.

The Big Adventure

Chapter Nine

There were a couple of big bridges over multiple waterways through no man's land and once we crossed those we were in India!

And what a difference! We had to rub our eyes several times to be sure we were seeing properly, but what we saw was real!

There were women and they were not wearing burkas!

There were women all over the place, dressed in beautiful colours, chatting and laughing as women do when they are together. The uniformed officer who collected our passports and the officer who stamped them were both women. Up until this moment everyone at every border crossing had been male. It took a moment for it to sink in. After leaving Turkey we had gotten used to the Arabic way of life, and women were rarely seen, if at all, but this was something totally different. We stood beside our bikes and simply stared at all the vibrant activity. We happened to be standing near a money exchange shop so went in and changed the last of our Pakistani Rupees for Indian ones.

Outside again we paused for a moment to absorb the colour, and the sound. Even the air smelt different. Well, perhaps that could have been imagination. We climbed on our bikes and slowly started down the street towards more open country on the road to Amritsar.

We were in the Indian State of Punjab where most of the Sikh people lived. Amritsar was the capital of the state.

Most of the men we saw wore beautiful turbans, apparently hand bound every morning. Uli and Theo had never seen a man wearing one of them except in a black and white film called The Tiger of Eschnapur starring Theo Lingen, one of our favourites.

As a ten year old at my grandma's house in Kuernbach I had seen and drank tea with Sikh soldiers who fought in the British Army. Her house was occupied by the British. At that time I had not the faintest idea that nine years later I would cycle through their homeland.

It was the middle of the day and we only had about 25 kilometres to ride before we reached the Hostel. Normally we would have rested at this time of the day because of the heat, but we wanted to get there during the day.

We rode through a couple of villages and still could not believe the different life from one culture to another. The countryside itself still looked the same with lots of rice paddies being planted. We passed fields of sunflowers that extended as far as we could see. There were some stands next to the road selling fresh fruit and vegies. When we stopped at one of them to buy some fruit we were served by a beautiful young lady dressed in a colourful ankle length gown. She also wore a red silk scarf loosely covering her beautiful black hair. She had a red dot just above her nose in the middle of her forehead and served us with a big smile. We thought she was the most beautiful women we ever put our eyes on.

Uli through clenched teeth said to us in Schwaebisch, "*dui daede uff dor schdell heirada!*" meaning "*I would marry her on the spot*".

The traffic was murderous and it took longer than expected before we finally reached Amritsar. We only had to ask once and found our way to the Golden Temple quite easily.

The streets were wide and we passed beautiful manicured gardens. One thing that disturbed us, and it was something we never expected; individual cows walking or lying in the middle of the street, holding up traffic. We had noticed a few cows walking in the villages we had passed through, but didn't take much notice. With all the people around them we thought they were being herded to a paddock to be milked.

We were wondering why the traffic had banked up on both side of the road and could not believe what we saw. Two cows lying in the middle facing each other, one in front of a bus, the other one in front of a big truck. We couldn't work out why no one gave them a kick in the bum to move them along?

How could we possibly have imagined that cows are holy and were worshipped all over India? But it wasn't only cows; every animal was holy, and cows were the holiest. We pushed our bikes along the footpath to get past the jam, but further along we encountered one walking on the footpath and had to go around it.

We spotted the Golden Temple in all his glory and headed straight

The Big Adventure

for it. The hostel was opposite a huge archway behind a big plaza leading to the Temple. Naturally there were people all over the place and not all men wore turbans. We saw heaps of poorly dressed people, but not many beggars.

A couple of young well dressed Sikhs approached us and asked if they could be of any assistance. They had seen us looking around as if we were lost. Being foreigners we stood out like dog's balls with everyone staring at us.

We introduced ourselves and so did they. They were brothers and studied at the Golden Temple, but were from Allahabad on the Ganges River, south east of Delhi towards Calcutta. The older Brother, Wasu, was the same age as Uli, the younger one, I forgot his name, was our age.

"We were told in Lahore to come to this Hostel," Uli said. "We were told accommodation was cheap."

They both nodded as they listened. "There should be no problem," Wasu said. "We are both staying at the hostel and have shared a room for the last two months."

"Follow us," the younger of the two said.

They led the way and we went inside with our bikes. The hostel was U shaped, three stories high wrapped around a large open courtyard, and there were hundreds of bicycles leaning against the walls.

"Looks like everyone here rides bikes," Theo commented as we stared at the stacks of them.

"We certainly came to the tight place," Uli said.

"Why don't you wait here while I sort something out?" Wasu said.

He walked through a door almost hidden by a stack of bikes and disappeared.

In no time he was back holding three cool opened Coca Cola bottles and handed one to each of us. It was heavenly! This was the first Coke we had since somewhere in Turkey. We didn't know the reason then, but all over the Arab speaking countries there was no Coca Cola for sale anywhere. You could only get a Pepsi. I almost downed the contents in one gulp.

Two elderly women had followed Wasu out and they pointed towards the back of the building. They smiled at us and took our empty bottles. We followed Wasu. We liked those two from the very moment they spoke to us and we somehow knew we could trust them. Wasu managed to get a vacant room exactly opposite theirs. It had three beds, but was too crowded for us with the bikes and the luggage.

"Easy fixed," said Wasu. He pushed their third bed next to his. "See, you can leave two of your bikes here."

Now we had enough space in our room to move around without stepping on each other's toes. Toilets and shower rooms were close by, which was very handy. We were hot, sweaty and dirty after having pushed our bikes through crowded streets to get here and we certainly needed a shower.

Wasu asked if we were hungry and Uli told him, we could certainly do with something to eat, but we wanted to have a shower first, to freshen up a bit.

The hostel was huge and only occupied by men, but not only by Sikhs. They came from all over India, mainly Hindus.

As if to explain the absence of women, Wasu said as we went to get something to eat, "There is also a hostel for women not too far away."

We wanted to light a cigarette, but noticed that no one smoked in the hostel. We asked Wasu about it and he would explain the different customs, as soon as we had something to eat.

We had to walk a fair distance away from the Temple to find a small eating place with room for the five of us to sit. There was no problem smoking on the street, and we quickly lit up cigarettes of our own. There were lots of other men smoking with weird contraptions and spitting onto the road saliva that looked like blood.

When I pointed that out to Wasu, he just smiled. "A lot of older men have red teeth because they chew betel nut. It's slightly intoxicating, but the juice from the nut eventually stains the teeth red. The longer you have been chewing the nut the redder the teeth become."

It makes them look gruesome when they smile, I thought.

They were also smoking thinly rolled tobacco leaf filled with pine needles.

I looked at the table next to us and the food had such an intense colour I figured it must be very hot. I nudged Uli and nodded my head towards the table. "I don't reckon we could eat anything like that," I said.

Uli turned to Wasu and said "We are not used to eating really hot food. Can you ask them not to put chillies in it?"

Wasu explained this to the waiter, when he ordered the meal. "I can't promise there won't be some chilli in it," he told us, "but it certainly won't be too hot."

Wasu and his brother then got up and told us to follow them. At the other end, next to the toilet, was a trough with slow running water where the brothers washed their hands. They asked us to do the same. We wondered why for a moment but then realised when we got back to the table what the reason was. A plate was put in front of each of us and the waiter scooped a big lump of steamed rise out of a pot on wheels and put it in the centre of each plate. Another guy came with a bowel of different stir fried vegetables. He scooped out some and placed it next to the rice on the plates. As soon as this was done another waiter placed some grilled meat with the ribs still attached on top of everything. Each of us was handed a big flat piece of bread. There were no utensils or cutlery on the table. We watched the two brothers tear the bread into small pieces which they used to scoop up the food.

In Arabia we had eaten a few times with the right hand only, and here we did the same. Uli and I enjoyed the food, even though it was still a bit hot. Theo got stuck into the rice and gravy ignoring the more spicy stuff. We drank lots of hot black tea which was served nonstop and which helped wash away the burning sensations from the chillies. Though there were no chillies in the food that we could see, I suspect it had all been cooked in the same bowls and pots and when served they made sure not to collect any chilli pieces. The food was still hot, but we managed.

It was very warm and humid with loud radio music playing. This music was totally different to the Arabic music we had heard. It was also very strange to our ears. It was only after we finished our meal when Wasu and his brother asked questions about our plans after Amritsar. We answered a few of them, but told them that we would like to show them our book next morning if it would be possible. They would love to see it and hear the rest of our story.

Wasu told us that they were studying at the University in Allahabad (about 400Ks south-east of Amritsar). Because of summer vacation, they were able to come to Amritsar to worship and learn more about their religion. They had been here for five weeks and were leaving for home in another three days.

We had finished our meal and the tea and washed our hands again. I wanted to pay for the bill, but Wasu said "Don't worry; it's already taken care of."

Funny I thought to myself, I didn't see any of those two paying for it earlier on.

Walking back to the hostel, we thanked them for their hospitality. Both of them smiled and told us they would be looking forward to showing us around Amritsar and especially the Temple next day.

Wasu started to explain the rules about their religion, but Uli patted him on the shoulder and asked him if he could tell us all about it in the morning. We told them that we'd had a big day and were very tired.

When we walked into the hostel his brother stepped into the office and came back with some water bottles. He handed each of us one bottle to drink during the night. We thanked them once more and entered our room.

"What do you think *buaba* (friends) about the reception on our first day in India?" Before we could answer he said with a big grin, "It can only get better!"

If it weren't for the ceiling fans sleeping would have been near impossible. Before finally falling asleep I thought about my friends and family back home. We are in India! I would have to write a letter in the morning to tell them. I couldn't help wondering what people would say when they receive the news. I felt like patting myself on the shoulder especially when I imagined my dad telling everyone at work.

None of us had the chance to sleep in next morning. Before daybreak the unusual music started blaring out and it seemed like there were hundreds of people chanting. Life certainly starts early in India.

I could easily have slept another couple of hours. Feeling stiff as we got up we hardly had time to put on some clothes when someone knocked on our door. It was Wasu, smiling, a freshly wound turban on his head and dressed in a long white robe.

"How did you sleep?" he asked. "Are you ready for breakfast?"

"We didn't expect to get up this early." Uli muttered. "We really need a shower and a cleanup first."

"That's okay," Wasu said, I'll come back in thirty minutes."

And he was back exactly thirty minutes later.

Breakfast was at the back of the hostel in a separate building. Students were everywhere, some eating at tables while many others sat on the floor around a big plate full of food. In front of the kitchen was a very long table with a variety of big hot and cold pots from which we had to help ourselves. We each had to get a plate, scoop some of the food onto it and then collect some slabs of flat bread. With the right hand we used pieces of the flat bread to pick up the food to eat it. Wasu's brother had already reserved a table for six (a friend of theirs had also joined us) and we sat there.

Finally we had some time to relax and get to know each other better. I had brought our book to show them and Theo brought a couple of our cards. I can't remember how many pots of tea we drank, but it felt like questions and answers in a class room. They could not hear enough about us and our adventures. I don't know how many times we told our story at different places. Some of the students looked at us as if we came from another planet. Well, not quite from another planet, but certainly from a country they had barely heard of and knew absolutely nothing about.

Being occupied by England for over 200 years, they knew just a lot about British history, but not too much about the rest of the World. They couldn't get enough of Germany, the war and our schooling, being an occupied country only nine years earlier.

They couldn't get over the fact that Theo at 15 and myself at just 16 had cycled to Africa and got sent back home by Interpol from Tunisia (we didn't tell them we were in handcuffs) Of course Uli with our other friend Konrad had made a similar tour one year later through France and Spain and got as far as Morocco (They came back after 4 months without the help of Interpol).

They almost fell off their chairs when they found out that I was born in Philadelphia and I had to show them my Passport. Some other of their friends joined us at the table, and with others standing behind us the questions came from all directions. They were very interested in our education so far and of course we told them that we were taking for our world tour before going to Uni when we returned to Germany.

Wasu, who asked most of the questions wanted to know why we were doing it on bikes? Uli quickly patted him on his shoulder and said, "Dear Wasu for several reasons. Firstly, we are not rich and have only limited finances. Secondly, we want to experience lots of different nations and learn about their cultures. Thirdly, we want to meet kind, hospitable, beautiful people like you, and we are extremely happy to make it to India so far!"

Uli certainly had a way with words! He always said the appropriate words at the right time. Uli got handshakes all round and Wasu smiled from ear to ear.

Theo told Uli in our dialect of German, "*Bauer des hosch widor amol guad gmachd*" meaning, "Bauer you did very well again!"

Glancing through some of the pages in our book, Theo explained to them about some of the people who we had met. If the music hadn't been blaring and if there had not been so much noise around us, you could have heard a pin drop; especially when we told them about King Faisal, Shah Reza Pahlavi and Queen Soraya.

How utterly surprised they were when they saw the signatures of President Iskander Mirza and the finance minister of Pakistan, whom we met only just over a week ago.

Naturally there were more questions from all sides and lots of excited chatter amongst themselves. As if it was the most natural thing for us to do Uli looked around and told every one of them, "When we get to New Delhi we will meet your Prime Minister, Pandit Jawaharlal Nehru!"

I couldn't suppress a smile as I, looked at those astonished faces. A few of them might have seen Mahatma Gandhi when they were young, but none of them had ever seen Pandit Nehru, other than in the news. He had been elected in 1947 and was the first Indian Prime Minister of Independent India. That's really all we knew about him then.

We also told them that our big goal was to reach Melbourne at the start of the Olympic Games in November. After a couple of hours we had made lots of friends!

We asked Wasu if we could go outside now because we were dying for a smoke, but really we just wanted to get away for a bit from all the noise and the questions.

We found a shady place outside under a tree and lit up, but it was already too hot to enjoy a cigarette. Finally being alone with Wasu his brother and friend, we were able to ask a few questions ourselves. It turned out that they lived in Allahabad, which including Benares, now Varanasi, are the holiest of cities on the Granges rive in India.

Their father and a couple of uncles had a restoration and stone making business there where they repaired, cleaned and restored old temples and stone buildings; and there were plenty of those all over India. Their friend who studied at the same Uni was a Hindu, but accompanied them to learn about the Sikh religion. They only had another three days in Amritsar before having to return home. Wasu told us that they wanted to show us as much as possible over those days and meet some influential people.

"We are all yours," Uli said and gave all three of them a hug.

We had hardly enough time to go to the bathroom before they were in front of our door waiting for us. As we walked across to the Golden Temple the crowds became bigger and bigger. There were thousands in the plaza in front of a big building with a large wall on either side. In the middle was a huge archway leading to the Temple.

What an awesome sight! The Golden Temple in all its might in front of us!

Entering the Golden Temple...

It wasn't as big as some of the Mosques we had visited, but it was incredibly awesome! And it had looked just as awesome for 400 years.

To me it looked like a beautifully carved huge golden nugget. There were three big entrances leading to the Temple with the main one facing the front of the Temple. You had to walk along some kind of undercover pier to get there. The 400 year old Temple was situated, dead set in the middle of a big square artificial lake of clean fresh water.

The crowed was enormous. I had never seen so many people worshiping in one place. There were young and old rich and poor side by side, and families with well behaved children. Wasu had told us that the Temple was washed every morning with milk and water.

He also informed us about the different customs of the Sikhs. They never cut their hair which was held by a small comb under the Turban. They wear underwear and carry a small dagger on their side. On their most used hand they wear a metal bracelet on that lower arm and they do not smoke.

After watching some of the worshippers wading in the water and washing themselves, Wasu led us out through another entrance. As soon as we were outside we lit a smoke. Stern faced, Wasu glared at Uli and me. "Did you carry those smokes with you through the temple?"

"Of course," Uli told him, "Where else would we carry them? Why?"

"I forgot to mention that Sikhs don't smoke. It is forbidden to carry tobacco inside the Temple."

"Don't worry," Uli said as diplomatically as possible, "next time we won't."

Wasu stared at us until without saying another word until shamefully we felt compelled to drop the partly smoked cigarettes which we pummelled into the ground with our feet.

Another view of the 400 year old Golden Temple

After lunch at the hostel Wasu asked, "Would you like to meet Master Tara Singh Ramgarhia to let him write in your book and take some photos?"

He was the leader of the Sikh at the Temple.

"We would love to meet the Big Boss," Uli told him with a smile. "It would be a great honour."

"You shouldn't ask for a sponsorship," Wasu explained, "because having a photo and writing from him in your book would be a big help to you on your way."

"But," Wasu added, "If you would be interested I can arrange for you to speak to the Amritsar Rotary Club members this evening. You would certainly get paid to do that."

"Of course we would," we said happily.

I didn't know what Rotary was at that time, but soon learned how important service Clubs were all over the world.

We emptied our pockets, to make sure that we had no smokes on us. I grabbed our book and a couple of cards with our signatures on the back and followed Wasu, who was by himself this time.

Before entering the Temple Wasu asked us about the tobacco?

Uli with a huge smile told him "No Wasu, we are clean."

Naturally he didn't believe him and felt all our pockets to make sure.

The whole area was surrounded by a big square wall with lots of different sized buildings in between. The Temple was right in the middle and one could walk all around it while worshiping. Moving through the crowd Wasu steered us towards one of the buildings which was part of the wall. It was about three storeys high and I assumed it was the Administration office.

My assumption was right. Wasu led us past a lot of busy office personnel and greeted all of them as if he was the boss. Up at the next level he stopped and talked to two armoured guards. One of them opened a door for us to enter. Inside it was just like an ordinary office with three desks and several comfortable chairs around a conference table where three people sat. One desk was occupied by two very attractive young ladies dressed beautifully in Indian costumes. The other one was occupied by a single elderly Sikh who greeted Wasu as if he was his son. We found out later, that it was his uncle. There was no one seated at the third desk but we could tell that it was the Master's desk. It had a big manager's chair behind it and on the back wall was a beautiful painting of the Golden Temple. There were also two big pictures of Queen Elisabeth and Prince

Phillip on either side of it.

The Master and two Associates stood up from the conference table to welcome Wasu who bowed, and so did we, before Wasu had introduced us. The Master greeted us with a beautiful soft smile and I couldn't take my eyes off him. I was mesmerised. He was dressed all in black, wearing a big black turban and had the most beautiful long, curly beard I had ever seen. What an incredible man! To me he seemed about ten foot tall and I could well believe that the Sikhs treated him like a God. They had known a fair bit about us, because Wasu's younger brother had been here a couple of hours before and told them about our travels.

After our customary glass of tea seated at the conference table I opened our book to browse through some of the pages. They all were taken by our journey; even the two young ladies were standing behind us, not wanting to miss a thing. The Master wrote in our book and shortly after Wasu stood up and we did the same. It was a joyful good bye and they all wished us safe travels. Another great man in our book: The leader of a

The page from our travel book with Master Tara Singh Ramgarhia and the words he wrote.

Uli, Fred, and Theo with Wasu and his brother.

very important religion who was like a God to the Sikhs!

Back at the hostel we had a quick shower and waited for Wasu and his brother to take us to the Rotary Club. We had to walk a fair distance past the Temple to reach a big old building that looked more like a Museum or an Exhibition building. It was surrounded by beautiful gardens. It was the Maharaja Ranjit Sing Hall, in Rambagh Gardens. The hall inside was more like a giant restaurant and was three quarters full with well dressed men. Most of them were Sikhs, but there were some Hindus as well as several European Gentlemen dressed in dinner suits. There were no women! The Rotary Club Members were mostly business men, doctors, tradesmen and politicians. They get together once a week to raise funds to help needy people.

We were introduced by the club President and asked to sit at his table together with several others. Wasu and his brother were seated at one of the other tables. Tea was served and with everyone talking the room was quite noisy. After a while the President stood and with a wooden mallet knocked on a small bell in front of him on the table and instantly it went quiet. We had to stand and bow our heads while the President said some words that finished with India and the Queen. Seated again someone else, presumably the Secretary because he had a lot of papers in front of him, started to fill everyone in what had happened during the past week. By the time he went through every page and answered heaps of questions, more than an hour had passed. I was getting bored because I didn't know what it was all about, but had to pretend to show interest. Once he finished and sat down waiters brought in a variety of plates with food, and the place became as noisy again as it had been before.

Through all this another guy had been studying our book and wrote down heaps of notes while asking questions to Uli who sat next to him. I had seen this guy talking to Wasu earlier on and I guessed Wasu had told him all about us. Another gentleman got up with an open tin in his hand, walked to the first table and pointed to one guy. He named him and told some kind of a story about this man and everybody started laughing. The guy everyone was laughing at had to put some money into the tin. I couldn't understand that if someone made jokes about a guy, why that guy had to pay money when the joke was on him. Many of the guys copped it and they all paid handsomely because when the guy came back to our table the tin was overflowing. A great way to make money I thought to myself.

Finally it was our turn when the guy who took notes got up to tell everyone where we were from. They were all anxious to hear our story and I had noticed Wasu and his brother answering questions. The guy did a pretty good job introducing us and telling them about our lives. I was amazed how much he learned in just a couple of hours. His questions were precise and our answers by now were precise also. During this time the Secretary wrote some nice words on their letterhead, which we glued in our book.

Unfortunately no one asked how we financed our journey which was a bummer, though we couldn't really ask for a sponsorship! We must have spoken for a good hour when the President on behalf of all the members thanked us very much for the entertainment. He and the others wished us well and hoped for a safe journey through India. We shook hands all round and started to follow a smiling Wasu who was waiting at the door way with his brother.

It was pretty late by the time we got back to the hostel. As soon as we were inside Wasu asked if he and his brother could come to our room for a few minutes.

The Big Adventure

We held the door open and indicated that they should sit on one of the beds. There were no chairs in the room.

"Well that was a great success tonight," he said while smiling from ear to ear.

He handed Theo a brown envelope. "Go on, open it," he said when Theo hesitated.

To our surprise the envelope was full with various Indian currencies.

Now we realised why Wasu had such a big grin. Apparently he had arranged it earlier on and told the Secretary that we were looking for sponsors. Some of the money came out of the tin which the joke guy had collected. Theo calculated the equivalent and it was just on US$200. We hugged both of them and thanked them over and over.

Wasu told us that they had arranged four more visits for the next day to meet more influential People. The more, the merrier I thought to myself! "But before anything else, first thing in the morning you must go to watch the Golden Book being carried into the Temple." Tomorrow was also to be their last day, before they had to return to Allahabad.

We slept well, but hardly were out of bed next morning when Wasu knocked on the door, telling us to get ready as soon as possible. The sun was barely up when we followed the three (their mate from home was with them again) of them to the Temple, already crammed with people. Many were being fed at a big kitchen outside the temple all paid for by the Sikhs and the City of Amritsar. There were men and women sitting on steps half submerged in the holy water, (we found out later that some of these people and their families came from far away).

But the oddest thing was how very quiet it was; not even the kids there made any noise. Usually with a crowd this size it was always noisy.

We were standing in the middle of the huge crowd, halfway in front of the Temple with our backs towards a big double door when it started to open. The first thing we saw was Tara Sing the Master walking towards the Temple creating a path as the people parted to let him through. He was followed by six Sikhs who carried a small stretcher, about one by two meters, on their shoulders. It was a beautiful handcrafted stretcher, with a one and a half meter high post on each corner supporting a ceiling looking like a small dome. Everything was painted in Gold, or more likely was plated with gold leaf. In the middle of it was a huge book resting on a laced pillow. The gold stretcher was carried into the Temple and placed in to the middle. None of us had any idea of what it was about, but what a great spectacle it was, and to be a witness to this is something I relish to this day.

The boy's took us back to the hostel for breakfast and so we could get ready to meet the people they had spoken of the night before. We could have had something to eat at the Temple, but there were just too many people and it would have taken too long for us to get anywhere near the food.

This time we took a couple of rickshaws, because Wasu and friends came with us. Wasu took us to the town Hall to meet with the Commissioner of Amritsar, but we had to meet the Deputy instead because the Commissioner was in New Delhi.

It didn't matter; the Deputy invited us in with big handshakes and insisted we have tea and biscuits in his office. After spending a couple of hours in his office telling him about ourselves and the journey, he wrote a few sentences in our book. I was flabbergasted by how Wasu was on such good terms with the Deputy and thought he knew just about every one!

Afterwards we visited a big photographic sound Studio, owned by a Father and his Son. We were there nearly two hours and when we left they expressed sadness for us not staying longer. This was followed by meeting the Principal and a couple of teachers from the Kalsa College in Amritsar. They would have liked it if we could speak to the students, but we told them we would be leaving next morning. Anyhow, the Principal wrote in our book and gave us a letter of recommendation for his friend, the Principal at the Kalsa College in Jullundur.

Wasu seemed to be in a hurry after we left the College. He told us he had made an arrangement with one more important person for us to meet. Crikey I thought to myself, Wasu is in full mode and enjoying every minute of it.

We only had to cross a couple of streets when the boys stopped in front of a big building, with several doorways. We followed Wasu up a couple of storeys, where he opened a door without even knocking. In a small reception room Wasu and his brother were greeted by a smiling young female who looked gorgeous. We were introduced and I noticed when she pressed a small button on her desk a door behind her opened as if by magic.

A tall good looking Sikh with a big grin had opened the door and took Wasu and his brother in his arms. Behind him were his wife and two younger children a boy and a girl. It turned out that the gorgeous lady was the boys' mother's younger sister.

The Big Adventure

We followed them into the other room which was very elaborate. It was a conference and lounge room combined. The conference table was full of good looking food and the gorgeous young lady was filling cups of freshly brewed tea. Wasu introduced us to his aunty, uncle and the children. We were asked to take a seat at the table and enjoy the food, which was absolutely delicious. Even Theo found enough to satisfy his appetite.

Now I knew why Wasu was in such a hurry to get here, because it was all arranged. Their uncle was the Minister of Reform, whatever that meant, and was all ears, as he listened to our story. Wasu had filled him in the day before and we were very happy to answer all his questions. I can't remember how many glasses of tea I drank, because every time my glass was empty the young lady would fill it up again! It was a lovely time and a fine gesture from the boys and their family.

We had not expected this great hospitality; could never even have imagined such a thing happening. How lucky we were to encounter Wasu and his brother more or less the moment we had arrived! After the Minister had written some words in our book, Wasu got up and started to say goodbye and thanked the family and so did we. They all walked down to the street with us and waved when our rickshaws left to take us back to the hostel.

Where had the day gone? It was already dark by the time we got to our room. It had been a long hard day, full of excitement and we achieved a lot and although we were absolutely exhausted we still had to decide the route we were to travel the next morning. Theo spread a roadmap over his bed and was studying it when the boys entered smiling.

"We got something for you," Wasu said, and threw two sealed envelopes on my bed. "Open them," he said, pointing to me, "I know what's in them."

The first one I opened was from the photo studio and had the equivalent of US$250 in Rupees. The second one had three one hundred US Dollar bills in it but no written note.

I looked at Wasu and with a big grin he said, "it's from my uncle and aunty."

We certainly had not expected anything like this. We couldn't find enough words to thank him. Uli was the first one to take them in his arms, followed by Theo and me.

We had a thousand questions to ask them, but Wasu held up his hand and stopped us. He told us that all the meetings had been arranged the day before and it gave them great pleasure having us meet some of their friends and relatives. Wasu handed me one more envelope, containing some handwritten notes. The first one was his home address and phone number in Allahabad, the second one was of a Temple in New Delhi belonging to Mr. Birla. We should go to this Temple to get some cheap, but good accommodation. The third one was a phone number of a reporter who writes for the Hindustani Times, and who was waiting for our call.

The boys informed us that they would catch a bus at ten in the morning straight for New Delhi where they would spend one day before heading for Allahabad. Apparently the boys' Hindu friend had to visit relatives there.

We arranged to have breakfast together and pack our bikes straight after so we could all leave at the same time. What a day it has been, and again we kept thinking what a great blessing it had been for us to meet up with those fantastic boys a couple of days earlier. We were on a high and had lots to digest. Without mentioning sponsorship to anyone we managed to finish up with close to 600 Dollars and that after only a few days in India.

Early next morning we had a big breakfast with the boys, surrounded by many of the other students who wanted to say farewell. Packing our bikes was done in no time and we were able to escort the boys to the bus stop. Needles to say that trying to pay for our stay at the hostel was fruitless, but there was a collecting box and we were able to donate at least ten bucks, which made us feel good. Amongst a huge crowd at the bus stop we hugged the boys and Wasu told us they would be waiting for us in Allahabad. With a big grin Wasu told us to enjoy New Delhi and boarded the bus.

We already had a rickshaw waiting to guide us out of Amritsar, towards Jullundur. Being back on the bike felt great, but it got hotter by the hour. Travelling wasn't hard because we had a slightly cool breeze coming down from the Himalayas, but after a while we had to rest under a clump of trees. We were only about 40Km past Amritsar, but I reckon we smoked more than a half pack of cigarettes by then. We were dying for some fags, having to restrain from tobacco around the Temple.

We found a secluded spot just before Kartarpur next to a big field of sunflowers. Sleeping on the ground again under a clear sky wasn't too bad and we had a reasonably good night. We were surrounded by lots of inquisitive people in Kartarpur next morning where we stopped for a breakfast of hard boiled eggs flat bread, fruit and tea. Most of the other food was obviously too hot for us.

We made Jullundur, one of the oldest cities in India, before midday and guided by a rickshaw had no trouble finding the Lyallpur Khalsa College.

"Have a look at this." Theo cried out. He was riding in front of us as we entered through a big open gate towards a well kept Administration building.

Somehow I wasn't greatly surprised, to discover we were expected. On the long steps of the building stood many students, boys and girls, most of them our age, some a bit younger. On top of the steps were the Sikh teachers with some elderly ladies next to them.

When we came to a halt in front of them we were immediately surrounded by most of the smiling students. They wanted to shake hands and asked questions, some even took photographs. The noise was deafening. We hardly knew which way to turn our heads, until we heard some kind of whistle and all went quiet. Most of the students then walked away towards different buildings until finally we were greeted by the Teachers and introduced by them to the Principal.

"Why the great welcome?" Uli asked the Principal and was told he got the news from his friend in Amritsar. We were expected around this time, because they had some spies on the road. They had seen us and passed on the word that we were on our way.

Some of the immaculately dressed ladies were teachers but two were secretaries. Our bikes were lifted up the steps and we followed them down a cool corridor before a door at the end opened and we were asked to enter.

It was a big room with two beds, two lounge chairs, a desk and big fan on the ceiling. One of the Teachers opened an adjacent door to a room with another three beds inside.

"These are some of our special guest rooms," one of the teachers said. "Toilets and bathrooms are along the corridor."

"Take some time to settle in," another said. "Someone will come along in about an hour to take you to meet the Principal."

Finally when we were alone, Uli said sat on one of the beds and said. "So Buaba, waas sagad dor jedsd?" meaning, "well boys, what do you say now?"

There was plenty of room for the bikes and luggage. Ulli and Theo shared the front room. After some freshening up we didn't have to wait long before we were taken upstairs to meet and be greeted again by the

Fred in Amritsar

Theo in Amritsar

Principal and staff again.

I had our book with us and a couple of cards, plus the recommendation letter from Amritsar.

The usual tea was served accompanied by bread and savoury dips.

The Principal wanted to know all about Amritsar and asked us if we would be willing to talk to his students in the morning.

"We would be delighted," Uli replied, because that would give us plenty of time to leave by late afternoon. After all the normal questions and answers, plus numerous glasses of tea, we were invited for dinner in the evening.

"As long as the food is not too hot," Uli quipped with a smile.

By late afternoon after a rest we met the Principal, his staff and a couple of teachers at the steps in front of the main building. There were buildings everywhere including a big sporting oval with included amenities. There was also a hostel for students from out of town. We set off expecting a long walk but in no time we were outside the school grounds in a street jammed with noisy traffic and people everywhere.

It was early evening but still very warm. Pushing through the crowds on the footpath we turned into an almost invisible side street. We followed them through into an old building and out into a huge back yard. Most of the yard was covered by a weatherboard roof held up by steel posts. There were no side walls, but there were rows of small bushes and lots of flowers in pots. There was a kitchen on one side of the yard and the rest was filled with rattan chairs and a number of tables of various sizes. By the time we were seated around one big table, the whole place was full.

The noise was deafening and the smell— unreal.

It wasn't a bad smell: on the contrary for me it was quite pleasant, but very unfamiliar. Sitting amongst so many sweaty people in this hot weather was a bit off-putting but the lovely but strange smells from the kitchen was a winner. We were really hungry.

The first thing we cherished was a beautiful cold bottle of Coke. Different dishes were served nonstop as one of the teachers explained what they were. Some of the dishes came in brass containers, some in clay pots and some dips in glass jars. There were different meat, vegetable and salad dishes, all accompanied with heaps of flat bread.

When I looked surprised at the number of meat dishes one of the teachers said "Except for beef, we are allowed to eat any other kind of meat." ...which immediately had me wondering just what kinds of meat there were in all the different plates son the table.

Several different dishes from the others were put in front of us.

"These have fewer chillies in them. Hopefully you will be able to eat them."

They were still hot as far as I was concerned, but Uli managed them easily. Theo stuck to salads which he saw had no chillies in them at all.

It was a great evening and by the time we got back to our rooms we were stuffed!

At the assembly hall next morning we were welcomed to a full house, similar to Lahore, except here we had just as many girls as boys, and the questions came thick and fast until eventually they ran out of things to ask after which we had some lunch and mingled with the students who miraculously discovered more questions to ask.

Our bikes had been packed before we went to the assembly hall, and after the Principal had written in our book and handed Ulli an open envelope, it was time to say goodbye.

Ulli counted close to 200 Dollars in Rupees and we thanked them for their generosity.

The Principal shook our hands once more and told us the college and staff had been more than grateful for having had us stay with them.

Once more quite a few students were waiting for us to lead us out of the city and after a few kilometres we were again on our own. The traffic was hectic but moving well and we felt great. It wasn't long before we stopped in Phagwara where we bought some drinks, bread and a few tins of food for the evening. About 10km before Ludhiana we crossed a big river and found a good camping spot alongside it. We slept soundly and by daybreak we were already on our saddles and riding along the highway. Ludhiana wasn't as big as Jullundur, but it took us a good hour to get through it.

Riding directly south, it got hotter as the days progressed and it got pretty sweaty under our helmets and around our Testicles! In the mornings we travelled reasonable well, covering mostly between 50 and 60km, but in the afternoons we were lucky to make 40km. We made it through Ambala and found a spot to rest for the night. After repairing a slow puncture on Theo's bike in the morning we rode through Ismailbad and stopped for lunch and a few hours rest at Pehowa. In all the small villages we rode through we were waved at and some boys and men cycled next to us and wanting to know where the heck we came from.

I dare say at that time no one had ever seen anything like us before!

We crossed Kaithal and camped about 20km before Jind next to a small canal. A quick breakfast in Jind next morning was all we needed to put a few kilometres under our belt before we stopped for some rest close to Rhotak.

We entered the town late afternoon and close to the middle we asked for a hotel and were told there were a couple of good ones only a short distance ahead right in the centre of town. Dodging cows and weaving through traffic, we picked the first one we saw, near a beautiful Hindu Temple. The smell of incense wafted all over the place. It was a smell we soon got used to and hardly ever noticed again no matter where else we went in India.

Theo went inside to check the prices while Ulli and I minded the bikes, surrounded by the usual onlookers. We had hardly finished a smoke when Theo came back with a well dressed clean shaven Hindu gentleman wearing white cap and long white gown. He was followed by four servants. Theo told us the price was reasonable. The servants lifted our bikes and carried them up a couple of steps into a pleasantly cool hotel foyer.

Just past the reception desk, along one of two corridors was an open door. We entered a big family room with a double bed in the centre and three smaller ones on the opposite wall. There was also a small couch and next to the door a small hand wash basin.

Heaps of room for us, our bikes and our luggage! We thanked them very much and Theo gave the main guy a few coins for their help.

Uli and Theo jumped straight onto the double bed which left me the choice one of the smaller ones. The big ceiling fan swirled the air around quite pleasantly, just as well, because it was still very hot outside. The toilets and bathrooms were a few doors along the corridor and it wasn't long before we stood under a welcome shower to wash the last three day's grime off our bodies.

Over the last couple of days we had left Punjab, the Sikh State, and had been travelling amongst the Hindu States, which are predominant across the rest of India. To this day in the back of my mind I still think that the State of Punjab is the most influential in the whole of India.

In the last few towns and villages we passed through there were more beggars and poor people sleeping on the footpath than before. We walked to a nearby market place, bought some fruit, cigarettes and ordered a couple of teas and enjoyed a smoke.

The Big Adventure

Having dinner at the hotel's dining room we told the waiter that our mouth was not used to such hot food. The rice and bread they served us was okay, but the lamb pieces and veggies were still very hot, especially for Theo. There were some hard boiled eggs, which Ulli and I left for him.

It wasn't very late after dinner so we decided to write some postcards and letters on the dining room table to post in New Delhi. We had brought plenty of postcards in Amritsar but never found time to write while there.

We slept well and after some tea and a couple of dips, we were on our way at sunrise. I had paid our bill the night before and we all thought it was quite reasonable and friendly.

It didn't matter how early we travelled on India's roads, they are always busy, especially close to a big city. When we rested around midday we were exhausted. We only made about 50km with still another 20 ahead. Twice we had to stop at railway crossings for long trains dangerously over filled with people. Every available space was taken, with some people even sitting on top of the roof. You had to see it to believe it!

After a couple of hours under some trees we hit the road again, but the closer we got to New Delhi the harder it became. It wasn't just trucks, cars, busses or cycles slowing down the traffic, it was Cows, believe it or not! We actually had to ride around several cows that had nothing better to do than rest on the middle of the road where they sat ignoring everyone and the chaos around them. No one ever disturbed them. They either went around them or simply waited until the cows decided it was time to get up and move. Unbelievable! We often had to push our bikes around such venerated living obstacles.

With about 10 kilometres to get to the centre of New Delhi we asked a vacant rickshaw driver if he knew where the Sri Lakshmi Narayan Temple (Birla Mander) was. Of course he knew, and immediately quoted a price to take us there.

Uli was about to accept the inflated price when a couple of the others called out to tell us they would do it cheaper.

We grabbed the first one because he told us he knew a better way to get there off the main road. He was right; there was still a lot of movement on the smaller streets, but no big trucks or busses. We followed him for well over an hour, passing some smaller Temples and nicely manicured parks, before stopping in front of a huge Temple.

Actually it was more like three Temples, a big one in the middle and a smaller one on each side, surrounded by beautiful gardens. A couple of carved white marble elephants were at the entry to the main building. The Temple was well set back from a wide busy road with a huge tiled walkway leading to a dozen or more big steps up to the Temple.

Ulli paid the driver who couldn't stop thanking him until Ulli waved him off with a smile. We asked some official looking uniformed guy if he knew where the hostel was. He pointed to the next corner where we spotted the building at the back of the Temple. Pushing our bikes through another large doorway to an open courtyard, we were greeted by several smiling men and women and one of the men maybe the same age as Ulli was saying "Welcome our German cyclists."

I was stunned, and from the look from my friends I think they also were. Here we were in the middle of New Delhi, India and were greeted like this, when not a soul knew who we were. How could they have known about us?

It didn't take long to find out. Apparently they had three visitors here staying with Mr Birla who owns this Temple (He was at that time the richest man in India) and many others all over India. One young Hindu, whose dad was a very good friend of Mr Birla and his two Sikh friends from Allahabad stayed here one night. They were on their way back from Amritsar and made a stopover in Delhi before going back home to inform Mr Birla of our arrival.

Suddenly it clicked, and we remembered the big grin on Wasu's face when he told us to enjoy Delhi. Their friend didn't have to visit relatives, they had this all planned and the surprise was perfect. By the time we realised this we had lots of people listening to our discussion and smiling at our dumbfounded but happy faces. The guy who welcomed us and a couple of others led us to the end of the courtyard and stopped in front of a brick building. Inside on the ground floor a door was opened to a room with three bunks in it and a couple of doors further was another room with a double bunk and plenty of room for our bikes. The welcome guy informed us that if we needed anything, just drop in at the front office. He also told us that Mr. Birla would like to meet us in his office around 10am next morning. There would be a reporter from the Hindu Times with him.

We unpacked our bikes, showered and changed into well overdue clean clothes. Sitting on the beds which were wooden bunks covered by a thin mattress and a pillow on top, I suggested we make some plans, but Ulli shook his head."Why so soon? We have to wait to see what tomor-

The Big Adventure

row morning brings first. Afterwards we can decide what plans to make."

I found it hard to sort out my feelings at that moment. After leaving Kohtak in the morning we were very apprehensive about what would confront us in India's Capitol City. What can I say; here we are sharing two rooms adjacent to one of the biggest Hindu Temples near the centre of the City.

We walked over to the office and asked the guy who had welcomed us to point out some shops and eating places.

"All along the side streets you can find everything you need. But be careful of the water. You should only drink water out of sealed glass bottles ore freshly squeezed fruit juices."

We thanked him, and laughing at that advice told him, "We are always very careful about what we put into our mouth."

We found a nice open eating place to have some bread, a couple of dips, a few teas and best of all, relaxing with a couple of smokes.

It was a great achievement to be here in New Delhi and we couldn't stop talking and reminiscent of our trip so far. It was fantastic to be enjoying life on our first evening in Delhi. We grabbed a couple of Coke bottles each and after paying for our bill we slowly walked back to the Temple. Sleeping on those bunks wasn't as bad as we thought it might be, but after sleeping many times on the ground in various countries, even hard wooden bunks seemed soft and comfortable.

Theo was already chewing on some flat bread next morning, fully showered and dressed before we had even moved. Uli and I did the same and by 9.30 we walked over to the office to be greeted again by the guy who had welcomed us (I shall call him W from now on).

"Do you live in this room?" Theo asked him.

"No," he said, "I live with my family in the next street, but I spend a lot of time here in the Temple to further my education."

We followed W across the street where he entered a several storey high stone building where he halted and spoke to two lady receptionists, who greeted us with big smiles. One of them begged us to follow her up to the next story to Mr. Birla's office.

Oh, I nearly forgot to mention that we were barefoot and so were most Indians. If they weren't barefoot they might have worn some kind of sandals.

Walking into one of the richest men's offices was not what we expected. On the contrary we were disappointed. Instead of Diamonds,

Gold and Glitter, there was nothing of the sort; it was extremely plain, furnished only by a couple of wooden desks, a big conference table and a few stationery cabinets. There were only two big framed pictures on the wall behind the conference table. One off Mahatma Gandhi and Mr. Birla shaking hands in front of the temple, the other one of Jawaharlal Nehru the Prime Minister of India.

There were already five men and one lady present and with us, W, and the receptionist the room became a bit crowded. As W introduced each of us it was easy to pick out Mr. Birla because of the picture on the wall. All the men were dressed the same in their white gowns and clean shaven, except one. This guy wore a European suit, but open shirt and held a writing pad in one hand, the reporter.

We were asked to take a seat at the big table. Tea was served and it turned out to be a really good conference. The reporter asked heaps of questions and so did the others. Everyone was interested in our book and the people we had met. Eventually someone asked what our plans were for New Delhi.

"Firstly," Theo said, "we would like to stay at the Temple for a few days, and if possible we would like to meet the Prime Minister, Mr. Nehru." He pointed to the picture on the wall.

"You can stay at the Temple as long as you need to," Mr. Birla said. "I will arrange for W to be your guide."

Well, we couldn't have asked for anything more. We thanked him and the others for their kindness.

Just before leaving Theo asked Mr. Birla to write some words in our Book, but he said "not now. Do what you have to do in Delhi first and before us leaving we shall have another meeting and I will write in it then."

That seemed a bit odd, but what can you do? We thanked him again for his wonderful hospitality.

On the way out, the reporter asked us if he was able to take a photograph of us with our bikes in front of the Temple. "No problem," we said.

He already had a photographer waiting for us at the Temple. He followed us back to our rooms and while we sorted out our bikes he studied our book and asked more questions.

All this time W was with us and I asked him if he could show us the way to the central post office after they took our picture. "Yes, but to get there we should take a rickshaw."

We pushed our bikes to the front of the Temple where the reporter introduced us to the photographer. What a sight I thought to myself. This magnificent building was only 20 years older than me, and standing next to it in brilliant sunshine surrounded by beautifully manicured gardens was unreal. This Temple was actually inaugurated by Mahatma Gandhi who was assassinated eight years ago in 1948 not far from where we were standing. After taking many pictures the reporter and the photographer wished us good luck and vanished into the crowd.

People paying their respects at the tomb of Mahatma Ghandi

Later we asked W if he knew where the Australian Embassy was situated and he told us he would find out. All in all, we had a good day and were very happy with ourselves.

Early next morning a loud knock on the door revealed a smiling W. He handed us a couple of newspapers. One of them, opened on page three or four had our picture filling half the page. We were elated.

The picture in front of the Temple was excellent and the article below was well written.

We were very happy about it and clapped each other on the shoulders.

"*So buaba jedsd sennor au no beriamd,*" Uli quipped. "*now my fellows, you are also famous.*"

By the time we walked to the front office we already had people smiling at us and everyone in the office shook our hands. W told us he had brought his bike and wanted to ride with us to the Australian Embassy, situated on the other side of the Gate of India.

After a bit of breakfast next door we grabbed our bikes, book, and passports, and followed W into the traffic. It wasn't easy following him weaving in and out of the traffic and after some time we called out "Stop showing off. We don't want to kill ourselves."

"Sorry, okay?" and he slowed down a bit. A moment later he pointed towards a wide boulevard with no traffic leading to a huge monument at the end. It was a monument called the Gate of India.

It reminded Theo and me of Rome where there was a similar building near the Colosseum. Apparently 82,000 Indian soldiers had died fighting in the British Army during the First World War. Their names were engraved in the walls of this magnificent monument and remembered by many people, leaving flowers and prayers. Uli took a couple of good pictures of Theo and me which I treasure to this day.

W told us we only had to ride a short distance to get to the Embassy. We entered into a more affluent part of the City, mainly office buildings with some displaying the national flags of other countries. We spotted the Australian one straight away, because we had seen it several times before.

W stayed with our bikes while we walked up to the third floor with mixed feelings. Would we be disappointed again? The whole floor seemed to be part of the Embassy but one door with reception and please enter written on it had the Australian flag mounted next to it.

Uli knocked and opened the door. We were greeted by a couple of Australian ladies seated behind a long counter on one wall with several chairs along the other one. The wall behind them was covered with framed photos featuring Australian motives, like Sydney harbour bridge, the red monolith in the middle of the continent, sheep getting shorn and huge farms with lots of cattle. There were also some bigger ones showing the ocean with beautiful beaches plus Kangaroos, Koalas and Emus.

Theo and me, in front of the Gate of India

One of the Ladies asked what she could do for us and handed us a form to fill out, an application for a tourist visa. There were several people seated in front of us, waiting to be called up. Twenty minutes went past and the same Lady asked us to follow her into another room occupied by one guy sitting behind a single desk.

We introduced ourselves and so did he in perfect German. This was unexpected, an Australian speaking our language and in a place like India.

He had our applications in front of him and whilst he studied them he told us that he was assigned to Bonn (the Capitol of Germany at that time) for 4 years and would be going there soon.

He also told us that he is in charge of all visa applications. He had seen our picture in the paper and was impressed with our story and couldn't believe that we had no visa for Australia. We didn't tell him we had tried in all the previous countries and were refused.

He asked the same questions as all the others and wanted to see if we had money to leave Australia.

"We've got more than enough," I told him confidently, and opened the pouch I had around my neck. As soon as I pulled out a stack of US Dollars he smiled and said, "never mind, I can see you have plenty." So I stuffed the money back into the pouch.

"Anyhow," he said, "I would love to hear more about your adventure, but I am very short on time. I have an important luncheon to attend.

Here we go again, I thought, another refusal.

"I will give you a three month tourist visa and I hope you will get safely to Melbourne."

I could hardly believe my ears.

He took a stamp and bang, bang, bang, we had our passports stamped!

He handed them to us, shook our hands, opened the door and almost in a trance we walked out to the reception. Finally we had our visas! I looked at Theo and Uli as if to say did that really happen?

Both the ladies in the reception had a newspaper each and wanted each of us to sign our photograph. "Happy to oblige," Theo said and scribbled his name across the bottom of the picture with a flourish. Uli and I did the same.

It wasn't until after we got outside where W was waiting with our bikes did it really hit us what had actually happened. We certainly were happy and some of the passersby must have thought there was definitely something wrong with us clapping each other on our shoulders and

The Big Adventure

W would look after our bikes while we went inside Parliament House.

squeezing W half to death. We had to celebrate and invited W for lunch.

Back at the Temple walking to the office, was another surprise. Someone from the West German Embassy had been waiting for a couple of hours to speak to us.

We always felt uneasy when we had to do anything with German officialdom, especially Theo and I. We immediately remembered our bad experience with them three years earlier. Uli asked him "what's it all about, something serious?"

"No not at all, on the contrary, the Ambassador would like to meet you at the Embassy tomorrow morning," he told us. "Would 10 am be convenient?"

"We would be more than happy to," Uli replied, "but how do we get there?"

"I will have an embassy car pick you up at 9.30am."

"We shall be waiting," Uli said and shook his hand to say goodbye and so did Theo and I.

By now we needed some more smokes and walked around the corner to relax over a glass of tea. We still couldn't grasp what was happening, and were still over the moon after getting our visa for Australia.

Journey of a Lifetime

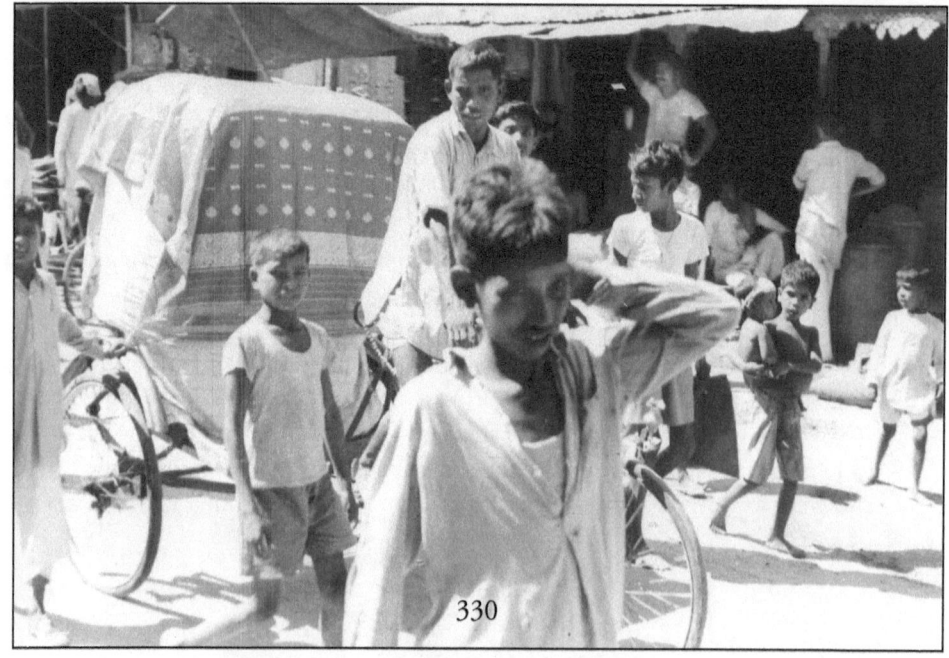

In the streets of New Delhi

"Meeting the German Ambassador in the morning... I'm not looking forward to it," Theo said.

"It sounds fishy to me." I was remembering how Theo and I had been treated on our first big adventure.

"We have to take the Bull by the horns." Uli said. "We don't have anything to worry about. We got our visas for Australia, so what do we have to worry about?"

Nevertheless, with mixed feelings we waited at the main street in front of the Temple and dead on 9:30 a black 300 Adenauer Mercedes pulled up at the curb right in front of us.

The same guy from yesterday greeted us and introduced us to the uniformed Indian driver who spoke fluent German. We drove past the Gate of India again and halted in front of a high white wall with a huge iron gate in the middle. It was only a few streets away where we were yesterday.

We walked through the gate towards a magnificent old stone building, almost a miniature palace, all white like the wall surrounding it. A pole with a big German flag hanging from it stood proudly in front of the main entrance. A wide door opened and we stepped into a huge reception hall with photographs of every major city in Germany hanging on the walls. No amount of money had been spared in furnishing this hall with lots of German artefacts hanging on the walls or standing on beautifully carved tables.

There was only one big reception desk where two German men and an Indian lady greeted guests and customers. Our escort walked towards another door, knocked and opened it for us to enter. Stepping confidently inside, we were greeted by an elderly well dressed Gentleman sitting behind an imposing desk. He stood up as we entered and came around to greet us, giving each of us a big handshake. He indicated that we should sit on the chairs arranged in front of his desk.

So, taking the bull by the horns, as Uli had suggested, we each introduced ourselves, telling him where we were born and educated. He was quite impressed when he found out that I was born in America and I had to tell him some of my story.

Apparently during the Second World War he was teaching at the University in Washington DC. He didn't have to introduce himself because facing us was a wooden name plate with Ernst Wilhelm Meyer engraved in gold on his desk. The door opened and the Indian Lady entered, carrying a big silver coffee urn and placed it on the desk. Then she came back with beautiful cups, saucers and another lady following her carried a plate of cakes.

This is unreal I thought to myself, it can't get better than this, but it did!

The coffee and cakes were delicious and it reminded me of Cafe Faas in Backnang. Herr Meyer was extremely interested in our adventures and was really pleased for us to have met so many different people.

Theo told him, as if it had already been arranged, that we were going to meet Prime Minister Nehru in the next few days.

"A very fine man," he said, "and a great Statesman, like the two of them." He turned and pointed to the two framed pictures hanging on the wall behind him. One was of Konrad Adenauer, the West German Chancellor and the other one of Theodor Heuss, President of the Bundes Republic.

I can't remember how long we were with the Ambassador, but it would have been at least two hours. It was a pleasure to meet a fine man like him and of course the whole time there we spoke in German. Finally he wrote some nice words in our travel book and wished us all the best for the future.

As soon as we stood up something incredible and unexpected happened. Herr Meyer took each one of us in his arms, gave us a warm hug and told us "You are much better Ambassadors than I could ever be. Germany and the world will be proud of you."

Then he pulled his wallet out and handed Theo two one hundred Deutsch Mark notes and apologised that it was all he had to help us.

Now this might seem be a bit farfetched, but it was 100% true. We couldn't believe it, especially since we had not mentioned finances at all.

Before walking out the door, Ulli told him we would write as soon as we get to Melbourne. We did send him a letter and included a newspaper article from the Argus, one of Melbourne's daily newspapers where we were on the front page. (When Theo and Hermann Gluecks visited the Embassy again three years later, Herr Meyer had joined the Bundestag in Berlin, nine months earlier).

We were driven back to the Temple in the same car. What a great feeling it was compared to earlier in the morning not knowing how we would be received. Passing the office W. waved us in and asked how it went, but we told him we had to have some tea first.

He yelled after us that he had some news for us on the way back. We had so much to talk about and by the time we finished and talked to some of the people a half a pack of smokes had gone. Back at the office we told W. mostly what happened, but didn't mention the money.

He asked us if we were interested in talking to the students at the University tomorrow or the day after?

"We had nothing planed," we told him, "except we would like to go to Parliament house soon."

"No problem," he said, "I will arrange for the Uni in the morning, "and I can accompany you to Parliament house afterwards."

"As good as done," Uli said.

We walked out the door back to our room to write some more postcards. By the time that was done W had arranged to be with us at ten in the morning. W. told us it would be a good idea for us to ride our bikes to the Uni next morning.

"That's okay," we told him, "what time shall we leave?"

"About 8:30."

"What? So early..." Uli was surprised he wanted to leave that early in the morning.

"Because of the traffic..."

That made sense. Traffic everywhere was horrendous.

Despite having to get up much earlier we were ready to hit the traffic on time next morning, with W. leading the way on his bike. Again we rode past the Gate of India and a few streets further on we passed Parliament house. When we arrived at the Uni there were people already waiting for us by the front entrance. This was a really big place, surrounded by a high and beautifully crafted iron fence. We pushed our bikes towards the Administration building and parked them in one of the cycling stands of which there were hundreds. We were greeted by lots of people, teachers, and students male and female. W seemed to know just about everybody and had to shake many hands.

The teachers led us into a dining room for tea and a bit of fruit before our talk. The Auditorium was bigger than all the previous ones we had been in, but by this time we were quite sure of ourselves. The place was full and we had to speak relatively loud to be heard. There wasn't too much of an introduction this time because everyone had read about us in the paper the day before. But the questions kept coming and coming! Of course they wanted to know how we managed to meet with Kings, Presidents and highfalutin people. They were very happy that we stayed at the Birla Mandir Temple and had met Mr. Birla himself.

One of the teachers asked with a smile on his face, if we are going to visit Mr. Nehru?

"Of course," Ulli said, "within the next couple of days."

I could see the teacher didn't believe the response, but Uli had stated it with such confidence that everyone in the audience gave us a standing applause. After signing several of the newspaper articles we finally said goodbye.

Outside it was boiling hot after the relative coolness of the auditorium.

"Are you still thinking of going to Parliament House," W asked.

"Of course," Theo said, "at least we shall find out if Mr. Nehru is in town."

Like any other Parliament House, this one was impressive with a short but wide street delineated with beautiful flowerbeds along the footpath leading right up to the big steps at the main entrance.

We were stopped by one of the guards, (there were several of them, all in white uniforms, each with a gun on their backs) who wanted to see our passports. After conversing with W we were allowed to leave our bikes next to the big steps and the guards would keep an eye on them. The entry hall was huge, lovely and cool and relative busy.

I had the feeling a lot of people had only walked in to get out of the heat for awhile. At the reception W spoke to a couple of officials for quite some time in some language we couldn't understand. They kept looking at us and one of them pulled our newspaper from behind the counter and they studied the picture.

After awhile W turned and gave us some good news. Jawaharlal (Pandit) Nehru, was in New Delhi, but would be extremely busy over the next couple of days. India had recently had a big State Visit a few weeks earlier from the Soviet Union with Nikita Khrushev First Secretary and Nikolai Bulganin Premier of the Soviet Union.

We could feel the excitement as people talked about it. Those two had certainly left their mark. One of the officials led us into another room and introduced us to a uniformed gentleman with quite a few decorations on his lapels. He had a big appointment book open on his desk. I guess he was in charge of visitors who wanted to meet up with different Politicians or the PM. himself. He was a jovial sort of a guy and very helpful. He even asked if we would like some tea which we accepted. He didn't mention the news paper, but I had the feeling that he knew all about us. He studied his book and told us there was a possibility in two

The Big Adventure

days time at 11.00 am, but he would confirm this with W at the temple. This proved that he knew about us because we had not mentioned to him where we were staying.

We thanked him for his time with us and we hoped to see him again soon. The two officials at reception asked how it went and W filled them in. Waving goodbye to them we walked outside, jumped on our bikes and headed for home.

Another exiting and satisfactory day! Well done, we told ourselves. We couldn't help feel excited about our impending visit with Mr Nehru.

Travelling earlier in the Embassy car we had noticed company names like Coca Cola, Supreme Motors Ltd, Philips Electrical, Studebaker Allied Motors and many more. We asked W if he could get us the addresses of these companies. Before we called it a night we glued a copy of our newspaper picture and article in our book in readiness for next morning.

With the list from W we hired a rickshaw to take us to Coca cola, the first one on the list. It was a distribution centre, a double story office building with a large warehouse at the back. The manager, Sender Singh, welcomed us with beautiful cold bottles of Coke, Theo's favourite drink. He was very happy to sponsor us on our journey and wrote some nice words in our book. I think we got close to 200 Dollars in Rupees.

We were as keen as mustard to make as much money as possible, especially since we had received our visas. We visited a number of companies and were welcomed by all of them. They all wished us good luck and helped us financially.

By the time we got back to our room at the Temple we counted close to the equivalent of 800 Dollars in Rupees. We had hardly distributed some of the money amongst each of us and stored the rest in my pouch when we heard a knock on the door.

It was W. to tell us that we should be at Parliament house by 10:30 in the morning. Someone had just called by and informed him of our appointment. He also informed us that someone from the University had called. In appreciation of our talk, some of the students wanted to take us to Qutub Minar, a world heritage site. "We kindly accept," Uli told him, "but the Prime Minister comes first!" We were overwhelmed at how quickly things were happening.

We couldn't believe that when Uli replied to one of the teachers question yesterday with, "we would see the PM in the next couple of days", we were about to do exactly that. It must have been an omen of some kind.

W told us "the best way to get to Parliament house again would be on our bikes in the morning."

"That's okay by us," we told him, "we'll be ready by 9:30."

We could hardly wait to have some smokes and some dinner. The excitement was almost too much to bear. We needed to calm down.

The next day we were ready early and looked forward to the big day ahead of us.

We dressed the same; brown shoes, long trousers and white tea shirt. W waited for us at the office, ready to jump on his bike. It was a brilliant day, hot with not a cloud in the sky. The traffic was heavy, but we still made Parliament house in less than an hour.

This time we did not have to show our passports and were greeted by one of the guards from two days ago, who again kept an eye on our bikes.

Walking to the reception desk through the cooler building felt pleasant and took some of the heat out of our bodies. One of the receptionists led us straight to the other office to be greeted by same friendly official in uniform we had met before. He made a few notes in his big book, got up and begged us to follow him down a long corridor. We passed several rooms with name tags on them before we stopped in front of a door with a guard on each side. They saluted to our official and one of them opened the door to let us enter.

It was a big room full of light with glass windows from floor to ceiling. We could look out into a beautifully manicured garden, with guards on each corner. It was more like a well appointed lounge room, with five or six small tables surrounded by small comfortable chairs like outdoor settings. A large cabinet by the side wall had stacks of fresh flowers on top and in front of the end wall stood a life size statue of Mahatma Ghandi carved in marble.

There were two other men in the room, both dressed in white robes, but no headgear and they were clean shaven. One of them was from the newspaper, the other an assistant because he asked us a lot of questions. About fifteen minutes later the side door opened and an elderly gentleman taller than I, strongly built, wearing a white linen robe to his knees and fluffy pants came in. He had no beard but sported a big moustache. He wore sandals and his head was covered with something that looked like an upside down small rowing boat made of linen.

He was followed by a tall Sikh wearing a white turban and long shirt

The Big Adventure

buttoned in front over fluffy pans. They were followed by one of the most power full men in the world, Jawaharlal Nehru, Prime Minister of India.

Mr Nehru was dressed in half a linen robe with a small thin jacket buttoned in front. His pants were pleated like rings down to his ankles. His head was also covered by an upturned linen boat.

The secretary introduced each of us and all three of them shook our hands and welcomed us to India. The first gentleman's name was Pandit Pant, Minister for the Interior. The Sikh's name was Gurmukh Nihal Singh, Chief Minister of the Sate of Delhi.

I was overwhelmed! Seven months ago we had left Germany as inexperienced young boys, and look at us now.

To this day I still find it hard to believe that those powerful men spent over an hour with us. They were sincerely interested in what we had done and asked many questions about our journey. Mr. Nehru wanted to know how we got on in India and we told him that the hospitality and the friendliness of the people were outstanding.

While Theo showed Mr. Nehru our book, I answered some of their questions. This gave Uli time to take a few discreet photographs. When Mr. Nehru saw the picture with us in front of our Temple, we could tell by his expression that he liked what he saw. Here stood the man who announced to the world, that Mahatma Ghandi had been assassinated. I could still remember as a twelve year old being told in school, but didn't know much about Mr. Ghandi at that time. As our time with him came to an end, he wrote best wishes in our book, stood up and shook hands with us once more. He wished us a safe journey and hoped we would make it to the Olympics on time.

With a big smile, he walked back through the same door he had used to enter the room. Mr. Pant asked if he could invite us for lunch in his office because he wanted to hear more about our lives. We told him we would be delighted. Before shaking hands with us Mr Nihal Sing wanted to know if we would be able to visit him at his office next morning? He would send a car to pick us up at 11am. The reporter, secretary and our appointment official left the room while the four of us followed Mr. Pant to one of the offices along the corridor.

A couple of staff members stood to attention while a servant entered through another door, with another pot of tea. Mr. Pant asked us to be seated around a big carved wooden table, and please enjoy some tea. Mr.Pant was interested to hear about our time during the war, the bombing raids and how people handled those bad times. Uli and Theo didn't

Journey of a Lifetime

Theo and I speak with a newspaper reporter as we wait for Prime Minister Nehru.
Prime Minister Nehru speaking with one of his Ministers

The Big Adventure

The first Prime Minister of India, Jawaharlal Nehru greeting us with a big smile as he entered the room.

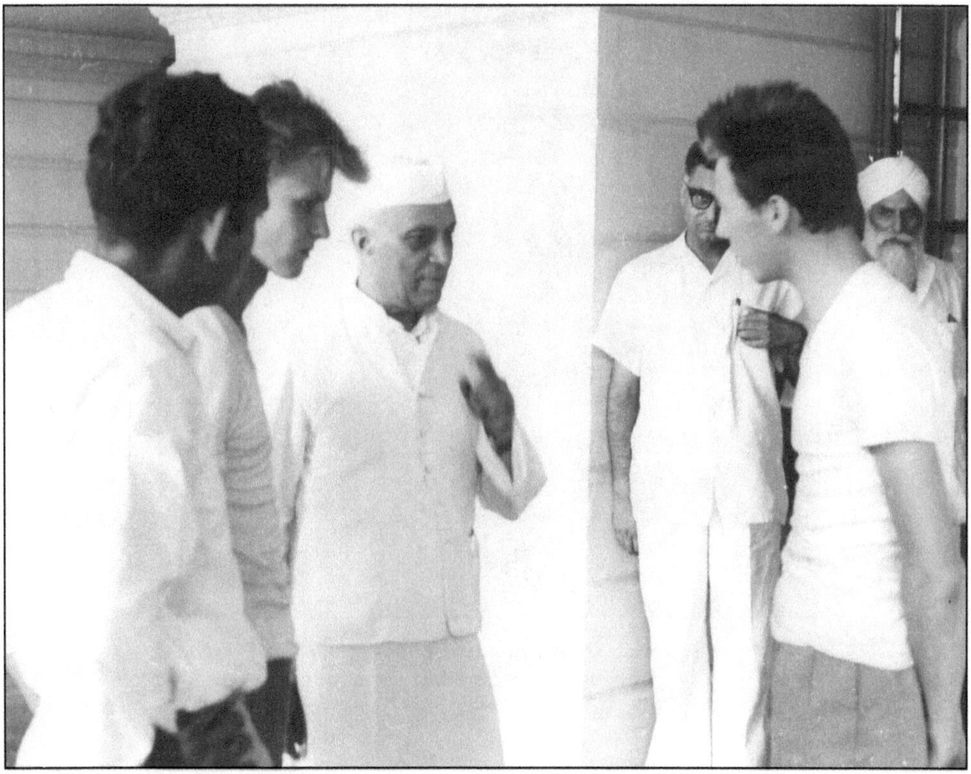

He took quite an interest in a book recording our travels before signing and adding some words to it.

New Delhi, Indien

All good wishes.

Jawaharlal Nehru
June 14. 1956

PRIME MINISTER'S HOUSE,
NEW DELHI.

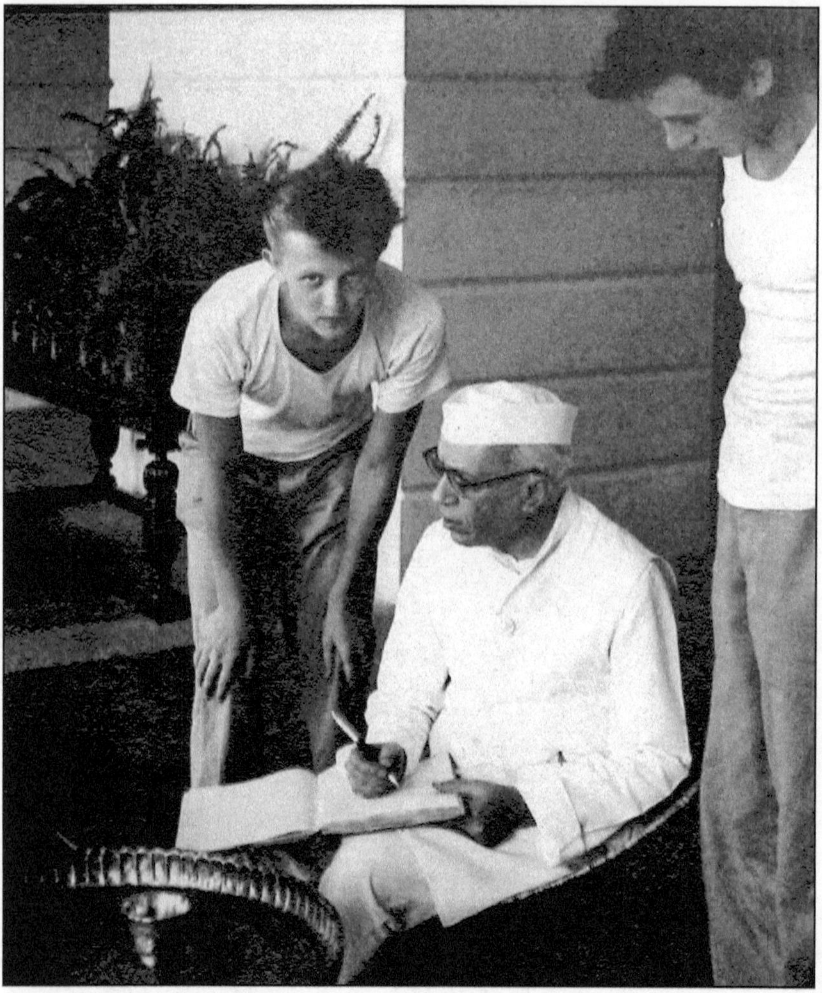

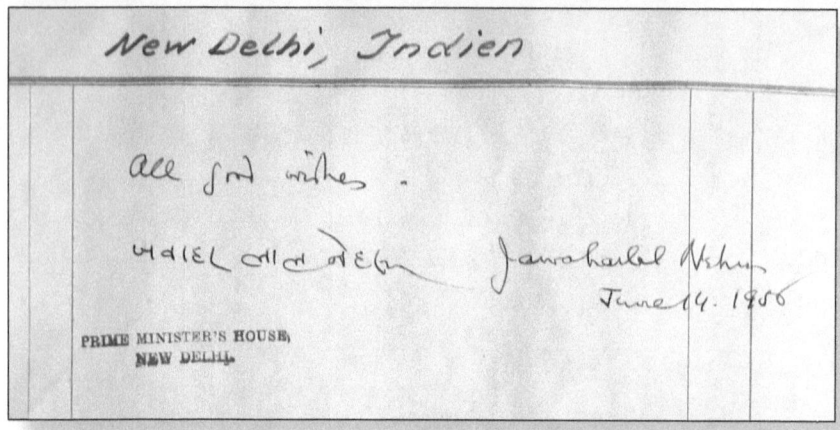

The page from our book where Prime MInister Nehru wrote us a message

get much of it in Backnang, but living in Stuttgart at the time my family and I lost everything. I was able to tell him that our fathers had to dig tunnels from one house to another to escape when they got hit, that fourteen people had died in the front house one night from one single bomb totally destroying their house. I also mentioned to him that to this day I can still see half burned bodies lying around when I snuck out in the morning. Some months later we got hit also and lost everything, except for one single red waterglass, which we found later in the rubble. Luckily my dad's mother found a small apartment for us in Backnang, where we could start again from scratch.

While I had been telling him this some small plates of different foods were placed on the table, with a damp cloth in front of us to clean our hands, because we had to eat with our hand. Naturally the food was hot and Theo had some problem, where Ulli and I got slowly a little more used to it.

Mr. Pant also wanted to know about the occupation after the war. Uli told him that on the 20th of April 1945 on Adolf Hitler's 56th birthday the American soldiers entered Backnang and instead of swastika's hanging out of windows to celebrate Hitler's birthday, one could only see white bed sheets hanging out. For us in Backnang the war was over!

More than three hours had passed before we jumped back on our bikes again.

Back at the temple we sat in W's office we talked about every minute of the past few hours. We also found out that W had met M. Nehru and some of the Ministers before, because they frequently visited the Temple to pray and meet with Mr. Birla.

It took me a long time to find some sleep that night. Theo had written earlier in the evening to the newspaper in Backnang and told them of our visit to M. Nehru and put a folded article with our photo in the envelope to be posted next day.

Again I wondered what our friends and the people in Backnang would think when they found out. I could just see my dad walking through the factory, being asked a lot of questions, by all who knew him and us.

W informed us next morning that he wouldn't accompany us to visit, because government cars are very small, they only carry three passengers. Anyhow he said, "I am quite sure you can handle it without me, but I will post your letters for you."

He was right, when the minister's government car pulled up it was small. Apparently, government policy was only to travel in economical cars, not the big American gasoline guzzlers. All the cars used were small English models. Even the Prime Minister and his Ministers were chauffeured around the same way.

This time our driver stopped at a side entrance, where our uniformed official greeted us like we had known each other for years. We followed him through a small doorway leading straight to the big corridor. The Chief Ministers office was only a couple of doors in front of Mr. Pant's. It was exactly 11am when our official knocked on the door, opened it and begged us to entre. This office was no different from Mr. Pant's with two small desks one for him the other for his secretary, and the same round conference table. I had the feeling that Indian politicians and public servants were very low key and didn't need to show off.

Mr. Sing spoke a few words with our official who returned to his office, and then he welcomed us with a big smile. It seemed an exact repetition of yesterday; we had the same food, talked mostly about the same subjects, except M. Singh wanted to know all I knew about the Sikh soldiers in Kuernbach just after the war. Theo showed him through our book and he asked questions about the heads of State we had met so far. He was very pleased that we had such a good time in Amritsar, especially meeting Master Tara Singh at the Golden Temple who was his friend.

While he was writing in our book two middle-aged Hindus entered without knocking. One was a reporter and the other a photographer. The reporter asked us to sit next to M. Singh and the photographer took a few pictures of the four of us. We didn't know these two but they knew a fair bit about us. I guess news amongst colleagues travels fast.

After more questions were answered they left and we started to make a move. Mr Sing wished us success in our travels and if we should ever visit again he would be pleased to accommodate us. We thanked him for his kind words and after shaking hands again we said goodbye. At our officials office the driver had waited to take us back. The official gave us each a big hug and we thanked him for looking after us so well.

Mr Singh with Prime Minister Nehru and his message to us.

Back at the Temple W was pleased that everything went great without him being with us.

"Someone called Sender Singh is going to call by shortly to meet with you again," he told us.

What a surprise. We wondered why the boss of Coca Cola wanted to meet up with us once more. We told W to bring him around the corner. "We'll be in our favourite little restaurant having a pot of tea and a smoke."

"I have also been in touch with the University and they are going to send a small bus around tomorrow morning to pick you up for a tour."

Wow!

After a couple of smokes and lots of water, Sender Sing walked towards us accompanied by a European gentleman. Sender greeted us as if he had known us for a long time and introduced us to his friend Karl Seidenather. Apparently Karl was born in Bamberg in 1914 and in the early 1920 his parents migrated to America and started a well to do business. During the Second World War Karl had to join the army and was stationed in Stuttgart during the occupation. I came across several soldiers like him at that time. Back in America his dad eventually sent him to India to establish a distributorship for their products. Over the last couple of years he and Sender became close friends. The reason for meeting us once more was simple, Sender had told Karl that we visited him at his office and Karl who read the article, wanted to meet us. He especially wanted to meet me because I was born in Philadelphia before the Second World War. He was eager to find out why I was bought up in Germany during the war. They also knew that it was going to be my 20th birthday and wanted to take us for dinner and a few drinks. We told them that we would visit Qutub Minar and Mahatma Gandhi's assassinations place next day, but the day after would be fantastic.

When we first saw the small bus next morning parked in the side street we couldn't stop smiling. It was a small International tray truck, with a canvas covered frame on the back, rolled up on both sides and back. Behind the cabin and along the sides, were long wooden frames bolted to the floor to sit on. A wide step ladder was mounted on the back to be pulled up when the truck was moving.

A smiling group of young people greeted us, amongst them the teacher who asked us if we are going to visit Mr. Pundit Nehru. There were two boys and three girl students plus the driver. One of the girls was Absolutely Stunning and Ulli fell instantly in love!

"*Heilandsblechle*," he said in a murmured voice, "*dui daede uffdor schdell pagga*," meaning "with God's will I would give this one a serve without hesitating."

They had all listened to our speech at the Uni, but we didn't recognise any of them, except the teacher. The step ladder was down and we climbed up to join those already seated on the benches, W included.

It was already very hot, but travelling on the open tray was relatively pleasant. On the way to Qutub Minar we stopped at Mahatma Ghandi's Assassination place, not too far from the Gate of India. A white memorial praying place was erected in the middle of a beautiful garden not far from a main road. A small concrete slab about five metres square was covered with white marble tiles. In the middle was a shoulder high obelisk with a carved bowl on top, also in white marble. The carved small fence around the perimeter was also white marble.

When we got there many people were paying respect, bowing and praying. Some even cried as they remembered the great man.

Not knowing too much about him at that time in my short life, I still felt sad watching all those people, old and young, rich and poor paying respect to the memory of Mahatma Ghandi. Our truck load of students also joined the people praying to the great man's memory.

When they had finished we jumped on the truck and headed towards Qutub Minar. On the way W told the teacher and students with a big smile about our visit to Mr. Nehru and of us having lunch with his Ministers. They looked at us in sheer disbelief until Theo showed them their writing in our book. They just could not get over the fact that three young cyclists like us, in Delhi for less than a week, had managed to achieve what we did. The teacher asked us if we could speak to the students once more to talk about our experience. We told him that we only had a couple of days left, but he could tell them all about it on our behalf.

Qutub Minar is a five story high Minaret and at 73 metres it is possibly the tallest Minaret in the world, at least the tallest we ever saw. It's set in a huge park next to a very old half ruined Mosque built close to a thousand years ago. There were several other ruins of ancient buildings with only a few archways still standing. The whole park was declared a UNESCO World Heritage site.

We spotted the Minaret a fair distance away and had to get off the main road to park a short walking distance, from the entrance. We could hardly wait to get into the park to get out of the sun and under some shady trees. Lucky two of the students carried a couple of baskets full of water bottles and a big watermelon. We had a great afternoon and the students together with the teacher and W couldn't show us enough of their heritage. This is fantastic I thought to myself, these buildings were erected by Moslems such a long time ago and here are Hindus proudly showing them off to us Christians. It told me that no matter what religion one believes in, great achievements of different nations are enjoyed by all.

Standing in front and looking up at the Minaret was quite a sight. I couldn't imagine how people could build something like this at that time. The first two levels of the building were made of bricks, the next two of marble and the top one of bricks. Only when we entered inside, could we make out the immense enormity and size of this building. The walls were very thick and each story had four or five openings to allow light to enter. A circular wooden staircase led from one story to the next.

The air would have been near perfect if it wasn't for the bats. There were big bats, hundreds of them clinging onto the ceilings and under the staircase. They were weird looking things, all asleep which was kind of creepy. Between the Minaret and an old archway surrounded by a steel fence was an Iron Pillar, also about thousand years old. This Pillar, about 10 metres high and never rusts. We were told that to this day they haven't figured it out how it was made so many years ago.

Seeing something like this was an eye-opener. We had a great day and by the time we got back to the Temple it was dark. It was a great farewell and we thanked them for their hospitality and to convey our greetings to everyone at the Uni. To finish of the day we invited W around the corner for some dinner.

I turned twenty while we were in New Delhi. In fact it was Theo who reminded me it was my birthday.

In the middle of writing the promised postcards to some of the people who had helped so far W knocked and opened the door. He asked if we could be at Mr. Birla's office by 10 o'clock with our book because he will be out of town for two weeks. Unfortunately W told us that he won't be able to accompany us, because he himself would be busy for a few hours.

"That shouldn't be a problem," we told him, "we know exactly where to go.

Qutub Minar

Journey of a Lifetime

One of the beautiful places where we stayed in New Delhi was the Lakshimi Narayan Temple.

*next page:
Uli amd me with one of our new friends, Karl, at Lakshimi Narayan Temple.*

The same smiling receptionist led us up to Mr. Birla's office and opened the door for us. It was a warm welcome again, being greeted again by this humble man with so much power. We had seen him a couple of times in the Temple, but had not spoken to him since our last visit. He begged us to sit with him at the conference table and I handed him our book. He was very pleased with all our achievements in such a short time in Delhi. He wrote something in our book and carefully closed it, and passed it back to Theo.

"I am very sure you will get to the Olympics on time. You have achieved so much already..."

He got up, walked to his desk, picked up a piece of paper and handed it to Uli.

"I know you are short of funds and need all the help you can get,' he said with a huge smile.

What he had given Uli was a cheque in Rupees, equivalent to US$2400.00 US.

"You can cash this at the bank not far from the Temple."

We could not believe what was happening to us and were dumbfounded by his extraordinary generosity. We knew exactly which bank he meant since we had passed it many times coming and going from the Temple. We were happy just to be guests at the Temple, and now this! We couldn't stop thanking him as he ushered us from his office.

We walked straight across the road to our restaurant for some lunch and a smoke. We had to digest what had just happened to us and read once more what M. Birla had written.

By the time we had returned to the Temple W was back at his office and wanted to know all about our meeting. We mentioned that M. Birla gave us a cheque but didn't tell him for how much and asked him to point out the bank just to make sure it was the bank we thought. We grabbed a rickshaw, which took us to the bank. Uli handed the cheque to a teller behind an open counter who then asked us for our passports. He told us to take a seat for a minute, because they had to prepare some forms to be signed by us. We hardly finished a smoke, when he waved us to the counter. Each of us had to sign a form under our passport number and then he counted the right amount in brand new notes, watched by another teller.

What a sight; my heart beat was on overdrive and so no doubt were Uli and Theo's hearts. He put the notes in an envelope, handed it to Ulli and we left the bank. We were Rich! This was definitely the biggest payroll we received so far, just on 800 US Dollars each.

We couldn't get back to the Temple quick enough to count it once more, plus we had to get ready soon to be picked up by Sender and Karl.

It wasn't long before W brought them to our room and we were able to tell Karl all about ourselves. Neither Karl nor Sender have ever met Mr.

Nehru or one of his Ministers and were very impressed and wanted to know all about our meeting with them. After looking through our book Karl could hardly wait to also write a few words in German. Karl was eager to hear my story of living in Stuttgart during the war years, about the three years of schooling before the air raids started in early 1943. He was astonished that my parents missed the last boat to go back to America in the middle of 1939. Apparently, when his battalion moved into Stuttgart they found the city totally devastated. He had gone back on a business trip six years later and couldn't believe the transformation the hard work of the German people had accomplished in so short a time.

Sender told us they would like to take us to the Claridges Hotel for some drinks to meet up with a few friends and to the Hotel Imperial for dinner later.

I grabbed our book and the five of us jumped into a big limousine without W; he would catch up at the Imperial later.

Several couples greeted us as soon as we entered the bar at Claridges, including the owner and his wife. Because I had told them it was my 20th birthday I got the most attention and best wishes and within minutes I had a cool glass of beer in my hand and everybody started singing happy birthday. Theo drank his usual Coke but was extremely happy also. After some time the bar was crowded and everyone knew what we were all about. Before we had too many drinks Karl told everyone it was time for dinner. Theo grabbed our book and the owner wrote a message in it. I think the Imperial Hotel at the time was the biggest and most modern Hotel in New Delhi.

There was a big table reserved at the Musketeer bar where a few of the people we had drinks with joined us. Just before the delicious food was served W joined us and stayed to the finish. I had a fabulous birthday and to this day I cherish their great hospitality, and I, along with Theo and Uli, shall never forget New Delhi!

Even with several beers in me I slept well and woke up feeling great. We had told W last night that we would give our bikes a tune up this morning and would start packing later in the day for an early start next morning. There wasn't that much to do, a good clean up with some oil on the chain and gears, and they were ready to travel. A last walk through the Temple, shaking hands with some of the people we had known, then it was time to have lunch around the corner.

W joined us and looking enigmatic he said, "I have a small surprise for you in the morning," but wouldn't let on what it was.

When we asked him all he said was, "You can leave your mail with me and I will post for you tomorrow. I will also be very sorry to see you leave. It has been the most fun…" he then left us to finish our preparations.

In the morning, packed and ready to say thanks and good bye to W, we did get hit with a big surprise. On the little side street, the small bus-truck from the Uni with our smiling teacher and driver were waiting. They had arranged with W to give us a lift out of New Delhi. We loved it. In no time the bikes were loaded onto the truck and W climbed up to join us. On the way out of town he pointed out lots of important things. The teacher and the driver sat in the cabin in front. It took a long time to get out of the City and out of most of the built up area into more open country.

After driving through a bigger village we were wondering when they were going to stop so we could get off. 60 kilometres south of New Delhi they finally stopped at a Small town called Palwal and invited us for a late breakfast. That suited us fine because we could sit out the heat and ride as far as Hodal in the evening. The farewell after a couple of hours with these guys was just great and we hated to see them leave, but of course they had to go back. Before they left W handed an envelope to Theo. "This is a letter of greetings from the Imperial Hotel to the Agra Hotel. Give this to the manager when you arrive." he told us.

We watched the truck until it disappeared into the traffic heading towards New Delhi.

And then we were alone again.

It was hot and very humid. While we had been on the truck moving along we hardly noticed it but standing on the roadside with our bikes we felt as if we were melting. There was no way we could ride for the next couple of hours so we found some large trees beside a roadside stall and sat beneath them where it was shady. We felt a bit sad leaving such good people behind us, but we had to look ahead. One thing was for sure, we had no financial problems anymore.

We enjoyed the shade under the trees, had a few smokes and studied our maps. We had plenty of water, tinned food and flat bread. When we jumped back on our bikes later in the afternoon it was glary and without our helmets and sunglasses we would have been in trouble. Even being off the bikes for a few days it didn't take long to find our legs again. Hodal

The Big Adventure

was only about 35 kilometres ahead and we rode through it before nightfall and looked for a camping spot about 20 kilometres beyond the town. We crossed lots of small waterways and most of the country side was full of small farms, where lots of buffalos were being used to work the land.

I found it quite remarkable that Buffalos had to work hard while Cows were worshiped and had the freedom to go anywhere they pleased. I wondered if Indians hoped that when they are reborn they would return as cows.

The further south we got we saw more and more huge vultures mostly sitting under or on top of big trees. They made horrible noises as we approached and waddled away if we got too close, sometimes barely able to lift their swollen bodies off the ground.

We made Mathura next morning before it got too hot and found a small hotel to spend the rest of the day and night. We thought it was better to arrive at the Agra hotel in the morning instead at night only 50km ahead. Rested and fit, we made Agra long before midday, riding next to the Yamuna River and had no problem finding the Hotel Agra.

They already knew that we were coming and the envelope from the Imperial hotel was only a formality. It was a lovely hotel right in the centre of the town and we got a beautiful room facing the gardens. Our bikes safely locked up and after a shower we felt great.

We liked Agra, firstly the welcome was great, secondly it seemed a flourishing small Town and thirdly, we were guests of the Hotel!

Another great thing about this Hotel was their kitchen; it had Continental food and we were able to cherish some non chilli hot dishes! After a great lunch we were itching to visit the Taj Mahal. The Manager told us to wait a few hours and they would drive us there after the heat had

The beautiful Taj Mahal

The Big Adventure

dissipated. They wanted to show us some of the important places by car, and then we could explore them the next day by bike.

What can I say; when I first stood in front of that incredible, beautifully shining white 400 year old building I had shivers running down my spine. How could one man build a Mausoleum like this for his favourite wife after she had died? Uli took lots of photos.

We were picked up by a big car and driven here passing a huge Fort built of red sandstone. Apparently Agra had been the Capital before Delhi and this was all part of it. We were driven through the rest of Agra and when we finally got back to the hotel it was getting dark. For dinner the three of us ordered Wiener Schnitzel, but we had the feeling that it wasn't beef. It tasted great and we were happy to be enjoying non Indian foods.

Early next morning we had our water bottles filled and headed first to Agra or Red Fort. We paid a few Annas to get in and some more for the fellow to keep an eye on our bikes. This thing was overwhelmingly huge, built mostly out of red sandstone blocks. There were separate buildings inside those big walls. We felt like ants and wondered how man could build something like this with just a pick and shovel hundreds of years ago?

It was already very hot by the time we got to the Taj Mahal and secured our bikes at the front entrance. It wasn't too bad under the shade of some trees and a slight breeze from the Yamuna River kept the humidity at bay. The Mausoleum was built of ivory white marble and it was an incredible sight glistening in the sunshine. It was built by SHA JAHAN to house the tomb of his favourite wife MUMTAZ MAHAL. We spent most of the afternoon admiring this magnificent building.

Back at the Hotel we were stuffed, hot and starving, but after another shower and a Schnitzel we felt great. The Manager had joined us for dinner and wrote in our book. He wished us all the best and safe travel for the rest of our journey, because he wouldn't be there in the morning to see us off.

Uli asked him about our bill and he told us not to worry, it was already taken care of.

We never found out who we had to thank for that.

At sunrise we sadly waved Agra goodbye and headed towards Kanpur close to 300 kilometres ahead. We followed the Yamuna River for a while through very productive farmland and stopped for breakfast at Firozabad some 40km from Agra and sat out the big heat of the afternoon. We had in mind to make Etawah by nightfall but passing through many small villages and dodging heavy traffic slowed us down. We made camp at a secluded spot next to a waterway about 10km before the town and slept as much as we possibly could.

The next day was pretty hard, because we wanted to make Kanpur to have some comfort in a Hotel. We didn't stop at Etawa for breakfast and just ate some fruit and flat bread while packing our bikes.

Well, we didn't make Kanpur either. It was too hard, hot and humid and we had to rest several times in shady places. We crossed lots of waterways and followed some rivers, leading to the big Ganges. There was no hotel this evening and we had to sleep again on the ground on our spread out tent, feeling morbid and hot.

The next day we didn't stop much and talked very little and had only one thing in mind, a hotel and a shower. With all the riding and sweating we had the same aroma as all the buffalos and vultures we had passed. It was dark by the time we found a hotel in a small town, Fatehpur, and after a long shower, some good food and a few smokes, we felt human again.

The next day as we made Khaga, where we decided to sit out the hot part of the day we got hit with the biggest surprise of all. Weaving through the traffic, looking for a suitable restaurant, we noticed lots of people waving to us and gesturing to pull over at the footpath. We couldn't quite work out what the commotion was all about, until we saw Wasu and his brother amongst the crowd, with big smiling faces running towards us.

We were dumbfounded when we got hugs and handshakes from our friends and some people we never met before. They led us around the next corner to a truck and bus depot. Next to was an eating place and we went in there followed by a by lots of people.

Our bikes were secured inside the eating place and we were seated on the floor behind heaps of fresh food served on big metal plates. Wasu, who was seated between us, introduced us to two of his uncles and a couple of his friends, who were having breakfast with us.

It was a real surprise to find out that Wasu had been aware of our movements ever since we had arrived in New Delhi. He and his family had known all about our whereabouts, passing through some of the small towns, and somehow knew exactly that we would arrive in Khaga this morning. They had also known about us meeting Pandit Nehru and the Ministers and read all the newspapers that had stories about us. Wasu had planned for quite a few days to surprise us here and had arrived in Khaga several hours earlier in one of his uncle's trucks to invite us for breakfast/lunch.

We never expected such a happy welcome in such a small town and could hardly digest what had occurred. It was just so unbelievable!

We didn't mind in the slightest, being driven to Allahabad on the back of an open truck, accompanied by such beautiful people. I can't remember what kind of truck it was but it was similar as the one which took us to Qutub Minar. There were hessian bags, stuffed with dried leaves on either side on the tray and plenty of room for our bikes.

It seemed that half of Khaga watched us load our bikes before climbing onto the truck. The two uncles were in the front, one of them driving, the rest were in the back with us. We couldn't quite believe what had happened; three hours earlier we rode into Khaga and now we were leaving on the back of a truck.

It was very hot when the truck left but with the nice breeze in our faces it was bearable. Naturally we had lots to talk about and the time just flew by and before we knew it we had passed through many small towns and hit the outskirts of Allahabad. It wasn't a big city, but was very impressive with big Mosques, Temples and even a Church. We passed a huge old Fort built next to the Yamuna River and then we saw the mighty Ganges, the holiest river of them all. Allahabad and Benares, now Varanasi are the two holiest cities in India, both on the mighty Ganges River, and every Hindu man women and child wanted to bathe in its waters.

Our truck drove through a big iron gate into a huge compound similar to the Uni in Lahore and stopped in front of an old administrations building. Wasu explained to us that it was the College where he spent most of his schooling, before going to Uni. His brother still had another year to do here and they had organised accommodation for us amongst the students. By the time we unloaded our bikes and luggage, a whole group of students and teachers shook hands with us and welcomed us to their school.

The uncles drove off in the truck but told us we would catch up with them and the rest of the family later on. Wasu, his brother and friends carried our bikes into the building followed by us and most of the other students. Passing a mess hall and a conference room, they opened a door leading into a guestroom with one double bed and two single bunks on top of each other. There was a bathroom and toilet through one door and another small bedroom with two single beds. It was late afternoon by then and Wasu informed us, he would pick us up in about an hour to

Wasu, right, with his father, left, with Uli, Fred, Theo, and Wasu's two brothers.

meet his family and have dinner with them.

"*So Buaba hod dor,*" Uli said, "*waas sagador jedsd? kaum zom glauba waas uff ons aellas zua kommd!*" Well my friends, it's hard to believe what's been happening to us!

After we freshened up, Wasu and one of the uncles picked us up in a limousine and drove us to a large house just a few streets away close to the river. Walking up to a garden we thought half of Allahabad was congregated there. So many happy people greeted us and shook hands and we could tell that Wasu and friends had told them a lot about us.

We were introduced to his mum and dad who owned the house, plus an older married sister and husband. There was also another younger brother and sister. Two of the uncles we had met, but there was another one and some aunties. With all their families and friends the huge garden was chock-o-block full of happy Sikhs and Hindus. Fruit juices and pots of tea were served to everyone by young women and men. A

The Big Adventure

couple of huge trestles and some tables stacked with delicious food were placed next to the house. After washing our hands at a washbasin we were handed a metal plate with some hot steamed rice in the middle and helped ourselves to the goodies. Everyone ate by hand and by that time we were quite used to it and got stuck into it because we had not eaten since Khaga.

It was a fantastic evening and I thought of Kavalla in Greece where we also had such a great welcome with young Spiro, his family and friends. By the time one of the uncles finally drove us back to the college we were absolutely rooted and hit the sack and slept instantly!

Wasu had told us during the evening that it was arranged for us to meet all the students and talk about our lives, the day after tomorrow.

We slept reasonably well under the fans but couldn't eat much for breakfast, still stuffed from last night. It wasn't long before Wasu and his uncle picked us up and took us on a grand tour of Allahabad in the limousine. I was amazed about the northern part of India, having more Mosques, Forts and other big Monuments built by Moslems so many years ago. Of cause there were plenty of Temples, but the Mosques were dominant. We did visit a couple of Temples and I must point out that from the first we saw we were surprised. Most of them had stone carvings of different animals cemented into the walls and Swastikas. Yes, Swastikas! We were amazed to see these symbols all over the Hindu Temples and we actually thought Hitler created it. We soon learnt that this symbol had been worshiped by the Hindus for well over a thousand years.

We drove along the riverbank where uncountable numbers of people submerged themselves to wash away their sins. We came past some big stacks of wooden logs, used to burn dead bodies. We parked at a small industrial area in front of a warehouse which turned out to be the family's workshop. Mum and dad were here, the uncles, a couple of cousins and a few ladies from last night, all working hard. It was a big place with many loud machines cutting different sizes of wood and stone blocks, an upstanding electric drill and even a small lathe. Heaps of sandstone and marble blocks of various sizes were set to be carved. Some very old figurines had to be repaired, after which they would returned to their original locations when finished. Although everyone worked hard they all seemed happy with what they were doing. There were trucks coming and leaving nonstop. It was obviously a very well to do business.

We were driven to a Temple which was being restored and shown a couple of building sites that were under construction. We parked in front of a big police station and were greeted by Wasu's uncle whom we had met the evening before. He was the Police Chief and we wanted him to write in our book, which he did. After a small lunch at a nearby restaurant we were shown some more important relics and eventually taken back to the school. Wasu informed us that we would have dinner at another restaurant later on in the evening.

Finally a couple of hours to ourselves, being able to study our map for the route to our next stop Benares, now Varanasi, 130km from Allahabad. By the time we had written some postcards and taken a refreshing shower, Wasu and his uncle picked us up again. There were at least five or six big tables being loaded with food and drinks at the restaurant and seated around them happy faces, most of whom we recognized. It was another great evening, but not as late as the last one, because we had to be at assembly by 10-am.

We were ready next morning for another day, a day which none of us have ever forgotten.

Assembly had already been over by the time we were picked up and to our surprise, we passed the empty assembly hall and were led towards the big entrance where in the front garden under the shade of the many huge trees, there would have been at least 300 Students clapping and waving to us. We felt privileged being there. A wooden plank on a steel frame for us to sit on was placed in the centre with all the students and teachers sitting on the grass in a semi-circle in front of us. There were plenty of girl students among them and we certainly had our eyes on the best looking ones.

Wasu and friends were sitting in between, probably making sure that everything went smooth. One of the teachers introduced us and told everyone about or lives and what we had accomplished up till now. Most of them had known some of it from the papers and of course from Wasu and his brother. While the teacher spoke about us, one of the students sat in front, and in pencil, sketched our bust in our book and didn't do a bad job either.

Uli got up, told them his name, where he was borne and in which Uni he was studying at. Someone even asked what subjects. Then it was my turn and when I mentioned Philadelphia as my birthplace, the questions came from all sides. By the time Theo had finished his story, we all became very relaxed and enjoyed ourselves immensely. After a while we were offered something to drink and being thirsty, we were looking forward to nice refreshments. Along with tea and water we were served something extra special.

Each of us was handed a metal drink container similar to a milk shake container holding about three quarters of a litre. It was the worst smelling and most horrible looking liquid I had ever held in my hand. It was yoghurt mixed with rancid milk and left standing in the sun for a couple of days. Mind you we were used to Maast in Persia, but this was totally something else.

We had seen people drinking this brew ever since we had entered India, but never had the pleasure of tasting it until now. During and after the war, our parents never poured milk which had gone sour down the drain. They made yoghurt out of it and we liked it.

Once we smelled and looked at the nearly overflowing containers we almost threw up. Our faces went ashen.

Theo said in our dialect *"des zeigs sauff I uff koin fall."* Nothing will make me drink this crap.

Uli replied, "*machad mor blos koin scheiss, seanor ned wia dia aelle uff ons glotzad ond wellad sea obs ons schmeggd.*" We must drink it because they are all watching us to see if we like their delicacy.

This was definitely one time where each of us could not talk ourselves out of a ticklish situation.

I looked at Uli and said, "I might give it a go," and holding my breath I took a small sip. I forced myself to look up and smile at all the students watching.

Uli did the same, but Theo wouldn't budge.

"There's no way out of it," Uli told him. "Everyone is watching."

And then the unthinkable happened. He held his breath, closed his eyes and gulped three quarters down in one go.

Uli and I had only managed a few sips, and Theo had gulped most of it down. Unbelievable! We had to congratulate him on his bravery. We slapped him wholeheartedly on his back mumbling "well done, well done."

Suddenly the students who had watched silently while Theo had contemplated his drink suddenly burst into a round of applause as he held up his drink container as if to say, "See, no problem." He was grinning from ear to ear.

What happened next you could never imagine. I have described seeing lots of vultures sitting in trees and along the curb side searching for dead animals hit by cars or dying of natural courses. Well, it was no different here. There were heaps of them perched in the tree branches above us, making sounds like wet farts. The sudden noise from the students yelling approval of Theo's effort with the drink startled them. With an awful squawk and much flapping of wings a heap of them took off from the branches above us.

As birds do when suddenly startled they shit themselves.

One of them just happened to fly over Theo's head and the shit it dropped fell right into his proudly upheld drink container. It caused an almighty splash as the shit filled the container to the brim causing whatever was left to splash up into Theo's face at the moment he looked down at it.

What an uproar!

Theo staggered back and almost fell over.

A couple of students jumped up and apologised profusely. Another one handed Theo a towel to wipe his face.

Uli and I struggled to keep a straight face.

And then of all things another student handed Theo a fresh container full to the brim.

Theo didn't know what to do with it. He looked at it dumbfounded.

I thought he was going to vomit.

I had quietly tipped out my drink in the confusion when no one was watching just in case we were asked to drink more, but that never happened. The drinks were soon forgotten, and put aside as we answered many more questions.

A young reporter from the local newspaper was present when this happened but didn't write about this incident! Apart from this mishap, the rest of the morning and the afternoon were most enjoyable.

Wasu and all his family spoiled us rotten and we didn't need our arms to be twisted to stay one more day. There was a nice article about us in the paper next morning and we enjoyed all the well wishes and hospitality, wherever Wasu and friends took us. We glued the article in our book and one of the teachers wrote underneath in Sanskrit.

All the Sikh men wind their turban around their head perfectly every morning and naturally, we had one wound around our heads too. It was hilarious and people couldn't stop laughing when they saw us Germans wearing turbans and bracelets on our arms.

Wasu came to our room later and wrote a full page in our book and we glued the picture underneath. He informed us that his family had organised a farewell party for us at their home in the evening.

It turned out to be a duplicate of the first one and we certainly felt as if we were part of this wonderful family. Wasu's uncle, the Chief of Police, told us to go straight to the Hotel de Paris in Benares where his friend the Commissioner would be waiting for us. He handed Theo a sealed letter addressed to the hotel. This was good news, and there was more good news from Wasu when he told us that they would give us a lift to Handia in the morning. It was very sad, with all the hugs, handshakes and well wishes when we finally were able to say goodbye. We didn't talk much before we went to sleep since we couldn't stop thinking about these wonderful people.

We didn't get away as early as we wanted, because half the college students and teachers were waiting to wave goodbye. It must have taken close to two hours before we had our bikes and luggage on the truck and slowly drove through the big gates and into the traffic. This time Wasu's father was driving the truck with one of the uncles beside him. Wasu, his brother and friends were on the back with us. Handia was only about 30km ahead but it was already very hot by the time we arrived there at lunch time. We had some light food in between lots of last minute conversations. This final goodbye was as sad as the one the night before. Wasu and the others hugged each of us for a long time before they climbed back onto the truck which soon disappeared into the distance.

We sat out most of the heat, but still covered close to 40km before we found a people free spot to camp overnight. Ever since we had arrived in India we were surrounded by an incredible amount of people, all kind of animals, and the ever present cows. Busses and trains were always overloaded and even had people sitting on top of the roof. Riding bikes through this mass of traffic and heat was difficult and quite often very dangerous. Perhaps we encountered so much life in the north because of the Ganges River and others flowing through some of the most holy cities. Perhaps the southern part of India is less populated.

After passing through a few villages and a couple of smaller towns we made the outskirts of Benares. We had a short break at a small market place before attempting to ride into the city. We wanted to get to the hotel as soon as possible so we grabbed the first rickshaw we saw to lead us to our destination, which we covered in just over half an hour.

Benares was larger than Allahabad and Hotel de Paris was a very impressive, Queen Victoria style building two storeys high, but massive in volume. Surrounded by beautiful gardens and shady trees, it was built in the middle of the city centre, two streets from the river. The rickshaw fellow guided us up a short driveway and stopped in front of two long steps made of white marble leading to the entrance.

I hardly had time to pay and thank our guide when two uniformed servants followed by two more, greeted us and welcomed us to the hotel. One of them told us that we were expected and he and the others were here to show us our room and help with our bikes and luggage. News travels fast. We had this letter from Wasu's uncle to give to the reception, but it wasn't even needed. In no time while hotel guests smiled at us we were led into a big beautiful family room. This special room had a double bed, two singles, a small table, a wardrobe and an adjacent bathroom and toilet. There was plenty of space for our bikes and luggage. One of our helpers informed us that Mr. Shiveshwarkar, the Commissioner would greet us at the lounge room in one hour. There wasn't much time to settle in if we had to be ready in such a short time, but we managed.

We were greeted not only by one elderly gentleman but by two accompanied by their wives. We introduced ourselves and with handshakes all round so did they. The Commissioner had brought along his close friend who also wanted to meet us. His friend owned a big steel company, which made cycle frames amongst their products. We were seated at a table and served some delicious fruit juices. I handed each of the men one of our cards and Theo showed them our book. Apparently the Commissioner's other friend in Allahabad had arranged for him to meet with us and had told him lots about our adventure. They couldn't get over us meeting all those head of states, especially having spent time with Pandit Nehru. The Commissioner had met Mr. Nehru several times and had even known Mahatma Ghandi.

We enjoyed their hospitality and it wasn't too long before the hotel Manager introduced himself and joined us. His name was Frank P Byrmel and he was English. Time just flew by. The Commissioner wrote some nice sentences in our book. The hotel manager also wrote in our book.

It had been a long day and we were stuffed, ready for a good night's sleep. The Commissioner's friend asked if he could show us his factory tomorrow and said he would pick us up at about 10am. Of course we told him we were looking forward to it and thanked them for their hospitality. The Manager walked us to our room and told us he would meet with us

The Big Adventure

at breakfast. It wasn't late, but it was great to lie down under those fans and we didn't wake up till early next morning.

Benares/Varanasi had many more Hindu Temples than Mosques. The Commissioner's friend picked us up after we had breakfast with the Manager and took us to his factory in a chauffeur driven limousine. It was a big place called ASIA ALLSTEEL situated a few kilometres north of the city in an industrial area. This huge factory had lots of separate sections, where steel was forged steel, to where they finished many different products, and it was hot. After the office staff served some us tea we were handed a helmet each and a safety vest to wear as we were shown through the factory.

The first section we saw was a warehouse with lots of goods being dispatched and loaded onto trucks. It was still okay here, but once we got further in towards the back of the factory it got hotter and hotter. We went through a section with lots of different machines manufacturing small articles from tools to steel framed furniture and bicycle frames.

By the time we reached the last two sections where hot furnaces forged different pipes and solid steel rods we were sweating like pigs. There were workers all over the place seemingly happy and getting on with their work not bothered at all with the heat, like us.

After walking through the last two sections in record time we found ourselves back in the office under cool fans. Our host turned out to be a very likeable, jovial person. He told us that his father had started ALLSTEEL many years ago in a small shed in another town where he was born. But it was our host and his younger brother who built this Factory, plus another big one further north where they made parts for railway and farm machinery.

A light lunch was served and we enjoyed a couple of relaxing hours telling him our life story. He wrote some words in our book and told us he had to take it next door to stamp it. It didn't take long he handed it back to Theo and told him not to open it until we got back to the hotel. After shaking hands with us, he informed us that dinner at the hotel was already organised for the evening, with friends. The limo took us back to the hotel and we couldn't wait to get under the shower once more. But first we had to open our book to see what he had written. Opening the page we counted six brand new US$100 notes. It took some time for us to settle our nerves. What a great guy we thought, handing us such a welcome present.

In Benares...

The Big Adventure

Taking a stroll towards the river later in the afternoon we encountered some incredible sights.

The moment the hotel was out of sight a bedraggled Hindu guy pestered us, demanding to be our guide.

"We don't need a guide," we said, but he kept following and pestering us.

Secondly a couple of musicians with a young girl wanted us to watch her dance.

There was a snake charmer with a massive cobra wriggling in front of his face who asked for money.

We gave them a few coins and received big smiles, except from the Tour guide.

"I am the best guide in the whole of India and the most trustworthy," he said.

"We don't need a guide," we told him again. "Go and pester someone else."

He wouldn't take no for an answer. He actually insisted that we look at and read a letter of recommendation he had received from other German tourists. He handed it to Uli who read it out to us.

"Dear country folks, beware of this so called guide, he is a bad man and only after your money, don't trust him and tell him to go drown in the river." It was signed by a couple of Germans from Bremen.

Uli had to keep a straight face as with a smile he patted the guide on the shoulder and told him how good the letter was. Handing the letter back he said, "Maybe we could use a guide for a while."

The man beamed at us.

"But not before you tell us the price."

Once that was negotiated to our satisfaction we kept our eyes and ears open and watched every move he made.

Across the street was a Temple called the Temple of the Apes which he wanted to show us first. We put a few coins in a plate to get in and a few more to purchase a couple of paper bags with nuts and dried fruit. It was a novelty to walk through the Temple accompanied by a heap of monkeys begging for food. Our guide seemed to know the history, because he kept explaining about different gods and some of the wood carved statues that were everywhere you looked. Every opening or doorway had a swastika carved into it which was something we still had not got used to. One level above was surrounded by a big cement platform held up by stone pillars. We sat on the steps, fed the monkeys and relaxed with a few smokes.

The Big Adventure

There were different Temples honouring a variety of other animals that our guide was eager to show us. He wanted to show us the activity by the river, but we told him it was too late for us and it has to wait till tomorrow. As a formality we asked him how much we owed him and were prepared to try and jack up the sum agreed on for the three hours he was with us, but could hardly believe it when he asked for less than he quoted us earlier. Theo paid him a bit extra and we told him to meet us next morning again to show us some more.

Back at the hotel we were smiled at by some guests and invited by the manager for the always welcome cool fruit juices. I had forgotten to mention that there was a small article and our picture in the Benares Paper early in the morning. It was written in Sanskrit and we couldn't read it, but we were told it was very good. We wondered if our guide had read about us and treated us differently. We would ask him in the morning.

After a refreshing shower, wearing long pants and clean shirts, we were ready for dinner. The Commissioner with his wife and two sons were already in the lounge when we entered, along with everyone else who had been there the night before. We were introduced to another two couples who were close friends of the Commissioner. While we were handed drinks, we took our morning's host aside to thank him for his wonderful generosity.

They all wanted to know about our walk towards the river. Uli mentioned the tour guide and they all laughed, when we told them what happened. The Manager led us into the fully occupied dining room where two of the biggest tables had been joined together. There were more than twenty of us. We were offered a cold beer which Uli and I readily accepted, Theo got his coke. We had great fun and it became fairly loud with everyone asking questions at the same time. The food was delicious and we certainly got stuck into it. The dining room was nearly empty by the time it was decided to call it a night.

The tour guide was waiting for us in front of the Temple and greeted us as if we were long time friends of his. He asked us "Why are you walking and not riding your bikes?"

So he had read the papers and did know something about us.

We pointed at the masses of people heading towards the river. It would have been impossible to ride bikes amongst them.

Halfway towards the Temple we heard loud noises like people moaning and pieces of wood being hit like a rhythm behind us. Everyone around us stopped moving and waited. What we saw was quite disturbing to us.

The traffic had stopped and the crowd made room for six guys carrying a homemade stretcher on their shoulders with a dead body lying on top. With three on each side each used their free hand to hit the stretcher with a short piece of wood as they walked at a brisk pace towards the river. They were followed by a compact mass of people young and old, all moaning and clapping pieces of wood together.

We stared at each other in disbelieve. What on earth was happening? We asked our guide and he told us to follow him.

It was a short walk to the river and what we saw was even more disturbing.

On the river bank in front of some very old buildings and lots of rowing boats were several stacks of wood about one and half meters high floating in the water. The dead body, covered in white sheets, was lifted up on top of one of the stacks, while the people on the shore in front of it continued wailing and moaning. The stack was set alight and very soon as it was in full flames. It was a ferocious looking fire with flames shooting high up into the sky. The burning stack was pushed out into Holy River where it swirled around in circles for a minute before a slight current took hold and it began to drift away.

We were astonished, never having seen anything like this before, and what was more surprising for us, life around us went on as if nothing had happened. The wailing and moaning stopped and all those people melted back into the crowds along the river bank. Not far from where we stood there were hundreds of people half submerged in the shallow water near the riverbank washing themselves and even drinking the slightly polluted but holy water. Every Hindu, wherever they live on Earth, wants to bathe in the Holy River at least once in a lifetime. On some of the boats where families lived we saw them throw their offal straight over the side, adding to the flavour of the river water.

Our guide hired one of the rowing boats to show us life along the river's edge and it was amazing. Every available spot along the shore was occupied by fully clothed people submerging themselves in the water. Some of the Temples and old stone buildings were built right to the water's edge with some food stalls in between. It was an amazing sight for people like us to see how different life was in India.

We had barely got back to shore after about an hour in the little boat when we heard more chanting, wood bashing and moaning coming towards us. Theo was in front as we climbed out of the boat onto the concrete landing. He turned and said, "...must be another dead body for burial." Well, it was a body to be cremated, but not a human body, it was a dead Cow! A bloody Cow!

Its legs were tied together with rope and it was carried on a long pole by six men towards another stack of wood. The crowd chanted and bowed when the cow was lifted up on top of the pile and set alight.

I couldn't believe what was going on around me. About an hour earlier a human body was burnt, and to us it was a big deal, but this was something else. Worshiping a cow in such a manner was beyond our comprehension. At that time we looked at cows for producing milk, beef patties and sausages, but today we see things in a different way and respect the law, tradition and belief of all the different people on earth. After seeing the burning cow being pushed on to the river, we needed time out to digest what had happened.

The Big Adventure

The Big Adventure

Journey of a Lifetime

Life along the mighty Ganges River.

Me, enjoying some time with Wasu and his brothers and sister.

Theo said "I wonder why we didn't see anything like this in Allahabad."

Uli said, "I suspect Wasu had no time to show us around the river there because he wanted to make some money for us instead."

We followed our guide through the crowd, past beggars and food stalls, away from the river to a quieter street with not much traffic. Next to a more modern Temple was a small restaurant where we were able to find a vacant table for the four of us. We ordered some freshly squeezed fruit juice and relaxed with a couple of well earned smokes. After some small nibbles of food our guide asked one of the servants to get him some paper and pencil. He wanted us to write him another resume as good as the other one.

Actually we got on with him extremely well and couldn't fault him at all and certainly learned a lot through him. Theo wrote him some very nice sentences in German, with our address being Stuttgart and the three of us signed it.

He was delighted. We made a point of telling him "if you come across some more German tourists, only show this letter to them, not the other one." He smiled and nodded, and I do hope he understood.

We had a look through the Temple next door and then it was time to say good bye. We paid him some extra and after long handshakes we walked back to our hotel.

By the time we gave our bikes a tune up for the long haul in front of us it was getting dark. Another shower, long pants once more and we were ready for our last dinner in Benares. The food was the same as the night before except there were no women or children only us men. It was a pretty sad good bye and the hugs and handshakes were never ending. We thanked all of them for their great hospitality and promised to keep in touch. Finally we got to bed, but with all the incredible things that had happened in the last couple of days, it took a while before I went to sleep.

We didn't need a rickshaw to guide us out of the city towards the main road next morning, we knew the way. We wanted to get away earlier but were held up by the Manager who insisted we should have a good breakfast and he had joined us. We knew that we were guests of someone, but didn't know who paid the bill. Uli asked him about it and we were told, "by the City Council, organised by the Commissioner."

We thanked him once more and walking past the reception, we saw that the newspaper article with our picture was nicely framed and hanging on the back wall.

Sassaram was about 130 kilometres east, but being hot and humid we only covered about 60 kilometres before we had to rest under some small trees to get out of the sun. We couldn't rest under the bigger ones because on most of the tree branches sat vultures dropping crap. We made Kudru late evening and found a quiet spot out of town. Our water bottles were full and each of us had a couple of cokes, some dried meat and some fruit, compliments of Frank Byrmel. Sleeping on the ground again was a bit hard, but lying down early still made us feel good in the morning and ready to hit the road. Sassaram was another 40 kilometres ahead and we made it in good time to have breakfast in the middle of town.

All along the northern part of India we crossed many rivers and smaller waterways all of which originated somewhere up in the Himalayas. The soils in this area were extremely fertile because of regular flooding and silt deposits from the rivers and were studded with small farms. There were no water restrictions on this part of India, but I believe in Rajasthan towards Pakistan, it was a different story.

We bought a few necessities and rested just before crossing the Soh River. Crossing it was a nightmare with all the traffic in two lanes on this long and narrow bridge. The bridge was solidly built and we could see why. The river wasn't very wide but it worked its way through enormous sandbanks at least a kilometre wide. We were told that during the rainy season the river was like an ocean, flooding the whole area and reaching half way up the bridge. It took a long time walking our bikes across and we had no hope of reaching Aurangabad before dark. We passed through a couple of small towns and several villages and camped about 10 kilometres before Aurangabad.

We had been travelling in a east south easterly direction and crossing all those rivers, water ways and lakes, was like travelling through a series of saunas. The 70 kilometres to Chouparan was more uncomfortable than other sections. What with the dust we collected and the constant sweating that wouldn't dry, it was painful sliding on the saddle in our sweaty undies from one cheek to the other. We could feel blisters forming and there was nothing we could do about it. We had to get under a shower as soon as possible and were happy to find a small hotel near the centre in Chouparan. Taking long showers after which we rubbed healing cream on our bums and groins, we certainly felt better. Our clothes were washed overnight and ready for us in the morning.

We left early to avoid the crippling humidity. Our aim was to get to Calcutta as quickly as possible but is was very hard riding and we had to

The Big Adventure

stop more than we would have liked to rest and to escape the horrible humidity that left us totally exhausted. We passed through many small towns and villages: Barhi, where we had breakfast, Bagodar where we had to take a long rest out of the heat, Dumri where we had an evening meal and camped out for the night, and on through the next day where just before Asansol, Uli's back tyre punctured, and an hour later my front tyre did the same. We camped by the Damodar River.

Riding alongside this river we were amazed how much sand and whole dunes were on both sides for many kilometres. Travelling was slow, the humidity unreal and each kilometre seemed longer than the one before. We couldn't quite make Burdwan and camped again next to the river and spent a very uncomfortable night lying on top of our spread out sleeping bags, near naked. Without a breeze the air was almost unbreathable. We could hardly wait for daybreak.

We wasted no time in Burdwan except for a quick breakfast. We followed a railway line from there and reached the small town of Dhaniakhali before midday. With just two hotels we picked the first one and had no problem getting a big room. We could have gone further towards Calcutta, but with only another 60 kilometres to go, we thought it would be better to rest, get a good night's sleep and be prepared for the big smoke early the next morning.

Waiting for dinner in the hotel dining room, a well dressed Sikh asked us if he and his wife could join us. "Gladly," we said and were about to introduce ourselves when he said, "no need, I know who are."

Now this was interesting, here we were in one of the smallest towns in India and someone knew us.

I suppose you could say "it's a small world," but this coincidence was odd to say the least.

Mr. R Mourli immediately explained that he was the owner of Tata Iron and Steel, a big Manufacturing Company in Calcutta, and he was a close Associate of K B Gupta and his ASIA ALLSTEEL in Benares. He and his Wife had driven through the northern part of India to visit customers in several big Cities. They happened to be in New Delhi when they read about us in the paper and were saddened when they missed us by one day at ALLSTEEL. It was only by chance that they had stopped at this hotel on their way to Calcutta to have a bite to eat and were totally surprised to see us here. How about that for a coincidence?

We had a great couple of hours together and the Mourli's invited us to catch up with them in Calcutta and gave us their address and phone number. They had to visit someone further to the north and wouldn't be back for three more days, but we could call on them any time after.

"Calcutta may not be as safe as New Delhi, so please be careful," they warned us. "You should call at the Salvation Army Men's Industrial Home when you get to Calcutta."

He wrote down the address for us. "Stay there for a few days until we get back. And tell the Manager Mr. Mourli sent you."

It took a few moments to digest this. Someone up above must be looking after us!

After the dinner and more tea, it was a big goodbye and best wishes until we see you in Calcutta.

We got another surprise early next morning. When I walked to the reception to pay our bill I was told it was paid. Mr Mourli had paid it after dinner before he left.

Unbelievable!

We felt great when we jumped on our bikes, excited to reach our last big City in India. With only about 60 kilometres to the centre we thought we would make it by midday, but we were mistaken. The road followed a railway line and for the first couple of hours we covered a fair distance even though the traffic was heavy. It was after midday when we stopped in Dankuni for some lunch with less than 10 kilometres to go.

Thick black storm clouds threatened us from behind as we reached a tributary of the Mighty Ganges and pushed our bikes over a big steel bridge. There were people all over the place and both shorelines of this river were built up with makeshift little huts where whole communities seemed to live. Even the footpaths were occupied with extremely poor people and we could see the living standard was near zero. We had seen poor areas in other large cities, but nothing like this. As soon as we could we mounted our bikes and got away fairly quick. We didn't feel very safe at all. The traffic was horrendous and the humidity was killing us. If we didn't find shelter soon we would get drenched when the storm coming up behind hit us.

To top it off, we didn't know where to go. The second rickshaw driver we asked knew where the Salvation Army was and said he would guide us there.

Our first impression of Calcutta wasn't very favourable, with so much misery, lots of deformed people and children, all begging. We followed the rickshaw for at least a half hour dodging busses, trucks, cycles and cows which always had the right of way. Our rickshaw eventually stopped in front of a big long building. A huge sign with big letters stating Salvation Army men's Industrial Home was perched on top of a double steel gate.

I paid our rickshaw guide a bit extra and got the first smile since before we crossed the river. We hardly made it through the gate towards the office, when the storm hit. Rain came down in buckets and in no time the streets were flooded. Had we been just five minutes slower we would have been drenched to the skin.

We got the second smile when the office door opened before we could knock and a young well dressed Hindu greeted us. He introduced himself as the Manager and wanted to know what he could do for us. Uli told him we were from Germany and on our way to Australia. He looked astonished, and from the look on his face he obviously found it hard to believe what Uli was telling him. We were still standing outside his office, holding our bikes. Several men had surrounded us while Uli was explaining, and that made me feel uneasy. Theo interrupted and told the manager that Mr. Mourli sent us here to find accommodation for three nights.

What a bombshell. That name was like magic. Their demeanour changed instantly.

Within seconds we were greeted with handshakes by most of the men around us and the Manager spoke to them in a dialect we couldn't understand and immediately some of the men ran off in different directions. The manager M told a couple of guys to watch out for our bikes while he ushered us into his office. We were offered some tea and M with a couple office assistants could hardly wait to hear about our encounter with the Mourlis. We told him what happened in Dhaniakhali and he could hardly believe that we had dinner with them.

Uli asked him "why are you so surprised?"

"Mr. Mourli is one of the biggest Steel and Mining Merchants in India," he said, "and without his very generous financial help this enterprise here could not function. Most of the men here work for Mr. Mourli or his Associates."

Now we understood why we were sent here in the first place.

It was no problem for us to stay a few days and our bikes and luggage would be safe in the storeroom next to the office.

This place was definitely no Hilton, but beggars can't be choosers.

We would often stop and talk to people we saw along the way.

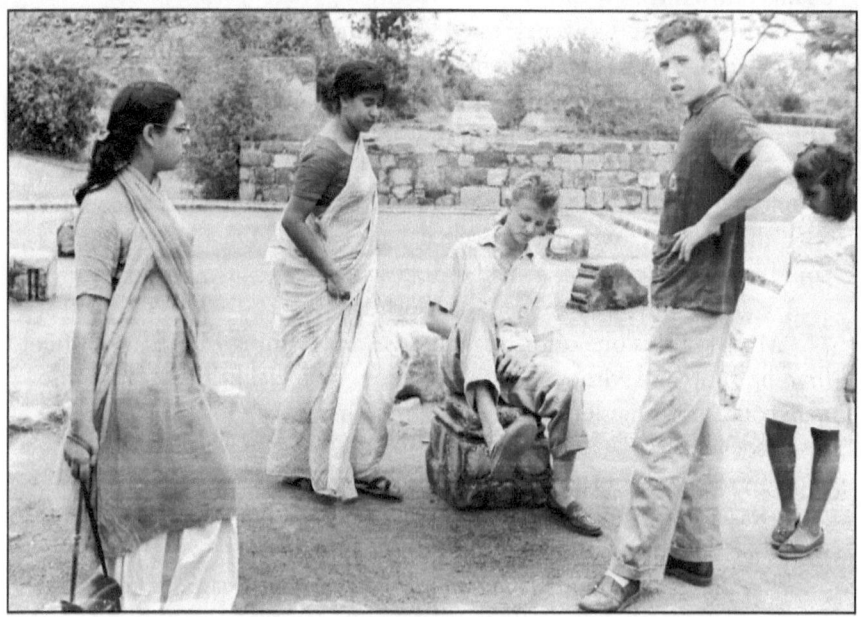

The building must once have been a big old factory or warehouse. It was solidly built of bricks and totally waterproof. Opposite the office was a rather big section where people could donate diverse things for less fortunate families. In the next section was a big kitchen and dining area, followed by bathroom facilities. On the opposite side were huge dormitories with mattresses scattered in disorderly fashion over the floor. There were some big fans hanging from the ceiling; otherwise one had no hope sleeping in these conditions. M. asked us to choose a mattress each and pick a corner in one of the rooms for one night.

"I will have a store room cleaned out tonight and in the morning you can stay there."

By the time we unpacked and stowed everything in the room where they took the bikes, the rain had stopped. The streets were still flooded but the sun came out and steam started rising off the wet areas. It was like a sauna.

M and some of the others were absolutely rapt when they found out we had met their Prime Minister. In the office under the fans swirling the air around, it wasn't too bad and we used it as if it was our own room. M organised some food from the kitchen and plenty of tea and fruit juices. The lights went out at ten o'clock M told us. Being a long day, we didn't mind that. We thanked M. and moved into our corner. By the time we had finished taking a shower in rather dubious bathroom there must have been at least twenty other guys sitting or lying on their mattress.

Theo was the first one to lie down, but after a few minutes jumped up swearing in Schwaebisch. "Jedsd leggad me no am Arsch, waas sen den des fer schaisliche Fiichor." "Now you can all kiss my arse, what are these unreal Beasts."

We looked, and from under his mattress came a myriad of bugs and lots of other creepy crawlies all trying to feast on him.

We turned our mattresses over and after shaking them we couldn't believe our eyes. The whole floor was covered with bugs running about looking for somewhere to hide. Uli grabbed a broom and swept them aside. This created a disturbance and the Indian guys wanted to know what was wrong.

They talked to each other in their dialect and we could see they became angry. They came very close and one of them asked "What are you doing?"

"What does it look like?" Uli said, "We are getting rid of these bugs."

"No you don't," the guy said, and then we got a lecture.

With no running water this was the only way to wash her hair.

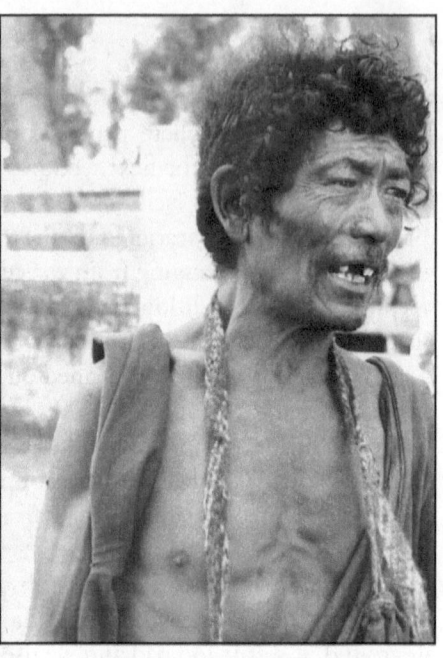

...and of course who can resist a snake charmer?

"How long have you been in India? Are you not familiar with Indian customs and religion?"

We told them that we are only travelling through and had not had a situation like this before. He explained that every animal, bugs, birds or insects were holy to all Hindus and they would not kill any living thing.

Well, we knew about cows and some other animals, but who would have thought about insects!

"Rich people have Sleepers."

"What's a Sleeper?" Uli asked.

"A Sleeper is someone who sleeps in the rich person's bed during daytime for the insects to feed on his body so later on the rich one could have a good night's sleep."

"You must be kidding," Uli said in disbelieve, but the guy was serious."

"You have a lot yet to learn about India," the man said.

This could have been a very ticklish and serious situation and we were glad that they accepted our apologies.

Needles to say we had another extremely uncomfortable night.

Even covering the mattress with our sleeping bags didn't help much and we looked next morning as if we had measles.

M and a couple of helpers were halfway finished cleaning out the storeroom when we entered the office next morning. He was shocked when we told him what happened and he could see that it could have come to a big confrontation. He explained again the customs of their religion, but assured us that there were no creepy things in the other room. Our move into the store room was quick and we felt one hundred percent happier and in a much better mood.

We asked M where most of the business offices, main Post Office, car dealerships etcetera were situated. "Calcutta is made up of many different cities and suburbs," he explained, "but the main centre of town is only a couple of mile from here. You could catch a train, but from here it would be better by rickshaw because then you could stop wherever you wanted."

He picked up a newspaper from his desk and opened the second page for us to look at. On half of the page was a picture of a huge cargo ship, with headlines above, Germany's New Frontier, Neuenfels on Maiden Voyage. Below was written that Neuenfels and her sister ship "Baerenfels" were Built in Bremen and were fitted with the latest technology in moving freight and accommodating up to twelve passengers in absolute first class. Neuenfels had only been here for two days and was expected to stay

Everybody worked hard to survive, especially the poorest, but the pride they took in work was enormous.

for over one week.

We asked M how far was it to where the ship was moored, and he told us nearly one hour by rickshaw.

We grabbed our book, passports, cigarettes, money and told M that we were having breakfast somewhere in town. It was hot and steamy with mean looking rainclouds covering the sky. We asked the first rickshaw driver we saw how much he wanted by the hour and he gave us a very reasonable figure, so we booked him for a few hours. I paid him some Rupees, told him to take us into the city and with a smiling face he pulled us through the traffic.

We were relatively relaxed, having found a place to stay and Calcutta seemed to make a better impression than it had the day before. We traversed a couple of smaller streets and entered a wide main road full of life and heavy traffic. There were big stone buildings on both sides and most of them were occupied by a variety of shops, restaurants and all kinds of repair businesses. No matter what was broken, somewhere here you could get it fixed. There were stalls all along the footpaths selling anything you could imagine.

We stopped in front of a better looking restaurant and told our driver to wait. There was no problem finding a vacant table and in such a big city being served without being gawked at by all the people was nice for a change. After a light breakfast and a couple of smokes we told the rickshaw driver to take us to where the German ship was moored. He was surprised when we told him the address because obviously it was quite a way, but pushed on with a smile, he was probably thinking of the money.

Had it not been so hot and steamy, with the sky full of angry clouds, we would have enjoyed the day. We passed lots of big parks with beautifully manicured gardens and some had massive old English mansions in them. We saw numerous office buildings with some of the world's bigger companies advertising their names above the entrances. Most of the names were very familiar to us and we were looking forward to visiting some of them. Turning down a couple of side streets we headed for the river and could easily see the harbour festooned with massive yellow painted cranes not too far ahead.

There was a lot of activity the closer we got, with small boats and some bigger ships navigating along the river, trucks coming and going through checkpoints. Manoeuvring through the traffic and passing lots of storage places with administration buildings in between, we spotted Neuenfels in the distance.

The very busy port of calcutta

What an enormous sight we encountered the closer we got. This ship was huge! Something we had never seen before. She was also beautiful. The hull was painted in a semi gloss black and the upper structure in a shining white gloss. We had never been to Hamburg or Bremen (Germany's major ports) and some of the bigger ships we saw crossing the Bosporus couldn't compare to this one.

High up on the very back on two flagpoles were the Indian and German flags proudly flying in the breeze. There were people all over the wharf with some well dressed looking like officials being greeted by uniformed men and led up the gangplank to visit. We found out later it was the Captain and a couple of his Officers who welcomed some high-ranking government officials and reporters to show them through the ship.

We told our driver to wait and pushed our way through the crowd and introduced ourselves to the two uniformed sentries, guarding the gangplank. How surprised they were, when we spoke in German and wanted to know what and why we were in India. It's always the same wherever we go; people find it hard to believe what we did, especially when we were without our bikes.

Uli showed them a few pages in our book and handed one of them our card and finally they looked at us differently. Both of them were in their late twenty's and seamen for many years. They had been in many ports around the globe and met many different nationalities, but never came across anyone on a bike so far from home. We asked them if we could go on board so we could feel a bit of home, but were told, "Not today, most likely tomorrow."

"We've been here three days," we were told, "and we haven't even started to unload. There's been nothing but official government visitors, businessmen and city councillors visiting. Who knows what they talk about?"

"Mostly bullshit," Uli suggested.

"You said it. This lot are the last, I think. Tomorrow morning they will start unloading freight. We'll show Captain Falin your card and if you could get here before midday the Captain would probably invite you to have lunch on board."

That was good news. "We don't have a problem with that," we told them while thinking we will come on our bikes so they can see we are for real.

We asked our driver to take us back the same way as we came to familiarise ourselves with the area. We wouldn't want to get lost on the way to the ship when we came back the next morning.

As we got close to our quarters, we asked the driver where we could find some shops and he told us there was a big Bazaar near where we are staying. We needed to buy some essentials and told him that when he dropped us off we would eventually walk back. I paid him well and we headed into the crowded Bazaar. We filled a couple of small paper bags and were able to buy some postcards. At food stall we had some freshly squeezed juice and enjoyed a couple of smokes. Back at the Salvo's we found our little store room nice and clean, and there was a small table and two chairs in the middle. We thanked M. and he was very happy after we told him that we will be meeting the Captain of the Neuenfels the next day.

On the way there next morning we had no problem managing the traffic and the weather also held, even though angry dark clouds hung threateningly above. There was no sun, but it felt as if we were in a sauna. Just as well there was a stiff breeze blowing across the water. It was eleven o'clock when we stopped at the gangway and were greeted in German by the same two smiling guards. Our bikes were secured behind the gangway and watched by one of the guards, while the other one asked us to follow him.

What happened next was unexpected. We certainly knew we were back in Germany. We were greeted as if we were the greatest sportsmen out of Germany. We had to shake hands with uniformed officers and other men dressed in overalls. The ship was spotless and still smelled very new. We were led straight in to the bridge where we were introduced to the Captain and the rest of the ship's brains. This was something totally new to the three of us, looking past the steering through the windows of this magnificent ship on to Calcutta's harbour.

After a lecture about the instruments, mechanics and specifications, we were asked to follow them. They led us down some stairs and along a never ending corridor to the back of the ship and then up a three or four storey high Infrastructure into a huge kitchen/ dining room with a beautiful bar and lounge chairs and next to it a small cinema. The levels above this had a gym, a library and lots of cabins. Several of the dining room tables had been pushed together and nicely set. We were motioned to take a seat and it didn't take long before we were served absolutely delicious food. There were half a dozen different dishes to choose from, but all three of us chose the Wiener Schnitzel and at that time it was the best Schnitzel we ever tasted. There were some beautiful deserts and cheese

The Big Adventure

Theo and Fred with Mr Fred Mitchel and his dog Rex.
Theo and Fred with M the manager of the Salvatian Army Hostel.

platters with coffee afterwards.

All I can say is we felt great. There would have been at least twenty personnel joining in at lunch and all of them wanted to hear our story. Uli started, Theo and I answered many questions of which some had to be answered twice. They just could not grasp what we had achieved so far, even the Captain asked a few very relevant questions. He was very interested about us meeting with all those heads of state we had visited and was very excited to write some kind words into our book.

When we finally thanked everyone for their great hospitality it was late afternoon before we managed to hop on our bikes. We were asked to visit once more, unfortunately we told them we had some other people to visit, before we headed for Burma.

Wearing our fabulous helmets, asking foir directions on the outskirts of Calcutta.

The Big Adventure

We didn't mention that we had to make some money for our journey ahead. By the time we got back we were fairly stuffed, especially after we had to tell M everything that happened. We knew we would be very busy next morning visiting the companies we had seen during our rickshaw ride, so after some tea and a couple of smokes, went to bed early.

M got us the same rickshaw next morning and after breakfast at the same restaurant we visited the following companies: Brook-Bond India Private Limited Tea and Coffee, The Good Year Tyre and Rubber Company, Walford Transport LTD., India Automobiles, Dunlop Rubber Co. India LTD. finishing off at Bata shoes Limited.

By then it was getting dark and we were pretty exhausted. Our reception was always friendly, kind and very hospitable. The financial help we got was overpowering and from Bata each of us received a new pair of shoes on top of financial help. Back in our room, away from M's inquisitive eyes we started counting the cash and opened three envelopes. We were simply overwhelmed by the generosity of all these people.

Our Rickshaw was waiting in the morning to take us for breakfast. Freshly strengthened we visited a beautiful old brick office building, several storeys high. It had WHIIE PRINTING in big letters above the entrance and on the front door a brass plate with The Titaghur Paper Mills Co.LTD on it. A well dressed Hindu Gentleman sitting on a small table, wrote down our names and pointed to a staircase leading to the first floor. Another Hindu Gentleman smiled, stood up and opened a door for us to enter into a large office as busy as a beehive. There must have been up to twenty desks with two or three people young and old, male and female at them, keeping very busy and noisy.

As soon as we entered everything stopped. It went dead silent and everyone stared at us. We were used to this kind of reception. Mind you, here we were dressed in short sleeve shirts, shorts with pockets stuffed with passports, cigarettes and matches. Our new Bata shoes we wore without socks, because of the heat. Uli carried his camera over his shoulder; I was carrying our book and Theo holding some cards.

We must have looked very foreign, not at all like their regular well to do customers. One smiling lady in full Hindi costume asked what she could do for us. I showed her part of our book and Theo asked her if we could see the Manager.

"One moment," she said, knocked on a side door and entered. It wasn't long before she came out, followed by a European in his thirties, blond and sporty, looking like a gentleman from England. He stared at us with a blank expression and I imagined that he was debating with himself whether to ask us to leave or hear what we came for. He decided to hear our story. He motioned us to follow him into his office which looked more like a lounge room. Next to a small desk was a round conference table surrounded by six comfortable lounge chairs.

After introducing ourselves Theo handed him our card and Uli started telling him about us as I put our book on the table. He introduced himself as Richard (I have forgotten his last name) from London. He asked us to take a seat and as I started to show him some pages in our book he became more fascinated by the minute. Suddenly he held up his hand and told us to stop.

He told us that he was commissioned as Secretary for five years to the Managing Director and owner of several paper manufactories and printing companies, Mr. Fred Mitchell. "I would like my boss to be part of your story," Richard said. "He's a great sports lover and sponsors the English and Indian National Cricket Teams."

Mr Mitchell's office was entered through the back of the building.

"It won't take a minute to go and get him. Make yourselves comfortable and I will have some tea sent in." He stepped through a door hidden by a long curtain.

We didn't know what to expect. Before we had time to become impatient the office door opened and the beautifully dressed lady and one of the office guys came in carrying a big pot of tea, half a dozen glasses and a tray full of cookies. They looked at us with astonishment. The fact that we were being treated like honoured guests and knowing that the Company Chief wanted to share tea with us was something they never expected would happen.

We guessed everyone in the front office wanted to know where we really came from.

We were on our second cup and had consumed a few cookies when the side door opened and Richard entered followed by a middle aged, tall heavy set Gentleman dressed in a tailored creamy white suit, white shirt, shiny black shoes wearing black rimmed glasses.

We stood up and Richard introduced us. Mr Mitchell shook hands with each of us.

The saying, "first Impressions don't lie", is certainly true. After that first handshake and friendly smile we felt as comfortable as if we were at home visiting a loved uncle.

I showed both of them through every page in our book whilst Uli and Theo answered all their questions. About half way through the book and lots of Mr. Mitchell's questions, we were asked to call him Fred. This we didn't expect, but with that big smile of his we felt quite comfortable.

Anyhow Fred and Richard couldn't get enough of our story and by midday we were asked by Fred to join them for lunch. Uli told them we would love to accept, but we had to see someone else soon. I asked him if he would be so kind as to write something in our book, but he said "not yet." He asked us where we were staying and what time we would be back there?

Closing our book I told him "we would be back by around four."

"Okay," he said, "I shall send my chauffeur to pick you up at five and bring you to my home for dinner."

We shook hands, thanked them for listening to our story, and for the tea and cookies. Richard escorted us out through the office and down to the footpath.

Actually we didn't know what to say; we sat back in our rickshaw with nothing gained and no writing in our book, but with an invitation for dinner.

We really didn't feel like visiting any more people, but stopped more or less out of habit at a company called Kilbourne & Co. Pty Ltd.

Our hearts weren't really with us when we finally met not one but two of the partners in the company. To our surprise, they were very hospitable, offered us some tea and wrote in our book. One of them asked if there was anything they could help us, and Theo told them the same story; that we were financing our own journey and relying on News Papers, Universities and some of the Companies they saw in our book for assistance along the way. Theo hardly finished when the other one opened a draw in his desk and counted out a good handful of Indian Rupees and handed them to Theo.

Our spirits lifted again! Having a light lunch and a couple of smokes at our breakfast restaurant, we told our driver to take us back to the Salvos.

As soon as we walked towards the office M ran towards us and excitedly told us, that Mr. Mourli had rung and would be here at three o'clock to meet up with us.

Things were snowballing a bit faster than we expected and we thanked M before entering our room to have another shower, count the money and change into fresh clothes. I can't remember how much we got, but

Theo had to count it twice to make sure and with a big grin handed it to me to put in our pouch around my neck.

We hardly had time to relax, to get our thoughts together when M knocked on the door. He asked us to come out to the office, Mr Mourli was waiting.

It was a very warm and happy welcome. Mr.Mourli introduced us to another well dressed Gentleman in a suit and tie who had accompanied him to meet us, a Mr. RL.Fripolli who was the Manager of the Great Eastern Hotel Ltd.

We thanked Mr Mourli for his great generosity, paying for our hotel in Dhaniakhali, and for recommending this place. He and his wife had only gotten back this morning after a hectic few days. He had made arrangements with Mr. Fripulli to meet him here to get to know us because they wanted to invite us for dinner at his hotel tonite.

Over tea organised by M we told them about Mr Mitchell's chauffeur picking us up at five.

"What a small world," Mr Mourli said, "Fred Mitchell and his Companies are good customers. Our paths frequently cross. "I'll have to organize something with him for tomorrow."

They stayed for about an hour, browsing through our book and asking questions about our adventure. Spot on five M told us the chauffeur had arrived. It didn't give us much time to get ready because Mr Mourli and Mr Fripulli had only just left. And on leaving Mr Fripulli invited us to stay for a few days as his guests in his Hotel from tomorrow onwards.

"That would be fantastic," we told him and thanked him very much.

There was a long black Humber Snipe Limousine waiting outside a well dressed Hindu chauffeur standing by ready to open the door for us to get in..

We wanted to make a good impression so we were dressed in long trousers and carrying our usual things. Our driver told us it would take about forty five Minutes, but he had to stop at the office on the way to pick up some papers. Uli sat in the front and told him to take as long as he wanted. Sitting in the back Theo and I enjoyed the ride. We felt as if we were someone very important being driven in such a beautiful, luxurious car. We travelled south one block adjacent to the river and saw Neuenfels still in port, its superstructure standing high above the buildings along the dockside.

Our driver pointed to Queen Victoria Memorial before he turned into a no-through tree lined street and drove up a beautifully manicured driveway to a very impressive double story brick house. He stopped under an awning in front of a superbly handcrafted front door. A young Hindu opened the car doors and asked us to follow him inside.

My first impression was do not touch anything and take slow steps. This place was like a Museum, with oil paintings on every wall along the hallway. The first painting on entering through the door was of Queen Elizabeth sitting on a big lounge chair and a uniformed Prince Phillip Standing next to it. The English flag was mounted next to the painting.

Fred Mitchell walked towards us with a well groomed bulldog called Rex by his side and greeted each of us with a strong handshake and a slap on the shoulder. He led us into a big lounge room furnished with old English furniture and it smelled old. It reminded me of my grandmother in Kuernbach; her lounge room had a similar almost mouldy smell.

Sitting in those big arm chairs with the ceiling fans circulating the air we felt comfortable. Fred clapped his hands and two young servants entered with big smiles to follow their Chief's orders. Fred told us we could have tea, fresh fruit juice or even a cold beer.

Uli and I opted for the beer and Theo for the juice. Fred also had a beer and we settled in nicely. We told him about Mr Mourli and Mr Fripulli and their invitation for dinner.

"Yes," Fred said, "I know both of them, but especially Mr Mourli. We do business together."

We told him that "Mr Mourli said he will get in touch with you in the morning."

"I Look forward to that," Fred said. "He probably wants us to have dinner together at the Great Eastern."

Many questions had to be answered about our travels and future plans.

"Our plan was to ride through East Pakistan via Dhaka and Chittagong into Malaysia."

I could see him shaking his head.

"We were told however that we would find this very difficult because the rainy season has started."

"It certainly has, and there are large areas flooded."

"So for this reason we were thinking to get a boat to take us across to Burma instead."

Fred didn't say anything but he led us into a dining room with lots of fine smelling goodies on the table. We were introduced to the two servants and to an Indian cook arranging the dishes on the table. All in all it turned out to be a great evening and we got to know Fred quite well. He had been in India since the early thirties, being sent out by a small printing company where he had learned his apprenticeship. He started in Delhi but after some years moved to Calcutta where he bought into an existing, nearly bankrupt printing firm. Over a few years of hard work he made it into one of India's biggest printing firms and by now owns three more in different cities. Before the war started he bought a small castle in Beaconsfield just outside London where he hoped to retire one day.

By the time the chauffeur took us back to the Salvos we were absolutely stuffed and hit the sack as soon as we got there.

When we came down in the morning ready for another day hitting the companies for funds and sponsorship M. informed us that Mr. Mourli would pick us up at 5pm.

We jumped in our Rickshaw to visit another company, the Great American Insurance Co. LB. It took a while before we were able to meet up with someone important and when we were finally led into a room, we found ourselves in a boardroom with seven men sitting at a big round table looking at us curiously. We felt quite silly standing there not really knowing who to address. This was a situation we had never encountered before, but thankfully they all stood up and one of them walked towards us holding our card.

He shook our hands, introduced himself and wanted to know who was who in the photo. He told everyone our names and we were greeted with big smiles by the others. Three of them were Americans, the others Indians. The one holding our card was the Director, the two associates were from America and the others were major shareholders.

Apparently we had disturbed a board meeting when they got our card, handed to the Director by the secretary from the front desk. They hadn't wanted to bother with us because they were busy, but looking at our picture they became curious and decided to meet with us and have a break.

The Director made some chairs available and we started to tell our story. They were all eyes and ears. When they found out that I was born in Philadelphia and would have been a US citizen, I had to tell my whole story. They were fascinated that we had taken on such an enormous journey at our age, and that we had and met with such great people, so far from home.

Naturally our financial situation was discussed and we mentioned that all the companies and people who had written in our book and helped us. While the Director wrote some kind words in our book, one of the Americans walked outside and came back holding a big envelope and handed it to me.

When we finally said goodbye and shook hands with all of them the Director told us that if our time would permit, we were very welcomed to visit them once more before we left Calcutta. I told him if it was possible we would.

Back outside again, just further down the road we noticed a big sign on a building, Hoare Miller & Co. LTD. Cast Iron Municipal Castings Manufacturer, founded 1920.

"That's looking good," Uli said, and we halted the Rickshaw.

It was the same as everyone before, they often did business together. He asked why those two hadn't written in our book and Theo told him they will tonite, at dinner. We would be having dinner with them. He was pleased to hear this and asked us to convey his regards to them. After writing a few sentences in our book the question about our finances arose and we all started talking together. He grinned and asked how much some of the other Companies had paid? Theo told him about Pro. Kilbourne & Co. Private Ltd not too far from here and how much they helped us. He also told him about the Great American Insurance Co.LB. "That's great," he said, "but I shall do a bit better." He opened his briefcase and took several big English Pound Notes from it, put them in an envelope and handed it to me. "This will help you wherever you travel, and you should wait until you get to Burma or Malaysia to change it, because Rupee's are no good anywhere else."

We thanked him many times and told him we would keep in touch, (we certainly did through Fred Mitchell). By the time we had visited a couple more offices and did relatively well, we needed a break.

M was in his office wanted to know about everything and we told him some of it. Back in our room we opened the envelopes and counted all the cash. We could not believe how much we had got in the past couple of days. We were beginning to like Calcutta more and more by the minute. With the US Dollars, English Pounds and German Marks we still had, we were looking forward to Burma and onwards. We would certainly be able to mange in better style than we had before. The foreign currencies we stored in my chest pouch, the rupees we split between the three of us.

We cleaned up, wrote a few postcards and it was 5pm and on the dot

M knocked on the door to tell us Mr Mourli had arrived. Mrs. Mourli was also in the car and greeted us heartily. Naturally they both were dressed beautifully, especially Mrs. Mouri. Uli had the pleasure to sit next to her and her husband in the back, Theo and I sat next to the chauffeur.

We were travelling in another luxurious limousine, hard to take!

A lot could be said about the Great Eastern Hotel In Calcutta, but again where to start? Since having used the sit down toilets at the Hilton in Istanbul a long time ago, we had been guests at several mighty Hotels. The great Eastern is one of those mighty ones, set in a park surrounded by beautiful manicured gardens and lots of different palm trees.

Actually I was surprised we didn't travel too far before our chauffeur drove up a long driveway and stopped in a big car park with just a short walk to the main entrance. Walking up a few steps to the entrance Mr. and Mrs. Mourli were greeted very respectfully by the uniformed employees who had curious eyes on us. Everyone was dressed in evening attire, except for us! We were led into a huge dining room where the walls were covered with original paintings with English and Indian artefacts underneath them. An Indian gentleman dressed in a black suit greeted us and guided us through the nearly packed room to a big table with four people already seated.

Fred Mitchell, Mr. Fripolli and Richard, the boss himself with his beautifully dressed wife greeted us as if we were long time friends. What a great evening we had, the food was unreal with Uli and I drinking beer and Theo his juices. To our surprise we got an incredible present from Fred and Mr. Mourli.

They had arranged with a shipping agent to get us a passage on a ship to Rangoon and both of them took care of it. Fred arranged to take us to the agent sometime in the morning with our passports, to get the tickets. On top of all this, Mr. Fripolli invited us to be his guests at the hotel for the rest of our stay.

This was a bit too much to digest for our young minds. We told Mr and Mrs Fripolli that we would rather stay at the Salvos because it is very easy to get around and they had done so much for us. Nevertheless, we thanked him greatly and after we had promised him to have lunch or dinner with them again he smiled bemused. I had a feeling why he found dit hard to imagine anyone preferring to stay at the Salvos rather than be guests in his magnificent Great Eastern Hotel.

Well, we did!

It was agreed that Fred would take care of us over the next couple of days and invited everyone for dinner at his home the following evening. M was waiting for us when our car pulled up and opened our doors. Mr. Mourli told us he would call by during next day to see that everything was okay. M. back to his office wanted to know everything that had happened and asked question after question. We certainly made a point of telling him that we were invited to be guests at the Great Eastern, but decided to stay here in his Hotel. He couldn't get over it. I'm sure he though there must have been something wrong with our brains.

As arranged Fred's chauffeur picked us up next morning, drove us to the office where Fred joined us on our visit to the shipping Agent at the harbour. As a matter of fact, the Agent's office was not too far from the Neuenfels and we could admire this mighty ship again. Even though the sky was heavy with dark menacing clouds announcing the monsoon hanging above her she looked Majestic.

The agent was well known to Fred and welcomed us. After filling in some forms and answering some questions, he told us there was a freighter leaving for Rangoon in three days. This was great news and we were very happy about this. We were even happier after we found out that Mr. Mourli's Company had paid for the cost.

Back at Fred's office we found out that Fred had organised our Burma trip with Mr Mourli and the Agent the day before. They knew very well we wouldn't be able to travel anywhere once the monsoon hit.

After morning tea I handed Fred our book and asked him to write something, which he happily did. Richard led us outside to the waiting car, after Fred told us that we would get picked up for dinner at 5pm.

We couldn't believe our good fortune. Earlier in the morning we were quite prepared to fork out a consider amount of cash for travelling by ship and now this. I emptied the pouch and we counted all the cash and found out that we were actually well off. Fred had written some lovely sentences in our book and we were looking forward to the evening.

It wasn't even midday yet, we decided to jump on our bikes and spend some time at our restaurant for lunch and a bit of relaxation. We just got back before one of those dark clouds opened up and within minutes the place was like a sauna. After having some freshly squeezed juices with M. we had a shower and at 5pm on the dot we got picked up.

The rain had stopped and with the windows down a bit it was bearable in the car. We certainly got a huge surprise driving past the harbour, no Neuenfels! She was gone. Six hours earlier she was still moored at the wharf. We felt a bit sad because we missed that bit of homeland, but started to feel great as soon as we arrived at Fred's house. They were all in the lounge room, Mr. and Mrs. Mourli, Richard, but instead of the Frippoli's being there we got a pleasant surprise. Mr. F. L. Puckridge greeted us with a big smile and introduced us to his English Wife. In no time Uli and I had a cold class of beer in our hand and Theo his juice.

We thanked the Mourlis for arranging our ship passage. "Don't even think about it," he said and told us that someone would pick us up at midday tomorrow to bring us to their home. Fred was the perfect host and time just flew by as fast as!

It was arranged, that we would spend most of next day with the Moulis and get together again for dinner at the Great Eastern the day after. It was fairly late by the time we were brought back, but of cause M was waiting and we didn't mind telling him what happened during the evening. As a matter of fact, we started to become quite fond of M. He was educated, friendly, couldn't do enough for us and he was the reason we stayed here.

Mr. Mourli had certainly picked the right man to manage this place.

Sure enough, just before midday next morning another chauffeur driven limousine picked us up and M opened the doors for us. It took some time to cover a few kilometres travelling north before we stopped in front of a big office building. A couple of middle-aged Sikhs opened the door and led us past a big sign reading TATA IRON and STEEL CO. LTD and into the building. Taking us through a couple of offices, past lots of staring eyes, opening a door where inside Mr Mourli stood up from behind a huge desk to greet us.

This office wasn't as elaborate as Fred Mitchell's, but still had photographs of Queen Elizabeth, Prince Phillip, Mahatma Ghandi and Pandit Nehru on the wall behind his desk. There were a couple of smaller desks next to his with two beautifully dressed women sitting at one and two younger Sikh's just starting to grow beards at the other.

Mr Mourli introduced us to them and we found that the two women were his personnel secretaries and the two boys were his sons being taught about the business. Some more chairs were put next to the big desk and after we were all seated around it we told our story.

I showed them page after page in our book, while Uli and Theo commentated.

Half way through we took a break for a snack. A few small dishes

The Big Adventure

containing different dips and skewered pieces of grilled lamb were served on a round table behind a partition. When we continued most of the questions came from the two boys who were eager to find out as much as they could about us.

I couldn't really blame them; they were the same age like us and had never been out of India. Mr Mourli wrote in our book and asked some very relevant questions, especially about the high profile people we had met and our planned route towards Melbourne. He was extremely pleased when he saw the photograph and writing of Master Tara Sing Ramgarhia the leader of the Sikhs in our book.

He pointed to it, showed it to his sons, the two ladies and I think to them this page was the most important one. Several hours later we were taken to a very old but beautifully maintained Temple with mostly Sikh worshipers. Mrs Mourli was waiting for us with more than a dozen people whom she introduced us to. Amongst them were a couple of absolutely beautiful young girls about our age eying us nonstop and of course we eyed them back. Walking slowly through the Temple, lots of different things were pointed out to us, but my mind was totally occupied with those girls, especially when one of them walked right next to me!

At the back of the Temple was a big hall full of people holding small plates of food eating standing and having a good time. All along one wall were at least a dozen big tables full of very delicious dishes. It was certainly exhausting with each one of us surrounded by different people all asking questions at the same time.

Even though we were tired we didn't mind at all. I felt like a Star especially with that beautiful girl by my side, clinging to every word I spoke.

It was very late by the time they were ready to take us back to our lodgings, especially with all the best wishes and handshakes from everyone. My hand was held much longer from this beautiful women and it would not be too difficult to fall in love! Mr. Mourli told us that they would pick us up for dinner at the Eastern next day as we got into the limousine.

It had been a full on day, but a very satisfactory one and it was easy to fall asleep.

With only one more day in Calcutta before the ship was to leave we decided to re-visit our Americans at Great American Insurance Company LB to say goodbye. This time it took only minutes to be ushered into the Director's office and with the blink of an eyelid, we had some glasses of tea in front of us. There were only three of them this time and we thanked them for their great generosity in supporting us so well. They brushed this aside wanting to know how we had got on in Calcutta so far. We told them about Mr. Puckridge, his generosity and the dinners we had at the Great Eastern and Mr. Mitchell. We mentioned that we would be leaving tomorrow for Burma by a Freighter. We also mentioned that Mr. Mitchell and Mr. Mourli paid for our passage. We told them that we had wanted to cycle through East Pakistan but couldn't because the rainy season had started. The Director offered to write a couple of letters to recommend us to good customers of theirs in Rangoon, which we gladly accepted. After telling them that we would arrive mid morning a couple of days later, they told us, "We will send a telegram to a couple of associates there. Arriving in a new country you might need some help when the ship docks."

They wished us the best of luck and hoped to hear from us when we reached Melbourne.

It had been a very hectic morning and it was nice to relax at our restaurant with a bite to eat followed by a couple of smokes. By the time we got back to the hostel M handed us a big envelope he had received from the shipping agent. It contained our tickets, some entry forms to fill in and a small booklet telling us about important laws in Burma. It also contained a smaller envelope with a small bundle of Kyats, the Burmese currency, and a note from the agent wishing us a safe journey.

M. took care of our washing and we were ready when the limousine picked us up at 5 pm to take us to the Eastern. It was a bit of a squeeze because the Mourlis had brought their two sons along. Fred and Richard were already there with a beer in hand when we arrived. Mr. Frippoli and his wife escorted the Puckridges towards us. To my big surprise another family arrived, one of Mr. Mourlie's beautiful secretaries her husband, their daughter and younger brother. The daughter just happened to be that gorgeous young lady from last night, who also made my blood pressure rise.

By the time we sat at a long table another English couple and a Sikh family with their young boy were introduced to us. As by accident it so happened that my heart throb sat next to me and made me feel as if I was in heaven. With great food drinks and conversation, time just flew. I had a bit of a grin when my beautiful dinner companion was served one of those rancid-milk things in a tall glass and seemed to enjoy it. It was an evening I will never forget.

Fred arranged to pick us up the next morning to take us to the docks where the freighter was moored. Finally we had to say goodbye to the others and it was a very sad feeling, having to leave these wonderful people. Unfortunately the Mourlis had to go on another business trip early in the morning and wouldn't be able to see us off.

The long squeeze of my hand by that beautiful girl would be remembered for a long time.

We had to promise everyone to keep writing and let them know if we made to Australia.

M. was waiting and we could see in his eyes that he was also sad to see us leave. Our washing was laid out on our beds and he sat with us for quite awhile, before he left us to our own thoughts. Packing the next morning didn't take that long and we had plenty of time to walk over to the Bazaar to buy necessities for the short duration of the sea trip. We were able to write a few postcards home from our last day in India and M offered to post them for us.

By midday Richard arrived with the chauffeur in the Snipe, followed by a small truck for our bikes and luggage. We offered M some money, but he wouldn't have a bar of it not even to post our mail. By the time our stuff was loaded a small crowd of people wanted to wave goodbye and some even shook our hands, as if we were part of them. M gave us a hug and we could see he had to suppress some tears. We noticed our rickshaw driver waving and we walked over and shook his hand and thanked him for his services. I had several notes rolled up in the palm of my hand and I was the last one to shake his hand. With a quick glance back as I walked away I saw his mouth wide open. He was waving madly and I knew this guy would have taken us all over India had we but asked!

We were taken to Fred's office where the small table was set and covered with heaps of goodies (our last meal on mainland India). We told Fred about the generosity of the agent, providing us with Burmese money, which pleased him. We also told him that we got heaps of Rupees and asked him if he knew a moneychanger?

"Sure," he said."Let's see how much you have."

We emptied our pockets and Richard counted all of it and told Fred there was close to fifty Pounds. "We'll take care of that," Fred said and gave Richard a wink. Richard immediately walked out to the front office and came back a few minutes later with an envelope in his hand. "I'll

In the background is the cargo ship that took us to Burma.

change the money for you," Fred said, "because in the street you would certainly be short changed."

When we arrived at the docks, I said to Theo and Uli, "You'd better keep an eye on me to make sure nothing happens to me. I'm carrying a bloody fortune, all our money hanging in a pouch around my neck."

They mumbled some incoherent answer.

"I mean it."

"You'll be fine," Uli said.

To our surprise, the Freighter was moored only about 500 Metres away from where the Neuenfels had been moored. It had probably been there before but we hadn't seen it because the Neuenfels was so big. The chauffeur drove us along the dock and stopped right in front of the gangway. Our bikes and luggage were already on board the agent told us. He had been there earlier to make sure all went well. We followed him up the gangway and were greeted by the smiling Captain and another uniformed officer, both English. This ship was a much smaller compared to the Neuenfels, but was also fairly new and spotless. Having never been on a ship this size before we were astonished by the size of the cabin and

the clean beds with fresh linen. But the best of all, there was a separate European toilet!

The agent informed us that it would take three nights before we arrived in Rangoon mid morning on the third day. Our bikes were secured in a storeroom just beyond the passenger cabins and our luggage was on the sofa in our cabin. There were five other cabins like ours on this deck and we weren't the only passengers. A cargo ship of this size was allowed to take up to 10 passengers; any more and they would have to have a doctor on board. Naturally these few passengers were treated like royals, because the price was double that of a passenger ship. All meals were taken with the captain and several officers and prepared by a couple of chefs and kitchen crew.

We didn't see much of the deckhands, all Hindu Indians; their quarters were up front, and they didn't mix with the passengers. Finally the big moment came to say goodbye to Fred and Richard. It was a very sad one; we had grown very fond of these people, who two weeks earlier we didn't know existed.

When they walked down the gangway and waved up to us for the last time we didn't know then, that Fred Mitchell would become a friend for the rest of our lives.

He visited us a year later when he was on a short business trip to Sydney and Melbourne, and when Zara and I got married he sent us a beautiful telegram from Switzerland and transferred two weeks wages for our wedding present. I must also add, when he retired in England Zara and I visited him in his small castle. Theo of course caught up with him many times and when Ilse and Theo got married, they named their son Fredrik after him. Fred even came to Germany for Fredrik's christening.

It was still daylight when a couple of tug boats guided our ship slowly out into and along the Ganges, but it was night by the time we reached the Bay of Bengal.

We also waved back at India, a gesture of thanks to her beautiful people, great Cities and the unbelievable hospitality we had received.

But soon we would be in another strange country.

We had no idea what to expect, but looked forward to it with much anticipation.

A note from the Captain of the Neuenfels wishing us a safe journey to Melbourne, Australia.

The Big Adventure

Chapter Ten

It didn't take long after we boarded for the ship crew to cast off and the ship soon made its way down the river and out into the ocean. By this time we had sorted our gear in the cabin. Venturing out onto the upper deck we were invited by one of the stewards for drinks and dinner in the dining room, where the captain introduced us to two elderly English couples on their way to Ceylon who had been on board for several days already, obviously enjoying the relaxed atmosphere and hospitality on board. The Captain also introduced us to his officers, the stewards and the kitchen crew. We followed the captain into a small lounge room that had a bar on one side, a tiny snooker table in the middle and along the other side, several small tables with very comfortable lounge chairs around them.

All of us were handed a strange cocktail consisting of freshly mixed fruit juices with a dash of gin. It tasted absolutely delicious; Theo asked if he could have his without gin. We were asked to relax for a while so the kitchen crew could prepare the dining room. And of course everyone wanted to know who we were and what our story was. Somewhere in the room was a record player stacked with records of Frank Sinatra playing softly in the background. Many of the songs we heard that evening will stay in my memory forever. In hindsight my liking of Frank Sinatra and his music probably is because of that first evening on the cargo ship. The dinner table was set for a dozen people, like a five star restaurant and the food, half English and half Indian, was delicious. We felt great! Because we were only a small group of passengers and we were all treated like royalty. The crew just couldn't do enough for us.

It was a pity the trip from Calcutta to Rangoon only took two days. I would love to have spent more time travelling on a ship like that.

We looked through our portholes on the last morning and discovered we were travelling up a very muddy river. The ship was flanked by a tug on each side. On both sides of the river jungle came right to the water's edge. We passed by several small settlements some of which consisted only of small wooden boats roped together with people living on them. By the time we had breakfast we were closer to civilization, passing more permanent settlements, and the traffic on the river had increased with boats everywhere. A couple of hours later we docked at Rangoon's harbor. After a final freshen up in the adjoining bathroom we packed our luggage and got ready to meet the customs officers who stamped our passports but didn't bother with the luggage. With handshakes all around, hugs and lots of goodbyes, we walked down the gangway and stepped on to another strange land.

The three of us by the lifeboats on board the cargo ship that took us Rangoon. With new friends on board the ship as it arrived in Rangoon.

The Big Adventure

By the time our bikes and saddlebags were unloaded, a small crowd of curious onlookers were watching. Towering above the locals a couple of tall smiling Europeans welcomed us to Burma. I thought they were Europeans, but as soon as they spoke I realized they were Americans. They told us they received telegrams from our American friends in Calcutta about our arrival and to make sure to help in any way possible. This was a welcome reception to a strange land, its different people and certainly customs, which we had not experienced before.

One of the guys stayed with us whilst the other fetched a small International truck open on the back and side which had been parked nearby. Our bikes and luggage were loaded on to the tray and whilst we were sitting on the back the two Guy's were chauffeuring us into the middle of Rangoon.

Sitting on our bums with all sides open, we got a bird's eye few of the city. Burma like a lot of Asian countries were under British rule at this time and we got used to all the different customs on our way, but Burma was something else. Traffic was still on the left and the architecture

had lots of British influence with big solid buildings, mainly built with red bricks. Driving along a very busy main street packed with American trucks, cars and smaller English ones, we passed a huge Pagoda and it was impressive!

Actually we had never seen one before especially with some men dressed differently, all in orange. They all had shaven heads and it appeared as if they just thrown this orange rope like a bed sheet around their bodies. They were Buddhists and studied in some of the Pagodas to become monks. We passed a Church, a Temple, but we didn't see any Mosques Even though there was a mixture of different nationals we didn't see any Moslem women totally covered.

We stopped at a car park in front of a tall building, at least five stories high, with the bottom part displaying the latest in American and English cars, behind huge glass windows. Above the windows in big letters was written Ensign Motors Ltd - Dealers in Motor Cars. Trucks. Spare Parts, Accessories 190-4 PHAYRE ST. RANGOON.

Jumping off the truck a small group of people welcomed us, shaking our hands and patting us on our shoulders. The bikes and luggage were unloaded and carried through a side door into a big office where our new American friends introduced us to more office staff, male and female, all of whom admired our bikes and luggage leaning against a wall.

Most of them were Burmese and full of beautiful smiles, but they seemed like midgets next to the tall Americans or Europeans. We had noticed that the people were quite small compared to us the moment we stepped off the cargo ship. (And almost every one of them, men as well as women, were smoking gigantic self rolled cigarettes.)

The women we saw did not cover their heads; they all wore black trousers with a white loose blouse reaching past their waist, and they had sandals on their feet. Men mostly dressed the same, but had their shirt tucked in. There was a mixture of different dress code in this office, including Indian, European men and women, even one very attractive young lady with her head covered whom we later found out was the boss's daughter, who was a Malaysian Moslem. He was a partner with the Americans in India and the two who picked us up were also involved in the car business.

One of the Americans led us into another office where we were welcomed by the Boss himself. I shall call him Khan; I think it was his family name. He was immaculately dressed in a light grey European suit, white shirt, brown bowtie and brown polished shoes that looked like they were

The Big Adventure

made from crocodile leather. He certainly stood out amongst a crowd, middle aged, quite tall and good looking. We found out later that he had been a very good cricket player a few years back.

It wasn't a big office; it only had a few desks with one of them occupied by a couple of sales men, one for the Boss himself and one each for the Americans. A small table off to one side was set with hot tea and several plates of sandwiches, chicken, lamb and beef, but no pork. Khan was absolutely rapt with our adventures and got more excited by the minute, the more he heard about the Moslem countries through which we travelled and their hospitality.

He offered us accommodation one level above the offices and to our astonishment our bikes and luggage had already been taken up and were leaning against one of the walls in a long corridor. One open door led into a beautiful apartment. It had a combined lounge, kitchen and dining room, two bedrooms and a European bathroom. How about that!

You never know your luck in a big city!

One of our American friends explained; "We have three of these apartment on this level, for relatives and very good customers from out of town."

That was impressive. Selling cars must be pretty good.

"Why don't you guys relax for a while? Settle in and I'll come back a bit later. There's a club a few streets up the road where we can go for some drinks."

By the time we unpacked some of our luggage and washed a few necessary things time just flew. After writing a couple of postcards and a small letter home, our friend knocked on the door to pick us up.

We were still wearing the shorts we had on when he picked us up at the docks.

"Do you think you could change into long trousers," he asked us slightly embarrassed. "We're going to the Cricket Club and they do have a dress code. They are rather strict," he added.

"No problem," Uli told him. We quickly slipped into our long trousers and our Bata shoes. "What about short sleeve shirts?"

"We don't have any long sleeved shirts," Theo said.

"Tuck them into the trousers and it should be okay."

Equipped with our book, passports, some cards and camera, we followed him down to the office. Our other friend was waiting and Khan wished us a great evening and told us he would see us tomorrow. The two Americans had organized to take us to a Chinese restaurant for din-

To my eyes, most of the artwork we saw was incredible, with fine detail and often brightly painted. It seemed strange at first but we got used to it after a while.

ner and Khan being Moslem doesn't frequent those because of the pork dishes.

It took only twenty minutes to walk to the club with our two friends in the lead. It was just like India where the streets were packed with over laden trucks, taxis, rickshaws, cycles, motorbikes and people pushing wheelbarrows fully laden with all kinds of stuff. The footpath was full of small stalls selling just about anything one wanted.

The only difference we could see was with the people in the streets. There were lots of Europeans, Indians amongst the local Burmese people, and there were many bald headed monks carrying a wooden bowl that contained food offerings from kind people. The only food they ate was what they could receive from kind passers-by in the streets.

We couldn't help noticing a lot of Chinese people as well as some mountain people with totally different features, plus Mongolians our friends told us when we asked where they came from. Uniformed police made us smile because they looked so out of place with all the armor around their belt.

"Do not underestimate them," our friends told us, "the police and soldiers are extremely fit and keep Rangoon pretty safe."

We walked past many big buildings erected of reddish type bricks and several Victorian style wooden mansions set in beautifully manicured gardens, hinting at an English heritage. We had crossed over four intersections, passed a couple of parks full of people with kids playing and running all over the place, when we sighted the club in front of a big sports field.

There must have been a game of cricket on because we saw some players walking towards the clubhouse. Our friends were greeted by several men and we were introduced to all of them. We had to write our names and where we stayed in a big visitor's book which was countersigned by one of our friends acting as our hosts. This was something we never had to do before, but like the old saying goes, every day brings something new.

Another thing strange to us was even though there were tables and chairs in the big room, everyone was standing in front of the long bar, holding their drinks. It wasn't long before Uli and I had a nice cold glass of beer passed to us and Theo his coke.

Several men and women were very interested in us and wouldn't stop asking questions which we gladly answered. Looking around this exclusive club one could tell that only well to do people were members. I felt great and for a few seconds my mind wandered back to some of the workers at AEG, my family and friends. I felt proud of ourselves and our achievements so far, and of meeting with all those influential people and being treated like adults.

We had barely finished a couple of beers when to our surprise we were told that a handful of gents and a couple of the ladies were going to join us for dinner. Amongst the men was a tall Burmese, like Khan and the other one looked Asian. We were later told he was Japanese, one Englishman and the rest were Americans. It only took a few minutes for us to walk to the Chinese restaurant; which was located in a shopping strip with lots of different eating places. We had never been to a Chinese restaurant before, nor had we ever eaten Chinese food, the surprises were never ending.

First of all, we had a couple of sticks placed in front of us and looked at them dumbfounded. Laughingly we were told they were chopsticks and Chinese, Japanese and several other Asian countries use them to eat with. We were told that most of the chopsticks were commonly machined out of wood, but many high class restaurants had them carved out of ebony.

Secondly, all the teacups, plates, saucers and soupspoons were all made of beautiful porcelain and were all hand painted. They had lots of different illustrations on them, animals like Tigers, Roosters, Dogs and Rats, but mainly different Dragons.

Thirdly, being seated at a big round table we couldn't grasp the amount of small and some larger plates with mouth-watering dishes being placed in the middle. One plate had been placed in front of everyone and a smaller bowl on it which was filled with some of those delicious foods.

We had great difficulties with those sticks, but were told to persevere, because where we were going, chopsticks were mainly used. Watching the others, we soon got the hang of it and had fun picking up small pieces like peas and clumps of rice.

It was a great evening and we got to know the others real well. We ate so many different foods that we had never seen before and with all the conversation which we had to make in English we were exhausted, looking forward to a good night's sleep. It did take me a long time to fall asleep because there was so much to digest, mentally and stomach wise.

When we came down the next morning the office was in full swing with people being going about their jobs. Our friends greeted us with outstretched arms and asked how we felt.

"Mr. Khan won't be in today, but he told us to tell you he wants to take you for dinner in the evening."

In the meantime they had arranged to take us to some of the people from last night to learn about their business. They wanted to take us around the corner for some breakfast, but we pointed to our stomachs and told them some fruit and a pot of tea would be more than enough. They felt the same way and were quite happy to lead us into the small kitchen-lounge, adjacent to the office. After a bit of fresh fruit and a cup of tea, we were ready to follow wherever they went. A taxi was already waiting in front and I must say we could hardly notice the small Burmese driver sitting behind the steering wheel in the big American Limousine. We only passed a few intersections before we stopped in front of a big brick building with a huge shop in front with what looked like a big warehouse behind. Above the entrance was a white sign with big black letters painted on it: JING HONG TRADING CORPORATION LTD. It was a hardware store with just about every tool, land machinery, lights, globes for cars and household, imaginable. One of the gents from yesterday greeted us and led us to a well appointed office at the back of the shop. His name was John C. Webster, and he was an Englishman, shareholder, importer and Manager of the firm.

Freshly squeezed fruit juice was served and John bade us to sit at a round table. He was extremely interested in our cycling achievements, because he had joined a cycle club in England when he was younger and actually won some road races.

We told him that Theo won a big race in our town, beating me by a whisker. We didn't tell him that the guy two hundred meters ahead of us had a flat tyre and had to push his bike towards the finish, and that we passed him ten meters before the finish line. We also did not tell him that there were only three of us in the race.

Anyhow, we had a good couple of hours with him showing us through his warehouse and taking us for lunch afterwards. Our friend told him we had to see the tall Burmese guy we met the night before whom he knew very well. After writing in our book, he wished us the best of luck and a safe journey. On leaving I noticed that he handed a small envelope to our friend, which he casually shoved in his pocket.

The tall Burmese guy was the manager of THE EAST ASIATIC COMPANY LTD, which imported and sold imported goods from different nearby countries. It was located next to a gigantic Market only a short drive by car. It was a gigantic warehouse, dealing in all kinds of imported goods from different countries and every shelf was packed full with tinned foods and spices from every corner of the globe. Freshly roasted coffee beans, dried fruit and heaps of different teas in open boxes, gave the warehouse a very exotic fragrance. The place was full of people swarming everywhere bargaining for and buying the products. The noise was deafening.

Our friend led us to through the warehouse to the end where there were several doors and without knocking opened a door with *private* written on it. It wasn't a big room, but well appointed being a private office and lounge in one. The tall Burmese man from yesterday greeted us like family and begged us to sit at a small table. His name was A. Aubye. Mr. Aubye was a sports fanatic, playing cricket for the club where we had drinks yesterday. Tea and different fruits was served and after telling our story he wrote in our book in Burmese.

When we had finished with our goodbyes I noticed Mr. Aubye handed a small envelope to our friend, which he casually slipped into in his pocket.

Outside our friend took us to the adjacent market for a cool beer, flat bread with dips and a couple of smokes. On the way back we saw a big billboard advertising 'The Crimson Pirate' with Burt Lancaster. He was one of our favorites.

"Do you think we could see this film?" we asked.

"We could do that tomorrow after your visit the big Pagoda." He told us.

Apparently it had already been arranged for them to take us to one of Asia's biggest Pagodas as well as the Thai Embassy for our transit visa.

Back in our room we had enough time to write some letters and postcards home and plan our next route through Thailand to Bangkok some 800 km ahead. We knew it would be a tough one with the rainy season about to begin and lots of rainforests for us to ride through. We were looking forward to Bangkok because we knew Thailand was a Kingdom and we surely would try to visit their King and Queen.

We barely had time for a cleanup and change before our friend told us that Mr. Kahn had ordered the driver to bring us for dinner with him and his family. Uli, sitting in the front asked the driver where he was taking us and was told "to one of Mr. Khan's restaurants, not too far away".

The Big Adventure

It was a fairly big place that had an Arabic flair, except for one big difference; there were lots of women with no face coverings there. They were all beautifully dressed, but their hair was covered by silk scarves. Some of them even wore slight make up and looked very exotic. There were waitresses and waiters, something we had not encountered anywhere in the Moslem countries we had come through. To this day I have not really found out whether Malaysia has more Sunnis or Shiite Muslims. Having religious freedom in the country I think there are more Buddhists than any other religion.

Mr. Khan and at least two more families occupied two big round tables in an enclave halfway along the restaurant. There were three empty seats for us. We were introduced to most of them, (their daughter we had already met at the office). There were three families, all Burmese. Mr. Khan, his lovely wife and a younger son, his sister's family with a couple of children, and Mrs. Khan's brother's family with two boys. Mr. Khan must have told them a lot about us, with perhaps some exaggerations judging by some of the questions being asked.

The food was served and we thought we were back in Persia or Pakistan. Within a short time the tables were full with lots of small and large plates all with different goodies. Needless to say, we ate with our hands, which we had finally gotten used to and had no problem ripping pieces of the flat bread and picking up small pieces of grilled lamb with it, some steamed rice and dunked it in some gravy, before shoving it in our mouth. There were heaps of mouth watering dishes to choose from; even Theo had no reason to complain.

It turned out to be another great evening and we enjoyed their company immensely. There was a hand washing basin on one of the walls, which we used several times and after some more tea and fruit, it was time to call it a night. After thanking all of them for their hospitality and shaking hands with everyone, they followed us on to the footpath to wave goodbye. Our driver had waited for us all this time. Back at the office where we were staying he wished us a good night and told us she would catch up in the morning.

The next morning started okay, but we certainly got some sticks thrown through our spokes, so to speak. After breakfast our friends were ready to take us to the Thai Embassy and afterwards to the Pagoda. Our smiling driver chauffeured us through heavy traffic to finally stop in front of a beautiful building surrounded by manicured gardens with a sentry at the front gate, next to the Thai flag. The whole street was manicured, with several different flags flying outside various buildings, all Embassies.

Two of our friends had accompanied us and we had no problem passing the sentry, after they had spoken to him. Inside we had only waited a short time before we were ushered into an office and greeted by an elderly uniformed Gentleman and a uniformed Lady, both smiling. They gestured for us to sit. Tea was served, and with some small talk over the Gentlemen asked to see or passports. He turned page after page and conversed nonstop with the Lady, all the time smiling.

We didn't think there was a problem from the way they spoke to each other, but then he turned to face us, and he was not smiling.

Dead serious he told us bluntly, "You won't get a transit visa."

We were stunned. This was like getting hit on the head with a cricket bat. I was so shocked I almost fell off the chair as I turned to look at Theo and Uli.

Uli explained how we had come so far with in most cases no problems at all.

"We need to cycle through Thailand to get to Singapore and Indonesia. And to get to the Thai border we need a Transit Visa."

"It is extremely dangerous in the northern part of Thailand. There are so many tribal wars going on. Any foreigners passing through would surely be kidnapped and killed."

We didn't know what to say.

"If you went into that part of the country you would never be seen again."

He couldn't have been more serious.

"You will have to find some other way."

What a letdown! This was definitely not what we expected. We had been certain there would not be a problem… and now this.

Funny though, our two friends were not one bit disturbed and urged us to sit in the car for the longer drive to the Pagoda. At this stage we couldn't have given a rat's arse about a Pagoda, we would have rather gone back to the office and studied our maps.

It was a very quiet trip. We hardly noticed the traffic, each of us occupied with his own thoughts. Without a visa, we certainly would not be allowed to travel the long stretch of border between the two countries or be allowed to exit Burma and enter Thailand further south. We had to put on a bit of a smile though to be polite to our friends who were trying hard to cheer us up.

Shwedagon Pagoda, also Golden, or the Great Dagon Pagoda is one of the biggest in the world and the closer we got, the more imposing it became especially with the sun shining on this magnificent building. It looked to me like a big golden Nugget. The closer we got the worse the traffic got and the slower we moved. It would have been quicker on our bikes.

One of the many Golden Buddahs inside the great Pagoda

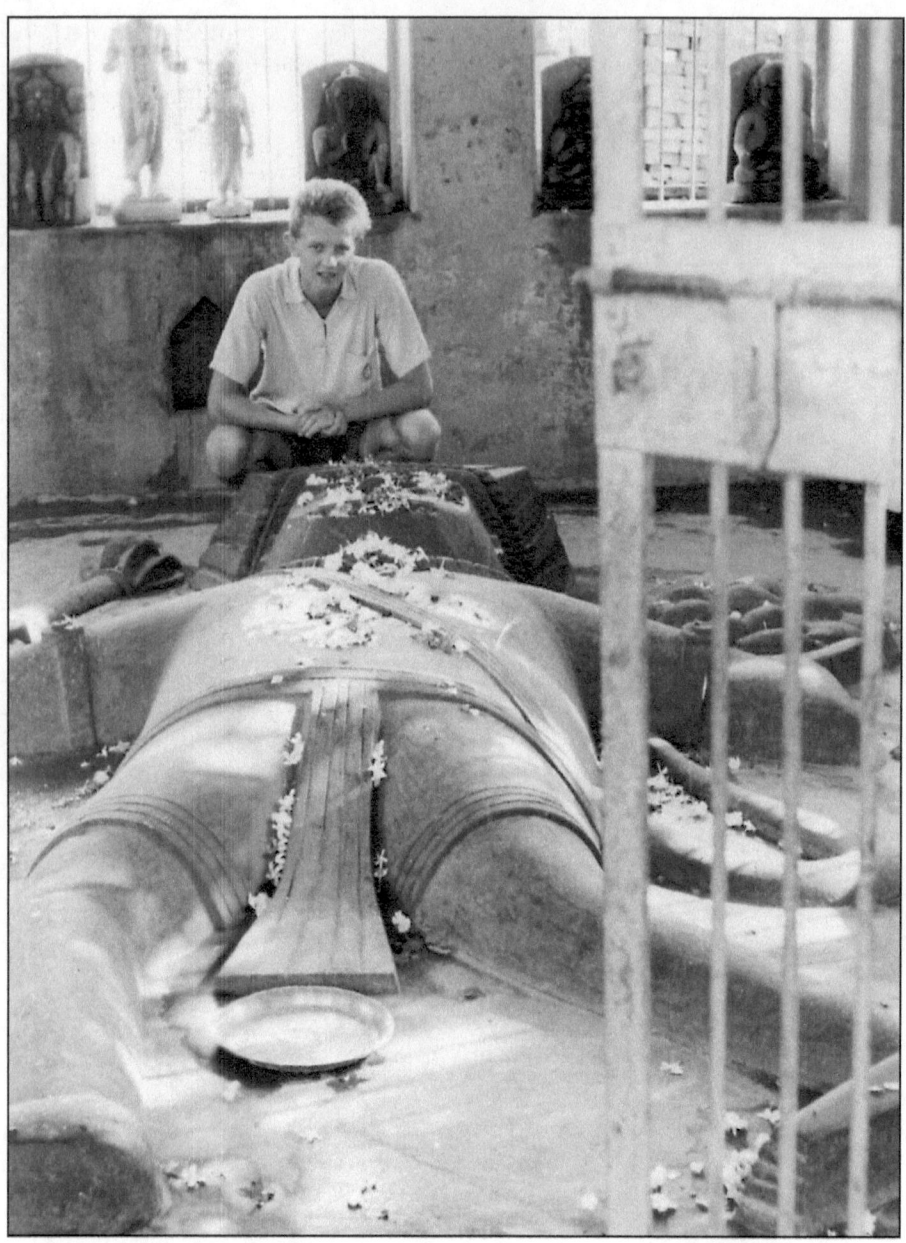

Inside the Great Dragon Pagoda, also known as The Golden Pagoda.

There were soldiers and police everywhere you looked. There were heaps of visitors, worshippers, monks and of course us.

The place was huge, and it was surrounded with shacks and smaller buildings. It was like a big village had been built all around the Pagoda with stalls all over the place, selling just about everything anyone could think of. Our driver dropped us off a short distance away so he could look for somewhere to park. We had to walk the rest of the way through the vendors and their stalls to the pagoda.

"Why are there were so many heavily armed soldiers and heaps of police on patrol?" we asked our friends.

They pointed to a heavy laden truck, with what looked like bullet holes along the side.

"Shot at further north by rebels," we were told. "It didn't stop to pay big ransom for permission to get through, so they shot at it. Fortunately they didn't hit the driver."

It was only then that we noticed quite a few cars with bullet holes in them. One even had a small hole with cracks radiating from it in the back window.

There were restaurants and different shops all over the place and our friends invited us for lunch in one of the better ones. Looking at our not so happy faces one of them put his tea down, looked at the others and asked "should I tell them now?"

"Tell us what?" Uli asked.

"What have we done now?" Theo said.

"Nothing, you have done nothing," he said with a big grin, "we had to bring you guys here first before we could tell you."

"Well," said the other one," it's quite a story. When the three of you arrived in Burma a few days ago and stayed with us, we all got to admire what you did and wanted to be of some help. After getting to know about your plans, crossing the northern Thai border to travel through Thailand, we knew it would be impossible by bicycle."

"Mr. Khan suggested we should arrange with some of our friends to help and find out a safer route to Singapore and they did. We had to keep this a secret because you would not have believed us. You would have thought we were trying to hinder you on purpose. You had to see and experience the danger for yourselves. We also knew that there was no way of getting the visa for Thailand, but we had to keep quiet until now."

We looked at each other not knowing what to expect next.

"Maybe you had noticed, that everyone we had visited who had written in your book handed us a small envelope," the first one said. "Over the last couple of days we have collected a considerable amount of money. As soon as you were picked up yesterday to have dinner with the Khans, we had a meeting about the best way for you fellows to travel. What we discussed then will be finalized while we are here now."

"And just what was that?" Uli asked. "Don't keep us in suspense."

Our two friends looked at us with big smiles. They were obviously enjoying this. They picked up their tea and sipped it slowly.

"Come on…" Theo said.

"You will be travelling through Malaysia," one said.

"And on your bikes." The other said.

"What!" the three of us cried out at the same time not comprehending.

"You will be well out of the danger zones, travelling to Penang on a small coastal freighter. Your visas will be organized tomorrow. We shall all know more about this when we get back to the office, but for now let's wander through and enjoy the Pagoda."

This was another shock to the system, but the more we talked about it the more real it became. It took time to digest: people we had never met before, had planned our new route, collected money and were extremely anxious about our wellbeing, and after noticing firsthand how dangerous it would have been had we tried to cross into Thailand, we took their advice. The only sad thing would be missing out a meeting with the King and Queen of Thailand.

The more we thought about it the better we felt. Going by coastal steamer and bypassing Thailand completely had not occurred to us. We were keen to study our maps of Malaysia as soon as we got back. Feeling a great deal better we walked through this magnificent Pagoda in bare feet, admiring the giant Buddha covered with thousands of fresh flowers. Everywhere inside the Pagoda was full of worshipers. We could have spent several days in and around this Temple and still wouldn't be able to see all of it.

Eventually we got back to the office and to our surprise some of the people we had met greeted us with big smiles, Mr. Khan included.

What a hello! They all spoke at once and wanted to tell us the latest news, which was at this moment better than selling trucks or cars. There was a road map of Malaysia unfolded on a table and Mr. Khan pointed to it. He told us that the only way to get through the danger zones was by ship. He also told us that after getting our visa next morning, the shipping agent would deliver our Tickets. Apparently the freighter delivered goods as far as Georgetown (Penang), stopping at several smaller ports reroute. The ship we were told would be sailing in the afternoon, the day after tomorrow. Studying the map, we discovered that it was a distance of nearly two thousand kilometres and would take several days.

The office was full of happy faces. I had a lump in my throat and had to push back tears. So much kindness was overwhelming and looking at Theo and Uli I could see they felt the same. By this time it was late afternoon and several people were leaving after wishing us all the best and we thanked them with all our hearts.

One of them remembering something we had mentioned earlier asked us if we would like to go to the movies later on to see The Crimson Pirate, to relax a little after so much excitement. Of course we told him, it would be great to relax a bit. We enjoyed the film even though we couldn't understand all the American dialogue, but the action spoke for itself. By the time we finally got to bed, we were well and truly stuffed!

After filling in a couple of forms, at the Malaysian Embassy next morning we got our visas in record time. They wished us a safe journey through Malaysia and were happy that we made the right decision, to leave by ship. Back at the office, Mr. Khan informed us that our tickets were ready to be picked up as soon as the agent could check our passports.

Both of our friends walked with us to get our visas because the Embassy was not too far, but the agent was down by the harbor. We went there in the big Limousine with our little driver. It took some time to weave through the traffic and the congestion at the harbor, before the driver stopped in front of a stone building.

A few steps up and we entered the agent's office, thinking we had walked into a pigsty. It was fairly big, but hard to describe. There were chairs all around four big desks with each of them chock o block full of papers, cardboard boxes stuffed to the brim, plus folders stacked on top of each other. There were filing cabinets against every wall, totally full. If the two guys didn't stand up behind their desks to greet us, we would not have noticed them.

There was no room for us to sit, because every chair was also covered with stuff. There was a stand up desk in the middle with a telephone, some exotic flowers in a vase and just enough room for a folder containing our tickets. How in god's name, could anyone find anything, in such a mess? Anyhow, the agent and his staff didn't seem to have a worry in the world and with smiles they effusively greeted us as we entered.

After making sure that our passports and visas were correct, the agent handed Uli our tickets.

"The freighter is getting loaded not far from here, right now" he said. "I am happy to take you there to meet the Captain."

It was the biggest ship in the harbor at that moment, but small compared to the one we travelled in from Calcutta. It would have been great to climb on board and meet some of the crew, but we could see they were too busy getting shipshape.

"The ship will be ready to sail by mid afternoon tomorrow," the agent informed us. "You should board by noon to be on the safe side. If they leave early and you are not there, they won't wait."

"We'll be there," we assured him.

The last evening with those lovely people was celebrated at the sporting club and they were all there, even M. Khan and family. It was a memorable evening and we couldn't thank everyone enough for their kindness. Numerous times we were told it was the right decision to leave by ship. We were also convinced that we did the right thing.

By the time we finally got to bed for the last time in Burma a feeling of sadness came over me and I found it hard to fall asleep. I knew we would never see any of these people again, but we would remember them and their kindness forever.

The excitement next morning was like being in a beehive with everyone buzzing around trying to help. After a light breakfast we finished packing, while our bikes were already loaded and secured on the truck. We didn't have to lift a finger to carry any of our luggage down stairs, it was all done. We must have made good impressions on everyone because they all seemed sad to see us leave. We asked Mr. Khan to convey our kindest regards to the Director at the Great American Insurance Company in Calcutta. If he hadn't recommended us to Mr. Khan and associates, who knows what the outcome in Burma and Thailand might have been.

It was a sad goodbye with all those well wishes, handshakes, lots of good advice and us thanking everyone one more time. Finally we got on to the back of the truck driven by our friends and it took off for the harbor and the waiting coastal steamer.

The agent and a couple of his staff were waiting and with their help we had no problem boarding. The Captain and a couple of his officers, all three of them English, greeted us and one of them showed us to our cabin.

Even though this ship was much smaller than the one before, it was fairly new and spotlessly clean. It had only six cabins for first class travelers, Theo and I shared one and Uli got one for himself. Apparently another three were occupied, one by an Indian couple with a young daughter, another by an elderly Englishman and two Malaysian students returning home in the third cabin, still leaving one vacant. The officer informed us that lunch would be served shortly in the dining room and we would be sailing would be not long after.

The goodbye from our friends was something special, not just handshakes, but effusive hugs and an invitation to visit them in America one day.

The cabins were small but they still had four bunks, two on top of each other and a separate bathroom. The toilet was the Asian style but immaculately clean. Our luggage we stored on the top bunk and Uli said he was quite pleased to sleep by himself for a few days. On our way to the dining room we thanked the agent who was just leaving and he also wished us all the best.

On this ship the dining room and lounge with a small bar was all one room but could be separated by a folding door. It was shared by the Captain, his officers and guests. The rest of the crew had their quarters at the bow. The Captain introduced us to the other passengers who had already been seated and with us seated at the table.

The food was European and Asian mixed and one could choose between chopsticks or knives and forks. The Captain also introduced us to an English chef and a Chinese one. We chose chopsticks to get the experience because, we were told, all the way through Malaysia and Indonesia they were mainly used.

It was about mid afternoon when we finally waved a sad goodbye to Rangoon and its wonderful people. The ship was escorted by a tug boat along the muddy river towards the open ocean. A few days earlier docking in Rangoon, we certainly didn't expect that we would be travelling by ship again, only this time away from it.

We couldn't stay long outside because it started to rain before we had gone very far. It was heavy and fell out of thick black clouds that looked as if they would come down on top of us. It was very humid, but in our cabins with the fans circulating the air, it was bearable.

The two thousand kilometre journey took a week because the ship made several stopovers along the coast and we didn't mind a bit! As a matter of fact, enjoyed it very much. As we travelled further south the rain started to ease and we got much more sunshine. We were seemed to be just ahead of the encroaching monsoon and whenever we looked back the sky was thick with storm clouds while ahead and the further south the sky was much clearer and sunnier. It was still very hot but the further south we travelled the less the humidity became.

We enjoyed the hospitality on board and made friends with all the passengers with whom we spent long hours exchanging travel tales and life stories while watching the distant coast and passing a few very beautiful tropical islands. The two students drew a map for us to show the location of a youth hostel in the port where we would disembark for Penang.

We had a great time on board, but it came to an end all too soon.

Uli and a laughing Buddah in Penan

"Malaysia here we come," Uli shouted across the water as the ship docked in Georgetown on the Island of Penang just after breakfast.

Our bikes and luggage were unloaded first and on the bottom of the gangway, we were greeted by two customs officers who checked our passports and stamped our visas.

We had to push our bikes to another security checkout, because the whole harbor was surrounded by a huge fence and then we were in a new country. Not having ridden our bikes for over two weeks, we felt great, even though it was only a short distance into the city.

Georgetown was fairly large and totally different to Rangoon, extremely busy, wider streets and different architecture. The first thing we came across was a big Church built with red bricks, surrounded by palm trees and a pathway leading to the front steps. On the opposite side was a big Mosque and further along a Temple. By this time we had to push our bikes on the footpath to be safe because the traffic seemed too dangerous. Between all those religious buildings were big wooden villas and stone buildings, all in English style. The footpath was very busy with many stalls displaying their wares. There were young children in different school uniforms and we didn't see any beggars like in India. Pushing our bikes past some exclusive shops and restaurants, we felt pretty safe and people always made a pathway for us to go through.

The whole footpath smelled of different spices, grilled onions, lamb and beef. Several policemen were directing traffic, but they were not heavily armed like those we saw in Burma and India. Malaysia being mainly of the Muslim faith was somehow different to the Arabic countries we had ridden through. Women dressed more like Europeans, with just a beautiful colored scarf covering their hair. Some of them looked stunning; with a hint of makeup we thought they could have been film stars.

While we were asking a policeman for direction to the hostel, we were approached by a young European in a navy uniform. Actually he wasn't European; he was born and bred in Sydney, a real Aussie. He was only a couple of years older than Uli and was one of the very few Australians we had met. John Tresidder and Frank Brazier, our cycling champions, were the first, and of course there were those few we met in various Embassies.

He introduced himself as Wayne and could not believe when he heard our story and how we were travelling to the Olympics in Melbourne.

When we asked him about the uniform, he told us "I'm a member of the Australian Navy, stationed in Malaysia. This is my day off duty. Whenever we leave the base we all wear a special going out uniform."

He asked what we wanted from the Policemen and when we told him he said, "come with me I'll find you accommodation. There will be no problem getting you a room for a couple of nights at the Australian Seaman's Club."

"Sounds good," I said.

We followed Wayne along a few streets and sure enough in one of the side streets we stopped in front of a huge, several stories high stone building displaying AUSTRALIAN SEAMANS CLUB in bolt letters over the entrance. The Australian flag was flying high and on entering we were greeted with the Australian Coat of Arms painted on a wall behind a big reception desk. Uli waited out front watching the bikes while Theo and I followed Wayne into the reception room. There were several people in the room and when Wayne introduced us they looked at us in disbelief. In no time the room filled up with more people, men and women of all ages, some in uniforms like Wayne and others in plain clothes. They all wanted to meet us. It was as if we just came from another Planet. The most important thing of course was that we were welcome to stay a few days as their guests.

By this time Uli was introduced and our luggage with the bikes were brought in, studied and debated, before being pushed into an adjacent room. It was lunchtime and we were invited to join most of them in the dining room. Most of them had already ordered lunch when they got news about us.

The menu was hand written with chalk on a big blackboard hanging on a wall next to a food server and long bar. Wayne told us to choose whatever we wanted and all three of us ordered pork chops chips and salad. The salad of course had no dressing and was very bland, but the chops and chips went down well.

It was only after we had a couple of beers (Theo some juice), had answered lots of questions asked by several people, that we were shown our sleeping quarters at the back of the building. Wayne, with the help of some others had already organized the last room at the end of the long corridor. It was a huge room with close to ten single beds in rows of three and we could take our pick. Our luggage was on one bed and Wayne told us that our bikes were safe in the room at front. The bathroom was fairly big also with a shower and separate European toilet. (All the toilets in the club were European).

Wayne offered to show us the way we would have to take in the morning to go to Taiping which we gladly appreciated. Catching a cab we had to cross over a big bridge to the mainland and followed the main street for a short time to the outskirts of the city. It was a very good road we were told, but very busy, and we would have to keep our eyes open.

Back at the club we were invited for dinner and drinks at the bar, to meet some of his mates who had finished their shift and were very thirsty. By the time we had dinner, everyone was standing at the bar with a big glass of beer in front of him and a smoking their butts off. A few tables were occupied by some women and men, all wearing uniforms. As time went on and we answered hundreds of questions, the mood became happier and happier.

All of a sudden one of the fellows hit another one, square on the chin and he fell backwards crashing onto an empty table. I totally freaked out and so did Uli and Theo, especially when another guy hit the first one, who reeled backwards, hitting the wall and then it was on. The one who crashed onto the table got up and hit another one and by that time a half a dozen fellows were punching shit out of each other. The three of us were standing behind Wayne and a couple of his mates, for protection.

They were holding their beers in one hand and cigarettes in the other, talking and laughing as if nothing happened. When they saw our scared faces, Wayne told us to have a close look.

"We call this 'Horseplay'" he said, "they don't actually hit each other."

Sure enough, as soon as we had a closer look, we noticed that when one of the fellows hit another one, he stopped an inch away from his nose or chin and the other fell backwards by himself. Well, we had never seen anything like this before, but we were told that Australians did lots of weird things not seen anywhere else.

As the years went past, I certainly came across many of those weird things.

In Penang

We didn't get away as early as we wanted the next day with all the handshakes and well wishes. It was mid morning before we sat on our bikes again.

I must add here that when Theo and I started in Sydney at the Ampol Trial two years later, we met Wayne again for a short time, just to exchange our addresses. Apparently he recognized our names in the program and managed to catch up with us just before the start. Unfortunately, we never did catch up, but I will always remember him and his Aussie Mates.

It took some time before we hit the bridge and it must have been close to midday before we could say goodbye to Georgetown. It was hot, but not very humid and it felt great to cover some kilometres again. On the last ship we had plenty of time to look after our bikes and they were in top condition. The traffic was heavy but more disciplined than in Pakistan or India. Taiping was less than a hundred kilometres ahead and we had only about ten to go when we found a nice secluded spot just off the road, beside a small waterway to put up camp.

Earlier on we had stopped at a roadhouse, exchanged a fair amount of money and ordered some food and Pepsi. The food was very tasty and to our surprise we were handed spoons, forks and chopsticks. We used the chopsticks instead of the forks and spoons to keep practicing and slowly we got the hang of it.

Putting up camp was relatively easy with our tent spread out and our sleeping bags laid on top. We soon learnt that was a mistake. Millions of mosquitoes swarmed all over us. Sleeping so close to a waterway we had asked for trouble. We didn't get much sleep that night. We were up again before daylight and back on our bikes in record time.

I had a few mozzie bites, but looking at Uli and Theo, I couldn't help laughing. They copped it badly and looked as if they had measles. Every bit of exposed skin was covered with red spots where they had been bitten.

"Serves you right for having better blood than me," I said when I had stopped laughing. "You remember in Syria how they didn't want mine, only yours?"

The mozzies must have thought Xmas and New Year had come at once! As soon as we arrived in Taiping we purchased a bottle of mosquito repellent and stopped at a market for breakfast.

On the road again we were extremely itchy, and riding our bikes became very irritating in the heat. Thankfully Ipoh was less than 30 km ahead. We decided to look for a hotel there and stay overnight and the thought of staying in a hotel spurred us on and we made the city centre before lunchtime. We didn't feel like sightseeing, but couldn't help noticing the very clean streets, the great architecture and the beautifully maintained Parks.

There were several hotels to choose from and some guy we asked for a good one pointed to the next building and told us it was one of the better ones. We pushed our bikes to a big entrance behind a bitumen roundabout filled with beautiful exotic plants. A very handsome Sikh in a white, spotlessly clean uniform greeted us with a very curious smile, not knowing, how to handle us.

He was a big strong man and one could guess he had some authority. As soon as we told him who we were and what we wanted to achieve, his face lit up and told us there would be no problem for us to get a good room. He lifted an arm and a couple of servants came running and he gave them some instructions. We undid our luggage and together with our bikes it was carried up to the reception where we had to show our passports and fill in a couple of forms.

Theo showed the man who had greeted us our book with Amritsar, the Golden Temple and the page with Master Tara Sing in it, and our stay was sealed. By this time the Sikh concierge told some of the guests who had gathered around us who we were and what we did. We were still standing at the reception answering numerous questions, but were dying to get to our room so we could do something about our itching.

We asked the concierge if it was possible to lead us to our room and answer the questions later. He actually apologized and we followed him along an open footpath with several rooms on one side and beautiful gardens on the other while the servants carrying our gear behind.

We didn't just get a simple room; no it was a beautiful furnished family room. Two bedrooms, master bedroom with an ensuite and separate bathroom with Asian toilet, immaculately clean. There was plenty of space for our bikes and luggage and we thanked our Sikh concierge for looking after us so well.

"My pleasure," he said. "Are you by any chance hungry?"

"Yes," we all said at once.

"Lunch has been served in the dining room, if you would like to go there now."

"As soon as we get organized," we mumbled. We needed to have a good cleanup first and treat those mozzie bites with some cream and repellent.

It didn't take long before we felt a lot better and were looking forward to a nice meal. But before going down to eat we had to sort out some money.

Since Pakistan and India our finances had accumulated considerably and we hardly had to spend much, being mostly invited. As far as we were concerned we were rich and just in case something should happen to me, I shared most of it between us. I had previously carried all of it in a pouch around my belly. We still had all our US Dollars, English Pounds and German Marks, plus there was a fair amount of Malaysian Dollars. The dining room was just past the reception in another section, but was nearly deserted by the time we got there.

We didn't ask for tea, but it was put in front of us with three small porcelain cups, which one of the smiling Chinese looking waiters filled. In this restaurant one had to ask for knife, fork or spoon, because there were only chopsticks on the table. We found out later, that it was a Chinese one.

It was easy for us to pick a couple of different dishes because on the menu there were pictures of all the meals and we only had to point to what we thought looked good. We managed quite well with the chopsticks because the meat and vegetable dishes were already cut into small pieces. There were hot chilli sauces on the table, but we didn't use any. The bill arrived and we were surprised how cheap it was for an up market Hotel.

We asked the concierge if there was a market nearby. We needed to buy a few items for the next couple of days. "There is a big market two streets up," he told us, "only a short walk from here." Then he added diffidently "would be possible to meet some of the guests in the bar later on?"

"No problem," Uli told him, "we would love to talk to the guests."

Now that our itching had subsided and with bellies full, we felt much better and enjoyed the short walk to the market. But just before we got there we spotted a small coffee shop back from the footpath with a few tables and chairs in front. Each table was shaded by a big canvas umbrella and only one was vacant, which we took. We just liked what we saw, water pipes on every table being smoked by men, mostly dressed as Arabs. They all looked at us and wondered where we came from, but all smiled when we ordered a pipe and coffee. It was very relaxing enjoying life in a strange country. After two pipes and more coffee we did our shopping at

The Big Adventure

the busy market and were back at the hotel in less than two hours. Even so it was late in the afternoon and the concierge told us that a couple of guests were in the bar already and some of the others will be there shortly. "As soon as we take our shopping to our room, we will be ready," Uli told him.

The bar was at the back of the hotel, beyond the restaurant, a small souvenir shop and a huge ballroom. It was similar to the one in Rangoon. Most of the revellers were standing at the bar, a beer glass in one hand, a smoke in the other. There must have been a dozen smartly groomed men and several well dressed women sitting at some tables. They were having a good time, but as soon as we entered it went all quite, but only for a few seconds and the handshakes didn't seem to end. In no time, we were introduced by a couple of Gents who got to know us when we arrived. It didn't take long, before Uli and I had a pot of beer handed to us and Theo his Pepsi.

We brought our book and a couple of our cards with us to show around and the questions were never ending. They were mostly young English fellows doing business in Malaysia and visited by their parents. They all were extremely taken by what we had done so far and what was in front of us!

During all this time the kitchen staff were preparing a big table in the middle of the room covered with hot and cold dishes from which we were supposed to help ourselves. This was a new experience for us and we enjoyed it. It was a smorgasbord. Only later in Australia did we find out what Smorgasbord meant. Anyhow, it was a wonderful evening and by the time we thanked all of them and got their well wishes it was close to midnight when we got back to our room.

All three of us slept in the single room, there were four beds and on one of them we had our luggage. There was no need to use the master bedroom.

Reasonable early the next morning after a light breakfast we went to the reception where we bumped into some of the people we had met the night before. The Sikh Concierge was also there. They all wanted to say goodbye and once more wished us a safe journey. When I asked for the bill at the reception desk we were told that we were guests of all those people. Apparently they loved our entertainment so much they decided to help by paying our hotel bill. A bit stunned, but happy as galahs we finally left and got back on the road again.

Kampar was only 40 km ahead, which we made in no time and decided to lash out a bit on brunch, tea and a couple of pipes. We were in great spirits and couldn't give a stuff about the heat or the traffic.

Slim river was about 70 km ahead and we had no problem reaching it by mid afternoon, stopping at a market place for some early dinner. Looking at our map, we saw that Kuala Lumpur was 100 km ahead. With still a couple of hours of daylight left, we decided to move on. We travelled next to a small waterway, but turned away from it a fair distance before putting up camp.(once bitten, twice shy) We rubbed mozzie repellent all over our bodies, and had a reasonably good night's sleep.

After breakfast in Kuala Kubu Bharu we pushed on and quickly reached the outskirts of Kuala Lumpur, but to get to the inner city took some time. One of the guests at the Ipoh hotel had advised us to look up the YMCA (Young Men Christian Association), where we could get cheap accommodation.

Kuala Lumpur was a much more subdued city than most of the others we'd been through, especially New Delhi or Calcutta; even Rangoon was very hectic. We didn't notice any one sleeping on the footpath nor did we see any beggars.

A street in Kuala Lumpur

After asking a couple of times, someone pointed to a double story stone building adjacent to a big Church. Next to the entrance was a board with YMCA in big letters written on it.

Theo and I went inside to be greeted by an elderly gentleman, dressed all in black who looked at us rather suspiciously. We were tired and rather scruffy after riding in the heat. He looked like a Priest and was probably thinking: *Almighty Christ, what did you send me today?* Uli stayed outside with the bikes.

It didn't take long for the two of us to convince him that we are decent fellows and looking at our card, he could hardly believe what we were telling him. While we were explaining several younger guys arrived and listened to our story. The elderly Gent (we found out later he was the Master) finally said we could stay a couple of nights. He pointed to some of the young men there and said something and immediately they went outside to help Uli bring our bikes inside. It took some time before we were shown a room, because by now we were bombarded with questions from all around us.

After some time the Master led us down the corridor and opened a door to a simply furnished room with four single beds. Toilets and showers were a few doors further along. Our bikes were leaned against a big table in a lounge room or study, for everyone to admire. Our luggage was stacked on the spare bed. Dinner, we were told, would be ready in an hour's time in the cantina and the Master asked if we would like to join them.

After we cleaned up a couple of guys led us to a reasonable dining room with a kitchen at the back. There were three long rows of trestles with at least ten chairs on each side. A number of people milled about selecting chairs. We had only met the few who had helped us with the bikes before and from the curious looks from the others it was obvious they were wondering who we were.

We were seated next to the Master and once everyone else had found a seat he stood up and introduced us and told everyone where we were from. After dinner he told them we would be happy to answer their questions.

To our surprise, it was a three course English meal: a bowl of soup with noodles followed by a plate with a few slices of meat in the middle, surrounded by steamed veggies, followed by a mixed fruit salad. It was quite ordinary after all the exotic food we had been eating on a journey, but was tasty and healthy, and we enjoyed it immensely.

But before we started to eat something which seemed a bit strange to me happened. The Master stood up and pointed to one of the guys along the table. Everybody then stood up including the guy indicated. We did the same, not knowing what was happening. And while everyone stood with heads bowed this young man then recited a beautiful long prayer and thanked God for our evening meal.

I was very taken by this, thinking about my earlier years in Stuttgart during and after the war. Most of the churches copped it badly; some of them were bombed into rubble. Later on in Backnang, we saw the churches only from the outside, walking past. Our generation had to work hard, or became streetwise in order to make a living one way or another. We certainly enjoyed the evening, answering all the questions and there were heaps of them, so it was almost midnight when we hit our pillows exhausted.

The next morning after some pieces of fruit for breakfast, the Master suggested we take a rickshaw to the General Post office, because it was a fair distance down the road.

The traffic was hectic, but more orderly than what we had experienced so far and our driver had no problem giving us a safe ride. We enjoyed it very much, somehow we found Kuala Lumpur much cleaner than other comparable cities and it was a relief to have no kids running next to us begging for money.

At the General Post office I paid the guy, but told him he could wait for us, if he wanted to. There wasn't much mail for any of us; just a few letters from our families, the bulk of our mail would be at the German Embassy in Singapore.

After posting some letters and postcards, we asked our driver to take us to a market close to the YMCA, where I paid him well. It was a pleasure to walk through the market after a light lunch and not be noticed. Every time we stopped somewhere with our bikes we always had a crowd of people around us. Purchasing some necessities for the next day didn't take long after which we walked back to the YMCA.

We were met by some old faces and some new people who wanted to hear our story and shake hands with us, We answered their questions for a couple of hours, but being invited for dinner again later on we had to call it quits because we needed to do a couple of minor repairs on our bikes.

Same thing happened at dinner except the thank you prayer was recited by another guy, but just as beautiful and the three course meal was

The Big Adventure

as good as the evening before.

Totally refreshed next morning we were raring to go. Singapore was drawing us towards it with huge magnets. We had enjoyed enormously the friendliness and hospitality of those young men from all walks of life and nationalities.

Seremban was only about 50 km ahead and even with Uli having a puncture we still made it just on midday. We lashed out on a big lunch to give us the energy to reach Tampin some 60 km further ahead. It wasn't an easy ride but we made it and went a further 20 km past Tampin by which time we were stuffed. We set up and camped for the night.

Malacca next morning was a breeze of fresh air, literately. Situated on the Straits of Malacca opposite Indonesia's second largest island Sumatra, a beautiful sea breeze cooled us down. We found ourselves a nice hotel not far from the harbor and after a good clean up we jumped into a rickshaw to explore the city.

Malacca was an exciting city, with Asian, English, Dutch and Portuguese cultures all thrown in together. Portuguese still seemed the most dominant, especially with the architecture even though it was the British who had been the most recent people there.

We used the rickshaw for over two hours and found Malacca much to our liking, but later in the afternoon we decided to have a few drinks and a couple of pipes at the harbor.

Having dinner at the harbor and watching the sun disappear over Sumatra was a great experience. It reminded Theo and me a bit of Sicily a few years earlier, except at that time we didn't have a razoo.

The hundred kilometres the next day were like a breeze and we took our time riding with the ocean on one side, jungle and coconut palms on the other, and stopped only a couple of times for food and drink. Even sleeping on the soft ground was a pleasure.

Scudai next day was harder, hillier and we had to cope with more traffic, but still made Scudai by late in the afternoon. With only about 50 km to Singapore we decided to stay at a hotel and freshen up to hit Singapore in our best attire.

Singapore, an island and a city, although part of Malaysia, was a separate State that had also been ruled by the British. It was now independent and had its own Parliament headed by Lim Yew Hock, Chief Minister of Singapore.

After an early start through heavy traffic and crossing a bridge, we

Jungle and coconut palms ... taking a break before crossing over into Singapore.

still arrived in the city, long before midday. This city was like a beehive, everyone seemed to be busy, even the elderly were running around doing something.

As soon as we hit the outskirts of the city we had to ask several times to get directions to the German Embassy. That was our most important address, because there we could get our mail and be amongst Germans again.

We finally arrived in front of a beautiful white painted double story stone building like a palace. It was set in immaculately manicured gardens. A big stone wall, with a huge handmade iron gate in front, surrounded the property. On one side of the gate there was a giant flag pole flying the German flag, on the other side was a large wide board with FEDERALE REPUPLIC of ALLEMAGNE in big black letters engraved into it.

We pushed our bikes the few meters to the building and leaned them against the wall next to the entrance and then we knew that we were in Germany.

Walking up the couple of steps to the entrance, the door opened and a middle aged German in a uniform asked us in English what we wanted and told us to shift our bikes around the corner.

Uli asked him "Why?" in German

"Because it doesn't look good, those old bikes against the beautiful building," he answered back in English.

"We are only here to pick up our mail," Uli said again in German, "and we will leave our bikes where they are."

"Well," he said with a smirk on his face, "if you don't move those stupid bikes I won't let you inside."

That put a sour taste in our mouths and we had no option, but shift our bikes around the corner where they were out of sight.

Once inside the big entrance hall it was very official with several desks on either side, and a big one in the middle with a Visitors sign in front. Without a welcoming smile, one of the women seated behind the visitors' desk asked what we wanted also in English.

When Uli told her in German that we wanted to collect our mail she told us in abrupt German to take a seat near the opposite wall. She handed Uli a piece of paper with a number on it. "Wait over there until the number is called."

We turned and looked where she indicated and there was only one row of seats with all but one of them occupied. There were also a series of vacant cubicles with small desks and chairs further in the room which we hadn't seen upon entering. There was a well dressed Indian family, a couple of young Chinese gentlemen looking very much like business executives, with a Jewish family seated next to them and several local people who looked vaguely Malay, and they all smiled at us.

Every time a number was called out, someone was led into one of the vacant cubicles at the back of the hall to be interviewed. When our number was called the stern faced women just pointed to an empty one and told us to take a seat.

Finally a well dressed elderly German greeted us with a half smile and placed a big paper bag on the small table.

"You're in luck," he said. "If you hadn't come in by the end of the week we would have to send them back."

"Are you serious?" Uli asked him.

"Dead serious," the man said.

We had noticed a small lounge room/kitchen behind the cubicles with some people helping themselves to some cooked food and it looked delicious. Uli asked the guy if it was possible to purchase something to eat.

"That's only for Embassy staff and guests."

"Can we meet the Ambassador?" Uli asked.

"Not without an appointment. And certainly not dressed like that." he said disdainfully. "You can always visit the German House where you can purchase a proper German meal."

"And where would that be?"

"I'll give you the address."

As soon as we got the address and direction to the German house, I grabbed our mail and without a goodbye we walked towards the front door. Uli stopped at the receptionist's desk and in a loud voice said to the stern-faced women, "thanks for nothing."

We totally ignored the uniformed fellow. As far as we were concerned he was only a shit kicker trying to feel important. We collected our bikes, but outside the gate at the flagpole we turned to have a last look at this beautiful building. We could not believe how miserable we were treated inside by our own Embassy staff.

It took awhile dodging the traffic and asking several times, before someone on the outskirts of the city pointed to a small cull de sack next to a park. Passing some very impressing buildings we stopped near the end in front of a double storey solid concrete well designed building, also flying the German Flag in front of a short driveway.

By this time we were pretty hungry and looking forward to a solid German meal and a cold drink. Entering through an opened doorway it felt quite pleasant. In one of the rooms someone was playing the piano and we felt right at home. We still looked pretty scruffy though. Even here the welcome by a couple of well groomed women behind a reception desk was a forced pleasantness. They looked at us as if we had The Plague.

"Why have you come to the German House?" one of them asked after looking us up an down. No doubt they thought that the sooner they found out what we wanted to sooner they could get rid of us.

"Because we were Germans, Uli said, "and we were hoping to get some food and read our mail."

We were each handed a printed sheet of paper.

"You are not members, so you need to fill out these forms."

We looked at each other, shrugged and looked at the forms.

"Do you have a pen?" Uli asked.

One of the women reluctantly passed a pen to Uli making sure she didn't accidentally touch him. It was so ridiculous I wanted to laugh at them, but I restrained myself.

We filled in the forms; put them on the desk along with the pen and waited.

The two women seemed nervous, but one of them took the forms and knocked on a door almost hidden behind them. When it opened she went inside. She came out a few moments later with a middle-aged guy, who without as much as a Guten Tag asked us to follow him.

He led us through a lounge room where the piano we had heard was being played and across a dance floor to a well appointed dining room where several people were having lunch. Ignoring the curious looks the guy pointed to a small table in a corner as far away as you could get from the other guests, turned around and talked to a couple of waitresses.

We sat there with long faces for awhile before one of the waitresses came over.

"The kitchen is closed," she said.

"Then why were we brought in here?" I said, and pointedly looked at a couple of people who were being served coffee and deserts.

"The gentleman who brought you in has arranged something for you to eat," she said. She turned and marched away only to come back a few moments later with a pot of tea, cups and saucers, and a plate of dried out sandwiches that may have been left over from breakfast. So much for a German meal! It was disappointing, but being hungry, we finished the whole plate in record time.

In between bites we could hear an argument developing between a big strong man in leather pants, a red shirt with white spots and the guy who led us to our table. We knew the big guy was Bavarian because of his attire and he became quite angry, pointing a few times towards us.

We couldn't hear what was spoken, but the other guests were listening in and started looking at us, which made us feel very uncomfortable. Some harsh words must have been spoken because the Bavarian stormed out and left the office guy standing red faced.

We didn't feel like opening our mail and decided to move on also and asked for the bill. The office guy told us it was okay; we thanked him with big smiles, got our stuff together and walked out.

Now what?

We were hoping to get accommodation at the German house but that was out so we decided to ride back into the inner city. Money was no problem so we thought maybe we should try a hotel.

Arriving at a huge roundabout next to Orchard Road, we had a brilliant idea.

I can't remember whether it was Uli's or Theo's, it certainly wasn't mine.

We decided to put up our tent and make camp in the middle of the roundabout… and we did! It only took half an hour to put up full camp with our German emblem in front and our bikes standing upright leaning against each other. We sat on our sleeping bags and enjoyed a couple of fags. It had been a long day, lots of things had happened and we were stuffed.

It didn't take long before we had our first visitors. People couldn't believe what they were seeing. Cars started to park opposite, cycles were pushed towards us and it didn't take long before we were surrounded by young and old.

We answered their questions but kept a look out for the law. We had seen several policemen directing traffic and we were sure, that before long we would be asked to move on, but it was not to be.

Actually, it was quite hilarious; earlier on our own people didn't want a bar of us and here right now we had created a small circus.

Two Chinese looking guys, each holding a paper pad in their hand

Camping in the middle of the roundabout

and a guy with a professional camera around his neck behind them, pushed their way through the crowd surrounding us. They were from the press and had heard about a commotion at Orchid Road. They were here to check it out. Once they saw our tent and bikes they became interested and asked if they could interview us. The crowd stood to the side while the photographer took several pictures of us in front of our tent.

We showed them our book and one could see the immense interest they showed in our achievement so far. One of them wanted to know all about the Heads of States we met and how we were able to meet them in the first place.

The photographer and after a while most of the crowd disappeared, but those two fellows stayed well into the evening only lit by a couple of street lights in the distance.

Even though it was very warm we decided to sleep in our tent. It wouldn't have created a good impression if we sprawled out on our sleeping bags in the open.

We were stuffed and didn't care about the warmth, and slept soundly until daybreak when we were woken by noises outside.

It was daybreak and looking through the opening of our tent we could see people walking towards us from different directions. Our shoes, shorts and shirts were put on in record time, a quick brush with fingers through the hair and we were ready to say hello.

We knew the first guy walking towards us which was a surprise because the day before dressed in Bavarian clothes he had stormed out of the German House. He introduced himself, but I can't remember his name, but he was known as the Singaporean Sausage King and he wanted to take us for breakfast. Now that was a turn-around.

Right behind him were Mr and Mrs.Akkerman from Augsburg who wanted to invite us for a home cooked German dinner. Watt & Akkerman had a huge Engineering company, servicing and repairing all the ships docking in Singapore.

We asked them (the Akkermans the Sausage King knew each other very well) how they knew that we were camped here.

That question was answered by two young Chinese-Singaporeans each holding a newspaper. They introduced themselves as students from the University and wanted us to stay with them at their campus. They showed us the newspaper opened to page 3.

We saw our picture under a big bold headline GERMAN CYCLISTS NOT WELCOMED AT THEIR EMBASSY.

The article was well written, even though we hadn't mentioned much to the reporter from the day before about how we were treated at the German Embassy yesterday. Half of Singapore would have read this by now. We had stirred the pot alright!

The Akkermans were quite happy when we accepted the invitation from the students and exchanged phone numbers for them to pick us up early evening after which they left.

More people arrived and watched us pack up our tent, but half way through, a big black Adenauer Mercedes limousine pulled up just across the road and three Embassy guys got out and walked over to us. We knew straight away they were from the Embassy because the dickhead who had interviewed us was amongst them.

The other two introduced themselves and told us every one at the Embassy was sorry about the misunderstanding and they would like us to be their guests as well as to meet the Ambassador.

"Hang on," Uli said, "you knew about us yesterday, but no one acknowledged us. You treated us as if we were vermin."

The three of them kept trying to make excuses.

"We shall be at the University," Uli went on, "and the Embassy can get in touch with us there if they want to."

How events had changed; several months earlier we were shit frightened of the German Embassies or Consulates sending us back home, like they did when we went to Africa, and today we practically told them to get stuffed. What a turnaround, telling them to get in touch with us!

The Sausage King had listened to every word and told them that he had cancelled his membership at the German house because of the way we were treated. They left with egg on their faces.

Our new Bavarian friend had arranged with the two students to follow us down the street for breakfast and afterwards they would lead us to the campus. Pushing our bikes off the roundabout we only had to walk a short distance, still followed by some onlookers, before we entered into a garden restaurant just off the footpath.

I must say our Bavarian turned out to be a great guy who was really concerned about our wellbeing and we kept in touch for several years.

After a great breakfast together with the two students he told us that before we leave Singapore he would pick us up to show us through his factory. We thanked him very much and he wished for us to enjoy Singapore, from now on! The two students grabbed a rickshaw and we followed them to the University which was only about three kilometres outside the city.

I don't know how they knew that we were arriving at this moment but a welcome committee was standing on the bottom of the few steps leading up to the main entrance. I suddenly remembered that while we were still talking to the Bavarian I saw one of the students wave to some guy on the footpath, who took off on a bike.

We were greeted by several teachers, male and female of different nationalities, all dressed in the same uniform. One English looking gentleman who was immaculately dressed in a grey suit, white shirt, brown tie and brown shoes, introduced himself as the Director. There were at least two dozen students around us, all smiling. Some had this morning's newspaper tucked under their arm. We certainly had caused a stir with this article making people aware of our achievement.

As soon as the director had read the paper early that morning he got his staff together and they had arranged with the two students to meet us. They were told to ask if we would like to stay with them at the campus because he knew all the students and staff would love to hear about our big Adventure. It was quite simple, as soon as we had confirmed the invitation they would give a third student standing amongst the people a hand sign. He raced ahead of us and confirmed it with the director and that's why the reception was there when we arrived.

By now we were quite used to telling two or three hundred students about our lives and answering their questions so it would not be a problem. We did it the very next morning with great success. The three students instrumental in getting us there plus a few others helped us with our luggage and led us to our quarters. This time we had to share the big room with about ten other students, our three included. The son of the Akkermans, Stevan, (Steve), came to pick us up and he wanted to show us Singapore before taking us to his parent's place for dinner. With two bathrooms in the quarters and separate toilets, we took advantage of both while our students went back to class.

Steve I guessed was at the most about ten years older than us, with an athletic build and a great smile. Coming from Augsburg he just loved it when we spoke in Schwaebisch (Swabian Dialect) with him, He had been working with his dad on and off for the last five years in his ship repair and engineering business at the wharf in Singapore.

Steve had a new Vauxhall four door English car and he turned out to be a great bloke! He showed us lots of important places and even stopped at a couple of markets to enjoy some beautifully fresh pieces of pineapple ice blocks. Those pineapple ice blocks had us really going; at every opportunity we gorged ourselves, in Singapore as well as later in Indonesia. By the time we finished up in Darwin we couldn't look at another pineapple and it took me years to get accustomed to them again.

The Akkermans' house was within walking distance to the harbor and their business. As soon as we walked through the front gate and into the house, we thought we were back home.

Mr. and Mrs. Akkermans greeted us very warmly and welcomed us to their home. Every wall was covered with pictures of German and Dutch cities and landscapes. Mr. Akkermans was Dutch. Many of the pictures showed Augsburg and surroundings. Most of the furniture was from home and even the beer Mr. Akkermans offered Uli and I was German. When Uli asked Mr. Akkermans how he got the beer, he told us getting it was simple. "When we repair a German Freighter we can get just about anything at no cost. And every one of them has a stock of German beer."

They led us to a back veranda shaded by two large beach umbrellas where we enjoyed our drinks, answering their questions while watching small boats dodging big freighters trying to moor in the harbor. Mrs. Akkermans excused herself to prepare dinner. We couldn't get enough of the scenery and the hospitality of our hosts.

Mr. Akkermans studied to be a ship's engineer in Rotterdam after the First World War, but because of the high unemployment rate in Holland he accepted a good job at MAN in Augsburg at that time, because Hitler somehow started to get things moving again. He met Mrs. Akkermans at MAN and she fell in love with the Dutchman. They were married and Steve was born in 1928.

Mr. Akkermans could smell the war coming and migrated to Boston with his family and started a small motor repair shop where he made a very good living, especially when America joined the war. Steve got a good education, studying to become a marine engineer.

During the last year before war's end he befriended Mr. Watt who had connections to a small engineering factory in Singapore and suggested they should have a look. Apparently some relative started it and was looking for experienced engineers to take over, preferably relatives, because he had no children. In 1947 Mr. Watt travelled to Singapore to check out the scene and a short time later, he wrote to the Akkermans and asked them to pack their bags and come with his family and help him to build up the business. He told them that Singapore under English rule was still very much under developed, but had a bright future, except it was hot! Mr. Akkermans sold his small business in 1948 for a good amount of money, took his family back to Augsburg and with heaps of US Dollars in his pocket bought a three family brick house in a nice area. Straight after the German currency reform went from Reich's Mark to Deutsch Mark; they bought the house as cheap as. Steve had no problem getting a good job at MAN to further his studies and whilst his mum looked after him and the house, his dad decided to check out Mr. Watt's invitation.

Everything turned out fantastic and after a couple of years of hard work the company was registered as Watt and Akkermans. Even though Steve had a great job at MAN he decided to join his father in Singapore. His mum had followed his father with most of the furniture and loved Singapore. They kept the house in Augsburg and frequently visit Germany and Holland.

Mrs.Akkermans called us to dinner, and I must say we haven't eaten like this since home! Handgschabde Schpaetzle (handshaved sourdough), shaved from a hand held thin board into boiling water for a few seconds, served with slices of roast pork, a special wine sauce and different salads. Uli and I hadn't seen Theo whack into food with such enthusiasm during our whole journey, but who is to speak, we did the same. This course was followed by a beautiful fruit cake and whipped cream.

Steve had arranged with staff at the Uni to bring us back at a reasonable time because some of the students who only heard about us wanted to meet us. No doubt they would have lots of questions they wanted us to answer which we would be happy to do. Before we said good night and thanked them for their hospitality Mr. Akkermans offered to show us through his factory during our stay and Steve would stay in touch to see when it was suitable.

At the Uni it was still lively because they had only finished dinner and lots of them waited for us to show up. As soon as Steve dropped us at the front steps a couple of the staff handed Uli a few notes as we got out of the car. One was from a A.J.JUGAS, Managing Director of Bata Shoe Co. Ltd. Singapore, next one from the German Embassy and the third one and most likely the best one for us was from Lim Yew Hock, Chief Minister of Singapore. They all wanted to invite us next day and when Steve had a look at them he couldn't believe what he read.

We knew we were welcomed by Bata, and the Embassy had to be sorted out, but we didn't know who the Chief Minister was. All we saw was Steve shaking his head in surprise.

"You just got an invitation to Parliament house to meet the head of Singapore."

"Meeting the head of Singapore was just what the doctor ordered," we told Steve laughing, and thanked him once more for what he had done,

Before he drove off he told us we would be very busy over the next couple of days, but to keep in touch so he could see how we are getting on.

We could just imagine what he was going to tell his parents.

We were going to keep this Parliament invitation a bit on the quiet, but by this time several students had walked outside and congratulated us, because someone from the office had leaked it. Most of the students and staff thought we were someone special and treated us with great respect even though we had arrived in Singapore only two days ago.

It had been a hard but exciting day and we declined to answer any more questions because we were tired. Furthermore it was already arranged that we would talk to all of them in the big auditorium after breakfast in the morning. It was easier said than done, sharing the room with five inquisitive students took some time before we fell asleep.

Because of the huge meal the night before we didn't feel like breakfast and after our morning ablutions we just grabbed a few pieces of fruit and walked over to the office where the Director and a couple of senior students were waiting for us.

"Someone from Parliament House called to tell us you will be picked up at 3 o'clock," the Director informed us as we entered.

"They certainly move fast," Uli told him looking at his watch, "it's just after 9 o'clock."

"We'll be waiting, of course," Theo confirmed.

"Speaking of waiting," the Director said, "the auditorium is already full... so if you would follow me..."

This one was a totally different audience. Instead of either Moslem or Indian students, here we had them altogether. Half the students were Chinese and I could see some European faces in there as well. Sitting again at a small table next to the Director and a couple of Teachers on a big stage in front of that large audience was quite nerve-racking, for me anyhow, but after one of the Teachers introduced each of us and told them a bit about our lives, I became quite relaxed. Uli as always was the first one to tell his story, Theo second and I with my American bit went last. While each of us spoke you could hear a pin drop, but as soon as I had finished hands went up in the air and questions were thrown at us from all directions. With everyone asking things at the same time we couldn't make out anything until the Director calmed everyone down and pointed at various individuals who asked their question for us to answer.

I felt enormously proud of myself and couldn't help thinking of my parents who spoke fluent English and how they would have loved to see their oldest son speaking to all those students and answering their questions in such a faraway City.

It was a total success, especially when we told them about the Heads of State we had met so far and when we mentioned that we were invited by Lim Yew Hock to visit him this afternoon, it nearly brought the house down.

During all this well wishing and handshakes, one of the Staff informed us that the German Embassy had tried to get in touch with us.

The Big Adventure

They wanted to invite us to something also this afternoon, but when they heard about Lim Yew Hock, they decided to postpone it for the next day.

Meeting Lim Yew Hock, the Chief Minister of Singapore, was an adventure in itself.

Not too many German youngsters like us, and definitely none from Backnang, were ever picked up in a chauffeur driven Government limousine and taken to Parliament house in their State, but we were!

We soon realized that we weren't being taken to Parliament house; Mr. Hock wanted to meet us in his private residence first to introduce us to his family. We found out later that he was put under pressure by his wife and three beautiful daughters who wanted to meet us before the Parliamentarians did, and we were rapt.

It was a warm welcome and we soon felt at ease, especially after holding the two oldest daughters hands, maybe a bit too long and being served a cool fruit drink. They were absolutely gorgeous! Mr. Hock was Chinese and his beautiful wife was Malaysian. Apparently there was another two year old girl, but we didn't see her.

Eulindra Lim was Uli's age and he couldn't keep his eyes of her and Theo and I loved looking at Shifley Lim who was our age. I had never seen girls dressed like these were before and none of us could keep our eyes off them. Eulindra wore a tight silk blouse, one shoulder free, displaying her perfectly moulded breasts. An ankle long black skirt with slits on both sides up to her thigh displayed her beautifully formed long legs.

Uli said later, "di hedde uff dor schdell vorgnudschd", meaning "this one I could have given instant cuddles"

Shifley wore a more modest dress, also showing off a great figure.

What a lovely family. We would never have guessed that Mr. Hock held the highest position in Singapore if it wasn't for the two sentries stationed at the front entrance and for the fact that we had been picked up by a parliamentary limousine.

Between sandwiches and fruit juices we answered a lot of questions mainly from the girls who were extremely interested in our schooling in Germany and wanted to know all about our classes with girls and boys mixed together. Uli's and my classes were evenly mixed with practically half girls and half boys, but they had to laugh when Theo told them that in his class there were 60 girls but only 4 boys.

As we showed them through our book M. Hock was summoned several times to answer calls and missed quite a few of our answers. We were there about two hours and as we were about to leave Mr Hock apologised for his interruptions and told us she had organized with his parliamentary secretary for us to be invited for lunch the next day.

It was still daylight when we were driven back to the University to answer more questions from staff and students who were happy to gossip nonstop, but eventually we managed to write some postcards and a couple of letters to send home. We wanted our families, friends and Backnangers to know what had transpired up until Singapore. We were in great spirits having been invited by the Head of State and his family to visit them, and falling asleep later we couldn't help thinking about his two beautiful daughters.

At 10 o'clock next morning we were picked up by the same chauffeur, but this time driven directly to Parliament house where we were greeted by two middle aged gorgeous looking Chinese ladies also with splits on each side of their skirts, reaching right up to their bottoms which we couldn't help noticing. We soon realised that the women who dressed like this were Chinese. The Malaysian women and other Nationals didn't display their treasures like this. With big smiles we followed them one flight up to Mr. Hock's office where we were greeted by several men and a couple more Ladies.

Lim Yew Hock, Chief Minister of Singapore with his family.
next page.
He wrote a message in our log-book with great flourish which we treasure to this day.

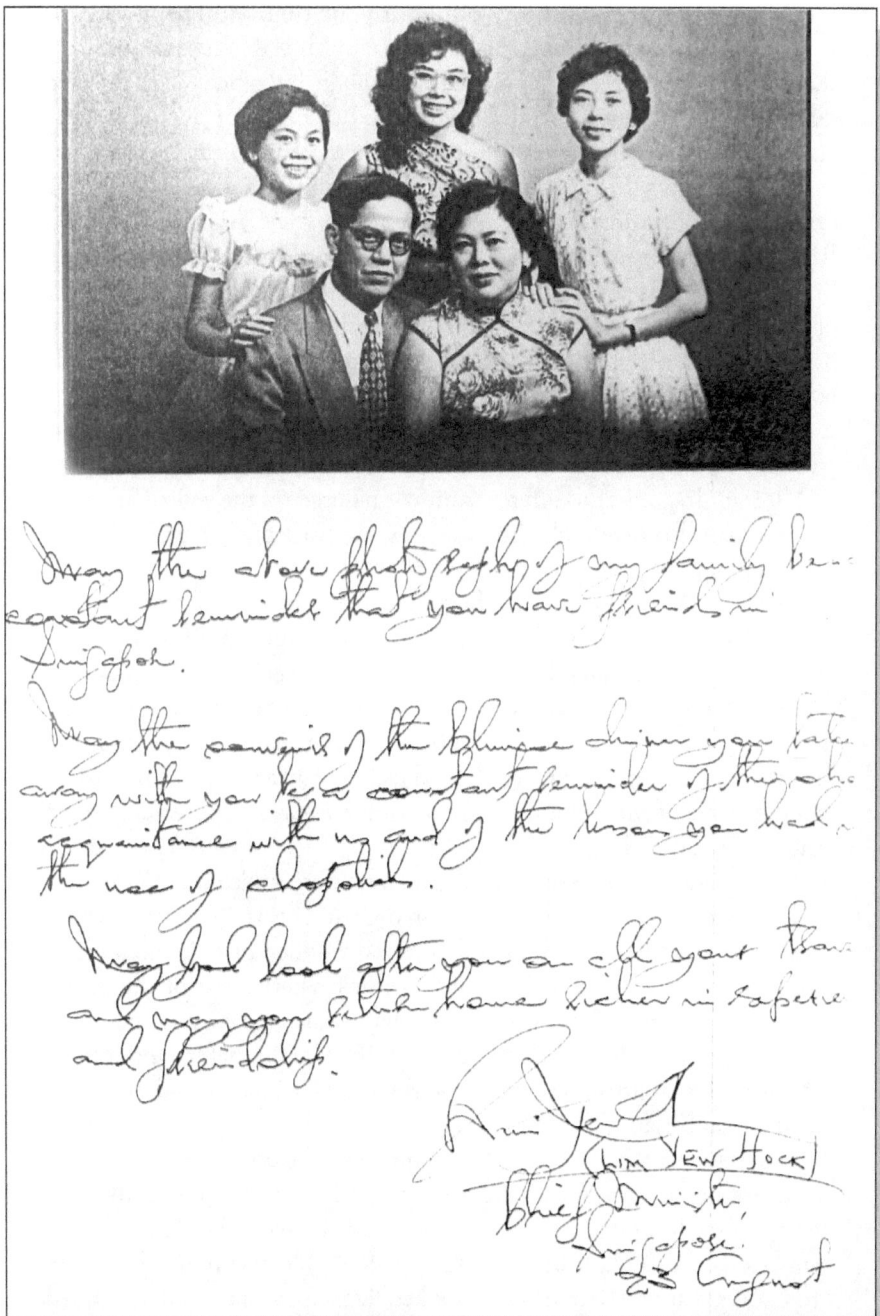

May the above photograph of my family be a constant reminder that you have friends in Singapore.

May the souvenir of the Chinese dinner you take away with you be a constant reminder of the acquaintance with us and of the lesson you had, the use of chopsticks.

May God look after you on all your travels and may you return home richer in experience and friendship.

(LIM YEW HOCK)
Chief Minister,
Singapore.
23 August

More and more people entered and Mr. Hock introduced us to all of them and told them about our journey. By the time Mr. Hock was able to write in our book, filling a whole page with his elaborate handwriting, there would have been at least thirty people in his office. We answered questions for over an hour and even signed a couple of our newspaper articles before Mr. Hock was told the restaurant was waiting.

What happened to us, must have been definitely a once in a lifetime experience; it certainly was for the three of us. The CHUA JOO SENG RESTAURANT was just across the street. I would never have imagined in a million years that we would be walking amongst thirty Members of Parliament to this restaurant to have lunch with Mr. Hock. He must have left just a skeleton crew back at Parliament House to look after the business of the day.

It was a Chinese restaurant, most likely one of the best in Singapore and the second floor was reserved for Mr. Hock. It was a beautiful room with lots of dragons and different animals painted on the walls. The waiters and waitresses were all dressed the same, wearing long black pants with a golden silk over garment.

In the middle of the big room were three beautiful big round tables carved out of black wood. They had lots of landscapes and flowers carved around the top and inlaid with pieces from mother of pearl. There was room for ten at each table. Each one of us had to sit at one of them. The tables were set very exclusively with beautiful porcelain plates, cups and a funny sort of a soup spoon with several teapots on each table. The cutlery had the name of the restaurant on each piece even the chopsticks which were made out of ebony.

It was hard for me to describe the many different dishes because most of them were new to me, but they tasted great! It was a fantastic experience. In the middle of the table was a round wooden plate about a meter in diameter and about five centimetres thick where most of the dishes were placed. It must have been set on ball bearings because one could turn it to get to the food. I never saw anything like this before and it must have been at least fifteen years later in Melbourne when I found out it was called a Lazy Susan.

Lucky for us we had practiced using chop sticks because there were no knives or forks. Some of the waiters served everyone pieces of a big steamed fish, head on, which was placed on the wooden plate, covered with green herbs and sweet sauce. At a smaller table next to us a guy all in white was taking the skin off what looked like a roasted duck and handed the pieces to some waiters. They in turn placed these pieces on small very thin pancakes with spring onions, pieces of cucumber and what we were told later was a sweet plum sauce. They served two pieces on a small plate to each person. They were eaten by hand and tasted delicious. To finish it all off we were served platters of freshly cut pieces of exotic fruit like pineapple, lychees and others which I had never eaten before. Something else tickled my fancy, after we finished this glorious lunch, everyone was handed a small rolled up white steamed towel to wipe their face and hands.

Another incredible thing happened to us, which we only learned some time later in Melbourne from our parents. Apparently several of those porcelain dishes which we ate out of were unwashed, wrapped in newspaper, put in cardboard boxes and sent to our homes. We were a bit surprised at the time, when a waiter had handed us a piece of paper for us to write our names and addresses, but we hadn't expect this.

About fifty years later I brought them back to Australia and proudly displayed them in our wall unit. Jill, our very close Singaporean friend tried a couple of years ago to find *Chua Joo Seng Restaurant*, without luck. Orchard Road is not what it used to be, every building today, is well over eighty stories high.

Back at Mr. Hock's office his wife and daughters were waiting to say goodbye once more and by the time we were taken back to the University it was late in the afternoon.

Several years later, Lim Yew Hock became Singapore's High commissioner to Australia, at that time Uli and I tried to find a way to meet him, but without success.

The Director was still in his office and called us in to hand us a couple of messages. The first one was from the Managing Director A. J. Jugas, of Bata Shoe Co. Ltd, who would like to invite us to visit and left a phone number to get in touch when suitable. The other from Dr. Hans Ulrich Granow, Deutscher General Consul German Ambassador, who was going to send a car next morning to pick us up at 10 am.

"What a turnaround," we told the Director, who by this time had ordered some tea. He offered to call Bata next morning to inform Mr. Jugas about our movements and we would get in touch with him. He was extremely pleased and couldn't get over the fact that we were taken for lunch by Mr. Hock. He had eaten at that restaurant but never in the big private room on top.

We were already waiting in the office next morning, when exactly at 10 am a big limousine stopped in front and a German uniformed chauffeur got out to greet us, this time in German, with a big smile. He told us Dr. Granow wanted to meet us at his home first, before he was to take us to the Embassy.

We did have slightly mixed feelings driving through a big open gate towards a double story house with a German flag in front, thinking about the reception we had two days earlier, but we shouldn't have worried. The Ambassador and his wife greeted us with Mr. in front of our family names, which we hadn't been addressed like since we left home.

First thing he wanted to know after we were invited into a big lounge room with a view to a manicured garden was what had happened at the Embassy. Uli told him exactly how we were treated by our country's officials and we could see that Dr. Granow and his lovely wife looked at each other, and they weren't too happy. Apparently he had already told his staff, that newspaper articles a couple of days ago were of no benefit to the German image. He apologized to us for their stupidity.

After some delicious fruit juices we answered their questions and told them about our lives and our adventures. Browsing through our book they became more and more impressed by the great people we had met so far. As soon as they found out that we'd had a long audience with King Faisal they both stood up and shook our hands. Apparently during the early war years they were in charge of the German Embassy in Baghdad and were very close to the Royal Family. They had known the future King when he was running around the palace as a three year old.

Of course they had met Lim Yew Hock several times, but always for Diplomatic Affairs; they never had lunch together. After writing a few sentences in our book, Dr. Granow looked at his watch and informed us that we were his guests for lunch shortly at the Embassy.

It was an absolute classic... When we walked into the Embassy behind Dr. Granow, through the door held open by the same idiot we had previously encountered; he didn't look at us. It was so ridiculous the way he tried to avoid seeing us. The receptionist inside greeted Dr. Granow but blushed when Uli, with a big grin, wished her a good day. It certainly was a tense few moments in the big room, there wasn't much noise and everyone seemed to be very busy. There were several people in the dining room and Dr. Granow introduced us to them before we were seated on one of the vacant tables.

There were three meals to choose from but all three of us ordered Wie-

The Big Adventure

ner schnitzel, a Pepsi for Theo and a German Beer for Uli and me. It was a meal for the gods to write home about. During coffee and cakes one of the staff we hadn't seen her before greeted us and handed over some more mail. By the time the chauffeur drove us back to the Uni, we would have spent close to five fabulous hours with the Granows.

Back at the university again the Director informed us that Mr. Jugas from Bata had rung and that they would like to pick us up for breakfast 9 o'clock the next morning.

"That would be great," we told him. We had enjoyed Bata's hospitality before and were happy to wear the shoes they had given us. With most of the students in class we finally got a couple of hours to ourselves so we could write postcards and letters home. There was a lot to write about because we hadn't written anything since Kuala Lumpur.

Steve Akkermans was already waiting for us when we entered the office just before 9am; he had rung earlier and was told that Bata was going to pick us up. He came to tell us that his mum would like to prepare another great meal for us and the whole family had a big surprise for us. By the time we had arranged for him to pick us up at 4pm a small English car with BATA painted on both sides pulled up outside.

Mr. Jugas welcomed us with open arms and a near perfect Austrian dialect. We thought he was Austrian but it turned out that he was a Czechoslovakian citizen born near Prague. He had studied in Vienna and married a Viennese several years before the war. They have two boys, both of them at the German school in Singapore where his wife was helping out.

Mr. Jugas was closely related to the founders of Bata and was asked if he would like to take over the Singapore operation and help out in Djakarta. They had known for some time that we would reach Singapore soon because telegrams and letters about us had been forwarded from the Bata companies we had visited previously. Because of the newspaper article they had known that we were here and after getting in touch with the papers did they knew we were staying at the University.

The breakfast at their canteen with a couple of Mr. Jugas' friends turned into a breakfast/lunch, with lots of European goodies and Asian fruits. In between a secretary handed Mr. Rugas a piece of paper which he signed and handed to me. It had some nice machine written sentences on Bata's letterhead, for our book.

Just before we were shown through the factory Mrs. Jugas with their two boys arrived and joined us. The boys were 15 and 18 years old with straw blond hair and blue eyes, like my brother. The older one was moving back to Vienna in a couple of weeks to study at the University and was looking forward to it.

Before being taken back Mr. Jugas handed me a piece of paper with the address of Mr. J. Huttner, the Managing Director Bata shoes in Djakarta and he would let him know of our arrival in Indonesia soon. They worked closely together because they each made different types of shoes which they exchanged so didn't duplicate each factory's work.

On the way back we asked Mr. Jugas to drop us off at Watt and Akkermans at the harbor where Steve decided to show us their very impressive repair shops. A short time later Mr. Akkermans jumped on his bicycle and followed us home, where Mrs. Akkermans was busy in the kitchen preparing the evening meal. After we had a few relaxing drinks while enjoying the sunset, Mr. Akkermans asked us how we were planning to get to Indonesia and when.

Uli told him, "We were thinking the best way for us would be to take a small ship over to Sumatra and from Palembang somehow to Djakarta."

"Not a good idea," he said straight up. "It might be the shortest way, but there are no small boats to take you to Sumatra except pirate boats. Besides, the place is still totally underdeveloped. There are no roads there. It would be too dangerous."

We just stared at him. So much for that plan…

"I've been discussing your journey with a few friends and our suggestion is you go by ferry. Every day a big passenger and freight ferry leaves Singapore for Djakarta. Some travel nonstop, and others service Palembang and some of the Islands in between. I often travel on them for business, first class, and believe me it's a great way to travel."

We didn't know what to say, but taking advice from people who know the area is always the best thing to do.

"We are always doing business with some freight forwarders so we could easily arrange a free passage for you. What do you think?"

"Sounds like a good idea," Uli said.

Before Theo and I could add to that that, Steve said, "All you have to do is pick a day and I'll arrange it."

We looked at each other dumbfounded. This was an extremely great offer we couldn't refuse. It was certainly unexpected. On the plus side it would save us valuable time! This whole journey was taking longer than we had expected and we were beginning to wonder whether we would actually get to Melbourne in time for the Olympic Games as we had planned. We didn't have to discuss it amongst ourselves. We immediately accepted and while thanking him several times Mrs. Akkermans called us to the dining room for another surprise.

The table was set and we couldn't believe our eyes when a grinning Mrs. Akkermans placed a big white porcelain soup bowl in the middle of the table, removed the lid and said, "Help yourselves gentlemen."

She had made Maultashen! (Translated it means Snoutpockets, which are a big type of ravioli, a great delicacy in Swabia. They can be eaten cold, hot in the soup or roasted and mixed with an Omlette.) That was our next surprise and we took full advantage of it.

By the time we finished and were served a Schnaepsle, to settle our stomachs. Of course Theo couldn't drink the schnapps. We had told them about our adventure with Lim Yew Hock and our lunch with the Ambassador, they were all ears. We decided to stay two more days and Mr. Akkermans would organize our passage by then. Steve said he would pick us up in one of their small trucks because the ferry terminal is not far from their workshops.

Most of the lights were already switched off for the night when we finally got driven back to the campus. Even though it was a pretty strenuous but beautiful day, we were in high spirits and it took us some time to digest everything and fall asleep.

Next morning it was was full on again, starting with some fruit and tea for breakfast at the office with the Director and staff. They were delighted when we told them what the Akkermans had decided to organize for us in two days time. Because of our willingness to talk about our lives to the students and staff which was highly appreciated, the Director said he would also organize accommodation for us in Djakarta.

He mentioned that one of his close friends is the Director of the University in the Indonesian Capital and he will inform him of our exact arrival. His friend and staff would be more than happy for us to stay with them and maybe we could speak to their students. That of course would take a great deal of pressure of us, especially arriving in a new country. We thanked him very much, also the staff for their hospitality and asked would he be so kind as to write a few lines in our book before we leave. At that moment the phone rang and after one of the staff answered, handed the phone not to the Director, but to Uli, who after a couple of seconds answered with a smile in German. It happened to be our Sausage King enquiring about our movements today and if it was possible he would pick us up soon to show us his factory and shop.

He picked us up in a VW kombi van with Sausage and Kitchen Dept. in big letters plastered on both sides and smelling like a smoke house. It had one row of seats behind the driver; the rest of the space was used for deliveries. Even though it was very hot and steamy, our Sausage King was still dressed in his Bavarian outfit and was happy to catch up with us again.

We only travelled a short distance towards the harbor when he slowed next to a big market and turned in to a small car park in front of a big shop full of customers. It was similar to our butcher, like Idler, Kuehnle or Gross back home, except this shop had some stand-up tables for customers to enjoy the delicacies, where at least six people were serving customers.

At the back of the shop was a brick building with a fairly large room divided into several smaller ones, each with different machinery and cooking equipment. We noticed about a dozen workers in there flat out producing the various sausages. Walking past these rooms we reached the office with a canteen and washrooms behind.

One of the wooden tables was already set for six, the three of us, the king himself. his manager and a friend, both German. It wasn't quite midday yet but there was already a big pot in the middle of the table up to the brim with hot water and full with white sausages. Next to it sat a basket with freshly baked pretzels and a couple of Bavarian sweet mustard pots. To top it all off, each of us, except Theo was served a half litre beer stein with a big white foamy head on it and the Lowenbrau emblem baked into the side.

It certainly was a feast, and drinking cold Bavarian beer out of those steins was heavenly! It was the first time since leaving Backnang that we were able to drink out of a stein.

Those sausages were absolutely delicious and the pot was emptied in no time to be filled several times more because some good customers were also asked to join us and listen to our story. Of course all the staff had their lunch with us and after a couple more steins of cold beer the atmosphere was electric!

We spend many hours with those lovely people, enjoying coffee and cakes a couple of hours later and by the time we decided to say goodbye, we were told, Leberkaese und Kartoffelsalat was being prepared. Leberkase is like Meatloaf, and is served best in a roll with mustard or on a plate with potato salad. We just had to stay a bit longer to enjoy this as an early dinner.

It was a perfect day! The Sausage King wrote something in our book and the goodbyes and best wishes for our journey from all those strangers was heart moving. To top it all off while walking to the kombi to be driven back one of the staff members handed each of us a small paper bag saying, "just a few goodies to have on the way."

We promised to keep in touch as we said goodbye to the Sausage King and we did send a long letter to him from Melbourne which he answered. Years later Theo caught up with him by chance in Muenchen where he was in a nursing home.

The University was still full of life when we got back and we barely had time to use the bathroom before being bombarded again with questions. Finally we were able to open our paper bags and smell all the goodies from the sausage shop. When I say smell, I mean smell, because everything in the bags was smoked and when inhaling, it hit my sense of smell like an old friend. With the salamis, smoked ham pieces and a couple of small liver sausages we certainly wouldn't starve over the next few days.

Uli and Theo in Singapore

Steve Akkermans had already phoned the Director, and by the time we walked in to his office next morning all was organized for us to leave tomorrow afternoon. That suited us fine and we were looking forward for a few hours to ourselves. We had some washing to do, our bikes had to be worked on and we were looking forward to visit one of the markets close by. Not once in Singapore were we able to smoke a water pipe, only the odd cigarette, without being seen. It wouldn't look good, lighting a smoke as sportsmen, especially in front of all the students.

After our chores were done and the bikes were in top condition we walked to the back of the market not to be seen and sat in front of a Malaysian eatery where we were served a big pipe joined to three hoses. With some small food dishes, a pot of tea, exotic fruits to nibble on and watching life going by, we felt great!

Packing our luggage, getting ready for next morning, didn't take too long and we were able to enjoy dinner and our last evening with some of the students. We could tell that some of them really enjoyed us staying with them and we felt the same.

By midday Steve was going to pick us up, so we told the Director in the morning we would jump on our bikes to see if there was any more mail for us at the Embassy and we would be back long before midday. The few kilometres were covered in no time and when we got there we leaned our bikes on the same front wall, this time without being molested. The uniformed dickhead acted as if he couldn't see us and the same receptionist blushed when she handed Uli a few letters and didn't ask us to take a seat and wait our turn.

It certainly was a sad farewell to say goodbye to all those wonderful people at the University, to the Director, office staff, a couple of teachers and to thank them for their hospitality. The Director told us that someone from the University in Djakarta would be waiting for us on arrival just before Steve turned up to take us straight to the harbor.

It was a huge ship and people everywhere were trying to get through customs and on board. We helped Steve to secure our bikes and some of the luggage we didn't need in our cabin into a special crate to be lifted on board. As first class passengers we were led to another gangway where one of the two customs officials quickly stamped our passports.

The Akkermans were already waiting to introduce us to the Dutch Captain, a close friend of theirs, and to a couple of Indonesian Officers. This would be our third ship, but this one was by far the biggest and busiest.

Saying goodbye to the Akkermans and Steve plus thanking them a thousand times took some time, before they had to disembark. They waited until the ship sailed and we waved until they were out of sight.

We also waved back to Singapore, which to this day is one of my most favourite cities in the world.

The Big Adventure

Chapter Eleven

"Sodelle, des heddador au ned denggd dass mors soweid schaffad," Uli announced in our dialect. *"You would never have thought that we would make it this far."*

As Singapore vanished into the sea behind us we were shown to our cabin and loved every bit of it! It was a family cabin with an adjacent guest or children's room, divided by a small bathroom and a separate squat down toilet. Theo and I shared a huge double bed and Uli picked one of the three in the next cabin.

We were spoiled rotten from the captain, officers, stewards, down to the kitchen staff and all of the first-class passengers. Being a huge ship, first-class was fairly big and most of the main meals were enjoyed with the captain who had told all on board about our adventures.

By the time we had crossed the Singapore Strait, passed some small islands, the sun was setting gloriously in the west and we felt we could just reach out and touch Sumatra.

For our first dinner on board we put on long pants, clean shirts and didn't look too much out of place. We certainly enjoyed the food which was placed on a long table alongside a wall in the dining room, like a big buffet. There was Indonesian rice, fish and lamb specials, plus Dutch smoked and pickled meats along with a variety of seafoods. We certainly had a ball, even Theo had plenty to choose from and was 'as happy as Larry'.

Just before lunchtime next day the Captain announced through loud speakers that we were crossing the Equator, entering the southern hemisphere.

Well, how about that? We were in the southern hemisphere, and so far from home we could hardly believe it.

It was an incredible sea voyage; three days and nights of sheer bliss being treated like Royals!

Sailing through the gulf of Thailand into the Java sea, passing heaps of big and smaller islands, with only a few clouds in the blue sky was unreal.

By the time we reached Jakarta everyone of course knew all about our lives and our big adventure. We reached Jakarta much too soon where once more reality very quickly set in.

Disembarking on the third morning didn't take long. Straight after our last breakfast a couple of immigration officers came on board to check our papers, stamp our passports and we were ready to leave. Naturally it took some time to say goodbye to the Captain, crew and some of the passengers, who all wished us well.

Walking down the gangway and stepping onto Indonesian soil was again a strange feeling; further and further away from home. No one took much notice of us while we waited for our bikes and luggage. Most of the people were busy working because we were still inside customs. It was a different situation once we received our bikes and started packing; curious looks and smiles abounded.

It wasn't crowded inside customs but as soon as we pushed our bikes outside it was bedlam. A huge crowd waited excitedly for family, relatives or friends to disembark. They laughed and yelled at people still on the ship, often waving furiously.

As first-class passengers we were some of the first ones to push through all these people and we were soon greeted by people coming towards us from two directions.

Firstly, a well-dressed elderly European gentleman welcomed us to Indonesia and mentioned his name was Joachim Ruttner. He was Austrian and the Managing Director of Bata in Djakarta. He was accompanied by a younger Chinese looking guy casually dressed, with a camera on a strap hanging around his neck who was introduced to us as Hong from the local press.

By this time four young Indonesian guys about our age greeted us in English and told us they were students at the University, and were here to welcome us and guide us back to campus. After a short discussion between Mr. Ruttner, Hong and the students in Indonesian, Mr. Ruttner informed us that he and Hong would get in touch with us at the Uni. the next day.

This certainly was an unexpected reception and we thanked Mr. Ruttner and Hong very much before they got into a waiting car. The stu-

The Big Adventure

dents flagged down a couple of rickshaws and we followed them as best as we could through the traffic which wasn't too bad, with police directing on every major crossing. It must have looked surprising; two rickshaws being followed by three strange looking cyclists. We did get some funny looks and lots of waves.

Djakarta certainly was a multicultural city, inhabited by people from many different nations. In the few kilometres to the Uni we passed a Mosque, a Temple, a Church, a Shrine, and further along another big Mosque. We knew that we were in a dominantly Islamic country, because many women had their faces covered. Passing a couple of busy markets, we finally turned off the main street and followed a high brick wall until we reached a beautiful wrought iron gate where a sentry waved us through. We headed towards a beautiful stone building similar to but bigger than the one in the Singapore University.

This time the welcome committee knew exactly about our arrival and greeted us very warmly. The director in Singapore of course hadn't told us that his great friend the Principal of this Uni was actually Indonesian, Moslem, tall, clean shaven and traditionally dressed. It just proved over and over again that it doesn't matter what race or religion one belongs to, we can all be great friends!

There were several teachers, men and women, different Nationals, plus a couple of Dutch teachers, who greeted us in fluent German. Two of the women were Moslem teachers, but they were dressed in white blouses and long black skirts without head coverings. I wondered if that was because of the Dutch influence over the years. As a matter of fact, we had noticed lots of beautiful young ladies and women, like in Malaysia without headgear, riding towards the Uni.

Our bikes and luggage were quickly taken care of and we were led to one of the guest rooms in the main building behind the office and not to the campus with the students. There were two family sized VIP guest rooms for special visitors and we certainly didn't expect to occupy one of these. Actually, it wasn't just one room, it was a whole suite! A small lounge room, two bedrooms, separate bathroom and European style toilet, plus a terrace next to a beautifully manicured garden.

Both Dutch teachers, the Principal and some students showed us through and wished us a happy stay at the Uni. We thanked them very much, but also told them that we would not have minded to stay on campus with the students in case they had more high-ranking visitors arriving.

"Don't even think about it," we were told. "We aren't expecting anyone else at the moment. Besides, as far as we are concerned you are high-ranking. Who else has done what you have done, met the important people you have met?"

Well, that certainly put us in a good mood.

"Take some time to freshen up and get used to the surroundings. We'll come back in an hour and take you for lunch."

We were taken to a much smaller dining room for staff and teachers only in the main building, compared to the one at campus for the students, which was huge. All our meals were taken in the smaller dining rooms while we stayed there.

We soon found out that we are in a different world, dominantly Moslem —not as strict as in the other Arab countries we had crossed— with several other religions included. Mainly Indonesian was spoken, but most of the younger generations spoke Dutch and English. The Principal Introduced us in English and told everyone as much as he knew about us. "But we all shall find out the full story tomorrow or the next day?" Which of course meant that we were expected to give a long talk or a lecture regarding out travels to all the students.

We had tasted some Indonesian food on the ship and didn't mind it at all, but here was something else. We were seated on a big round table with the principal, one of the Dutch teachers and a couple of gorgeous looking office ladies. The food was served like in a restaurant. Mostly different rice dishes (called nasi goreng, which is traditionally fried and mixed with different vegetables, lamb, beef or seafood) were put in the middle of the table for everyone to help themselves. Some smaller bowls with steaming fish fillets and hot meat were placed next to them and the aroma was over powering.

Being novices, we just watched the others and soon got the hang of it. We could choose whether we wanted chop sticks or cutlery but we opted for the latter because eating rice with chop sticks was still too hard for us. Tea and fruit juices were on the table, but no alcohol. Over freshly cut pineapple, mango and some other strange fruits we had never tasted before it was decided we would speak to the students next morning.

Naturally, we couldn't wait to collect our mail at the general post office and the Dutch teacher asked a couple of the students we had met earlier that morning to lead us there on their bikes, which they didn't mind at all. It felt great riding our bikes without our heavy gear behind us and we had no problem weaving through the traffic following our two show-off's. It was a fair way. We crossed several big intersections and several wide waterways before they stopped in front of a big stone building at what seemed to be the center of town.

Our two friends stayed with the bikes, while the three of us searched for the poste-restante counter, which was at the far end of a long corridor. After showing our passports we collected a heap of mail and couldn't wait to get back to read it. We asked the mail man where we could change some money and he pointed to the right counter. Because we were unsure of what financial or other help we would get as we travelled further into Indonesia we decided each of us would exchange a fair amount of US Dollars for Rupiah's and were advised at the Uni that Jakarta and Surabaya had the best exchange rates.

Back at the Uni we thanked our friends and went straight to our room, sorted our mail, started reading and replying to the most important ones. The reason why we got such a lot of mail was simple, we had written to everyone explaining that after Jakarta our next post office would most likely be Melbourne.

Once we got back from the post office we found out only lunch and breakfast were served in the Uni dining rooms. But that was fine by us. It enabled us to wander through one of the nearby markets to look out for a small eating place where we might also be able to smoke a couple of water pipes, before nightfall.

We could hardly get over the diversity of the different looking people we saw everywhere we went. We thought we've seen it all, but this was somehow unexpected.

We noticed boys as young as fourteen or fifteen years of age smoking in front of everyone and no one took any notice. Back home we had to be eighteen to smoke openly otherwise we got a kick up our arse. We noticed that most Indonesians were relatively short compared with Europeans, and we also noticed some elderly Europeans, probably Dutch, holding hands with some beautiful, but two heads shorter Indonesian ladies.

Being without our bikes no one took much notice of us and we could observe without being bothered. Something else we noticed; just about everyone was smiling and there was no loud music blearing out as had occurred in some of the other countries we had visited, and even though the market was very busy, people were not rushing about madly. We started to like being in Indonesia.

We were well prepared for everyone at 9.30 next morning, but I still had some creepy feelings in the stomach region when we walked into the fully packed Auditorium and were greeted by a cheering and clapping Audience.

This Audience, was totally different to the one in Singapore where most of them were Malaysians, Chinese, Indians and some European students. Here we had a big mixture of many Nationals, but mainly Indonesians, Chinese, Dutch, plus lots of half Dutch and half Indonesian.

We got a big surprise when we were led to the table facing the Audience. Mr. Ruttner and Hong the Journalist were seated there next to a couple of teachers and the Principal. They greeted us warmly. Apparently, they had been in contact with the office to find out about our moves and were told that we would speak to the students this morning and were asked to take part. We would be sitting next to them.

This time the Principal introduced us and told everyone a short history about us, before Uli got up and started talking about his life, which he did by now without a hitch. Theo took nearly twice as long, because he added something about our earlier odyssey through Italy to Tunisia. I also interjected with comments on it. Hong took quite a few photographs and scribbled notes in a pad on his lap. Question time was just as hectic as Singapore, but one question stood out and it came from a beautiful young lady. She stood up and asked, "Are you going to visit President Sukarno?"

Uli who was the smoothest talker said, "We would very much like to, but we're running out of time. We still have to make our way towards Semarang and Surabaya within the next couple of days before the rainy season makes travelling impossible."

It must have been close to three hours and I am sure it would have gone much longer but the Principal finally stood up with a big smile and thanked us very much on behalf of the students and the Uni. This was followed by a thunderous round of applause which made me think that we were getting better at this every time we did it.

Back at the office we were served freshly cut pineapple pieces and other fruits, while all the staff and a couple of teachers thanked us once more. Mr. Ruttner and Hong were very pleased to be part of the activities and Mr. Ruttner invited us to visit his factory, if time permitted.

"No problem," Uli told him, "just give us a few minutes to grab some letters and postcards we'd written to post on the way."

The Big Adventure

Hong was missing by the time we got back to the office and Mr. Ruttner told us in German, "Hong has a few urgent things to do, but will catch up with us sometime later."

Mr. Ruttner was driving the latest two toned (White, with a red top) three-cylinder DKW and was happy to show us his latest acquisition. Posting our mail on the way didn't take too long and we hardly wasted any time in the post office.

Traffic was fairly smooth, but if there weren't so many policemen directing it at every crossing it would be bedlam. Passing lots of different shops, eating places, a big manicured park, cycle and other repair shops we turned into a driveway and stopped in front of a big impressive looking stone building.

It was an old building, not long ago totally restored, which made it look very modern, compared to some of the shabbier ones nearby. On the front wall in large letters was PERUSAHAAN SEPATU BATA N V. DJAKARTA.

The smell of fresh leather as we entered the front of the building was overwhelming. Such a beautiful smell! And like the previous Bata stores we had visited, every shelf was packed full of shoes, but in this case, mainly sandals.

Mr. Ruttner introduced us to some of the sales staff, then led us into a big office where we were greeted by a beautiful tall Indonesian Dutch lady, speaking fluent German. Mr. Ruttner introduced her as his wife. Lucky you I thought. She was smiling and holding the newspaper from Singapore with our article in it. Mr. Jugas from BATA had posted it to them a few days earlier.

This was a very busy place and we were surprised, when we were led through the office, past a canteen and through a back door into a large warehouse, how big it really was.

"This place is only used for storage and dispatch of goods," Mr Ruttner said. "Our factory is in a big industrial area outside Djakarta."

Mr. Ruttner insisted that we should try new walking boots, similar to the ones we had on, even after we mentioned that the ones we had on were still in reasonable condition, but we certainly didn't argue.

We were invited into a dining room where one big table was beautifully set up by kitchen staff, overseen by Mrs. Ruttner. Two other gentlemen were standing by the table. Smelling the fine aroma coming out of the kitchen, I wondered what we would get served and started to feel hungry. The two other gentlemen were business associates and had been asked by Mr. Ruttner to be his guests for lunch, to meet us and hear more about our adventures. He had already told them some of our story and they were eager to hear more. One of them was English and the other Singaporean so we had to converse in English.

Being seated with such nice people felt great and whilst enjoying some freshly squeezed fruit juices we answered all their questions. It wasn't long before we were served with another surprise; a Wiener Schnitzel! In Indonesia! It came with all the trimmings; French fries, pieces of lemon, finely sliced potato and cucumber salads. Well, this was certainly not expected, but it went down really well!

Not long after the table was cleared and coffee with freshly baked cakes were being served when Hong entered with a big smile.

"I have some good news," he said. "Ibu fatwamati, first Lady of Indonesia, would like to meet you at her residence tomorrow morning."

Hong got the idea for us to meet Ibu Fatmawati, after one of the students had asked if we would meet their President, and he just went ahead and arranged it!

Unfortunately Dr. Sukarno, The President, was on a state visit to Washington DC. invited by President Dwight D Eisenhower. Hong thought that Ibu Fatmawati was the next best person for us to meet since The President was unavailable.

This certainly was great news and really something to look forward to next morning.

"I don't know what to say," I said.

He grinned at us. "Don't say anything."

"We can't thank you enough," Theo said.

"It's all about the news," Hong said. "I'm a reporter and this is a great story." He held up his camera and notepad. "I will come for you tomorrow morning at nine thirty in a rickshaw, but I want you to follow me riding your bikes. I want to take some pictures with you holding your bikes while meeting with our First Lady."

The rest of the day passed quickly and before we knew it we were thanking everyone for their beautiful hospitality and especially Mr Ruttner who gave us a lift back to the university.

Life sometimes plays incredible tricks and we couldn't believe that the first person walking towards us as soon as we entered the Uni was the young female student who asked if we would meet their President. When we stopped to greet her Uli said, "You'll never guess what has happened."

She studied the three of us with curiosity.

"We are going to meet the First Lady in the morning, and it's all your fault."

"That reporter from the newspaper arranged it after you asked us would we be meeting President Sukarno."

Her eyes opened wide with astonishment.

"He's on a State visit to the US but we are going to meet his wife instead." I said.

She just stared at us. She seemed very pleased but didn't know what to say.

"She's a very nice lady," she said after we started to walk on into the uni.

By the time Hong arrived in the morning we already had our bikes looking their best and were very excited to meet the President's wife.

Following Hong's rickshaw was relatively easy, but it still took sometime before we got out of the main city and reached an outer well to do area with less traffic. Passing some stately old homes set well back from the road and surrounded by beautiful gardens, we enjoyed our ride. It was warm and humid with a slight breeze coming from the sea. We felt great as we rode along this important road lined with tall palm trees on either side.

We spotted the President's place from a short distance away because there were two armed sentries, one standing on each side of the entrance of a long driveway leading towards the residence. Hong exchanged a few words with the sentries and they saluted when we pushed our bikes past them. We automatically saluted back.

A short distance along the driveway the three of us had to show our passports to a well decorated officer who waited for us outside a small guard house. He shook hands with Hong and us, and said we should leave our bikes there. He also told the Rickshaw rider to wait inside with some guards, and then he accompanied us to the villa to meet the First Lady.

She was so beautiful!

To this very day I have treasured that moment, being welcomed by Indonesia's most powerful Lady, with the biggest smile.

As soon as we walked through a big double doorway into a large foyer with several doors on each side Ibu, —I shall call her Ibu from now on because it means Mother— walked towards us and gave each of us a big handshake while Hong introduced us to her and the others. Yes others... we soon noticed that Ibu was surrounded by some family members and friends all smartly dressed. Not one of the ladies had any head coverings.

We felt instantly at home and were offered a seat at a massive round table stacked with bowls full of different fruits and juices. While we answered lots of questions, Hong kept taking photographs from different angles. After Ibu had written some kind words in our book, Hong handed his camera to one of the ladies to take a photo with him in it.

Theo, Uli and Fred with Indonesia's First Lady, Ibu Fatmawati as she looked through our travel journal. Hong, the reporter stands behind Fred.

Time flew by as we were enjoying ourselves immensely with these beautiful people. If Hong hadn't suggested it was time to leave we would have stayed all day. It certainly was a heartwarming goodbye and everybody wished us the very best and hoped that we would get to the Olympics on time. In front of the Residence, Ibu wanted Hong to take some photos of her with us and our bikes, "to show the President," she said with a big smile.

Fred and Uli with Ibu Fatmawati and our bikes.

Theo with Ibu Fatmawati and a family member.

This is my favourite photo of the First Lady.

Once that was done we followed Hong back to the Uni. and invited him for some coffee or tea, but he declined saying he still had "lots of work to do, an article to write, photos to develop…"

He took Uli's address back home in Germany and promised to send some of the pictures he had taken today. He also wished us all the best, and we promised to keep in touch once we reached Melbourne.

The Principal invited us to his office for tea, anxious to find out about our time with Ibu. He congratulated us for such a successful morning. "The four students who welcomed you at the harbor would like to show you the way out of Djakarta next morning on their bikes. They would like to ride with you as far as Bekasi, if that's okay with you."

"No problem," we told him. "We look forward to having some company on the way out."

"It would certainly be a big help since they know the roads in and out of the city. It would save us a lot of time." Uli said.

He too took Uli's address and told us that he would send a letter for our book home and a copy to his friend in Singapore.

Our bikes were in top condition and packing our luggage wouldn't take too long.

Looking at our map we started to get more exited in the knowledge that after Surabaya we only had to ship over to Bali and hopefully get a coastal ferry to Dili, because it looked as if the closest point to Darwin would be from Timor. Little did we know at that moment that our plans would be shattered once we reached Surabaya.

We packed our luggage and loaded our bikes for an early start in the morning.

Well that was wishful thinking. The four students were waiting for us next to their bikes when we came out, but so was half of the Uni. Students were surrounding the entrance and they all wished us farewell and shook hands with us once more. The Principal, some staff members and a few teachers (especially) the two Dutch ones, insisted on shaking hands as they thanked us for our informative talk and wished us all the best. We of course responded by thanking them for their hospitality and so by the time we finally jumped on our bikes it was well after mid-morning and very humid.

Having the four students guide us through the traffic and out of the city was certainly appreciated; it saved us a lot of trouble asking for directions and we made good time.

Bekasi was only about forty kilometres ahead and our students really put on a great performance. They wanted to show us how good they were and for a while kept up a good pace in front of us, but after about ten kilometres they started to slow down, and halfway to Bekasi we shot past them, and after a couple of kilometres they were so far behind we had to stop so they could catch up.

"You don't need to accompany us all the way to Bekasi," Uli told them.

"If you do," Theo added, "you probably won't make it back before nightfall."

They seemed relieved to hear this. It was obvious if they continued as they were, they would only hold us up. The ride was harder than they had expected. They already looked exhausted, but had been embarrassed to give up. Once we told them they should go back, that we would be fine, they perked dup and wished us all the best.

We watched them ride back towards the city and finally we were by ourselves again.

By the time we hit Bekasi it was hot and very humid. We stopped at the first shady eating place to sit out the worst of the heat. Bekasi was just a small town, very clean, mostly Muslims, but with lots of Dutch European flavor. The thing we noticed straight away, even though we got some stares and smiles, was we didn't get pestered and could relax.

We didn't feel much like eating, but had some fruit and a couple of Pepsis anyway. Once we had cooled down a bit we went on to the next town. The forty-five km to Cikampek were no problem, except Uli had another front wheel puncture only ten km out of Bekasi, but we still made Cikampek well before sunset.

We could have gone on for another hour towards Subang City and camp off the road, but decided to lash out and look for a hotel because money was no problem. At the first one we stopped they looked at us as if we were ghosts. They had no room for the three of us but pointed further down the street to a bigger more modern hotel which we soon found out was managed by a Dutch couple.

Even though it was probably the best hotel in town and after everyone had wondered where we came from, we were told at the reception by the Dutch gentleman that we could stay. The price wasn't too expensive and we were helped with our luggage and led to a family room on the ground floor which had a double bed, two singles, one on top of each other, with an adjacent toilet and bathroom. Our bikes could be stored safely at the back of the hotel in a storeroom. After a shower and a change of clothes, we were ready to hit the dining room, for a well-earned dinner and some pipes.

By this time the sun had set. It was still very humid and warm, but sitting under the cooling fans hanging from the ceilings we felt quite comfortable. The dining room was situated in another section of the hotel with big glass doors open onto a beautiful terrace. It was surrounded by big terracotta pots, each with different exotic flowers planted in them.

The dining room was already half occupied by the time we entered. We were led to a small table on the terrace by the Dutch lady who also acted as a waitress. We did get a few stares from guests at other tables, but nowhere near as bad as what we were used to and that suited us fine. The lady handed us the menu, which was a double-sided sheet of white paper with the different dishes written by hand in Indonesian, Dutch and English.

There were several Dutch specialties, like pickled herring fillets with different salads and hard-boiled eggs, or whole smoked herring and mackerel, all with mouthwatering condiments. Most of the dishes were Indonesian and every dish was accompanied by specially prepared rice.

We really enjoyed the way our meals were served on small trays from which we helped ourselves and we could choose whether we wanted chop sticks, or a knife and fork. We chose the latter. With beautifully mixed fruits for dessert, cups of tea and a couple of pipes afterwards, we felt blessed.

We were up early the next morning so we could head to Cirebon, about 150 km away, before the morning heated up too much. Once the sun got up and the humidity settled, riding bikes was a very sticky business. We were hardly dressed when there was a loud knock on the door. Theo opened it and the broadly smiling Dutch owner walked in to our room.

"Good morning gentlemen," he said cheerfully as he held up an opened newspaper with Ibu and us on page three.

He was very excited. "You have to stay another night," he said, so he and their guests could get to know us better and listen to our story in more detail.

Naturally we told him that we would love to stay, but we were running short of time and had to get to Australia as soon as we could. We still had a long way to go.

It was a great photo with Ibu in the middle holding our book. Uli was behind her with the officer on his left and Hong on his right. Theo and I stood either side of her. The article was written in Indonesian and the owner of the hotel told us it was very good.

This was not expected, because we hadn't thought that Hong would write about us so soon. It pleased us immensely that our fame had reached as far as this small town.

The Dutch proprietor and his wife insisted that we have breakfast with them. They understood that our time was limited, and regretted that they hadn't realized this the day before or they would have asked more questions so they could get to know us better.

It was a big breakfast and when we were ready to pay for our bill and jump on our bikes, we only had to pay for the room. Just before waving goodbye our Dutch host handed Theo the newspaper and told us he would get some more.

Subang City was only about 40 km ahead. The road was hilly but we still made good time and stopped there only for a drink and a brief rest, but amazingly we got lots of smiles, waves with people pointing towards us. We smiled back.

It was still sometime before midday, but we knew that the further 100 km Cirebon would be no easy matter, especially in the heat and humidity.

I find it difficult to write about my feelings for Indonesia; it was somehow strange, but not strange in a bad way, on the contrary, it was strange in a very positive way! It was totally different to the other countries we had passed through, much more subdued, much quieter, no over laden busses or dangerously driven trucks and no screaming or yelling, but hard-working people, getting on well with each other. They must have been very religious, because every larger town we came through had several Mosques, Temples and the odd Church.

The first couple of hours out of Subang City were hilly and tough, but the road was good and the traffic manageable. It was very warm and getting warmer and incredibly humid as soon as we got on to the open plains where there were rice fields as far as the eyes could see. Water was certainly no problem with all the small creeks we had to cross and for a few hours we followed a long river, with heaps of palm trees planted on either side. Like in India we saw farmers leading buffalos plowing fields half submerged in water, with women and children following and planting rice. With only about 30 km to Cirebon, we stopped at a truck repair and petrol station to replenish our water supply and have a couple of Pepsis.

We made Cirebon well before sunset, sweaty, uncomfortable and sliding from one side of our saddles to the other, (in later years the Aussies would call it sweaty balls) but we congratulated ourselves for one of our longest days. Still, it was great to see the blue waters of the Java sea in the distance again.

Cirebon City seemed to be larger than Cikampek, with lots of very busy shops, several markets, beautiful old buildings, people everywhere. The air had a slight smell of fish mixed with a salty sea breeze, a nice change from the moldy smell of wet jungle. We soon discovered that Cirebon City's main industry was fishing.

This time it was harder to find a hotel because more people were recognizing us, wanted to talk to us, especially when we pushed our bikes along the foot path when the road became congested. Finally, we asked someone where to find a good hotel, but still had to walk a fair distance, before we came to most likely the best hotel in town. It was set not far from the road, surrounded by big palm trees with a wide cobblestone driveway leading to the front entrance.

We were greeted and welcomed by an immaculately dressed Indonesian gentleman in a white uniform. He introduced himself as the head porter and was happy that we had chosen this hotel because lots of people here had read about us in today's paper. We parked our bikes near the main entrance, as always, like a pyramid with one standing upright and the other two leaning on each side of it, (they always stood very solid). The porter called over two other uniformed men and told them to stand watch by our bikes while he led us inside to the reception.

This welcome was totally different to the one from the night before in Cicampek, where they hadn't heard of us until this morning. As soon as we walked through the big entrance towards the reception desk several men, some in uniforms, others in European suits and a couple of gorgeous looking Indonesian ladies dressed in national costume, smiled and welcomed us. One of the suited gentlemen introduced himself as the manager and he would make sure, he told us, that our stay in his hotel would be a happy one. He also told us that we would be his guests for dinner once we had checked in to our room and refreshed.

"Refreshed is the right word," Uli said. "We need to get rid of the sweat and grime after our long ride."

Everything went like a charm. While our bikes and luggage were brought into the foyer, we had to fill out a small form. Our passports numbers were registered which was the first time in Indonesia. We didn't even ask about the price of the room, all we wanted was to get under a shower.

We were given another big family room and our luggage was brought in on a small trolley and laid out on one of the spare beds, all without us doing a thing. Our bikes, we were told by the porter with a big smile, had been stored at a safe place and monitored.

"*Heid wirds deior*" Uli said, "*it's going to be costly.*" "*abor bei so amma servis isch des scheisegal*" "*but with a service like this, who gives a crap.*"

He stripped off and was first in the shower before Theo and I had even started to take off our grimy clothes.

It took about an hour before we were in our 'evening attire', starving and making our way back to reception. In front of the big reception desk were our bikes leaning one behind the other, with a couple of receptionists telling guests who were admiring them about the bike's story. As soon as we started walking towards them we were bombarded with questions which we were happy to answer.

Word had spread like wildfire that the foreign bike riders who had met The First Lady were here, and by the time the manager, his lovely wife and two young sons led us to the big dining room, it was packed. With smiles and waves all around us, we were led to a big round table, half occupied by couples introduced to us by the manager.

It was a wonderful evening with all these lovely people, answering so many questions and stuffing ourselves with delicious food, served in lots of small bowls and one pot of tea after another. Enjoying a couple of pipes afterwards we answered plenty more questions about our lives in Germany, our adventure and a lot of questions were asked how we met Ibu. Even guests from other tables joined in and eventually everyone wished us all the best, a safe journey to Australia and by the time we hit the sack we were stuffed.

Along the way from Djakarta to Surabaya

Theo sampling some bananas in one of the many villages we passed through.

Sometimes it was hard to leave a village as we always had crowds of people wanting to know all about us.

After a well-deserved good night's sleep, we were looking forward to reaching Tegal City 80 km further along by midday. Our host invited us for breakfast but we had to decline and thanked him again for the lovely evening we'd had.

Surprise, surprise, by the time we were packed, ready to leave and wanted to pay our bill, it was only a small amount. "Just to keep the books in order," we were told.

We thanked everyone, waved goodbye and headed towards the open sea, towards Tegal City.

It was quite enjoyable riding with a slight breeze coming from the sea not too far away. We had to go slow in places because of road works. Stopping at a couple of very small townships for refreshments we still made Tegal City before midday for a good brunch, in a small restaurant by the sea.

Looking at our map we decided to make the other 70 km to Pekalongan City and book into a hotel before it became too hot and humid. It would be easier then to travel 90 km to Semarang City the next morning.

We had been spoiled by soft hotel beds and hot showers and no longer felt like camping by the roadside anymore.

Filling our bottles with clean water and paying our bill we headed for Pekalongan City.

Everywhere we went, wherever we stopped or stayed, we were made very welcome, and this was certainly because of our meeting with the First Lady Ibu, with her kind words and reported in the newspaper article along with our photograph in the paper.

Initially it was a pleasant ride by the sea. For a couple of hours and we made a fair distance until the road turned towards some kind of jungle, with huge trees and a dense canopy where the sun had no chance of filtering through. It seemed as if we were riding through a dark tunnel. The cars and trucks on the road couldn't see without using their headlights. It became very dangerous because drivers on that road would not be expecting people to be riding bikes. With the likelihood of being hit from behind by a truck we had to switch on our dynamos to have both head and taillights working or else no one would see us in the darkness.

Thankfully the traffic moved at a relative slow pace and everyone was watching out for each other. I must say, as dangerous as it was, we didn't come across one accident, or anyone yelling at each other. Finally, out of the tunnel we were greeted by a not very friendly sky and it looked as if there was some bad weather behind us. Before we had turned into the jungle there had been masses of cumulus clouds in the sky, but now they had turned into big black rain clouds ready to drop their load.

After several kilometres we came to a wide river spanned by a single lane bridge. There were trucks, busses and cars banked up for a long way on either side. At both ends of the bridge there were uniformed men holding walky-talkies sorting out how many could cross at any one time. Lucky for us we could weave through the traffic and join a group of motor bikes in front to get through with the next lot. You could smell the rain in the air and the river under the bridge was a series of swirling dirty brown whirlpools. You wouldn't want to fall in, that's for sure.

We had less than 10 km to go once we crossed the bridge and we peddled like we hadn't peddled for a long time to reach Pekalongan City, which we did and found a hotel just before the rain and the storm hit. It came down in buckets and seemed as if it would never stop. Had we not made it on time, I think we would have been in big trouble.

This hotel was no match to the one we stayed at the last two nights, but we were incredibly happy to have a roof over our heads. This hotel was managed or owned by a Chinese family and every one, workers or guests, looked Chinese. We were greeted with big smiles and were told in broken English, that they only had two rooms available, both with two single beds. At that moment, we couldn't give a hoot, even if we had to take three rooms, it was only for one night and we needed a good rest.

It was a fairly old hotel but well looked after and spotlessly clean. Both our rooms were opposite each other. We didn't have to show our passports, nor did we have to fill out any forms and nobody asked us where we came from or where we wanted to go. Of course, it had to do with the language, not understanding each other very well. There were strange looks when we unloaded our bikes and pushed them in to our rooms; Uli in one room with two bikes, Theo and I with one in the other.

By the time we had a shower and felt better we were looking forward to dinner and a couple of pipes. We were disappointed when we finally sat at a one of the dining room tables and were told they don't have water pipes, only cigars and cigarettes. We each lit a fag, looked around the room and to our surprise, saw other guests drinking beer.

"Yes," the waiter said. "It's Chinese beer."

"We have to try this," Uli said laughing and ordered one for me, one for himself and a Pepsi for Theo.

What a great drop this beer turned out to be. It tasted just as good as ours back home and in my latter years I drank it often with some of my friends. Most of the dishes had photographs on the menu so we had no difficulty ordering a couple of different ones with steamed rice on the side.

It turned out to be a very quiet, relaxing evening. We were not being bothered by anyone. Even though we had some stares when we entered people quickly lost interest and turned back to what they were doing. We couldn't tell what language the diners were using only that it wasn't Indonesian. It sounded different. We didn't use German either, we spoke in our Swabisch dialect as we discussed what lay ahead of us.

We felt great next morning and ready for another long ride. We were happy that we had stayed at this particular hotel because we'd had a beautifully undisturbed night's sleep and felt completely rested. Paying our bill before leaving we were pleasantly surprised. We had occupied two rooms but they only charged us for one. In any other more modern hotel we would have paid for using two rooms.

It had stopped raining during the night but when we left the hotel early in the morning it was still very overcast and humid. It certainly looked like it would rain at any moment which was not a pleasant aspect to look forward to as we started to ride out of town. We had about 100 km to Semarang ahead of us.

Batang City was only about 10 km from Pekalongan, but we still stopped for breakfast and to fill our water supply. We had been told that except for a few small villages, there would be nowhere to get food or drink. And there were lots of road works all the way to Semarang.

Most of the way to Semarang was a small nightmare. For the majority of the distance the road surface was gravel, relatively smooth, but hard to ride on while it was wet because the wheels tended to sink in a bit. There were many potholes and corrugated surfaces caused by rain runoff and traffic, and we kept expecting to get a puncture or two. Surprisingly none of us got any punctures. Every so often we rode past road workers repairing pot holes, by shoveling gravel from the side of the road where it had been washed away into the holes to fill them. They tapped it flat with their shovels, but I figured that when the rain came down again all their work would be washed away.

We were travelling in an easterly direction not far from the sea and were told by one of the road workers who could speak some English that a big highway was being built a few kilometres inland. Once that was done this road would be forgotten about. It wasn't until we reached Kendal, that the road got better and the last 20 km to Semarang had a bitumen surface which made it much easier on us.

Semarang was a small town, living mainly off sea produce. However, there were rice fields everywhere and lots of great fruits. There were two small hotels in town. At the first one we had no luck, but the second one had no problem finding us a couple of rooms. It was owned by an Indonesian family and they were very excited as soon as they spotted us riding towards their hotel, because they too had read the newspaper article.

Several of the younger people spoke reasonably good English and we felt instantly at home. No show of passports, nor did we have to fill out any paperwork and we could see that they were happy accommodating us. The rooms were simple, but very clean and it didn't take long before we had a refreshing shower.

On the way to Semarang...

A Market in Semarang *Washing clothes along the roadside*

This one was a Muslim hotel. Most of the men and women were dressed in traditional costumes and all the women had their heads covered. We were invited for a couple of pipes in the dining room, with tea and later on for some dinner. By the time big round tin plates full of different dishes were served the dining room was full. Every man and his dog had heard that we stayed in this place and they all wanted to hear our story.

Again, we had a great evening and again we only had to pay for one room, but were told that the road towards Kudus City was constantly under repairs, especially the stretch after that to Rembang. They were right. The 60 km to Kudus, with Theo having a puncture on his rear wheel, took over three hours before we finally saw the town. We were stuffed when we got there, not so much from riding our bikes, but more from frustration, the humidity and the road works. To top it all off, we had just missed a barge that would take us across a big river, because the new bridge they were building further up was only half finished and was not usable. We had to wait several hours for it to come back so it could repeat the crossing.

When we finally got to Rembang it was already late afternoon and we needed a shower as soon as possible. Not far from the small harbor we found one managed by a Dutch gentleman and his Indonesian wife and they too were pleased to have us as their guests.

Once again there was no paperwork to be filled in, nor passports to be shown, but there was the promise of a nice cool beer before dinner. A big family room with a spare bed for our luggage and our bikes leaning against the wall in the corridor, was all we needed. Uli and I were certainly looking forward to our promised cool beer and as soon as we had our shower, the three of us marched over to the dining room to sit with our Host and family. The beer was Golsch and we had to put a small bit of ice in a big glass to keep it cool. Theo got a pineapple juice and he was happy with that. In one way it was quite amusing, in a Moslem hotel only there was only tea or coffee, but in a Christian one, there was as much alcoholic drinks as one wanted.

After a great dinner, a couple of pipes and answering lots of questions, we slept well, but we weren't looking forward to the next day. The same story; the road towards Tuban was always under repair, because it was still a long way off before before the new highway would finished. And we still had to cross several big rivers by barge, something we weren't looking forward to if our previous crossing was anything to judge by.

The Big Adventure

After paying only for our room we got away early next morning and even riding on the bad road, we still made the 20 km to Lasem for an early breakfast without any problems.

The next 80 km towards Tuban were tough!

Firstly, we had to ride several kilometres along the side of a mountain covered in tropical jungle before we reached the sea again, and the road works were never ending. I lost count of how many small creeks with bridges we crossed. Four big rivers also had to be crossed on barges before we finally reached Tuban City. It must have taken us close to six hours for the 80 km and it was already late afternoon before we found a hotel, again managed by Dutch people.

The hospitality was the same as the previous nights and even this far away from Djakarta people still wanted to know how we met Ibu and we still answered dozens of questions during and after dinner. After a good night's sleep in a big family room, the owners insisted that we have a big breakfast in the morning. Apparently, there were only a few small villages on the way to Gresik City 70 km ahead. We were each given a small parcel of different fruits, some flat bread, all wrapped in banana leaves and our bottles were filled with fresh orange juice when we paid for our room. The owners never charged for the dinner the night before and they were making certain we would have enough provisions to see us through the roadworks on the road ahead. How good was that?

It was a threatening day, humid and hot with rain clouds covering the sky, and the thought of how much we would sweat in the humidity was depressing, but we pushed don regardless.

About 10 km from Tuban the road veered away from the sea and we had to ride through solid jungle on bad roads. To top it off, I copped a small screw in my front tire and had to pump it up several times before we reached another big river, where I could mend it while we waited for the barge to take us across to Brondong by the sea.

Even though Brondong was a small village it still had a market where we could refill our bottles and being next to the sea, a slight breeze from the water was highly appreciated. The next 20 km to Pedesan were relatively comfortable and we reached it by midday. We finished our food parcels, filled our bottles and set off for our next leg to Gresik, 30 km further ahead with a quarter of it through jungle again.

As soon as we entered the jungle it got so humid we were instantly covered in sweat. Travelling in a southerly direction, away from the sea, there wasn't a breath of wind and riding on the muddy road took every skill we had mastered to stay on the bikes. About 20 km before Gresik we had to cross another big river by barge and were lucky to be the last passengers on board without having to wait. We reached Gresik by mid-afternoon for a well-deserved cold fruit juice and a pipe. From there, the 25 km to Surabaya were a breeze. With lots of traffic on a double road we had an easy ride. Finally, we had reached civilization again, plus it didn't rain.

Uli and me somewhere near Semarang with two beautiful friends.

Chapter Twelve

I always have fond memories of Surabaya, especially when I remember that a beautiful young lady, half Dutch half Indonesian fell madly in love with me...

We found a nice hotel near the center of town, but as soon as we got off our bikes and pushed them towards the entrance we were greeted by several men and women dressed in white uniforms. It must have been eight or nine days since the article appeared in the newspaper, but these people acted as if it was from this morning. They told us that they were very happy that we picked this hotel. By the time we finally reached reception to be greeted by the Dutch manager we had about a dozen people around us.

It was getting on dark and we desperately needed a shower and our dirty clothes washed. No problem the manager said and his Indonesian wife told us that we could have a big family room and our washing would be ready again by the morning.

Here we had to show our passports and fill in some documentation, but we never asked why we didn't have to do that at some of the other hotels we stayed at.

We were pretty knackered after a hard and sweaty day and spent a long time under the shower. I must say we were rather elated afterwards, because we felt reaching Surabaya had taken an almighty effort. We had to celebrate with a good meal and a couple of drinks. We also felt that we were closer to reaching our goal, especially if we could get a freighter to Denpasar and on to Dilli.

A knock on the door, and our dirty washing was picked up and taken away. Another knock straight afterwards and the manager was at the door asking us if our bikes could be shown at reception and if he and his family could invite us for dinner in the dining room.

"Thanks for inviting us," Uli said. "We're just about ready to come down anyway… and we don't mind you showing our bikes at reception. They are a bit dirty and do need to be serviced, but if you want people to see them…"

The dining room was full and everyone sitting at the tables smiled as we passed. Some people even waved and said something in Indonesian which we didn't understand, but it sounded very friendly.

The manager and his wife were standing with several people next to a long table at the far end of the dining room and after introducing us begged everyone to be seated. Like every evening in hotels we stayed at this one turned out to be just as good. The food was great, the Grolsch went down well, and the couple of pipes afterwards made us feel very relaxed. We answered every question and even signed a couple of the articles which someone had handed to the manager from one of the other tables. By the time we got to bed we felt great.

The next morning, after our washing was brought to the room we went down to talk to the manager.

"We would like to stay a few more nights here," I told him.

"That's wonderful," he said. "You're very welcome."

"We need some directions to get to the harbor," Theo said.

"Because we want to find a freighter that can take us to Dili," Uli added, "or at least to Denpasar where we could find another ship to take us to Timor."

"I think you should go to the police headquarters and ask there. They will give you the best advice."

"Is it far from here?"

"I think you should take a rickshaw. It is a long walk."

We grabbed our book, passports, a couple of cards and got a rickshaw right outside the hotel.

It felt great, being in freshly washed clothes and in civilization again after the long journey from Djakarta and we were looking forward to exploring Surabaya with its many different nationalities, Mosques, Temples, Churches, and so much different Asian and European architecture.

Police headquarters was next to what looked like parliament house or the town hall in a beautiful old double story building. There were a couple of police cars and some motorbikes parked in front. I paid the rickshaw and we entered the cool stone building, where a uniformed policeman who couldn't speak English begged us to follow him. He guided us towards an office door, put up his hand to motion us to wait and without knocking, entered. After a short time the door opened and our guide begged us to enter and left.

We found ourselves in a medium sized room relatively well furnished with a big photo of President Sukarno and Ibu hanging on one of the walls. We were greeted by five police officers, three men and two good looking policewomen all dressed in immaculate uniforms, all of whom spoke good English. The oldest of the men had several medals on his uniform and it turned out he was the sergeant.

They knew who we were before we even introduced ourselves.

"Welcome," the sergeant said. He pointed to the picture on the wall. We all read the article about you meeting our First Lady."

The sergeant offered us a seat at a big conference table and after a short while the policemen who had brought us to this room entered with a couple of glass jugs full of fresh fruit juice. Before we could say what we wanted we had to answer, as so often, questions about our journey, but more specifically they wanted to know about us and our meeting with Ibu. While we were still answering questions, a tall Chinese man dressed in a European suit entered and introduced himself as Dr. Oen Hok Sing, Doctor of Police and also asked some questions. By the time we finally were asked why we were here, a few more men and a couple of women had entered.

"We are hoping to get a coastal freighter to Denpasar and on to Dili" Uli said. "Looking at our maps, it seems to be the best way to get to Darwin. They told us at the hotel to come and ask you for advice."

Suddenly there were no more smiling faces. The Sergeant asked if he could look at our Passports. We handed them to him and he showed the others a couple of empty pages and they all conversed in Indonesian.

"Firstly, you don't have a Portuguese visa for entering East Timor. You can't get this here. You must go to Djakarta."

Our faces started to fall.

"And secondly, travelling down there is absolutely too dangerous."

"What do you suggest we do then?" Uli asked.

"There are only two ways to get to Australia," Dr Sing said. "Either by plane from Djakarta to Darwin, or by ship to Perth. To do either you will have to go back to Djakarta."

Well, this was certainly a blow to our plans. The thought of riding all the way back after what we'd been through to get here was certainly depressing.

"And one other thing," Dr Sing added, "You also need two inoculations which I see you haven't had yet." He was looking at our medical book and not the passports. "They won't let you enter if haven't had them. My advice is that you stay here a few days while I organize the inoculations for you. Once that's done and I have signed the certificates, you can catch a train back to Djakarta and try your luck there."

By this time our heads were spinning, especially when one other elderly Dutch gentlemen in European clothes introduced himself as the official Police Dentist and kindly offered us a furnished house next to his for a few days. Thankfully someone offered us a cigarette to calm our nerves.

The Dutch Dentist, Dr. Janssen, was married to an Indonesian and they had German neighbors who were on a vacation in Germany and their house was empty except for the house keeper. He told us we would be more than welcome to stay there for a few days so we could save on hotel expenses.

It was hard to take it all in and we still felt quite stunned. Going back to Djakarta was difficult to accept, but at least there was a train we could take for the return trip so we didn't have to ride.

The decision was a foregone conclusion; we would take a rickshaw back to the hotel, check out and ride our bikes back to the police station where we would have some lunch after which we would follow Dr Janssen back to his house next door to the vacant house belonging to the German couple on holiday in Europe.

The hotel manager was disappointed that we were leaving, but pleased that we had such a good reception at the police station. Packing was quick and at the reception our smiling host pointed towards the wall behind him and there was our article framed and hanging on the wall. He only charged us a small amount as a book keeping fee, rather than charging us for the room.

A bit over half an hour when we got back, a big table was set chock-o-block full with deliciously smelling food. There were still half of the people present to enjoy the food with us, our doctor and dentist included. Our bikes stood upright in front of the building, watched by several police and admired by a small crowd of onlookers while we were stuffing ourselves inside. Dr. Sing was going to give us our first injection the next day and the other one the day after. That meant that we had to stay in Surabaya for at least another three days.

Once the food was almost gone Dr. Janssen grabbed a rickshaw and we followed him on our bikes to his house. It was only about three kilometres away and we had no problem following him, but half way there he stopped in front of a stone building and told us to wait for a couple of minutes. Apparently here was his dental surgery, where at the Police station he only had a small consulting room. He came back less than five minutes later and found we already had a small crowd around us wondering who we were.

Ten minutes later we turned into a no-through road with houses on one side and lovely gardens on the other. Half way along we stopped in front of a big old house surrounded by palm trees and what looked like garden plots with lots of different herbs and vegetables. Dr. Janssen paid the rickshaw driver, opened a big garage door next to the house where we could store our bikes and motioned us to follow him into the house.

The house looked a bit like an old-timer from the outside, but it was totally modern on the inside and the best of all, we were greeted by three beautiful ladies, Mrs. Janssen and their two daughters. Mrs. Janssen was approximately my mother's age. The eldest daughter, Kemala, was a year younger than me, and her sister was another year younger again. Why I remember Kemala's name is simple, she smiled like a goddess, looked like a star, and over the next few days fell very much in love with me.

Seated in the shade at the back of the house some cool juices were served by an elderly housekeeper and his wife, while Dr. Janssen told them what he knew about us so far. He spoke in a mixture of Dutch and Indonesian, but a short time later we all spoke English and the questions never stopped. Kemala conveniently sat opposite me and never stopped smiling. Every time she asked a question it was always directed at me. By the time we were shown the house next door and moved our luggage into it, the sun was nearly setting.

As soon as we entered the house we thought we were in Germany. There were photographs from all over Germany hanging on every wall, and it looked as if most of the furniture came from Germany as well. Dr. Janssen introduced us also to an elderly couple, who were the housekeepers and lived in a small house in the back yard. It was a large home, very comfortable with four bedrooms, three of them with separate showers and sit-down toilets. The main bedroom also had a bathtub. A very large living and dining room with separate kitchen, plus a small office made the house seem bigger inside than it appeared from the outside. How lucky we were to be able to stay in a place like this!

Every bedroom had at least two single beds, one even had three and that was the one for us, even though we were offered one each, we felt we should only use the one with three beds so as not to abuse the hospitality.

Inside the house Kemala had not left my side and asked me lots of questions about my private life and I happily answered. It was obvious that she had a bit of a crush on me. We hardly got organized and were left alone for a short while, when Kemala came back to let us know that her mother had the table set for dinner and wanted us to join them.

By now our heads were really spinning; we simply couldn't get over so much hospitality. What would the future bring?

It had been a terrible feeling when we found out that we were unable to continue the way we had planned. It would have been the greatest disappointment of all time if we got stuck in Indonesia and somehow had to find a way back home again. But there was nothing we could do other than to make the best of our stay in Surabaya. We could worry about making new plans when we got back to Djakarta.

After a relaxing evening with several different tasty dishes, we enjoyed ourselves immensely and really got to know this lovely family. By the time we finally got to bed we were exhausted. It took me a long time to go to sleep with too many things to digest and of course thinking of beautiful Kemala. During the evening Dr. Janssen had suggested we should take a rickshaw sometime in the morning to Police headquarters for our first injection.

I can't remember what the other two injections were for, because the German Dr. in Yazd had given us Small Pox, Cholera and Typhoid.

He welcomed us next morning in his small office next to a fairly large operating room and had one of his secretaries order some tea for the four of us. Yes, four of us, because Kemala insisted she come along to take us to the movies afterwards. Apparently, she had already seen it and it was called Artists and Models, with Jerry Lewis, Dean Martin, Dorothy Malone and Shirley MacLaine. We had never heard of them, but she said it was very funny. Little did we know that those stars would be part of our lives over the next fifty years.

It certainly was a funny movie, even though it was dubbed in Indonesian, with Dutch sub titles below. (But over the next few years I got to see the original American version twice more in Melbourne.) The best

With the very lovely Kemala who fell madly in love with me.

part for me was sitting next to Kemala, holding hands and rubbing knees. The next couple of days were sheer bliss for me because Kemala hardly moved from my side and I would have loved to stay for another month or two longer.

As soon as we had our last injections the following morning and our booklets stamped by Dr. Sing we went to the railway station with Kemala as interpreter to find out about a train to Djakarta. There were several to choose from but only one of them did a direct route to Djakarta, stopping only in some of the bigger towns. That was the one for us, leaving at two pm the day after tomorrow. We bought the tickets but had to pay extra for first class with sleeping compartments for two nights. It made a big hole into our finances, but we could exchange more US dollars in Djakarta.

This meant we would be one extra day in Surabaya, and that made Kemala and me very happy. She informed us that her parents thought we would leave the next day and had booked out a big Chinese Restaurant for this evening. They wanted some of their friends and relatives to meet us, plus several people from Police headquarters and their families also came along.

It wasn't a huge restaurant but by the time we had arrived there was only one unoccupied table for our hosts and us left. What a welcome; so many hands had to be shaken from young and old, male and female, different ethnic backgrounds and different religions. It was overwhelming and it must have been close to half an hour before we finally got seated.

Lots of different dishes with delicious tasting food were served and we had no problem keeping up with everyone using our chop sticks. It was an unforgettable evening and in later years we often talked about it and the great hospitality we received in Surabaya as a whole. After answering lots of questions, it was fairly late by the time everyone wished us well for the rest of our journey and hoped we would get to the Olympics on time. We were the last ones to leave with our hosts and we were happy, when we finally got back.

Having more less a free day, we got stuck into our bikes after breakfast next morning to give them a good clean and service, plus our house keepers offered to wash some of our clothes and to clean our sleeping bags. After lunch Uli and Theo decided they would write some letters home and cards to some of the people we had promised on our way, while Kemala would show me parts of Surabaya.

Kemala about to hop into the rickshaw she organized for the two of us. Being small it meant we had to sit very close to each other.

The beautiful carving of Balinese Dancers that Kemala sent to Germany for me.

Kemala and I jumped into a rickshaw and she showed me half of Surabaya, led me through several markets and even brought me a present; two beautiful Balinese dancers carved out of black wood weighing close to three kg.

"There's no way I can carry that with me on a bike." I wanted to convince her not to buy it.

"I'll send it to Germany by post, and you can collect it when you get home again."

Which she did by the way. It took close to thirty years before I was able to bring it back to Australia and it has a special place in our home.

We had a wonderful afternoon together and made it back just in time for dinner with her family and my friends. Of course Uli and Theo wanted to know whether something unusual had happened while we were alone for such a long time, but a gentleman never tells. I kept them guessing!

It was a sad farewell next day at the railway station, before we boarded the train to say goodbye.

Packing didn't take long and loading our bikes after breakfast was no problem. Saying good bye and accepting all the well whishes from the family and their neighbors, even some friends from the night before, took a long time. Finally, we rode along following three rickshaws with the whole family guiding us to the station where we had less than an hour before departure.

Several guys in uniform stored our bikes in a lock up room before leading us to our compartment where there was plenty of storage space for our luggage.

One last hug to all and a long cuddle between Kemala and me. I had to promise her a hundred times that I would keep in touch, then with a couple of whistles from the steam engine we boarded and waved back to Surabaya which to this day I have never forgotten.

I never thought at the time, that thirty years later I would export canned Abalone, my own 'Ocean Gold' Brand, for several years to Surabaya. Unfortunately, I never managed to get back there again, but returning has always been on my bucket list.

It was a very modern train and our two first class wagons were less than fifty percent occupied, and all the way to Djakarta we had one compartment for ourselves. There was a dining room, open twenty-four hours, and a sleeper compartments with beds on each side of the gangway. Two on top of each other, secured through a pull-down curtain, also several toilets and shower rooms.

It took some time, before we actually realized that we were leaving Surabaya with its wonderful people. We were preoccupied with the grinding thought that plagued us for the last few days; what will happen in Djakarta and will we ever make it to Melbourne?

Being on a fast-moving train with nothing to do other than stare out at the passing landscape we finally settled down and enjoyed some of the tropical fruit Mrs. Janssen had given Uli wrapped in a parcel just before we boarded the train.

We checked out the dining room and decided to spend most of the time at one of the tables writing letters and postcards while enjoying the landscape and being by ourselves again. After an hour the train stopped for a short while to take on cargo and several passengers. After that it didn't stop until we got to Madun.

Moments after we stopped it got dark. In the tropics as soon as the sun goes down it almost instantly goes dark. We never quite get used to that. Anyway, we enjoyed a dinner of nasi goreng mixed with finely cut meats and veggies. The dining room was only half full with different Nationals, but mainly Indonesians with families. Watching the activity on the station through the windows we couldn't figure out why the train had stopped for so long at Madun.

Theo asked one of the waiters and he told us that the train would be there until midnight. That's all he knew. "If you would like to go to bed, you can do so at any time."

"We might just do that," I said. I asked him for the bill and was pleasantly surprised when I saw how little it was, definitely no rip-off.

After a cramped shower in the small bathroom I climbed into the top bunk. Theo took the one below, Uli the one on the opposite side. I don't know about them but it didn't take me long to fall into a deep sleep. I just felt a small jolt when the train started again, but went back to sleep instantly and didn't wake up until we reached Surakarta early in the morning.

By the time Theo and I got up Uli's bunk was empty. We found him enjoying breakfast and writing postcards in the dining room. Breakfast was included in the ticket price, only lunch and dinner were charged separately. We certainly took advantage of this and had as big a breakfast as we could so we could skip lunch.

Meeting new friends on the train... here I am telling these lovely ladies all about our travels.

There was another long halt and Theo and I stepped out on to the platform to see why. There were masses of people everywhere carrying all kinds of goods passing them up to be loaded on to the train. There were also more passengers getting on. Truck after truck pulled up loaded with goods which had to be emptied on to the freight wagons. It was steaming hot with the air so damp and heavy we could hardly breathe. We watched for a while, but the stifling heat was too much and we got back into the train where our first-class room at least had circulating fans overhead which made it quite bearable, especially with the doors closed.

Late afternoon we finally arrived in Yogyakarta, a relatively big town, and had another long wait, but by now we were used to it. Yogyakarta certainly played some importance to me fifteen years later when our great friend Konrad came to visit and stayed with us for three months. Konrad was a stonemason and had a two-year contract through UNESCO to restore the Borobudur Temple, just a short distance north east of Yogyakarta. Borobudur is the world's biggest and most beautiful Buddhist Temple and we were so close to it but had no idea of its existence at the time when we were there in the train.

It was another long night but after a good night's sleep we arrived in Bandung very early and halted only for a couple of hours. By the time we'd had a leisurely breakfast, it was time to get our gear together and as the train continued on to Djakarta we wondered what the next few days will bring.

The station in Djakarta was huge and there were people everywhere. It took a while before we were sorted out and had our bikes organized and packed. Feeling a bit lost we weren't sure what to do. Arriving by ship as we had done before and with people waiting for us had been a lovely welcome, but this time there was no one expecting us. The station was so large we didn't even know which way to find the best exit.

"We should ask one of the stewards on the train," Uli said, so Theo and I stood by our bikes while Uli headed back to the train.

I was just thinking we would have to change some dollars because we were running out of Rupiah when Uli reappeared. "He said we should try Hotel des Indes. It's not too far from the center of town."

We got out of the station and approached the first rickshaw driver we saw. There was a long line of them waiting for passengers. He knew the way to the Hotel des Indes and in very broken English we explained that we wanted him to lead the way so we could follow on our bikes. After telling us the price we agreed without bargaining and had no problem following him through the busy traffic. After a couple of kilometres he stopped in front of the driveway to a very good-looking Hotel, which we thought would probably be too expensive for us.

As soon as we paid the rickshaw driver he turned and vanished, and we had no option but to walk our bikes up the driveway to the hotel front entrance. A couple of uniformed guys came out of the reception.

"Welcome to our hotel," one of them said in good English.

"You made a very good choice," the other one added. Both were smiling expansively.

"Not so fast," Uli said. "Firstly, we have to find out the price, and then we shall decide what to do."

"Please follow us," one said while the other added, "you won't be disappointed."

Theo and I stayed with our bikes while Uli followed the two guys in to the reception, taking along our book and a couple of cards.

We had two smokes before Uli and a European dressed man, followed by the two uniformed guys finally came back out, all smiles. The European dressed man was no other than a German from Friesland, the north eastern part of Germany and was the Director of the Hotel. He greeted us in his home dialect. He came from Shortens and had a contract for five years to build this hotel into a successful enterprise.

He remembered the newspaper article very well and was surprised to meet up with us, thinking we were already on our way to Australia. Uli told him about our mishaps. He said he would be delighted to have us in his hotel, plus he would give us special rates.

All this dialog was in German while we stood by our bikes in front of the entrance. A small crowd of curious onlookers soon gathered around us until we were escorted into the Hotel, bikes and all, where here in the big city we had to fill in a form and our passports were registered.

We were given a big family room on the ground floor just past the reception and our bikes were put in a small store room at the end of the corridor.

"*Heilands blechle, was sagad dor jedzd, mor sods ned Glauba, was uff ons zua kommd,*" Uli said in our dialect as soon as we were alone in our room. "Jesus Christ, what do you say now? It's hard to believe what's happening to us."

D (the director of the hotel whose name I no longer remember) invited us for lunch, but we declined because we'd had such a big breakfast on the train, but we told him we would appreciate it if he could phone the newspaper and see if he could get in touch with Hong?

We had a double room with a european toilet, lots of space for our luggage, and we couldn't believe our good fortune. What would have happened if the guy in the train had given us the name of a different Hotel?

Not long after lunch there was a knock on the door and when I opened it, one of the unformed guys asked if we would like to join Mr. D for coffee or tea with some of his guests. It was early afternoon but we certainly liked the invitation. Uli grabbed our book and we followed him to the dining room.

A couple of tables had been pushed together and occupied by several people who were introduced to us by D. The three vacant seats left were for us. Though they were guests of the hotel they were well-known to D who acted almost as if they were family members. Most of them were from out of town, but every time they were in Djakarta they would stay in this hotel and had been doing so for years. They'd had lunch together and D had told them a bit about us and they thought it would be nice to meet us and hear our story, from our own mouths.

Coffee and tea were served with freshly baked cookies, and a couple of glass bowls with fruit salads were put on the table for us to help ourselves. One Chinese couple in Djakarta on business from Singapore couldn't believe that we had been invited by Lim Hew Hock for lunch with most of his Parliamentarians and wanted to know all about it.

Right in the middle of answering their questions we got hit with a huge surprise! One of the waiters came to our table and whispered something in D's ears, who immediately stood up and excused himself for a moment, and with a smile followed the waiter. He came back two minutes later accompanied by a smiling Hong and we nearly fell off our chairs. This was totally unexpected. We were more than pleased to catch up with him so soon.

D had phoned the newspaper and got on to Hong, inviting him for lunch, but Hong declined because he had an assignment at that time. He couldn't believe his ears when D told him we were back in Djakarta and told him he would be there as soon as possible.

By the time he'd finished shaking hands with the three of us and clapping us on the back, a chair was put at the table for Hong. We had to tell him all about our experience over the last two weeks and why we had to come back to Djakarta. By this time more guests had gathered around the table to listen in and everyone was fascinated.

We told Hong about our disappointment, that we might not be able to reach Australia, because we couldn't afford flying to Darwin nor going by ship to Perth or Melbourne, which would take too long anyhow.

He took a brief look at his watch then said, "Leave it up to me. Maybe I can pull a few strings. I will have a chat with Ibu and tell her of your problems, okay. I have to get back to the office to finish a story for tomorrow's paper, but I'll be in touch in the morning. Okay?"

"Sure." We all nodded enthusiastically.

We also excused ourselves, telling everyone we had to get to the post office to collect some important mail before it closes. Actually, it was a bit of a lie; we didn't want them to know that we were on our last Rupiahs and had to exchange some of our dollars. Anyhow, we wanted to post our mail which we had written on the train.

We thanked D. for organizing the meeting with Hong and for the lovely afternoon with his guests. He stopped a rickshaw and told the driver where to take us, then to wait and bring us back to the hotel. We changed all our Dollars and some German Marks. We figured the English pounds we still had would be easier to exchange in Australia than Marks.

Back at the hotel D asked us to be his guests for dinner, seeing that we couldn't make it for lunch. We gladly excepted, because we liked this guy, especially after what he had done for us so far.

Back in our room we finally had time to ourselves and started to feel much better, especially after meeting up with Hong. After a couple of smokes and a shower we were looking forward to another great evening and it turned out to be exactly that.

By the time we entered, the dining room table had been extended with the same people from coffee time, plus several more including an elderly German couple who were relatives of D. The food was fantastic, a mixture of German and Indonesian goodies, all served in small pots and bowls. Marinated herring fillets on top of Nasi goreng, small lamb pieces on steamed rice, heaps of green steamed veggies and even a couple of bowls with Bavarian potato dumplings in a chicken and a beef broth. All in all it was a great meal!

Hong, with camera, Theo and I, and other guests in front of the Hotel des Indes.

Hong joined us for breakfast next morning with some very good news. He'd certainly been a very busy boy.

He had been in contact with Ibu a short time before coming to join us and she was looking forward to meeting us at her home in a couple of hours. He also informed us that Mr. Ruttner would like to meet up with us again, after he had told him yesterday evening that we were back. He had also called by the Uni just before and the Principal was more than happy to help us out and look after us again to save on hotel costs. Busy indeed!

D was quite happy as soon as we told him what had transpired and was impressed to hear that we were going to meet Ibu again. He offered us a free night and another invite for dinner, because he could see we were going to have a big day ahead and would like to hear all about it. No problem Hong told him, he would arrange with the Uni. director that we would be there next day.

We jumped on our bikes and had no problem weaving through the traffic, following Hong's Rickshaw. When we got there he said, "You might have to find your own way back. I have to leave early."

"Don't worry," we told him, "we could find our way back blindfolded by now."

The Big Adventure

The welcome at Ibu's was unreal. They were totally surprised to see us again, expecting us to be close to Australia by now. They couldn't stop smiling and kept shaking our hands as if they couldn't believe we were there.

Some of the same people as before were still there shaking our hands like old friends, plus a couple of new once we were introduced to. The big round table was already set and full of food, because it was lunch time and we were invited to take part. Even with our mouths full of food, Ibu and all the others wanted to know all about our travels through Indonesia since she had seen us last time,

We could see in her eyes how disappointed she was for our inability to get further than Surabaya, but she was very pleased for the hospitality we had received. Except for a few questions, everyone listened intently when we told them about the wonderful people we had met on our way to Surabaya and how so many of them knew about us through the newspaper article with Ibu.

By this time Hong excused himself, telling everyone he still had a lot to do, but hoped to catch up with us sometime in the evening. Ibu walked him to the entrance and it took several minutes, before she came back in with a certain smile in her eyes.

We didn't take much notice, still busy answering questions. We had several lovely hours and just before we jumped back on our bikes Ibu told us that she would try to help us as much as she could. We thanked her many times over for what she had done already and headed back to the hotel to be welcomed by D.

D was very excited to find out what happened, because in all his time in Djakarta he only saw President Sukarno and Ibu Fatmawati once at some kind of a parade. They were sitting in the back of an open limousine and waving to the people. Apart from that one time he only saw photos of her printed in newspapers or magazines.

"*Unglaublich*." "Unbelievable," he said several times in German after we were seated for dinner and told him all about our time at Ibu's residence. It certainly was hard for him to digest and he told us laughingly that he might buy a bike and cycle back to Germany, hoping similar doors would open for him also.

"That would be fantastic," Uli said, but we told him in a nice way; "You might just be a bit too old for it and not used to riding a bike anymore."

Hong didn't make it but left a message to say he would see us again in the morning. Anyhow D and his guests were very pleased that Ibu, was trying to help us and he would be very pleased if we could keep him informed, after we check out. By the time we hit the sack, we were stuffed.

None of us wanted breakfast in the morning other than a bit of fruit and some tea, which we had served in our room. We didn't waste too much time before we started packing, because we knew Hong would be along fairly early.

Well, it wasn't Hong who knocked on our door just after we finished packing. It was our two cycling students barging in to give us big hugs, very happy to see us again. We were incredibly surprised. Apparently Hong had arranged with the Director to send the two students to guide us to the University because he was still busy, but would talk to us as soon as possible after we got there.

D was already busy behind his desk fare welling some of his guests by the time we came to the front with our luggage. Our bikes were already outside standing next to the students, who had wanted to come by bike, not by Rickshaw, to greed us. As promised, D only charged us for one night. Looking at the bill we were sure that even for the one night he hadn't charged us the full amount. It hardly took any time to load our bikes, but the farewell to D and some of his guests took a while. We thanked D and told him we would call by in a few days to let him know what was happening.

Following our students was no problem and it took about twenty minutes before we rode through the big gates, waved through by the sentry and welcomed as if we were long lost sons. We didn't even make the front steps of the building before students came running towards us with some teachers behind them, one of the Dutch teachers included. Everyone wanted to shake hands and were very happy to see us so soon again.

This welcome of course was different from our first one, because everyone had read the article and it had been debated during school hours about whether we would get to Surabaya without too many problems. None of the students knew anyone who had done this journey on a bike before. Naturally, they all wanted to hear about it, and as soon as we were welcomed by the Principal and the others the Principle asked if we could speak to the students one more time. We were given the same room as we had before and by the time we entered our smiling students had already taken care of the bikes and our luggage was on the spare bed as before. It was as if we had never left.

After a quick freshening up, we made our way to the Principal's office where a number of people waited. We had just sat down and answered a couple of questions when Hong, accompanied by a uniformed officer opened the door, shook hands with the Principal, introduced the officer and spoke in Indonesian, whilst looking at us.

Suddenly everyone stood up. They were all grinning and smiling. We had no idea what was going on, but we stood up as well. We didn't know whether to smile or what! Then Hong turned to us and introduced us to the officer who turned out to be one of the bodyguards for Dr Ali Sastroamidjojo, who, Hong told us, was waiting at his residence to meet us in an hour's time.

Dr. Ali Sastroamidjojo happened to be the 8th and 10th Prime Minister of Indonesia. He was also Indonesia's first Representative at United Nations and first Ambassador to Canada, America and Mexico. Apparently, Ibu had organized this meeting and asked Hong to go to the Minister's residence to arrange a time, and now arriving in a Government chauffer driven car he was here to pick us up.

Everyone was exited and forgot about asking questions because this was great news. We hardly had time to digest what was happening. One minute we were relaxed and comfortable, the next moment everyone was congratulating us and telling us to hurry. We barely had time to walk back to our room, grab our book and a couple of postcards before minutes later we were sitting in the back of a black limousine with Hong in front and the officer driving.

It was a fair distance to the outskirts of Djakarta, and we sat back and enjoyed the drive. We found ourselves in a similar area to where Ibu lived. It was nicely landscaped and full of beautiful homes. The Minister's residence was easily seen because it had a huge Indonesian flag flying on a big pole in front. This time we didn't have to show our passports. The officer waved to the two sentries as he drove straight past the guard house, to stop in front of the big residence where a couple of men in traditional dress immediately stepped forward and opened the door for us.

This place was bigger and much busier than Ibu's home. We could see lots of activities taking place with several people, male and female, occupied with whatever they were doing. Big pictures of President Sukarno and Prime Minister Dr. Sastroamidjojo were hanging on the walls. By the time our officer knocked on a large door for us to enter Hong told us quietly, "we made it right on time."

There were several men and a couple of ladies in the expansive room, which was the Prime Minister's daily office. It didn't look any different to most other offices, except for its size.

We had seen a photograph of the P.M. and knew straight away who he was. Hong walked towards him to introduce us and the rest of the people. The handshakes were warm, the smiles sincere and we felt instantly at home. Hong had spoken to them in Indonesian for a short minute, then the P.M. turned towards us, pointed to the big round conference table and said in English "Please, sit down."

No one in the room knew who we were or what we had done apart from the Prime Minister who had spoken to Ibu about us and was more than interested enough to invite us to visit him at his home. He told the other people there that something interesting was about to happen. When we walked in their faces lit up because they had all read the articles by Hong and recognized us from the pictures in the newspapers.

We didn't know who they were but soon realized that they were somehow important. The two middle aged ladies were wearing head scarves and traditional costumes, the men were all in uniforms.

We were hardly seated when questions started to come from all sides, especially after Theo had shown some of the most important pages in our book. They were extremely impressed when they realized how many heads of states we had we had visited, because they had also met them.

The P.M. told us that on various state visits, he had met King Faisal, the Shah and Queen Soraya, Iskander Mirza, and Jawaharlal Nehru. "I have also met with Lim Hew Hock on many occasions," and he indicated a couple of people around the table, adding "some of the people here have accompanied me on those occasions."

But the way he looked at us when he said that gave me the impression that he found it hard to believe. "Yet here it is," he said and picked up our journal to read the message Lim Hew Hock had written to us. Everyone in the room found it hard to digest that young fellows like us could reach Indonesia on pushbikes. Not only that, they could hardly believe that while riding through those different countries we had managed to meet so many very important people at the same time. But the proof was there in our travel journal, along with the words each person had written.

The prime Minister passed our journal to the others once again so they could have another look before tea was served and several fruit platters put on the table. While Hong took pictures and scribbled in his note book, we had to tell in detail about our journey to Surabaya and back. We could clearly see how pleased they were, especially when we mentioned how well we had been treated and looked after during those few days in Surabaya and meeting up with those great people.

Naturally we mentioned our plight, not being able to reach Australia through the Islands and we were back now trying to find some way from Djakarta.

"Ibu is trying to arrange something through the Government regarding that matter," the PM mentioned, which secretly got us very excited, but visibly we didn't show anything because there was no certainty about it.

The three of us with the Prime Minister Dr Ali Sastroamidjojo just before leaving.

Well over two hours, and after The PM. had written some lines in our book, we reluctantly had to leave. Everyone wished us all the best and thanked us for the great conversation.

Hong stayed behind. We were driven back to the University in the same government car. As we were thanking our uniformed driver several university staff members wanted to take us straight to the Principal.

"We have to go to our room quickly for some urgent matters," Uli told them, "but we will be there very soon."

They looked confused for a moment but stepped aside to let us rush up to our room.

All three of us were busting for a pee and but had hung on because we felt shy and didn't want to ask if we could go to the Prime Ministers toilet while we were at his residence.

Relieved, and back at the Principal's office we got a lovely surprise; Mr. Ruttner was sitting next to the Principal and he welcomed us back. He wanted to pick us up for dinner later on. More questions had to be answered, firstly to finish off getting to Surabaya and now we had to tell them all about our time with the Prime Minister. Everyone wanted to see what the PM had written in our book.

Mr.Ruttner was still there when Hong arrived to tell all of us that we were going to meet Dr Subandrio, the Foreign Minister and Deputy Prime Minister under President Sukarno, at 10am in the morning, and Vice President and one time PM., Dr. Mohammad Hatta and his wife Rahmi at 3 pm. Things certainly were happening, all organized by Ibu and Hong.

Wow! We hardly had time to scratch ourselves with everything happening so fast.

Our biggest concern was how we could get to Australia as soon as possible. We still had no clue about how or when that would happen. We hardly had a moment to even think about it. All we could do for the moment was to allow ourselves to be swept along by events that seemed to happen spontaneously around us.

We were certainly not disappointed when we walked in to Dr. Subandrio's residence and met this great man exactly at ten o'clock next morning. Hong had already arranged earlier on with the University to take us in their mini bus and the driver was instructed to wait for us however long it took. Hong, as always, introduced us and we followed Dr. Subandrio into a smaller very comfortable office where he asked us to take a seat at a round table to enjoy some of the exquisite fruits and tea already set out.

We didn't really feel like eating much after the great meal we'd had the night before with Mr. Ruttner, his beautiful wife and another Austrian couple in an up-market restaurant, but we certainly enjoyed some of this fruit.

Dr. Subandrio turned out to be a wonderful person who showed great interest in what we were about, and told us that he had also met the

Heads of States whom we visited. He also told us that Ibu had mentioned our plight to him a couple of days ago. He was very anxious to hear the rest of our story. This gentleman treated us as if we were his sons, but unfortunately, after Hong took several pictures, we had to say good bye. He told us that he would get in touch with Ibu and the Vice President whom we were going to meet later on. After many thankyous and handshakes, we finally got back into our bus which took us back to the University. We didn't know that we would meet Dr. Subandrio one more time several days later.

Dr Subandrio writing a message to us in our travel journal.

Back at the University we barely managed a visit to the toilet before we were sitting in the bus once again, this time to visit the Vice President of Indonesia at 3pm. Actually, while President Sukarno was in America Dr. Hatta was the Acting President.

I can't remember whether we were ten or fifteen minutes early, but we were greeted by a beautiful Lady dressed in half European and half traditional clothes. She was accompanied by a ten or eleven year old girl. After Hong had introduced us to Mrs. Hatta and her daughter she informed us in good English, "Mr. Hatta is just finishing his prayers and will be with us shortly."

She led us into a lounge or living room where there was a big couch, several lounge chairs, and a large round table with at least a dozen chairs around it. The walls were covered with paintings. At two of the corners nearly as high as myself stood beautifully painted vases. Several Balinese carvings were placed on small hand carved tables alongside the walls. By the time we had walked through one door, Dr. Hatta, dressed in a grey European suit, white shirt and black tie, walked in through the opposite door and greeted us with big handshakes and a welcoming smile.

Like all the great people we had met — they all had some kind of an aura which set them apart from ordinary people — Dr. Hatta was no different. He wasn't a tall man but his eyes, it seems, were able to look into one's soul without blinking leaving a long-lasting impression. This man wanted to know every detail about us, especially our schooling and what made us take on such an epic task to cycle to Australia. He also wanted to know everything about my American history.

He couldn't get enough of our Indonesian travels and we could see how pleased he was when we told him about the fantastic reception we got on our way and the friendliness of all the different people. Many times, he translated to their daughter who was sitting next to her mother. Mrs. Hatta only asked the odd question, because she went out of the room a couple times to organize some fruit and several pots of tea.

"What about your future plans after you reach Melbourne?"

"We will most likely cycle back to Germany," Uli said, "through New Zealand, South and North America and work for our passage on a Freighter from Canada back to Germany. We want to visit as many different Nations as possible and learn all about their customs. I'm thinking we might write a book when we get back."

Theo and I looked at each other. We'd never discussed that before. But it was a good idea.

Except for Ibu and Lim yew Hock, the Acting President and his wife spent more time with us than any other Head of State or Parliamentarian. The time just flew by incredibly fast and it must have been close to four hours by the time Dr. Hatta had written a few sentences in our book and finally wished us all the best for the future. We thanked him, Mrs. Hatta and their young daughter for their hospitality.

We never mentioned our financial problem to Dr. Hatta, because we knew that Ibu had already informed him. Besides, Hong had mentioned to us earlier that the Acting President might not want to be bothered with matters that others were handling.

Dr Hatta who was Acting President of Indonesia while President Sukarno was on a State visiut to the US, with his wife Rahmi.

By the time we got back to the University— on the way back Hong was dropped off at his office — the two Dutch teachers were waiting for us at the Principal's office. The others had gone home. It had been arranged for us to give another small talk at ten o'clock in the morning and both of them were asked to see if it was suitable for us to do it. we assured them that it was not a problem and finally, after an exhausting day, we finished back in our room.

It turned out to be not a small talk at all; on the contrary the auditorium was packed with students and lecturers with some even standing in the aisles and the questions bombarded us from all sides. They all thought it was an incredible achievement, us riding our bikes as far as Surabaya, especially on those bad roads. Several of the students actually came from some of the towns we rode through, like Cikampek, Subung City, Tegal City, Tuban City or some that we'd stayed in overnight.

How their faces glowed when we told them how well people received us and the hospitality in the hotels we stayed at, and the few great days we had in Surabaya. Nearly three weeks earlier they all had read the newspaper article and couldn't get over the fact that we were guests of Ibu Fat Mawati, Dr. Hatta and some of the other Ministers, as soon as we had returned from Surabaya. They felt very sorry that we couldn't get to Australia via Timor and wanted to know about our future plans.

"We really don't know yet," we told them. "There are only two ways to get to Australia from here, either by plane to Darwin or to Perth, or by ship to God only knows which port. In the next few days we should have an answer."

Towards the end of our talk which lasted nearly three hours, Hong arrived and told everyone that we were invited to meet Mr. Yusuf Wibisano, at 3pm in the afternoon, Dr. Sarino Mangun Prano at 10am next morning, and after that we were going to Ibu Fat Mawati's place for lunch. That made everyone even more excited.

We had only a short time ago spoken about meeting all these high-class people and here was Hong with news that we were to meet more. Mr. Yusuf Wibisano was the Minister for Finance and Dr. Sarino Mangun Prano was the Minister for Education in Dr. Ali Sastroamidjojo's second Cabinet.

Hong had to leave, but told us with a big smile from one ear to the other, that he would meet up with us at three o'clock. There wasn't much time to relax. By the time we had some lunch with the teachers the University's driver told us he would pick us up shortly because it would take close to half an hour to get to where he had to take us. After a bit of a cleanup we were on our way again.

Mr. Yusuf Wibisano wasn't really the type one expected to be a Minister, especially one of such a high position and huge responsibilities. He was young, very casually dressed and extremely athletic. I thought to myself maybe thirty to forty years old. Hong didn't have to introduce us. Mr. Wibisano shook hands with each of us and asked us for our names and without any difficulties introduced us to some of his staff, some of whom were in uniform.

It certainly was a warm welcome and we felt instantly at home, especially when we were offered delicious fruit juices. We gladly answered all his questions, in particular the ones about our education. He seemed quite impressed about our Apprenticeships and told us with a big smile, "You should come back to Indonesia, marry a beautiful girl and settle here."

And immediately I thought of the beautiful Kemala who had so lovingly showed me around Surabaya. I told him jokingly, "I might just take up that offer."

And he laughed. "You'd be very welcome," he said.

We enjoyed the couple of hours with this gentleman very much, but time just ran away from us and eventually Hong gave us a blink of his eye, meaning "it's time to leave."

Before we said goodbye and received all the well wishes, Mr. Wibisano told us that he was aware of our problem and he was sure that the Government might be able to find a solution. After taking some photographs in front of the residence we shook hands all round and were driven back to the University. Hong stayed behind.

I am holding our travel journal and standing next to Mr Wibisano. Hong is leaning casually against the wall.

We finally found ourselves alone in our room, but not before we had to relate in detail what happened to some of the teachers and office staff. We certainly felt exhausted, but still decided to walk up to the market place the same eatery where we had been before where we could eat some small rice dishes and enjoy a couple of pipes. We needed to unwind and let the whole experience sink in. When we walked back to the university there was little movement, and hardly anyone around which meant we could get back into our room without being pestered with more questions.

We knew we had to get up reasonably early, and just as well because as soon as we had finished our morning ablutions and got dressed, one of the office staff knocked on the door and asked if we could come to the office soon.

It was just on eight o'clock, but the Principal and all the staff were already busy and greeted us as like old friends. As soon as we had finished shaking hands with everyone The Principal said, "Hong rang and asked me to tell you that Minister Prano would like to welcome you on your bikes."

"We are happy to ride our bikes there," Theo said.

"Hong will meet you there, The Principal added.

The same students who had ridden their bikes with us before came into the office.

"We'll ride ahead and show you the way," One of them said.

"Then you'd better get a move on," the principal said.

"It could take us an hour to get there," one of the students said.

"No time for breakfast then? Uli asked.

"We go immediately," we were told.

It did take an hour, not because of the distance, but because we had to weave through so much traffic. Even though our students led us through many small side Streets, short cuts, it still seemed to take forever. As soon as we got out of the big city traffic and into the open more affluent area we got to see some of the sights. Turning into a side street that we recognized, we knew exactly that Ibu's Residence was only a few kilometres further ahead and we would have no difficulty finding it ourselves.

The two guards in front of the driveway leading to Minister Prano's residence greeted us with big smiles and we thanked our students for guiding us. One of the guards escorted us up to the Residence, but asked

Uli with a big smile, if he could push his bike towards the Residence.

"It's all yours," Uli said and stepped away from his bike as the guard took hold of the handlebars. We were greeted at the front entrance by several men, some in uniform and a couple smartly dressed in European suits. There were also two smiling well dressed women holding hands with a couple of young children watching us curiously as we leaned our bikes against each other in front of them. One of the suited gentlemen told us that we were expected and he would take us to meet the Minister.

"What about Hong?" Uli asked him.

"Hong will catch up with us later on," he said

Once inside Dr. Sarino Mangun Prano greeted each of us with a very firm handshake, after we had introduced ourselves. Most of the people from outside followed us into a big room looking partly like an office or conference room. Needless to say, the reception was the same. As with all the others there was lots of fruit and tea served; except here there were more people listening to our story.

Most of the questions were asked by the stern-faced Minister of Education. He just looked like a school teacher, which in fact he had been for most of his life. He mentioned to us that he had been to Holland and England to look at their school system, but had not been able to get to Germany as yet. They all were surprised when we told them that most of our classes had more girls than boys and they couldn't get over the fact, when Theo told them, that his class had sixty girls and only four boys.

We thought our meeting went extremely well and there were smiles all around after the Minister had written some very kind words in our book. Finally, as we were about to leave the Minister wanted to inspect our bikes. He couldn't stop himself from smiling when he saw our bikes neatly supporting themselves standing upright in front of the Residence. When the well wishes were over and we were going to walk our bikes to the front gate, the Minister wanted to see us ride towards the guards at the gate.

"Of course," Uli said and hopped onto his bike and started riding down the long driveway. Theo and I did the same and and when we got to the front gate we turned around and waved to the Minister and the other [peole still standing by the front door. They waved back enthusiastically, and then we were through the gate and after another wave backwards we hit the road and headed towards Ibu's Residence. We had no trouble finding it and it only took about twenty minutes before we turned into Ibu's Street.

There was a lot of commotion in the street with several armed soldiers in front of the entrance and a couple of Police cars parked opposite. We were certainly surprised and wondered what was going on. We were nervous about continuing on so we stopped a fair distance away.

"Should we turn around, and come back later?" Uli asked.

Theo just shook his head.

"This might not be a good time to visit…" I said.

"I mechd bloos wissa was do drenna loos isch!" (I would just love to see what's going on inside!) Uli said aloud to himself. But before we could do anything several of the guards in front of Ibu's entrance gate noticed us standing in the middle of the road and gestured for us to come over.

"I guess we'll soon find out," Theo said as we started riding towards the guards at the entrance gate.

All along the driveway towards the residence cars were parked, a couple of police cars amongst them. There were people all over the place, most of them smiling at us as soon as we pushed our bikes past the guard house and along the driveway to the residence. Right near the front entrance there were two big shining Limousines with Indonesian flags mounted on top of the radiator.

Suddenly things were happening very fast. An elderly uniformed gentleman greeted us in perfect English then commanded some younger men to hold our bikes. He begged us to follow him inside. The place was full of people and everyone greeted us. No, Ibu didn't give us a big hug, which I half expected when She came towards us, but grabbed our hands and shook them warmly. She introduced us loudly to all around us and told everyone in a few minutes what we had done up until now. While people clapped and smiled warmly, she let us into another room along the corridor which we hadn't seen before, and got hit with one of the biggest surprises we had encountered so far.

It was a relatively large office with several desks, one huge oval table and plenty of chairs all about the room. The big surprise was the people. We saw a smiling Hong taking photographs, then two unbelievable Gentleman greeted us warmly; Dr. Subandrio, whom we had not expected to see again, greeted us warmly. He introduced the gentleman next to him as the Minister for Planning, Djuanda Karlowidjaja, whom we were supposed to visit in a couple of days' time. (I think Djuanda Karlowidjaja became Prime Minister several years later).

Our heads certainly were spinning, not expecting anything like this commotion, especially when the Principal from the University and the couple of Dutch teachers also greeted us.

Everyone was standing, shaking hands with us and wanting to know all about our adventure, even though most of them already knew about us. The excitement and the questions didn't stop until Ibu picked up an envelope from one of the desks and all of a sudden there was dead silence. You could have heard a pin drop. Ibu held the envelope up to the smiling crowd.

"Several days ago," she said, "The Indonesian Government purchased these air tickets from QANTAS, for a flight from Djakarta to Darwin, for Ulrich, Theo and Friedrich."

She turned around with a flourish and handed the envelope to the dumfounded Uli, and we looked just as stupid, not having a clue what to say.

While everyone in the room was applauding loudly, she told us only the Ministers, who decided as soon as we had visited on our first day back knew about it. Hong of course knew, but none of the others here knew until now. "The flight will be leaving in three days' time."

We didn't know whether to cry or smile. It was simply overwhelming… so much kindness. It was a relief to have that burden off our shoulders. Ibu, with a big grin on her face was the first one to congratulate us. Her ten-year-old daughter clinging to her arm — I am sure she was the one who became the first female Prime Minister of Indonesia in mid July 2001, Megawati — added her congratulations to those of her mother.

What a wonderful afternoon, mixing with all these people patting us on our shoulders, congratulating us and seemingly just as happy as we were. Dr. Subandrio with his body guards, had to leave shortly after the announcement. He wished us well again and told us that his office had posted a document for our book to Uli's address and he promised to keep in touch, and he did. (Three or four years running, Uli's parents received Xmas and New Year's Greetings from him and we answered back.)

Djuanda Karlowidjaja, was next to leave with his guards, but offered to write in our book and wish us a safe journey and a great flight to Darwin. He had known for a few days, what had happened and knew we were going to meet several Ministers who also knew but were not allowed to say anything about the tickets. We were supposed to visit him next day, but he thought it would be better for him to come here today, because he knew we didn't have much time, before we had to leave. After writing some nice words in our book he told us with a big smile, "it was beautiful to see the surprise on your faces when Ibu handed you the tickets."

Because the Principle and both teachers could see that it would take some time before we were to leave they offered to take our bikes back so we could catch a rickshaw later on. A short while later we saw them shaking hands with some of the people before leaving. We ourselves had to shake so many hands afterwards; people wishing us health and a safe journey, before the crowd slowly dissipated.

It had been a sensational day!

We felt incredibly elated knowing that we would reach the fifth Continent and now it was pretty certain we would make it to Melbourne and the Olympics on time.

Sitting here writing about this moment after all these years brings tears to my eyes.

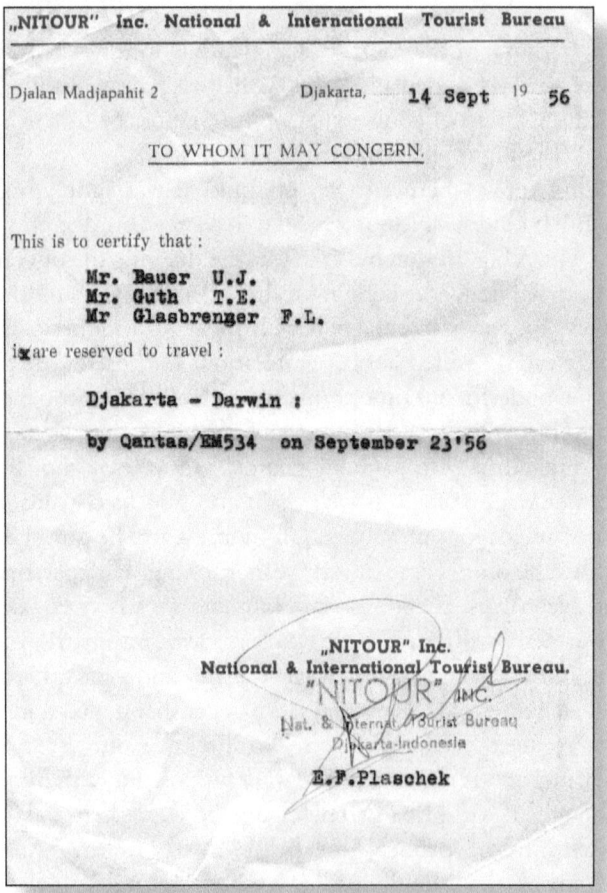

The official letter of authorization for our flight to Darwin.

The Big Adventure

It was dark by the time we finally were able to say goodbye, Hong had left as soon as we had received the tickets, but told us he would be in touch. By the time we walked to the Guardhouse a rickshaw was already waiting to take us to the University. We asked the rickshaw guy to drop us off at the market next to the University; we had to digest this day over a couple of pipes.

We decided that we would pack next day and slowly get ready, but visit Ibu once more about lunchtime the day after to say goodbye. According to our tickets, we were to leave the day after, mid-morning, on Qantas/EM534 on September 23,1956. I couldn't help thinking, it was on my Grandma's birthday.

I must have slept like a log. by the time I woke up Uli was in the shower and Theo had already written several postcards to Singapore, Rangoon, India and home, with the great news. By the time we walked to the office and canteen the whole Uni. knew what had happened and the well wishes didn't seem to end. We didn't waste much time at breakfast because now that we knew what's ahead, there was some important things still to be done. Firstly, we had to take some of our dirty clothes to the laundry to be ready by tomorrow. Secondly, our bikes had to be given a good service. And apparat from that I had more cards to be written and posted, especially a couple from me to Kemala.

By midday the office staff informed us that Hong had rung and explained he was busy all day but he would meet up with us at Ibu's tomorrow. We jumped on our bikes to post our mail and exchange several English pounds for Australian currency. After the post office we decided to call in at the Hotel des Indes to tell D what had transpired since we last saw him and his friends, as promised. We also wanted to say goodbye. D was full of smiles when we pushed our bikes through the entrance and welcomed us with open arms and sure enough invited us for lunch. We had brought our book with our ticket inside to show him, plus all the writing from the different people. He was rapt and so were some of the other guests who decided to join us in what turned out to be an extended luncheon.

All good things come to an end and finally, after so many well wishes, we had to say goodbye to another great person and some of his guests and staff.

"As soon as we get to Melbourne," we told him, "we will write." And we did. Theo received a couple of replies in Footscray where he was boarding.

Back at the University our clothes had already been washed, ironed and neatly placed on one of the beds in our room. We knew they wouldn't charge us, but Uli walked over, thanked them and pressed some Rupiahs in one of the fellow's hands.

Our bikes were ship shape and ready to cover the long distance from Darwin to Melbourne and having cycled our last kilometres in Indonesia, we started packing.

Having had such a late lunch, we felt like a couple of more pipes at the nearby market, not realizing that they would be our last ones for many years. Afterwards we walked over to the campus and spent some time with the students, again answering a lot of questions, before going to bed and dreaming of Australia.

We had only one more day in Indonesia!

The next morning the realization that our time with these beautiful people was coming to an end really hit home. We simultaneously felt depressed to be leaving while at the same time excited because our journey was entering its last stages. We would be in Australia the very next day. Entering the principal's office just after breakfast he introduced us to a Dutch gentleman. This man was part owner of the travel agency that had organized our tickets.

"It's a pleasure to meet you," he said as he shook hands with each of us. "I'm here to tell you that
 the airline will send a van at six in the morning tomorrow to take you and your bikes to the airport for our nine o-clock flight."

"We'll be ready, don't worry about that." Uli said.

With packing just about done we slowly got ourselves ready for our last visit to Ibu's.

We grabbed a rickshaw and enjoyed every moment, lighting a fag and reminiscing about the weeks and months behind us. It felt great being saluted like the President himself as the rickshaw took us past the guards, and as far as the guardhouse without being stopped. I paid the driver with a good tip.

Compared to a couple of days ago the place seemed nearly deserted. There were a few people working in the gardens and one guard stood in front of the entrance. We didn't see anyone until we entered the Residence where we were greeted by Ibu and her daughter and a couple of servants. The table in the room was stacked with lots of goodies. Hong had been here earlier for a short time we were told, but would be back again later.

Even with all this great food and drinks on the table, everyone seemed to be picking only little bits here and there, us included. As a matter of fact, the whole afternoon was somehow subdued, not like the other day. We all sensed that today will definitely be the last goodbye, and that perhaps we would never see any of these wonderful people ever again. No doubt the same thoughts were in their minds. It was very difficult to say goodbye.

Hong arrived and spent the last couple of hours with us before leaving. He told us he would be at the airport in the morning to make sure everything would be ok. This time Ibu put her arms around each of us and so did the other women, plus the men who had come to say goodbye could hardly stop shaking our hands.

It had been a very sad day and sitting in the same rickshaw (the guy had waited) on the way back. We hardly talked until we got back to the University. We still answered heaps of questions before we finally finished up in our room for our last night. Knowing that we had to get up early, we finished our last-minute packing and hit the sack reasonably early in the hope of getting a good night's sleep.

I finished up having a miserable night, turning, tossing and dreaming, and wondering about what lies in front of us I finally got to sleep only to be woken with a loud knock on the door. It was five in the morning and I could have slept all day. Uli and Theo had the same kind of night. The moment we got out of bed the excitement about flying in an airplane for the first time in our lives overcame all the tiredness. We dressed in a flash and headed to the dining hall for an early breakfast where we knew manay students would be waiting to say goodbye.

Just before six a large van with QANTAS in big letters written on both sides, stopped in front of the University where we were waiting with our bikes and luggage.

The van had three rows of seats in front and a big luggage compartment in the back to be entered through wide rear doors. The driver with two helpers, all Indonesians had our luggage stored and bikes tied to the side walls of this large rear compartment in less than five minutes and by exactly six o-clock we waved goodbye to these wonderful people.

Theo and me with the driver of the Qantas van. Uli is already inside ready to go to the airport.

The airport was not too far away, but it still took more than half an hour before we got our gear unloaded in front of an administration building with Djakarta in big letters written on it. Whatever Indonesian money I had on me I gave to the van driver to split between him and his mates. As soon as they drove off, we saw Hong, Mr. Ruttner, plus a handful of uniformed guys with Qantas written on their arms, walking towards us.

Mr. Ruttner greeted us with a huge hello and Hong introduced us to the Qantas guys. They took charge of our gear and led us into the airport. We were surprised at the small amount of people in the big hall and reached the counter almost immediately to be served by several Qantas employees. We had expected huge crowds, like when we had arrived at the harbor, but we soon found out that flying in the fifties was extremely expensive. We were stunned when we found out how much it had cost the Government to pay for our tickets, and told Hong to thank them once more. Our Passports and tickets were checked and our seating arrangements were handed to us.

We could see our plane not far from the building getting last bits and pieces done to it and our excitement grew bigger and bigger. This plane had started in London three days earlier, we were told, and its final destination after Australia was New Zealand. We watched our bikes and luggage being loaded on to the plane and we knew that within a few hours we would set foot on the red continent Close to an hour passed before we were told to board. We followed a couple of stewardesses walking us across the tarmac to the plane. Also following us were two well-dressed gentlemen and an elderly couple with two young boys.

It was a very sad goodbye again and Mr. Ruttner promised to look us up in a year's time. He expected us to be back in Germany but we weren't. Our parents had written to us later after he had been in touch with them.

Hong, like us, had tears in his eyes when we hugged each other. He promised to send the articles he had written to Germany, which he did, and Theo had sent him copies of our articles in the Age and Argus newspapers in Melbourne as soon as they were published.

What a great birthday present Theo would get the next morning, being able to let Backnang know, that we had arrived.

The plane was three quarters full with very tired looking people and some children sound asleep cuddled up on their seats covered with blankets; no wonder since most of them boarded in London. It was a huge plane, to us anyhow, with three seats on either side of a central aisle. One of the stewardesses told us that we could take a whole row of seats further towards the back, to get two windows. That put us several rows back from the four big engines and it wasn't long before they started firing up.

Exactly at nine o-clock a big tractor pulled the plane to the runway. It left us there and the pilots immediately increased power to the engines. We started along the runway going faster and faster and a few minutes later we were airborne and waved Indonesia goodbye. Taking off was not very pleasant. My ears started to ache more and more the further we flew upwards. Uli and Theo were also rubbing their ears. Kids were screaming and a couple of stewardesses quickly came along handing out sweets to suck on. Apparently, this was supposed to equalize the eardrums. It didn't make any difference to me. A passenger a couple of rows in front turned and told us to press our nostrils together and blow hard, and sure enough with what seemed to be an almighty pop of my eardrums I felt a great relief. The others did same and the pain in their ears also disappeared.

Not long after that we were served sandwiches and a cup of coffee on a small tray which we had to balance on our lap. Once the trays were taken away we settled in and changed seats frequently to look out the windows, admiring the beautiful scenery passing down below us. Gazing through the small windows we had been told that we would fly east, back over the whole of Java and we should look out for Surabaya, Bali and some of the Islands.

We did see Surabaya in the distance, plus the other places, but half

Flying over Java's volcanic terrain.

way into our flight, perhaps somewhere over Timor, something peculiar happened.

Uli sitting by himself at the right-side window deep in thought, Theo gazing out the left one and myself sitting next to him, thinking about Kemala. Suddenly Theo turned around, poked me in the side and yelled over to Uli to come over.

"*Glotzad amol do zom Fenschdor naus ond guggad was aus dem aussora Moddor raus kommd?*" "Have a look what's coming out of the outside motor."

Small flames were shooting out of the motor… getting bigger by the minute.

Uli said with a very stern face, "maybe the plane will catch fire too." He tried to get a stewardess's attention.

We saw one coming slowly towards us, but she stopped several times to talk to other passengers who had noticed the same as us. By the time she came to us the flames were getting bigger and bigger.

"There is nothing to worry about," she reassured us. We could clearly see she was forcing herself to smile. "In less than two hours we will be landing in Darwin." And saying that she quickly turned around and walked back towards the front of the plane.

She pulled a curtain across behind her as she entered the first-class section. A moment later a man's voice came over the intercom.

"There is a small problem with one of the engines," the voice said with a calm measured tone. "I can assure you there is absolutely nothing to worry about."

"Nothing to worry about…" Uli said. "There are flames shooting out of the engine."

The passengers in front of us were all crowding the windows to catch a glimpse of the fiery engine.

"We will be in Darwin in an hour and a half," the voice continued, "and the weather is perfect.

"It's getting worse," one of the passengers yelled.

"Why doesn't he shut the engine off?" another asked.

…but the captain's voice kept rambling on about how he and the crew would take a nice rest in Darwin.

He talked and talked but no one was listening. They kept staring out the windows at an engine now totally engulfed in flames. I think he wanted to give the appearance that having a flaming engine was a normal occurrence. He didn't want the passengers to worry so he rambled on about life in Australia all the while gradually taking the plane lower until we were flying only a thousand feet or so above the water.

By now all the passengers were sitting on the edge of their seats. No one was asleep anymore and some of them were praying. We all knew this guy talked a lot of crap. He was just trying to keep everyone calm.

"He's probably shitting himself as much as we are," Theo said.

"Hey, I can see land over there," Uli said.

Looking beyond the flaming engine I saw a thin green strip on the horizon.

"Please return to your seats and fasten your seat belts," the captain's voice said over the intercom.

The stewardesses reappeared and went along past all the occupied seats making sure we were all strapped in for the landing.

We expected the plane to crash and skid along the runway, but it was a very smooth landing. There was a slight bump as the wheels hit the runway and the three remaining engines roared as they were throttled down and brakes were applied. The plane came to a gentle stop and was immediately surrounded by fire trucks.

"Please remain seated," the voice said.

The fire trucks sprayed masses of foam over the totally burned out engine. A couple of police cars and two ambulances pulled up near the front of the plane.

"Please remain in your seats," the voice said again.

Chapter Thirteen

After about fifteen minutes the doors were opened and the stewardesses indicated that women with children were to be the first to exit down the steps. They were quickly followed by the elderly. Because we were at the back of the plane we were the very last and looking down from the top of the steps we saw some people kneeling down kissing the ground.

The whole plane had to be emptied. The passengers who were continuing on to New Zealand also had to vacate. Several trucks pulled up at the rear of the plane and all the luggage was unloaded. Those going on to other parts of Australia and then on to New Zealand would be put onto another plane later in the day.

Looking up we clearly saw the damage this engine had caused. The wing on either side of it was buckled and scorched and we thought how lucky we were that the fuel inside the tanks in the wing had not exploded. We were also lucky that Darwin had been so close. If the plane had to fly any further the wing would probably have fallen off. This plane was parked a fair distance away from the runway and the airport terminal buildings in case of fire or explosions.

It was only when we reached the Administration. building we were told that the pilot had only one chance to land because the engine would not have survived another jolt. If we'd had to go around for a second attempt who knows what would have happened had it fallen off before or during landing. I don't know what happened to the NZ. passengers, but one thing was for sure, this plane was not flying anywhere for a very long time.

The trucks were unloaded in record time and it didn't take too long before we got our bikes packed and our luggage tied down. We had no problem getting our passports stamped, but were told to follow a grim looking uniformed man through a side door where big letters painted above the door proclaimed Security and Customs.

Welcome in Australia.

We could hardly believe what happened next. Each of us was ordered to go to a separate table and told to unpack our luggage.

"Why do we have to do that?" I asked.

"We need to inspect your luggage."

I heard Uli ask "inspecting for what?"

"For illegal imports," he was told abruptly.

We had to empty our pockets and take off our shoes, while at each table an inspector emptied all our packs and spread out the contents. One of them even spread out our tent.

They didn't give a hoot, after we told them, where we came from and what we done so far. And today, after ten months of traveling and nearly crash landing in a plane with a burning engine, they couldn't have cared less. They couldn't find anything because there was nothing to find. But because we'd questioned them they were pissed off.

"You'll have to take the tyres off your bikes," one of them said.

"What!"

"We need to see what's inside the tyres."

Up until this moment we had remained fairly calm, but that was just too much.

"You're joking," Uli said in a loud voice. "In all the countries we have passed through nothing like this has ever happened."

"This is Australia…"

"If you want the tyres off the bikes then you can take them off yourselves," Uli said. His voice was louder than ever. "And when you find nothing you can put them back on again."

I saw the man start to look very angry. He certainly didn't like being spoken to like that. Or worse still he didn't like the fact that we were challenging his authority.

Before the confrontation could escalate further a side door flew open and another guy with a couple of medals on his uniform demanded to know what was happening.

"They want us to take the tyres off the bikes," Uli said before the customs officers could say anything. "And I told them if they wanted that they could do it themselves, and put them back on again, because I'm not going to do it."

He looked at the officers. "Is that right?"

When the guy who had demanded that Uli take the tyres off his bike started to explain, the man raised his hand and the officer shut up.

"Let them go," he said. "You want to give this country a bad name?"

The Big Adventure

And that was the end of it. We quickly repacked our gear and left.

We rode out of the airport to what appeared to be a highway and stopped under a sign that said: Darwin 5 ½ miles.

It was a glorious but very hot day and if we hadn't been treated so badly, we would have felt pretty good. Well, we had made it to Australia and were really looking forward to a cool drink in Darwin, the Capitol of the Northern Territory. But before we could get back on our bikes we all were covered in flies.

"What kind of place is this?" Theo said as he spat a fly out that had got into his mouth.

They were crawling all over us, buzzing around our faces and we had to keep brushing them out of our eyes.

We jumped back on our bikes and started riding towards Darwin, and as we rode along we left the flies behind.

There was nothing but tall grass from which came very loud noises like crickets make. Further away from the road there were scraggly trees and sometimes giant mounds of dark grey earth. We had no idea what they were.

As we rode towards Darwin there was no traffic, no overloaded busses or trucks, and certainly no rickshaws. We saw no animals on the road except for a couple of stray dogs. The few cars and trucks that passed were all American or English manufactured. It was somehow strange, as we neared the outskirts of the city passing wooden houses on stilts, most of them with nice gardens in front, but some definitely in need of repair. But one of the strangest things we came across and didn't know why was all the bicycles had their handlebars facing skywards. Another strange thing we encountered on the way into the city; we saw a few white and black men wearing strange hats, riding horses. We expected Darwin to be much bigger, especially the inner city. There were a few bigger buildings like banks, the town hall, a couple of hotels and several pubs, but nothing like you would expect to see in a big city. This was like one of those old towns in the wild west that you saw in American films. I expected to see a gunfight at any moment. Especially when we stopped in front of the first hotel/pub, and saw a long log mounted across two poles, with at least a half dozen, saddled horses tied to it.

Being thirsty we stopped and leaned our bikes on the wall of the building opposite the horses and entered where the word BAR was written above the entrance. There were also two other entrances, one with rooms to let and the other one said ladies lounge. What happened next was quite incredible and to this day it gives me great pleasure telling people how we were treated on our first day, but at the time we didn't know what hit us.

We entered and found a huge room with a long wooden bar along one side and very rough looking men standing or leaning at it, with several barmen behind, filling their beer glasses nonstop. The room was half full of smoke and lots of those guys were rolling their own cigarettes. Several radios were blaring words which we couldn't understand. In one of the corners stood a guy with a big leather bag in front of his belly hanging on two straps from his shoulders. it looked like it was full of money, because we saw that several men were handing him money and receiving a bit of paper with something written on it.

All this we noticed waiting for one of the barmen to serve us while we were waiting behind a couple of guys listening to radios. Finally, one of the barmen yelled across and asked what we wanted and Uli yelled back holding up three fingers, "three cokes please."

We were actually looking forward to a Coca cola, because most of the time we could only get Pepsi cola.

"What do you want?" the barman yelled once more cupping his ear with one hand.

"Three Coca colas please," Uli yelled back.

All of a sudden, the radios went quiet and everyone looked at us, especially when the barman yelled out. "What, you want fucking coke?"

Uli nodded.

The barman yelled back, "If you want fucking coke, go across to the fucking milk bar, they will sell you fucking coke." With that he walked further away along the bar to serve someone a real drink.

Amidst all the laughter we walked outside and stood next to our bikes, dumfounded over what had just happened. We certainly didn't know what the word fucking meant, we had never heard it before, except a couple of times at the seamen's club in Penang, but didn't take any notice. It certainly didn't sound as if it was meant to be nice.

We walked our bikes across and down the road a bit to another shop, presumably the milk bar where we bought and enjoyed a couple of cokes each, still asking ourselves, what had happened? Standing outside the milk bar next to our bikes smoking a cigarette, contemplating whether to go back to the airport and see if we could get a flight back to Indonesia, a young blond fellow walked towards us and greeted us in German.

He had been driving past and had seen us coming out of the pub and pushing our bikes across the street. He parked his car and wanted to know what three guys with fully loaded bikes were up to. He had a feeling that we were German, looking at our bikes, with the dynamos mounted on the frame, with front and back lights, all requirements under German laws.

"I am Eugen Daube from Mannheim," he said in a dialect affected German. "What are you fellows doing here?"

When we told him he could hardly believe that we had cycled all the way from Stuttgart, but were being treated like shit in Darwin. He told us that he and his wife had been here in Darwin for the past two years. He was a carpenter and his wife was a nurse.

"I would love to hear your story."

"No problem," Theo said.

"Why don't you come around to my place? You could stay there for a bit... and I can tell you all you need to know about Australian customs."

Uli humorously copied his Manheim dialect and with a big laugh told him "we would be very happy to get out of a not so happy situation."

With a big smile he tried to copy our Stuttgarter dialect, of which he had no hope. "Follow me," he said.

We pushed our bikes behind him to his parked car, a Holden with a small trailer behind loaded with lots of different tools. He had just finished a job, and was on his way home when he spotted us. He was still wearing overalls and was looking forward for a nice cool beer.

"I'll drive slowly so you can easily follow. It's near the harbor a couple of miles away, that's all."

We had no problem at all and were happy to get away from this stupid pub. Like most of the houses theirs was also weatherboard with a big carport next to it. A couple of palm trees and some nice flowers filled the front garden. Being Sunday, Eugen's wife Helga, (a good-looking young lady) was more than surprised when she saw him pulling into the driveway followed by the three of us. As we got off our bikes a few of the neighbors opposite came out to have a look. He gave Helga a big kiss and it didn't take long for him to explain the predicament we were in. With a friendly smile she shook hands with each of us and welcomed us into their home.

Behind the carport was a big garage more like a workshop, and behind that in a fairly big back yard was a small building like a big party room. This was a small bungalow for guests. After unpacking our bikes in the garage, Eugen and Helga helped us carrying our luggage into the bungalow and Eugen pointed out that he had built it himself.

We followed them into a very comfortable lounge room with a small kitchenette. Beyond was one double bedroom, another one with two beds one above the other, and through the last door was a shower and flush-toilet, ideal for a whole family.

Before they asked us to join them in the main house, Eugen explained that we were lucky to have a flush-toilet, because until only four weeks ago they still had to use the outhouse and crap into a special bin which was emptied once a week. He had been very busy lately and had no chance to demolish it as yet, but would do so soon. Apparently across the street the houses still had to wait a couple of months yet to be connected to sewage pipes.

Following them inside their house was another experience we hadn't counted on. We had to step up a couple of steps from the back yard to get into the house. Eugen held the back door open to let us in. Uli stepped in first, but after a couple of steps, turned around with a look of horror on his face. He pushed Theo who was behind him backwards and yelled out, "Snake."

Theo staggered backwards almost falling over. I couldn't believe what had happened to us since we had left Djakarta. The plane we were in almost crash landed with a damaged engine, then there were the unfriendly customs officers, the nasty bartender in the pub, and now a bloody great Snake!

To get into the house from the backyard we had to walk through the laundry where there was a big trough next to a bench against one wall. Between a small washing machine and a big ice box was a gigantic snake curled up on a woven mat. It lifted its head, opened its mouth and we saw its forked tongue flicking in and out.

This was just too much.

Helga and Eugen burst out laughing as they saw the looks of consternation on our faces.

If this is what we could expect in Australia we should turn around now and go straight back to Indonesia. The three of us stood outside the laundry door, not knowing what to do next.

"This is our pet python," Helga said. "You must not be afraid of it." She bent down and stroked its head. "It's completely harmless."

"What would you keep a big snake like that for?" I asked.

"It keeps the rats and mice away. The neighbors' cats don't bother us either."

"Come on," Eugen said. "Come inside and we'll have a beer."

We stepped into the laundry keeping as far away from the snake as possible.

Eugen opened the icebox and we could hardly believe what we saw. There was a big block of ice in the middle and it was surrounded by several of the biggest beer bottles we had ever seen.

Eugen grabbed one of those gigantic bottles and looking at our astonished faces, held it up and laughingly said, "this is the famous Darwin Stubby."

We walked through the kitchen where Helga handed each of us a glass and we finally finished up sitting in the lounge room. Eugen poured cold beer into the glasses and we sipped cautiously.

Surprisingly, it didn't taste too bad, and Uli and I drank it all down with enjoyment. Theo explained he didn't drink alcohol so Helga immediately squeezed some fresh fruit juice for him. She brought in a big plate of square cheese junks and slices of a doughy white bread and sat down to join us. Finally got around to hearing their Story.

They had known each other since school in Manheim and got married five years ago. Eugen was three years older, was a qualified carpenter and Helga was a qualified doctor's assistant. Both of them had no problems getting an assisted two-year package to Australia. They arrived in Sydney in early 1953 and both of them had immediately got well-paid jobs. They were also quick to learn the Australian language. After a year in Sydney they heard that Darwin, being a pioneer town, had huge possibilities. They also heard that it was a cosmopolitan place where many different nationalities mingled together. It wasn't really what they expected when they got there. It was in fact a rude shock. Darwin was the place where the worst possible people ended up; there was nowhere else for them to go in Australia. But they got used to the place and fitted in quite well and now they are very happy and would want to go anywhere else.

We were extremely lucky to have met both of them, because to this day, we always wondered what would have happened to us if those two hadn't changed our minds about returning to Indonesia.

After hearing our story and looking through our travel journal, they both convinced us that we must make it to Melbourne and the Olympics.

"You must not compare Melbourne with Darwin, or Darwin with the rest of Australia. Once you leave here it's an unspoiled continent and people everywhere are very friendly."

It was dark by the time Eugen lit a fire under a large steel drum. "This is our BBQ," he said.

While Helga prepared some salads, Eugen put five big steaks and a heap of sausages on the top of the hot plate and it didn't take long for the burned smell had our mouths watering.

It was a great Australian outdoor meal and we enjoyed it immensely. Having had nothing but Asian food for such a long time, this was the best meal we'd had. With a full gut, and beer that was a bit stronger than we were used to back home, we slept like logs that first night in Australia. We did look under our beds before going to sleep as well as first thing next morning, just in case that giant snake had found its way into the room.

Helga had another day off and made a substantial breakfast for us while Eugen, who worked mostly for himself, offered also to take a couple of days off, to be able to show us around Darwin before we left. Breakfast consisted of bacon and eggs with baked beans, plus buttered toast and black tea with condensed milk.

"This is a typical Australian breakfast," she said when we sat down at the table.

We were certainly happy to have toast, because the white bread without being toasted was very doughy.

Over breakfast Eugen tried to explain to us variations in the use of the word Fuck or Fucking. Go and get Fucked, what the Fuck? or I am Fucked, plus, several other sentences with those words. He "They are only used by men and are bad swear words, and they used in just about every sentence; but never in front of women or children. You'll get used to them, plus the word Bloody."

Clearing the kitchen table, we studied our road map and Eugen gave us some valuable advice.

"You should stock up with lots of canned food and dried bread, plus heaps of water, because there are not many places to purchase that between here and Alice Springs. There are even fewer, if any, between there and Adelaide. Take as much as you can carry."

Looking at our roadmap it seemed a very long way from Darwin to Adelaide. Surely there would be somewhere along the way where we could replenish our supplies. There was limit to how much we could carry on our bikes.

"What about finances?" he asked. "You won't find anywhere to change foreign money on the way so you should change all your English pounds and US dollars here in Darwin first. No one in the Territory will accept anything else but Australian currency. If you run out you could probably get a job somewhere, but then you would miss getting to Melbourne for the Olympics."

We listened carefully because we assumed, he knew what he was talking about, having been here for a while already.

"You should also be very careful when you stop in some of the towns along the way. Never walk into a pub or a shop or a milk-bar and leave your bikes outside. They might not be there when you come back out again."

We looked at each other wondering what the hell we had got ourselves into.

"The best places for you to stop would be the service stations along the way. They sell food and drinks and it would be much easier for you to watch your bikes."

He had a look at our bikes and was surprised how robust they were, and considering how far we had travelled on them, how well-looked after they were.

"You should have seen them when we arrived in Surabaya three weeks ago."

Before driving us around Darwin he offered to take us to a bank.

While Eugen drove us to several places Helga accompanied us as our tour guide. The first place we stopped for a look at was the large harbour. There were quite a few big navy ships moored to an enormously long pier with two uniformed sentries guarding the entrance.

"The Japanese bombed this harbour and made one hell of a mess. A lot of ships were sunk and when the tide goes out you can easily see them. The water drops about three metres. This was only about fourteen years ago and ever since then some navy ships have been permanently moored here. Most of Darwin was destroyed at the time and everyone fled south expecting the Japanese to land, but they never did, they just bombed the place."

Before walking onto a couple of piers on the opposite side of the harbour, we passed a big sign with a picture of a crocodile on it. Underneath, it said NO SWIMMING. That was a new one for us.

Eugen pointed at the sign. "Don't swim anywhere in the northern part of Australia or camp next to an inlet, or you will get eaten!" he said.

Along the pier there were several smaller, wooden clinker fishing boats with small motors in the middle, surrounded by heaped fishing nets on both sides and some crab pots in front travelling out of the harbor to their fishing grounds. This pier was mainly for commercial fishing boats with some big steel trawlers getting worked on also. The other one led past a big clubhouse to an enclosed smaller bay for private members where several beautiful luxuriant sea-going recreational cabin cruisers were moored.

After we had seen a couple of well-kept parks with big bronze statues in the middle, plus walking through the main street to the strangely modern Commonwealth bank where we changed our money, we certainly could see why Eugen and Helga liked being here. With all the restoration and new work to be done he certainly wouldn't run out of work. And of course, trained nurses could get work almost anywhere.

"We want to work and save as much as we can for a few years, then maybe we'll move back to Sydney, or perhaps to Brisbane."

"We may even go back to Germany," Helga said.

"Why not Melbourne?" Uli asked.

"Too bloody cold," was the short reply in English.

We walked past some shops and stopped at what they called a hardware shop, (apparently, they were most of the important shops all over Australia) where Eugen bought each of us a water bag made out of hessian, which looked like the material they made potato bags from. The water bag was surrounded by a small steel frame with a couple of hooks to hang the full bag on any bumper bar, especially on trucks, where wind blowing through it as the vehicle drove along kept it cool. It would hold approximately half a gallon and to fill, or empty it, you had to close it with a cork pushed into a spout.

Another important thing they bought for us was a kind of a fine net to hang loosely over our well used tropical helmets to be tied at the neck to protect our faces from the extremely annoying bush flies inland. We had already encountered those damn flies when we left the airport. Persistent and horrible, you couldn't just brush them away, you had to wipe them off your face. We were most grateful for those gifts because we would never have thought of such things and we would certainly have suffered because of that.

On the way back to the car Helga stopped at a baker shop and brought several apple pies to have with cream, plus a cake for Theo's birthday. She planned on serving these when she made coffee once we got back home. Yes, it was Theo's 20th birthday, but with all the excitement Uli and I hadn't thought of it. Helga must have heard us mention it during the evening before. Eugen brought more steaks for another grill that evening and after driving past another park we took a different way back home.

The apple pie was delicious and I really got the taste of it once we settled in Melbourne and every time I enjoyed one my thoughts went back to those wonderful people we met in Darwin.

We had a lovely afternoon for Theo and another great evening, especially after our hosts had invited another German couple who wanted to meet us. They had been working in Darwin for several years and had helped Eugen and Helga immensely when they first arrived here. After hearing our story, we all were invited for lunch the next day at their place, but without Helga who had to work. But she would be there for the outdoor grilled steaks in the evening.

I can't remember if we stayed three or four days with them and the Python, but we certainly got to like them.

We did learn a lot from them and it was certainly a sad goodbye, leaving early on that morning, after Helga had prepared another huge breakfast and being assured once more, laughingly, that "Darwin is not like the rest of Australia."

Helga had to go to work and after lots of thanks, we followed Eugen, who offered to guide us onto the highway. When we stopped to say goodbye, he put five one-pound notes in Uli's hand. "You will need all the cash you can get," he said, before shaking hands with each of us. "Good luck," was the last thing he said as he got into his car and drove off to work.

We were alone again and with a long way to go from one end of the Continent to the other. Eugen told us that this whole Continent, which was only a bit smaller than the whole of Europe, had only between 12 and 13 million people and was largely uninhabited inland and unexplored, but it had nearly as many sheep and cattle, plus many more Kangaroos than that.

Our water bottles on the handlebars were filled, and so were our water bags fastened to the frame, but with the extra food adding to the weight, we had to push pretty hard to keep moving, but then we were extremely fit. On the outskirts of Darwin we had seen a road sign telling us we are on highway 1 and it was 75 Miles to Adelaide River. That didn't seem so far, but what we forgot was that in Australia it was miles and not kilometres. 75 miles was actually further than we thought.

It was already very warm without a cloud in the sky, but we were well covered. One other thing Eugen had mentioned was to "watch out for the Australian sun." I remember telling him that we had learned our lesson in Karachi, and we would be careful.

The road was narrow but very good to ride on and without much traffic we did very well. We rode one behind the other and covered many miles before we stopped for some water and a couple of smokes. We were instantly covered in pesky flies but the netting over the helmet and our faces kept them from annoying us too much. Helga's big breakfast kept us going nearly all day.

We certainly felt the vastness of this huge landmass, and the loneliness very quickly.

Our only companions were big birds, eagles I think, that feasted on dead animals, mainly Kangaroos run over by vehicles during the night. It was several days before we saw live ones in the distance. We had to cross several rivers, but didn't stop beside them because we were told that there were also fresh water crocodiles in the rivers and creeks. The land around us was dry but starting to green up as the wet season approached. Eugen said we could sit and watch the grass grow during the wet season. It would grow several inches a day until it was sometimes six feet tall. I'm not sure we believed him, but in any case, we wouldn't be there when the season started. We would hopefully be somewhere much nearer to Melbourne which was a long way further south.

The very few heavily loaded trucks that passed us blew their horn and the drivers gave us big waves, no doubt wondering who they had passed, blinking their eyes a couple of times, thinking that people on bikes must be some kind of vision. Not one of them slowed down or stopped. They just kept barreling along the road with the bigger ones almost blowing us off the edge with the wind they displaced as they went past.

With approximately twenty miles to go, we would have made Adelaide River easily, but a big all-wheel drive Land rover pulling a small trailer behind passed us and stopped ahead. We pulled up behind him to see what he wanted. An elderly uniformed man got out, and shaking his head he asked, "where the bloody hell do you fellows think you're going?"

"We're going to Melbourne," Uli told him.

He burst out laughing. When he finally stopped he introduced himself as Pete Wilson, Officer in charge, Police Station, Adelaide River, Northern Territory.

"You are coming with me and you can stay at my place, I have to hear this story."

"So far so good," Uli said laughingly in English to him, "getting picked up by the law, when we had not such good experiences with it on arriving at the airport."

It wasn't long before we had our bikes loaded on the half empty trailer and the luggage behind the seats, and we were on our way.

Adelaide River turned out to be a small place, every house, was built with weatherboards, even the police station which was adjacent to a big wooden building, acting as a bar, repair shop, restaurant and service station. It had a huge sign on the highway with the words Golden Fleece written on it with big letters that could be seen miles away.

Sergeant Wilson was a fine man and looked after us very well. He was married to a New Zealand lady, but she had gone back for several weeks to visit relatives and wouldn't be back for a couple more. He introduced us to his household lady, a tall but skinny Aboriginal woman who I thought must be totally under nourished.

This was the first Aboriginal women we had come across, even though we had seen men and whole families of Aboriginal people in Darwin. We didn't have the chance to talk or meet any of them in the short time we were there. This lady was very friendly, no doubt wondering why her Sergeant had brought along someone different than the drunks he usually collected and made sleep it off in a cell.

As soon as we had unloaded our bikes and luggage, he told us that we could have a bedroom each, because there were five of them. Laughingly he said, "one never knows what the un expected will bring." I certainly agreed with that thought.

Sitting in the lounge room with a cool pot of beer in our hands, Theo with fruit juice which the lady served for us, he wanted to know all about us. We had told him some of it in the car and he asked lots of questions. We had a great evening and the more we were with this man, the more we got to like him. Of course, not to forget his housekeeper, who grilled and prepared a great meal for us.

Actually, Sergeant Wilson was the first Australian we had stayed with in his house, and it had to be a policeman. He loved Theo's and my story, about getting caught by Interpol in Tunisia and could hardly believe our age at the time. He was completely thrilled with our achievement so far and mentioned that once we were ready leave Melbourne for New Zealand, to get in touch with him for some addresses.

The bedrooms were simply furnished, but each bed was surrounded by a thin net, because of the mosquitos. All three of us slept well and after a quick shower in the morning, breakfast was already on the kitchen table and our sad thoughts about Australia, where rapidly vanishing.

Sergeant Wilson had already written in our book and over breakfast, mentioned that the road from Darwin to Alice Springs was built by the Americans in 1942 after the Japanese had bombarded Darwin and was perfect all the way. He also mentioned that we could camp safely off the road and advised that we should erect our tent because of mosquitos, but to watch out for snakes, near waterways.

We were in great spirits and after telling him that he had changed our thoughts and impressions of Australia, we thanked him and the housekeeper for their great hospitality. We told them we would keep in touch, jumped on our bikes and took off towards Pine Creek. Forty years later we travelled through Adelaide River again, by car this time, and were told that Sergeant Wilson had retired many years before, taking his whole family to New Zealand.

Forty years later we travelled through Adelaide River again, by car this time, and were told that Sergeant Wilson had retired many years before, taking his whole family to New Zealand.

We had no problem covering many miles and didn't stop until we reached a place called Hayes Creek, which existed as one big wooden building that housed a pub, cafe and store, plus a couple of fuel bowsers in front. We stopped for a bottle of coke and a couple of smokes, and then didn't stop anymore until mid-afternoon when we reached Pine Creek, which was about the same size as Adelaide River. I think it was in Pine Creek where we tasted our first milkshake and liked it very much. It came in lots of different flavors such as chocolate, strawberry, pineapple, vanilla, caramel, as well as others we couldn't name. There was even one flavor that was a blue colour. We also had some sandwiches, made with white doughy bread. An After that we decided to keep going to get closer to Katherine. That didn't happen because it suddenly got dark, pitch black, almost as soon as the sun set.

None of us could hardly remember the last time we slept in our tent — except for the one night in Singapore in the middle of the giant roundabout — but with about 40 miles still to go to reach Katherine we veered off the road and made camp. We didn't encounter any snakes or spiders, but were certainly glad about the mosquito nets; these little bastards would have had a feast otherwise.

Uli woke us up early in the morning.

"Have a look," he said. He pointed towards the thicker forest further in from the road and sure enough we saw our first Kangaroos, not just one or two, but a whole herd of them in the distance just sitting there and looking around. A couple of them made a few tentative hops, but mostly they just stood there at the forest edge.

Without a cloud in the sky it warmed up very quickly and without wasting too much time, we were back on our bikes, leisurely riding towards Katherine which we reached by midday.

Sergeant Wilson had mentioned that Katherine, Tenant Creek and Alice Springs, had camping grounds, and they would be the best places for us to camp. Katherine was situated on a reasonably big river and was quite busy with a fairly big shopping center next to the highway. The camping and caravan park were situated beside the river and we headed straight there. It wasn't very busy and after paying a small fee the lady in the office pointed to a vacant block.

"You can put up your tent over there," she said, and we did.

This camping ground was fairly big with a huge toilet block adjacent to a laundry and shower cubicles. The office had a small shop with just about everything a camper would possibly need.

Some men were sitting by the river bank drinking beer and we actually saw a guy catching a decent sized fish.

Uli went over to them and asked, "aren't you worried about crocodiles?"

"There's no fucking crocks here," one of them said.

"There's a few freshwater crocks somewhere here, but they don't bother you." Another said. "It's the salties you have to look out for."

When ULi looked puzzled, the man went on, "you know, those big salt-water bastards that live in the Adelaide River up near Darwin."

"And all over the top end," the first man added. "They haven't worked their way down as far as Katherine yet. Too many hunters up there who take them for the skins."

Later in the afternoon after doing some washing and having a nice shower, we asked at the office where we could get something good to eat.

"There's a fish and chips shop in the main street," the woman who booked us in earlier told us. "It's very good. They get fresh fish from Darwin every second day. And if you don't go for fish there's a café over the road that makes the best hamburgers anywhere."

We had no idea what a fish and chips shop was, but didn't really fancy it when we saw all the people walking out of the shop tearing open parcels of newspaper, ripping into it like seagulls.

"They wrap the fish in newspaper?" Theo said.

"I'm not sure I like that," I said. "Let's have a look at the café?"

Entering the cafe was a different story. We were greeted with a superb smell and our taste buds started to work overtime. Before we could even think of sitting down, an elderly lady approached us. "Do you want takeaway or would you like to be seated at a table?"

Not knowing what take away was, Uli said "seated," and she pointed to the only vacant table. She also pointed to a blackboard hanging on one of the walls. It was a list of meals served.

"Do you want something to drink?"

Uli ordered three cokes.

We studied the board and were surprised at how many different hamburgers there were, plain, with lettuce, bacon, one or two eggs, with onions, tomato sauce, or the lot. There were other things like steak sandwiches, also with all the complements. We had never heard of a hamburger as being something you eat, so we studied some of the other patrons and realized that a hamburger was comprised of a soft bread roll cut through the middle, buttered on both sides, filled one side and closed on top with the other. After getting our cokes, Uli ordered three with the lot. "No onions on mine," Theo said, and the lady amended what she had written down in her notepad. They came on plates and were accompanied with piles of crisp chips. Absolutely delicious!

I dare say, we didn't regret it! For many years, whenever I had a hamburger I would always say, "This is not as good as the one we had in Katherine." Perhaps it was because that one was our first one ever, or perhaps because we were just outright hungry.

Bright and early, with refilled water bottles, we waved Katherine goodbye and headed for Mataranka, which we easily made by mid-afternoon. We put up our tent next to a warm spring where hot water bubbled up from deep underground. It was too salty for us to drink but it didn't bother the kangaroos. There were plenty of them around this area with abundant food and fresh water. And where there was water, we knew there would be mosquitos, and we certainly had to cover ourselves well that night.

Early next morning we headed towards Daly waters, another two hundred miles south. It took two days to get there and again we camped just off the road.

The road was flat and riding a bike was not much of a problem, unlike in Asia where the roads are choc o bloc. One thing we couldn't get over were mountains of empty beer bottles every fifteen to twenty miles beside the highway. Someone told us later on that they were from the thirsty workers who built the road many years ago.

The two hundred and thirty miles to Tennant Creek took longer than expected. First off, we encountered literally clouds of those pestiferous bush flies and had to cover our heads with the net, and on top of that, we had two flat tyres on the first day and another on the second, for no apparent reason. We thought, if we started early and put a couple of hard days into it, we would get there in two days, but when Uli had the first puncture on his back wheel, which took longer to fix because of the bloody flies, and then I had one a couple of hours later, also the back tyre, we knew there was no hope.

We camped off the road and had barely been riding for a couple of hours the next morning when Uli had another one on his back wheel.

"Again!" Uli said as he prepared to fix the puncture. "I don't believe it." He swiped at the flies that immediately formed a cloud in front of his face. I could feel them crawling all over my back, so it must be the sweat that attracted them. And in this heat you couldn't avoid sweating.

It was almost the same time we'd had the punctures the day before. Maybe we had been riding too hard. Maybe the wheels got too hot. I bent down to touch the bitumen and discovered the surface was hot enough to cook an egg. We decided to take it easy and make Tennant Creek next day.

We did make it late in the afternoon a day later than originally expected and headed straight for the caravan park located behind an Ampol service station. We could hardly wait to get under a shower. Putting up the tent didn't take long and after washing sweat drenched clothes we were downright hungry.

When we asked, who made the best hamburger, a half dozen hands simultaneously pointed across the road to Bob's Eat-in or take-away. We didn't say Katherine's was better because this one was just as good, and eating inside, we escaped the flies. We noticed that every restaurant and shop had fly screens on windows and doors, even private homes had them.

It was a bit over three hundred more miles to Alice Springs, and we were eager to get there.

We were well prepared for the three days it took us, and with the advice given to us by Eugen in Darwin and Peter Wilson in Adelaide River, we knew that farms and service stations were far and few in between. We slept in our tent twice and made it to Alice Springs late afternoon on the third day, stuffed. Except for one puncture on Uli's bike, we experienced two things. Firstly, even though the days were quite warm, the further south we got the colder the nights were. Secondly, only a few miles before Alice Springs we passed a sign that had a line painted across it with the words Tropic of Capricorn above it. Once we passed that sign, we left the tropics and entered a more temperate zone. But it was still bloody hot during the day. Alice Springs was only a few miles ahead.

Alice Springs, close to the center of Australia! And we were elated.

We felt that we had crossed the half way mark, and it wouldn't be long before we would arrive in Melbourne.

At the caravan park next to a big truck park, service station and roadhouse, we were told if we wanted a hamburger, we should hurry next door, because the cafe would close shortly. We could put up camp later. We certainly were the last ones to be served, but we didn't have to wait long to get our burger with the lot and again we didn't complain. We had booked for two nights because we knew it was a very long way to Andamooka and we needed a good rest as well as having to stock up with things to eat, water and so on.

We were just about to order some breakfast at the cafe next door the next morning when four rough looking bearded fellows introduced themselves and sat next to us around the table and laughingly told us some bad news. "You won't be riding those bikes past Alice Springs".

They had heard about our adventure from the cafe owner whom we had told we were riding our bikes to Melbourne.

"No fucking way," one of them exclaimed, "this is the fucking end, nothing but fucking sand and fucking bush, as far as Port Augusta." and the others put their thumbs downward, shook their heads.

"He is fucking right you know," another said. "There aren't any roads."

"What do you mean no roads?" Uli said. "It's marked on our map."

"Sure it is, but there's no road. Not even a track you can follow. It's where they're going to put a road."

"One fucking day." And they all burst into laughter.

We looked at each other in disbelief.

This was a big blow to the system, we had known that it was going to be hard for us, but most of the people we had spoken to had never been to Alice Springs. Even Sergeant Wilson mentioned that it would be difficult and we may have to find an alternative.

"We have no choice," Uli said. "We're trying to get the Melbourne for the Olympic Games. We've cycled all the way from Germany, and through lots of difficult countries. A bit of sand isn't going to stop us."

"Yeah, I added. "We rode through the desert in Iran."

"Now don't get your nuts in a knot," the spokesperson said. "There are more ways than one to skin a cat." He patted Uli on the shoulder. "Why don't we have some breakfast together and you can tell us all about yourselves. You never know we might just come up with a fucking solution."

They ordered grilled lamb chops, two fried eggs a couple of small fried sausages, baked beans, bacon rashes and buttered white bread, for all of us. That's one hell of a breakfast!

We told them some of our life story and we could see how interested they were. They didn't interrupt us with questions. They listened intently while they ate their breakfast.

Bill was the spokespersons name and he was the one who told us the good news, but he waited until we had finished breakfast and were drinking a coffee. By this time we knew they were interstate truck drivers.

"There are two possibilities," Bill explained. He pointed to one of the fellows, the one with red hair and a beard. "Firstly, you could wait for Bluey." Bluey nodded and smiled at us. "Or you could travel with me."

"It will be a week before I get back from Darwin," Bluey said.

"The trucks are loaded and they'll be off as soon as breakfast is done. Bluey's truck is the only one that has room for you all and your bikes. But that would be only after he has gone to Darwin and is heading back empty to Port Augusta. He'll pick you up here on the way back."

"So we would have to wait a week here until he comes back?" Uli asked.

"Right. There is an alternative though. You could travel south with me early tomorrow. It won't be as comfortable, but you would save a lot of time."

The three of us jumped up at the same time and grabbed Bill's hands to thank him for such good news.

"We are used to a bit of discomfort," Theo told him.

But none of us had any idea of just how uncomfortable it would be.

One of them paid the bill and we followed them to where their trucks were parked, loaded and ready. We watched Bluey and the other two starting their trucks which were incredibly loud and blew out clouds of dark exhaust. One after the other the trucks edged out into the street and slowly headed north to Darwin.

"Follow me," said Bill. He headed towards the truck servicing workshop on the other side of the road.

When we saw Bill's truck we realized how uncomfortable the trip would be. It was a Comer, an English truck with a single cabin for two, with a big loading platform on double axles at the back. It had a huge amount of empty oxygen and gas bottles lying lengthwise on top of each other. They were stacked like pyramids to the top and fastened down by several thick chains. On both sides were two lock up compartments, mostly for tools and spare tires, but there was one for luggage and cooking utensils. On front of the cabin on top of the solid bumper bar were big steel girders welded together and bolted to the bumper bar. We had never seen anything like that before.

"That's in case we hit a kangaroo or a camel," he explained when he saw us looking at it.

"We don't have those in Europe," I said.

"What? Bull Bars? Or kangaroos?"

"None of that," I said, not knowing what he was talking about.

"I'm just doing a service and some minor repairs before we leave tomorrow. I want to leave at daybreak. Are you up for that?"

"We'll be ready," Uli said.

"It'll take two nights and three days to get to Port Augusta. I'll be stopping at Oodnadatta, Andamooka and Hawker, on the way. There isn't anywhere else anyway."

He told us we could store our luggage in one of the truck's lockers, plus we should purchase some tinned food stuff to take with us, but our water bottles we should fill in the morning. We did all that and in late afternoon we had dinner with him, another one with the lot.

Bill slept in his truck and was already up and waiting for us when we arrived at daybreak. He greeted us with a big smile.

"Let's get loaded," he said, "we have a long way in front of us."

Grinning from ear to ear, he said, "You need to vote on which one of you will ride up in front with me first."

That's right, two of us had to sit on top of the stacks of gas bottles. Theo and I decided that Uli, being the oldest, should be the first one to ride in front.

After storing the last of our luggage and tying our bikes to each side of the bottles, Theo and I climbed on top and waved Alice Springs goodbye, heading south just as the sun started to rise in the east. It was a smooth ride until the sealed road finished and Bill had to choose one several tracks carved into the red sand by many trucks like his. Suddenly everything vibrated and rattled as the truck bounced over corrugations across or along the track.

We used our sleeping bags tied on top to one of the bottles as cushions to sit on and even though it was still a hard seat it wasn't too bad at the beginning. We had to be rugged up because of sun and wind burn and it very quickly got hot and uncomfortable. Bill said we would stop after every hundred miles for a short rest, and so one of us could swap with the other in the cabin with him. He wanted to make the 350 miles to Oodnadatta before nightfall, so the rest was only a few minutes each time.

After a couple of hours we absolutely regretted the choice we had made. Our bums ached! Even though we were sitting on our sleeping bags, underneath was pure steel, and with the continuous bouncing our buttocks started to hurt. You would have thought that after sitting on our bike saddles for several months our bums would be used to it, but there is a big difference between a relatively soft saddle and vibrating steel!

Still, Bill had told us that it was going to be a rough ride. We just couldn't imagine how rough! Had we not been pressed for time we would have waited for Bluey to pick us up on his way back from Darwin.

It was a great relief to stretch our legs and drink some cool water. We also enjoyed a couple of smokes, (Bill rolled his own). Theo being the youngest, had to do another 'shift' on top, this time with Uli whilst I was able to rest my bum on the soft seat in the cabin with Bill.

Bill turned out to be a great bloke, a real Aussie tough guy. Every second word was Fuck or Bloody. His grandparents migrated to Australia from England as newlyweds and settled in Port Augusta. As a miner his grandfather prospered well, investing in real estate and creating a big family, mainly around Port Augusta. Bill himself did very well, owning this truck, plus another three. It certainly was a huge relief for my buttocks, sitting on the soft seat and out of the wind. I wasn't looking forward for my next turn on top of the bottles.

Surprisingly, it wasn't just sand, as we were told. "On the contrary," Bill explained, "after the rainy season the whole Australian bush is covered in beautiful colors. There are wildflowers everywhere."

We were also told that Australia only had kangaroos, plus Cattle and

Sheep Stations, but apart from heaps of kangaroos we also saw lots of camels, donkeys and wild dogs. "Fucking dingoes," Bill said. "They're everywhere."

"In a few weeks' time, maybe even by the end of this week," he added, "all the dry river beds and lakes we cross will be flooded and no one will be going anywhere. It could be up to four months before you could get to Alice Springs again, so it's good you decided to come with me now. If you'd waited for Bluey to come back from Darwin you might well be stuck there with him for four months. Although I don't really expect the rainy season to start for a couple of weeks yet."

Time just flew and for me and the hundred miles were covered too quick, before I had to swap with Theo and sit next to a not too happy looking Uli.

It didn't take long before I got miserable again and didn't really care about the beauty of this great unexplored continent we were travelling through. My backside hurt so much it was unbearable. I don't think Uli and I said more than a dozen words together. We continuously nursed our bums, shifting from one cheek to the other. We were mighty glad when it was time for another rest.

"It's only eighty miles to Oodnadatta," Bill said as we stood by the shady side of the truck.

"Are we stopping there?" I asked. I thought a stop so we could walk around and stretch, ease our bruised bums would be a good idea.

"No, I never stop there... well, not unless I have to."

He didn't elaborate and before we could ask anything else, he said "Alright, come on. Enough rest. Time to get moving while there is still some daylight."

He jumped back into the cabin followed quickly by Uli whose turn it was up front leaving Theo and me to climb painfully back up onto the pyramids of gas bottles.

We soon guessed why he didn't want to stop at Oodnadatta. It looked as if this remote run-down village was occupied mostly by Aboriginal people who stared suspiciously at us. Bill would have lost hours answering questions about the couple of not very happy looking, strange guys he had sitting on top of his empty gas bottles and the bikes tied to the side of them.

It was Theo and I who were stared at, when we finally drove through this small settlement in second gear, across a narrow railway track, past a small railway station, a couple of brick buildings, some wooden houses and a relatively big repair and refueling station. Several Aborigines on horseback, plus a couple of Aussies, waved at us and we waved back. Bill told us later that they were stockmen.

It was still daylight when Bill stopped next to a dried-up river and told us to gather plenty of dry wood to keep a good fire going.

"It's a bit hot for a fire, isn't it?" Uli asked.

"It keeps the bloody flies away, Bill said. "And later on, the fucking mozzies. Besides that, you'll appreciate a good fire very soon."

We had no idea what mozzies meant. He saw the look that passed between us and he smiled. "Mosquitos, it keeps the mosquitos away," he said.

"Ahh!"

It had been a stinker of a day, far too hot to be sitting on top of a stack of gas bottles, but we had no choice. At least as the truck was moving there was enough of a breeze to keep a bit cool. But as soon as we stopped the heat would hit you like a furnace. However, as soon as the sun went down the temperature started dropping and Bill was right, we really did need that fire going all night. The further south we went, the colder the nights got even though the days were super-hot.

If it wasn't for my sore bum it would have felt quite romantic sitting around a campfire, with Bill boiling water for tea and telling lots of yarns. We had plenty of food and by night fall it was just us, a sky full of stars and the buzzing mosquitoes were kept at bay by the fire.

Sleeping on the soft sand was quite comfortable, but it soon got cold and we had to sleep in our sleeping bags. And to be on the safe side we covered our heads with the nets. Twice I had to get up for a pee, but by the time I rushed back, my testis and backside, were already being attacked by those bloodsuckers. Thankfully, the next morning I was first in the cabin and got some relief.

Bill had slept in the cabin but was already brewing tea at daybreak and had a good fire going again. It didn't take us long to get ourselves organized to join him, but not before he handed us a small spade, some toilet paper.

"You have to dig a hole to bury your shit," he said. "Off the track somewhere. I don't want to drive over it as we leave."

I was mighty glad, that it was my turn first in the cabin; better still when Bill told us he wasn't going to stop until we got to William Creek, some 170 miles ahead. Back with Bill again, was a pleasure and I could nurse my bum to prepare it for my next turn on top.

On the way, Bill pointed to a couple of tracks leading to Homesteads with thousands of acres of land, mainly for cattle and sheep. Bill also told me while rolling a cigarette with one hand, and with a proud smile from ear to ear, that "Australia has some cattle stations that are bigger than England."

William Creek was situated next to a narrow railway line and it turned out to be one 'hotel' pub, a big workshop for servicing motor vehicles and farm machinery, plus a small camping ground.

Bill greeted several rough looking guys after we'd stopped, truck drivers like himself, and it seemed every second word in their conversation was fuck, even when he introduced us to them.

"This pub is famous for its hamburgers, steaks and chips," Bill told us. "They have the best cold beers too," he added.

I looked around and thought there can't be too many people living close by. If the place was famous it had to be advertised by people like him or some of the adventurers that pass through here.

We walked into the bar which was certainly cooler than outside. It almost seemed windy because several huge ceiling fans were going full bore blasting air down onto us. There were a dozen guests standing at the bar or sitting at several tables.; more people than I imagined lived in the whole settlement. After ordering three pots of beer and a coke for Theo from an elderly friendly lady behind the bar, Bill upended his glass and drank the beer in one gulp. He shook his shook his head and immediately ordered another beer. Then he turned and looked at us. "The first one always tastes shithouse."

It tasted alright to me, though it was very cold. But he was dead serious. He sipped the second glass and smiled. "Now that's better," he said, and then wandered off to talk to some of the people in the bar. I couldn't help noticing that nobody used the work fuck or bloody and I found that peculiar. Perhaps it was because there were several women in the place.

Sitting by ourselves eating hamburgers with the lot (and they were good), Bill came back and I asked him why nobody swears in a pub?

Well, I certainly received a lecture. He swallowed the last bit of his burger, took another gulp of his pot and turned towards me, his eyes sparkled angrily. "What do you think we are?" he said looking me straight in the eyes, "uneducated idiots? I don't know about Germany, but here in Australia we do not swear in front of women, the elderly or children, and if we catch some guy swearing in front of them, we give him a kick up his arse."

He stood up, walked to the bar and ordered another round, and paid for everything.

The next 170 miles to Andamooka were sheer torture, and I felt for Uli who had already endured the shift before, but still he had to laugh about the lecture I got from Bill. "Snegschde mol helsch hald dei bleede gosch, no wirsch ned zamma gschissa," he said to me. "Next time you must keep your inquisitive gob shut, then you won't get lectured.".

Because of the three pots I'd had I felt a bit light-headed and for some reason the two of us kept talking about old times to keep the pain of sitting on top of those gas bottles at bay.

Andamooka is an Opal mining town where fortunes are made or not, but even the not-so-lucky ones still make a reasonably good living. The area is absolutely flat, and hard as cement. All the mines and the holes had to be dug by hand with pick and shovel, extremely hard work.

Sitting on top of the gas bottles as we drove into the place Uli and I could see hundreds of holes everywhere, with mounds of dirt and gravel next to each hole. The deeper the hole, the bigger the mound beside it.

Andamooka, must have been the arsehole of Australia; there was absolutely nothing to do except dig for Opals and repair machinery, trucks and cars. We passed some miner's huts, big tents and several caravans erected next to the holes dug in search of Opals.

Bill stopped a couple of miles past Andamooka where we were to camp for the night. Uli and I were off the truck before Theo and Bill opened their cabin doors. As soon as he got out Bill grabbed a machete, and just off the track chopped down a few small bushes for a camp fire.

"We could have gone another ten or twenty miles," he told us as he piled up the chopped branches for the fire. "But we would end up at Lake Torrens. There's fuck all there though."

A lake would be nice, I thought.

"No plants, no bushes, no grass. It's a dried-up salt-lake."

I wasn't sure what a salt-lake was, but dried-up sounded right. Looking around, I could hardly imagine anything more dried up than where we were right then. It was still hot enough to feel the sun burning onto our backs and shoulders. And the slight wind that gusted from time to time blew eddies of fine sand and dust up into the air.

"I usually stop around here somewhere whenever I'm on my way back."

Camp was quickly established and even though it was still daylight a reasonable fire was lit, not because it was cold but because of the relentless little bush flies that swarmed over you the moment you stopped moving.

"We should get to my place about mid afternoon tomorrow," Bill said while we sat around the fire.

"We'll have to leave early though. It's about 170 miles from here but the good thing is that the last 70 miles is sealed and we'll go a lot quicker. And from there on it's sealed all the way to Port Augusta and to Adelaide."

We would be awake at the crack of dawn anyway so leaving early was fine by us.

"You're welcome to stay at my place to rest your sore arses," he said and chuckled heartily.

Apparently, he had already arranged it with his wife with whom he kept in contact via two-way radio. He was always talking on the radio to other truck drivers and friends, so everyone always knew where everyone else was in case something happened.

We slept well and long, but it got noticeably colder during the night and it was nice for Bill to still have the fire going at daybreak. He already had a pot of tea ready when we woke up.

As soon as we did our hole digging and cleaned our campsite, we were off, with Theo and myself on top. Bill was very conscientious about leaving our campsite clean. After moving the truck, he shoveled the rest of the fire into a small hole which he dug and covered it with soil. Except for the tire tracks, no one would have guessed, anybody had camped here overnight.

After some miles we encountered a totally dry lake which must have been Lake Torrens. Bill drove onto the lake followed the edge of it for some distance. It was a relief to be traveling on the smooth dried out lake surface, but after a couple of hours we were back on the corrugated track again and bouncing up and down on our very sore bums. I was mighty glad when Bill stopped just before the sealed road. It was my turn to be inside the cabin and I jumped down the instant the truck stopped. No more squatting on bloody bottles for me because the next stop was Bill's home. Even sitting in the cabin, my bum still ached, and I don't think I could have lasted one more day of torture like we experienced sitting on top of those bloody gas bottles.

Port Augusta is situated on the northern end of Spencer Gulf and seemed quite busy, and compared to Darwin very prosperous, clean and civil. Bill told me that the living standard in Port Augusta was one of the best in South Australia. It had a well-established fishing industry, and there were several different mines nearby mainly extracting iron ore. There was a big iron ore smelter in Whyalla and a lead smelter in Port Pirie, both places not too far away from Port Augusta. The streets were wide and on each side were mostly weatherboard houses painted in different colors, which made the place cheerful.

Not far from the harbor, Bill turned into a small industrial area and stopped in front of a big warehouse. "This is the end of the road," he said and switched off the engine.

What a great feeling it was, knowing that we would be riding our bikes again soon.

A few fellows in overalls started to unload the gas bottles from truck and it didn't take long before we had our bikes and luggage. We could hardly distinguish one from the other. Everything was covered in red dust. Bill got his small truck which was parked behind the warehouse and everything we had was loaded on the back to be taken to Bill's house a couple of streets away looking across the Gulf.

We were greeted not only by Bill's lovely wife, but also by Bill's parents who lived next door, plus the neighbors on the other side. We were instantly offered cool drinks which we gratefully accepted. They all understood why we didn't want to sit down. Laughingly they comforted us and told us that we wouldn't feel any the pain by the time we reached Melbourne.

I could write so much more about Port Augusta and those wonderful people, especially Bill and his family, who looked after us as if we were one of them. We stayed all afternoon getting cleaned up, servicing our bikes and enjoying a BBQ in the evening. That night we slept like logs. The soft beds offered to us were heavenly.

After one more relaxing day, Bill opened his road map and gave us lots of advice about the roads and suggested that we stop at smaller towns in the evenings because most of them had camping grounds. He showed us on his map highway eight, which once we were on it from Adelaide we would automatically finish up in Melbourne. By evening our bikes were packed and we were ready for our last leg to Melbourne in the morning.

Early next morning after a good breakfast, we sadly said goodbye to these lovely people.

Fifty years later, on the exact same day, on my way along the Canning

Stock Route I again visited Port Augusta. By this time it had grown to a big City and I couldn't find Bill's house, nor the big warehouse. My travelling companions knew all about our story and enjoying a counter meal in a pub, we raised our glasses and remembered Bill, his family and friends.

Even though it was going to be relatively warm, Bill warned us that we should wear long pants, because along the southern part of Australia, the weather could change suddenly. "One minute you'll be hot, and the next suddenly you'll be freezing." We didn't believe him until later when we experienced those sudden changes for ourselves.

Back on our bikes again felt great. Even though our bums were still bruised and sore, the eighty Miles to Port Pirie on good roads alongside Spencer Gulf was no problem. Except for a cool south westerly breeze, we travelled through a couple of small villages where we stopped for a couple of smokes and made Port Germaine early in the afternoon, where we relaxed with a 'one with the lot'. The 15 Miles from there to port Pirie we covered in no time and did find the camping place just off the highway and had a good, but relatively cool night.

The 85 miles next day took as away from Spencer Gulf, and travelling to Port Wakefield situated on the St Vincent Gulf we found travelling certainly harder. Leaving the sea, we had to ride through some hilly, but very interesting country, passing what looked to us like big sheep and cattle stations. We rested for a short time at a small at a clean and affluent looking village called Crystal Brooks. By the time we had reached the sea again at Port Wakefield and found the camping grounds, a south westerly was blowing hard and strong and we had to endure a cold night.

The next day was pretty miserable; cold with a slight drizzle, and to top it all off Uli had to mend a slow puncture. Travelling the 75 miles to Adelaide took us nearly all day, because riding on a slightly wet surface we had to be extra careful. But the closer we got to the Capital the more we felt like we were in civilization again. We rode through increasingly larger and bigger populated places until finally we arrived in Adelaide, very cold and wet.

We turned into a big caravan and camping ground that had a large sign in front advertising single and family cabins with shower and washing facilities. Because we were here well before the high holiday season, we were given a family sized cabin for half price, and mighty glad we were too.

The room was cozy and heated. We soaked our weary bodies in a good hot bath and had a great sleep. After a hearty breakfast the next morning we emerged to find the weather was still miserable.

But it wasn't very far to Hahndorf, a wine making area where plenty of German families lived.

It was pretty hilly and we really had to push a bit from time to time but we made it much quicker than we had thought. It was only 15 odd Miles to Hahndorf and well before midday when we got there only to be greatly disappointed. I don't know what we expected, but the three of us had in the backs of our minds that this town would be like many of the smaller wine making towns along the Neckar River near Stuttgart in Germany, an area we were very familiar with, but it was nothing like that.

Hahndorf was just a little fake German look-alike village surrounded by lots of vineyards, and no one spoke good German and many didn't speak any German at all. We pushed our bikes along the footpath, entered a couple of shops and tried to talk to several people. Most of them couldn't understand us. One elderly man even told us to speak English. "You are in Australia now. You have to speak English.". I think he told us that because he had trouble making sense of anything we said in German. It would have been much worse had we spoken to them in our local dialect, Schwabish.

Well, that was certainly a disappointment. We decided to push on and looking at our map we saw Murray Bridge was only another 60 miles. Even though the road was slippery and very hilly we made good time.

Murray Bridge, situated on the mighty Murray River, was big enough for several camping grounds and all ready for their summer trade, and after asking some people we had no problem finding the best of them with a cabin again. A couple of Milk bars were still open where we could buy some supplies. We were told at reception that we will have to sleep in our tent the next night, that there wasn't a camping ground until Border town or Kaniva, and to stock up with some supplies.

Early next morning we followed the Murray for about 15 Miles and stopped at Tailem Bend in front of a cafe advertising The Best Hamburgers in town. We just had to stop and order one with the lot for each of us. That was our breakfast. They were pretty good too!

Leaving the Murray River and travelling in a south easterly direction it got colder. We'd left the rain behind and the air was dry with a slight breeze, which made it seem even colder. We travelled past lots of freshly sown hectares of land as far as our eyes could see and Uli as a half gardener told us that those big farms would do extremely well. The soil here appeared very rich and fertile.

Once we had left the Adelaide hills, riding along the beautiful and rich countryside was enjoyable, but lonesome. The traffic was certainly not like in Asia, with the occasional truck blowing its horn to warn us. Here there weren't many cars on the road at all. Our bums quickly became accustomed to the saddle again and the pain subsided.

Reaching Tintinara, only resting at a couple of very small towns, we decided to get as far as Keith, but with about 10 miles to go I got a puncture on my front wheel and while I fixed it, Uli and Theo put up camp far enough off the roadside to be not visible from cars driving by, and opened a couple of tins of food for dinner. We couldn't get dry wood for a fire so we ate the food cold, straight out of the tin. We also had to endure a very cold night.

With a stiff westerly pushing us along next morning, we only stopped at Keith for a couple of smokes and made it to Bordertown by lunchtime starving. After lunch and some more pedaling, we put up camp several Miles past Kaniva. Here in the southern part of Australia we saw lots more Kangaroos than further north, especially early in the mornings and in the late afternoons.

After another cold night in the bush it didn't take long to reach Nhill early in the morning for breakfast. By now we were longing to get to Melbourne, to meet up with our friends and enjoy a few weeks of civil life. We only stopped at Dimboola for a milkshake each and a couple of sandwiches made with very doughy bread.

In Horsham we found out that they didn't have cabins at the camping ground, only spaces for caravans and tents. That was disappointing because we were looking forward to a nice warm room. At reception someone told us that Ballarat, on the way to Melbourne, had cabins. Looking at our map we decided to head for Stawell while there was plenty of daylight left, to get closer to Ballarat. We figured that we would have to sleep in the tent either way, and it would be closer to a cabin next day. We didn't quite make Stawell and by the time we had put up camp and opened a couple of tins, we were very tired. It certainly had been a mammoth day.

Getting to Ararat was no problem next morning for breakfast and we pushed on to Beaufort for lunch. Although we had not seen the sun for the last couple of days, we still enjoyed the freedom of this undulating countryside, especially the huge variety of bird life and the fact that we hardly saw anybody anywhere except in the small towns we passed through.

What disturbed us though were the killed or badly wounded animals scattered along the road. They were mostly kangaroos, but there was also the odd koala. Such beautiful animals… Unfortunately, we also saw some badly wounded kangaroos limping amongst the bushes along the roadside but there was nothing we could do. I wondered if drivers deliberately targeted these animals when they saw them on the road. Surely there couldn't be so many accidents. Perhaps the metal frames welded on the front of trucks and cars in the country weren't to protecct the vehicle, but were to kill animals without damaging it. *What a horrible thought.*

We made Ballarat and found a camping ground next to a large lake, but it was closed to the public. We were told to try the one on the other side of town. When we asked why it was closed, they explained to us that they were getting the area ready for the Olympics. Lake Wendouree was where the small sailing races were to be held… so that explained all the work and activity going on around the town. The place was like a beehive with workers everywhere.

Finally, we started to feel excited. We were getting close to our destination, and close to the Olympic Games. After all our travelling, all we had been through, we were almost there!

We did find the other camping ground and were lucky to get one empty cabin, but got a shock when they told us the price.

"Because of the games," we were told. They had to modernize and double the size of their ground, and someone had to pay for it. We were probably the first to be hit with the higher prices. We also were getting short on cash, but had to take the cabin to make ourselves relatively respectable before riding into Melbourne. At this stage in our long journey we looked like bums!

After a great shower, some dinner and sleeping in a warm bed, I never occurred to me that the night before, near Stawell, would be the last night for me to sleep in a tent for many years to come.

The last leg to Melbourne was certainly one of the toughest. We weren't alone on the road. There was a lot of traffic and no freedom to ride where we wanted. We were told to take care, and the best we could do was stay close to the edge of the road and ride in single file.

It wasn't too bad on the open road, but riding through the smaller and bigger towns the traffic backed up. We were forced to weave through it.

We had left Ballarat fairly early, stopped in Balan briefly for a light breakfast, and made Bacchus Marsh by midday for some lunch. The more miles we covered the more excited we got. We were also running out of cash.

Bill from Port Augusta had told us to stay on highway one until Murray Bridge, then change to highway eight; it would lead us automatically to Melbourne. He was dead right.

We passed through some 'outer villages'; Melton, Deer Park and Sunshine, before getting onto what was called Ballarat Road to head into the city of Melbourne. Coming down the hill we crossed the Maribyrnong river and got hit with another unforgettable sight. The traffic had halted and we had to push our bikes along on the footpath. We soon saw to our amazement that the holdup was because there were thousands of sheep all over the place. The road was filled with them. No car or motorbike or even pedestrians could get through them. What were they doing all over the road? We were in the middle of a major city, there shouldn't have been anything like this happening...

Apparently, we discovered later, opposite the huge race course was Melbourne's big abattoirs, and the sheep were being herded in there for slaughtering. A mile further up was a railway station where a goods train had unloaded the sheep. A couple of guys walked leisurely in front leading them while their two dogs did all the work behind them, racing back and forth to keep the sheep close together. Even after the road was free for traffic to move, we still had to push our bikes along the footpath to the big cross road. The road we had been on was full of shit, and smelled to high heaven. We were glad when we left that area behind.

We followed a green tram all the way into the city, past a huge marketplace to the end of the line where it stopped opposite a beautiful old stone and brick building; Melbourne's central railway station. (Flinders Street Station.)

We walked around the building, crossed the Yarra river which was much bigger than the one we crossed earlier, and headed along a magnificent tree lined boulevard, St Kilda Road. We road along the side road and finished up at a huge roundabout where a policeman directed traffic. Around the other side we noticed a big hamburger shop and headed straight for it. With our last Shillings and several pence, we just had enough for one with the lot and a coke each.

We asked where Southey Street in Elwood was because Theo had the address of Mr. and Mrs. Wachtel, which is why we wanted to go to Elwood. We were told it was not too far from the bay. According to the map we were shown we had maybe a mile and a bit to ride.

It started to get dark by the time we found the place. It was much bigger than we expected and we quickly discovered it was a guesthouse rather than just a private residence. Theo knocked on a thick handcrafted old wooden door, hitting a hinged brass knob against a cast iron plate.

The door opened, an elderly man looked at us for a few seconds, closed the door again and we could hear him yell, "Frau Wachtel vor der tuer stehen drei Fremde," in German, "Outside are three strangers."

Moments later it was opened again by Mrs. Wachtel who was followed by her husband exclaiming in perfect Swabian dialect, "Meine drei radler, do sendse endlich, welchas isch dor Theo?" "My three cyclists, had finally arrived, which one is Theo?"

Mrs. Anna Wachtel was born around the turn of the century, not far from Backnang and became close friends with Theo's mother, but unfortunately her father was Jewish. She had married Mr. Wachtel, a local, but they had to flee Hitler's mob, migrating to Australia in 1935. During all those years she had kept in touch with Theo's mum. Both of them had to work very hard during the war, bringing up a son and finally after the war, they established the guesthouse, serving Swabian food, plus having mostly German boarders.

Mr. Wachtel told us that all the rooms at the guest house were taken, but invited us to sleep in one of the unfinished double story houses which they were building across the road. They were at lockup stage, with the interior only half finished and we had to sleep on the floor. That did not matter to us, but we were happy that in the one where we stayed the toilet and bathroom were finished. Our first night in Melbourne was not too bad, a bit uncomfortable on the wooden floor but on top of our spread-out tent and in our sleeping bags, no problem.

A young Bavarian fellow called Georg, Uli's age, entered next morning, introduced himself and told us that Mrs. Wachtel invited us for Breakfast. Georg became a very close friend, especially to Uli and finished up working with Hermann and Uli at the snowy mountain project.

The dining room was full and we were greeted extremely well and had to answer hundreds of questions from guests who were fascinated by our achievement. The Wachtel's had already told all the guests about our incredible (to them) journey. Mr. Wachtel also informed us that one of the reporters from the daily newspaper, Steve, whom they know very well, would call by later during the day to interview us.

Steve arrived just after lunch and filled several pages in his note book about our adventures.

"I'd like to write enough to fill the middle pages of both The Argus and The Age."

These were the two newspapers he worked for as a freelancer.

"Unfortunately, because of the Games. we have to write stories about all the arriving athletes. Look I can't be sure exactly how much I write about you will be published. Perhaps, when all the commotion is over, they'll accept a more in-depth story…"

All we could do is go along with whatever he suggested and hope for the best.

"Would it be possible for you to ride into town tomorrow morning so I can have a couple of pictures taken?"

"Happy to do it," Both Theo and I exclaimed.

"We can meet in front of the Town Hall in Swanston Street."

"No worries, we'll be there."

A time was set, and Steve went on his way. We went back to our quarters and gave our bikes a good clean up, with George's help.

The next morning, after dressing in suits so we looked presentable, Uli told us it would be better if he stayed here and spent the time to search for our friends.

"You'll miss out being in the photo…"

"Doesn't matter, does it?"

"No Problem," I said. "We'll be back in not time."

It only took us about twenty minutes to reach the Town Hall where Steve was waiting with another guy with a very impressive camera hanging around his neck.

After taking several pictures riding by the Town Hall in both Swanston Street as well as crossing Swanston Street while riding along Collins Street, we followed both of them inside where we signed our name in a huge book and an official handed us three tickets for opening day to the Olympics.

When we got back to the guesthouse about one and half hours later Mrs. Wachtel told us that Uli was able to get a lift with George on his scooter to West Footscray. "They should be back by lunch time," she said. Apparently, one of the boarders had told Mrs. Wachtel that a young man from Backnang was a member of the Skat (card) club somewhere in Geelong Road, and the two of them had gone looking for it.

Fred and Theo arriving in Melbourne in 1956... riding along Collins Street. The Melbourne Town Hall, where later they met the Mayor, is in the background.

They found it not far from the Footscray Football Club, and were told by the owner that it opened every day from 4pm and a George Schad from Backnang played there regularly, and he would certainly be there later that night.

"I only know a Guenter Schad," Uli said, "not a George Schad."

"Let me think, yes, now that you mention it… it is Guenter. Guenter Schad. He goes by the nickname of George."

"Please, don't tell him that I was here looking for him when he comes in. I want to surprise him when I come back later on."

"'s okay by me," the owner said.

When both of them arrived a couple of hours later, Uli sporting a grin from ear to ear, could hardly contain his excitement. He grabbed our hands and shook them vigorously. "Well, we found the first one," he exclaimed.

He was certainly pleased when we told him about our pictures being taken, even more so when Theo handed him a ticket to the Opening Day Ceremony for the Olympic Games.

About half past four we jumped on our bikes and followed George on his scooter and it didn't take long to reach West Footscray where George stopped in front of a big Edwardian house next to a service road parallel to Geelong Road.

It turned out to be a bit more than just a card playing club. They were playing for money, and not just men either, there were several women playing there as well. There were four big rooms and every table was occupied. Nearly everyone was smoking like a chimney, and some guy was serving drinks.

We spotted Guenter sitting at a table with three other guys and a woman.

He had his back towards us and when Uli tapped him on his shoulder and said "*So du aldor seggel, jedzd semmor do*"— "Now you old dickhead, we have arrived", he looked up and dropped his cards. It was obvious he never expected any of us to show up in Australia.

It certainly was a big surprise with lots of hugs and handshakes and Guenter introduced us to the others at his table as well as to everyone else nearby. He told everyone about us and we were welcomed and offered a drink and smoke.

Guenter excused himself for a minute to make a phone call and within a short time Hermann Foell (Hermann the bloody German) and Horst

Phitzenmaier (Phitzy) burst in and welcomed us profoundly.

It must have been at least an hour before the card games resumed and during that time arrangements were made regarding where we should stay. Horst (Phitzy) was lodging with Erna Rumpf, the lady who was sitting opposite Guenter, and her Husband Fritz and family, and she offered for me to board also at her place in Edgar Street west Footscray. Uli and Theo would board with Guenter and Hermann not too far away, in Epsom Road Ascot vale. So it was all settled and we had somewhere to go.

An elderly Berliner Gentleman introduced himself as Fritz Schwab and wanted to know all about us. He even came outside to admire our bikes. He took a hat and collected 13 Pounds and 12 Shillings for us, nearly two weeks wages! It took 30 years for our paths to cross again and then I found out that his father was Jewish and he'd had a miserable life in Berlin dodging the Nazis! We became close friends for many years and I paid him back with interest for what he did for us!

Elated at having met our friends again, we followed George back to the guesthouse with Horst offering to pick us up next day. We knew that we were going to be taken care of for the next two months that our visa lasted.

We truly had arrived at our destination, and on reflection it hardly seemed possible that we would have done it had we known what lay ahead of us at the start. But we didn't know, and because of that we did it. We embarked on our journey of a lifetime, and would never ever regret one moment of it.

Not one of us guessed at dusk after reaching Southey Street and getting off our bikes that we would never ride a bike again!

After the Olympics, our continuing journeys took different turns, but we have stayed close friends for all our lives.

I became a Bus driver for a few years during which I met my future wife Zara and her family. Not long after marrying Zara I became a keen skin diver, and then later, a professional Abalone diver and Processor.

And the adventures have never stopped…

Inside the Melbourne Town Hall, Councillor Curtis looked through our travel journal before adding his own words and signature to it. Theo is looking over the Councillor's right shoulder.

Acknowledgements:

This book is for my great friend Uli, who unfortunately is no longer here to see it. He has gone to heaven on the ultimate journey all of us must take, and part of me is missing. I hope he took a travelling book with him so the Almighty and His Son can write some nice sentences about us in it and look after him.

I would also like to thank Theo, who eventually returned to Germany and married my first cousin, for his assistance in remembering parts I had forgotten. He is always only a phone call away. It is fortunate that he rescued the photos seen in this book from being destrroyed during an acrimonious divorce between Uli and his first wife. She had thrown them out into the garbage along with other things belonging to Uli. The great tragedy is that there were thousands of images that Uli took during our epic journey, and most of them will never be seen by anyone because the negatives no longer exist.

Last but not least I thank my wife Zara for correcting many of my English grammar mistakes and her brother John for editing this Book.

Friedrich— Fritz — Fred Glasbrenner.

*...some pages from our travel journal
with approximate translations...*

" *Djauh berdjalan banyak dilihat* " = *orang yang banyak merantau banyak pula pengetahuan dan pengalamannya.*
 Long walks are seen a lot, which means, people that are wandering about gain a lot of knowledge and experience.

   Dr Hatta, the then acting President with his wife, wrote the above message in our book.

Djakarta, Indonesien

Many succes all of You
God bless You
Bey, bey
                Kind regards
                    from
                    Ibu
                Fatmawati
/ The First Lady of Indonesia
    15 Sept. 1956

I've hereby attached my picture and give it to Theo Guth, Ulrich Bauer and Frederich Glasbrenner, gentlemen of Germany who are going to Melbourne to attend the Olympic Games by cycling, as my appreciation of their huge spirit to reach their dream.
Jakarta, 1 Sept 1956,
Prime Minister of Indonesia,
Mr Ali Sastroamidjojo

For those who may have trouble reading the handwriting above, below is a transcsript.

We are very much pleased to meet these young German cyclists who came to our studio. It is always a great pleasure to meet people like such youngsters from abroad who are going around the world to participate in the Olympics at Melbourne. They visited the Sacred Temple of the Sikhs which has got no consideration of Caste and Creed, poor and rich, low and high. The Golden Temple is the place of worship to all the Humanity. This Sacred city of Amritsar is the homeland of the Sikhs.

We wish them good luck, success and prosperity in their difficult task.
signed by Bagwati Sing and his father on the 1st of 6th, 1956.

New Delhi, Indien

All good wishes —

प्रतीक अच्छी देने   Jawaharlal Nehru
June 14, 1955

PRIME MINISTER'S HOUSE
NEW DELHI.

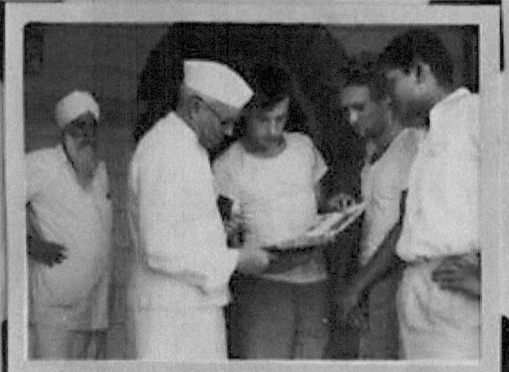

RAJ GHAT

New Delhi, Indien

[Urdu handwritten text]

14.6.56

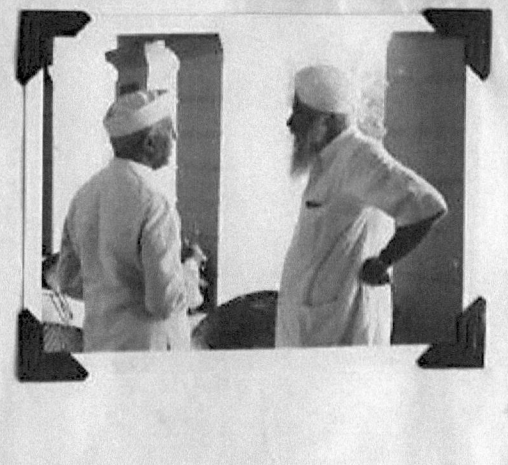

www.ingramcontent.com/pod-product-compliance
Lightning Source LLC
Chambersburg PA
CBHW021756220426
43662CB00006B/77